OKINAWA AND THE U.S. MILITARY

T0339231

OKINAWA
AND THE U.S. MILITARY

Identity Making in the Age of Globalization
With a New Preface

MASAMICHI S. INOUE

Columbia University Press *New York*

Columbia University Press
Publishers Since 1893
New York, Chichester, West Sussex
cup.columbia.edu

ISBN 978-0-231-13890-1 (cloth : alk. paper)—ISBN 978-0-231-13891-8 (pbk. : alk. paper)—
ISBN 978-0-231-51114-8 (e-book)

Library of Congress Control Number: 2016948443

Columbia University Press books are printed on permanent and durable acid-free paper

Printed in the United States of America

Except when otherwise noted, the photographs that appear in this book are the author's.

The poverty of politics and culture in Okinawa. In order to receive money from the government, my people let the matter drop even when a girl was raped by the military. They may not mind offering another sacrifice to do the same. The prayers of old women have never been heard. The oceans and mountains, objectified as lucrative sources of income, have gone to ruin. Spiritless men spend time and money idly by drinking *awamori* liquor and gambling. Spoiled youth crashed into a palm tree on Route 58 to die. Luxuriating in the windfall income Tokyo has been paying for Okinawa's military land, people no longer have any independent soul. The poverty of [politics and culture in] Okinawa. I would like to face this poverty when I write.

——Meroduma Shun (1996: 29)

CONTENTS

Contents

ILLUSTRATIONS

Illustrations

PREFACE TO THE 2017 EDITION

This new preface, written for the paperback edition of *Okinawa and the U.S. Military: Identity Making in the Age of Globalization*, reflects on this book's values and humble contributions. In addition, it summarizes the development of the U.S. base problems in Okinawa in a historical perspective, with an emphasis on those issues that have taken specific shape since the manuscript for the first edition of this book was completed in the mid-2000s. Furthermore, it presents a hypothesis regarding the ongoing transformation of Okinawan identity for future research.

Three Incidents: Unequal Relations of Power and History

On May 19, 2016, as I began preparing this new preface, a former U.S. Marine in his early thirties was arrested by Okinawa Prefectural Police for abandonment of the dead body of a twenty-year-old Okinawan woman. The suspect had a job related to computer and electric wiring at Kadena Air Base (Sato 2016). At the time of writing, details of the crime are still unknown, but the police investigation indicates that the suspect had been hanging around an area of Uruma City in central Okinawa looking for women for a couple of hours in his car. He found this particular woman, who was out for an evening walk, and hit her with a stick from behind with intent to sexually assault her.

It is still unclear whether or not he raped her. Apparently, for fear that his crime would be brought to light, he murdered her with a knife, put the dead body in a suitcase, and abandoned it in a wooded area approximately twenty-five kilometers (fifteen miles) away from the woman's residence ("'Bōkō Hakkaku Osore Satsugai' . . . " 2016).

Following the discovery of the victim's dead body, deep sadness and anger permeated Okinawa, triggering a series of grassroots activities that led to an all-Okinawa rally of protest and mourning attended by 65,000 Okinawans on June 19, 2016. In advance of this rally, Okinawa Governor Onaga Takeshi visited the scene where the victim's dead body had been found in order to pray for her soul. The governor apologized for "being unable to protect your life. Our administration has failed to establish a mechanism to prevent a crime like this from happening" (Okada 2016).

This tragedy has reminded many Okinawans of another disaster: the 1995 gang rape of a twelve-year-old Okinawan schoolgirl by three U.S. servicemen, discussed in detail in this book's introduction and chapter 2. This incident also set off rallies and organizing, culminating in an all-Okinawa protest. Here, too, the then governor apologized for failing to protect the victim.

Further, compare these two incidents with what Okinawans collectively remember as the "Yumiko-chan incident" (Asato 2000, Fukuchi 1983, "Special Feature . . . " 2016, Yomitan Village 2008). On the evening of September 3, 1955, Nagayama Yumiko, a six-year-old kindergartner living in what was then Ishikawa City in central Okinawa, went missing while she was watching eisā, an Okinawan folk dance that marks the end of the Bon festival. On the following day, she was found dead in a vacant field near a military dumping ground in then Kadena Village. The September 4, 1955 edition of *Okinawa Times* describes "her slip sliding down to her left arm and her lips tightly held" (quoted in Asato 2000). The victim's dead body, beaten by heavy rain before it was discovered, showed signs of sexual assaults. The suspect was a sergeant in his early thirties who belonged to Kadena Air Base. In a resolution addressed to the U.S. military, the Ryukyu Legislative Council expressed Okinawans' indignation in the strongest terms: "As it became clear that the girl was [sexually] assaulted [before being murdered], the entire Okinawan population has developed animosity and resentment [toward the U.S. military]" (1955, quoted in Nakano 1969, 126). The protest against this crime was interwoven with an emerging island-wide struggle against forceful seizures of Okinawan land by the U.S. military. These events prompted what came to be called the *shimagurumi* (all-Okinawa) resistance, which mobilized, at one moment in 1956, more than 300,000 people across Okinawa (Okinawa Prefectural Peace Memorial Museum [OPPMM] 2001, 127).

These three incidents took place more than sixty years apart in different historical contexts. Still, the similarities are striking: the most vulnerable—women and children—were the victims; large-scale protests followed each incident; and Okinawan leaders expressed anger, regret, and remorse on behalf of Okinawa at large. These similarities must be understood against the background of the prolonged presence of the U.S. military in Okinawa. The articulation of this historical background is one of this book's major contributions.

One particularly important aspect of historical background is the Battle of Okinawa in 1945, in which Okinawans—long discriminated against by mainland Japanese, who saw them as economically backward and culturally different (Rabson 2012)—were sacrificed to protect the mainland of the then Empire of Japan, and an estimated 150,000 people, a quarter of the Okinawan population, lost their lives (Arashiro 1994, 254). Many were killed in a barrage of U.S. bombs and artillery fire. Others died of starvation and disease. Still others were driven by the order of the Japanese military to kill their own parents and siblings before committing compulsory suicide to maintain their honor as imperial Japanese subjects. In some cases, retreating mainland Japanese troops executed local residents who used the Okinawan "dialect" (incomprehensible to these troops) on the suspicion of spying for the U.S. military (OPPMM 2001, 68–78).

Many of the U.S. bases on Okinawa originated during and after this battle as staging grounds from which to attack and watch the Japanese mainland (Nakano 1969, 1). For instance, the U.S. military seized and expanded bases that had been created by the Imperial Japanese Army to form the foundations of what we know today as Kadena Air Base, Yomitan Auxiliary Airfield, Ie Jima Auxiliary Airfield, and other facilities. The U.S. military also requisitioned a vast stretch of privately owned land to create the original forms of what we know today as Futenma Air Station, Camp Zukeran, and other facilities. The landowners were put in refugee camps set up by the U.S. military; upon returning, these war survivors found their land enclosed and converted into military bases (Arasaki 1995, 17–36; Okinawaken Sōmubu Chiji Kōshitu Kichi Taisakushitu 1998, 26–133; OPPMM 2001, 126).

The havoc extended into the postwar period from 1945 to 1972, during which the U.S. military maintained direct control of Okinawa. In the 1950s, the U.S. military seized additional Okinawan land with "bayonets and bull-dozers" (as Okinawans have described it), transforming this semitropical archipelago into the "Keystone of the Pacific" to confront and contain communist threats. The Yumiko-chan incident took place in the midst of these land seizures. In 1972, when the United States returned administrative rights over Okinawa to Japan, the U.S. military remained in Okinawa to defend the "free world." At the same time, U.S. bases on the Japanese mainland were reduced and reorganized in response to the rise of anti-base sentiments there, triggered by accidents (e.g., a military airplane crash into a university campus in 1968) and the negative economic impact of the bases, which blocked development of the areas they occupied. Consequently, after the Okinawa reversion, approximately three quarters of the facilities for the exclusive use of the U.S. forces in Japan came to be concentrated on Okinawa, which accounts for only 0.6 percent of Japan's total landmass (Okinawaken 2015a, 18–23).

To placate Okinawans' frustration with this situation, the Japanese government paid ever-increasing sums—an amalgam of various forms of aid, investment, and subsidy from Tokyo, including ground rent for Okinawan land used for the U.S. bases—to Okinawa from 1972 on. These funds were provided in the name of *hondonami*, that is, of "assisting" Okinawa in catching up with the Japanese mainland in terms of infrastructure and economic development. Even after the end of the Cold War, Okinawa was forced to shoulder the disproportionate burden of U.S. bases in exchange for continuing government funds because the Asia-Pacific region, according to the U.S. and Japanese strategic planners, remained "an area of uncertainty, tension, and immense concentrations of military power" (Department of Defense 1995, 2). The 1995 rape incident occurred against the backdrop of this large-scale presence of the U.S. military in post-reversion Okinawa.

The fundamentally unequal relations of power between Okinawa and the U.S. military over the years are visible in the ways in which the crimes committed by the U.S. military personnel—i.e., uniformed service members, civilian employees of the U.S. military, and their families—have been handled in Okinawa. While comprehensive crime statistics during the period of the U.S. military control are not available, 5,367 crimes, including 504 atrocious crimes such as homicide and rape, were committed by U.S. military personnel in just the five years from 1964 to 1968. This indicates that on average more than 1,000 crimes, including more than 50 atrocious crimes, were likely to occur every year from 1945 to 1972 ("Fukkimae Beihanzai Nen 1000ken . . . " 2011). And yet, during this period, Okinawa was allowed to arrest U.S. military personnel only for crimes committed in the presence of a policeman; it had no legal right to investigate or to otherwise exercise jurisdiction over them. In effect, Okinawan life was included or contained in a naked system of violence but excluded from protection of the laws, as in *bare life* defined by Giorgio Agamben as "something that is included [in the social system] solely through an exclusion" (1988, 11), that is, through "its capacity to be killed" (1988, 8).

Since the Okinawa reversion of 1972, crimes committed by the U.S. military personnel against Okinawans have decreased. From 1972 to 2014, there were 5,862 crimes, including 571 atrocious crimes (Higa 2016); on average, fewer than 140 incidents, including fewer than 14 atrocious crimes, occurred every year. This reduction can be explained by a number of factors. First, since the Okinawa reversion, U.S. military personnel have been at least partially subject to the criminal and civil justice procedures of Japan due to stipulations of the Status of Forces Agreement (SOFA); these procedures became a deterrent to crime. Second, the decline of the power of the American dollar vis-à-vis the Japanese yen has made it increasingly difficult for U.S. servicemen to use Okinawans (particularly women) for entertainment (e.g., prostitution) (Tanaka 2015); the reduction in personal contact between U.S. military personnel and Okinawans resulted in fewer crimes by the former against the latter. Third, the U.S. military have improved their education programs for servicemen, though they remain far from perfect (Abe 2016).

In the midst of the crime reduction of U.S. military personnel, however, the legal power of Okinawan authorities over them remains limited. For instance, after the 1995 rape incident, even though Japanese/Okinawan authorities had the primary right to exercise jurisdiction according to SOFA, the Okinawa Prefectural Police's request for the transfer of custody of the three accused U.S. servicemen was denied, also according to SOFA, because this request was made prior to indictment (Nichibenren 2014). This kind of special treatment of U.S. military personnel is an indication of the continuation of fundamental inequality between Okinawa and the U.S. military. In Okinawans' eyes, the 2016 murder of a twenty-year-old Okinawan woman has confirmed the vulnerability of "bare life" in Okinawa.

From Okinawan "People" to Okinawan "Citizens"

In spite of unequal power relations throughout modern Okinawan history, this book refuses to depict Okinawa simply as a passive victim. Instead, the book attempts to capture, from an ethnographic perspective, the active production of Okinawan identity—the collective sense of being as Okinawans—by Okinawans themselves within and against changing structures of power. This ethnographic perspective is enabled by the fieldwork that I conducted for fourteen months from the summer of 1997 through the summer of 1998 and additional fieldwork I performed thereafter. The primary site of my ethnographic investigation was Henoko, a sparsely populated eastern coastal district of Nago City in northern Okinawa. Henoko is home to Camp Schwab, a U.S. Marine Corps base created in the late 1950s in the midst of the *shimagurumi* (all-Okinawa) resistance. The focus of my fieldwork was Okinawans' efforts, beginning in 1997, to stop the planned construction of a new U.S. military facility in Henoko. Complemented by historical analysis, this fieldwork-based ethnographic exploration is one of this book's major contributions. More specifically, it allows me to address the shift of Okinawan identity from one generated by the oppressed Okinawan "people" under U.S. military control in the 1950s and 1960s to one articulated through the political-cultural styles and sensibilities of affluent, confident, and planetary but still grounded "citizens" with diverse backgrounds in the 1990s.

Speaking schematically, the "people" in the 1950s and 1960s were poor and subjugated, united by the shared hardships of the war (1945) and the U.S. military control of Okinawa (1945–1972). These experiences were the basic building materials of an Okinawan identity of resistance. More specifically, the Okinawan "people" consisted chiefly of the first generation, who experienced the total destruction of their life-world in the war and transformation of their life-world into the site of a gigantic military base complex in the era of U.S. control of Okinawa. They were supplemented by the second generation, who experienced the U.S. military rule but did not experience the war. The year 1955—when approximately 69 percent of the population fell into the first generation (who were ten years old or older) and 31 percent into the second generation (under ten years old) (Sōmushō Tōkeikyoku 2011)—is a useful reference point for when the Okinawan "people" began to establish themselves as the key social actor in Okinawa. They were the ones who shared anger and helplessness when the Yumiko-chan incident occurred. They were the ones who, often calling themselves "beggars" (Arasaki 1995, 52–57), protested land seizures by the U.S. military and mobilized the *shimagurumi* (all-Okinawa) resistance. The "people" also played a central role in organizing the Okinawa reversion movement in the 1960s and beyond.

"Citizens" of the 1990s, on the other hand, were produced in a new socio-economic context: Okinawa's affluence. By contributing to the dramatic improvement of social infrastructure, an upgrade in the standard of living, and the steady expansion of job markets, particularly in the secondary and tertiary industries across Okinawa, Japanese governmental funds for infra-structure and economic development helped Okinawa make poverty a thing of the past (Kurima 1998). The average per capita income of Okinawans in the 1990s became higher than some of the G8 countries, including Italy and Canada, even if it remained the lowest in Japan. Indeed, due to the power of the Japanese yen, Okinawans became wealthier than U.S. servicemen. In the process of Okinawans' transition from "people" to "citizens," the Japanese view of Okinawans as different and backward was transfigured. In particular, through the so-called "Okinawa boom" in the 1990s, Okinawa—now embed-ded in the comfort of a modern middle-class lifestyle (e.g., air conditioners, concrete houses, cars, and fast food restaurants) and packaged in the touristic images of tropical beaches, blue skies, and resort hotels—signaled a difference that mainland Japanese no longer disavowed but rather actively consumed. To be sure, this boom relentlessly commodified "exotic" Okinawan life, but it also helped Okinawans gain confidence. The rise of the social movements in the 1990s was, at least in part, attributed to this confidence.

Unlike the Okinawan "people" of the 1950s and 1960s, Okinawan "cit-izens" consisted of the first generation, which had experienced both the war and the U.S. military control; the second generation, which had expe-rienced the latter but not the former; *and* the third generation, which had experienced neither. By 1995, Okinawan "citizens" were clearly formed: approximately 27 percent of the population fell into the first generation (who were fifty years old or older), 38 percent into the second generation (twenty-three to fifty years old), and 35 percent into the third generation (under twenty-three years old) (Okinawaken Kikakubu Tōkeika 2016). This generational composition enabled the first generation to transmit their direct experiences of the war and the alien rule, and thereby establish such experiences in Okinawa's collective memory across generations. Also notable was the production of the globalized citizenly discourses such as the promotion of peace, protection of the environment, and empowerment of women, developed mainly by the second and third generations. The mixture of direct experiences of the war and the alien rule by the first generation on the one hand and discourses of peace, the environment, and gender produced by the second and third generations on the other, formed the building materials of Okinawa's citizen identity of the 1990s, as demonstrated by the social movements of that period.

For instance, in a protest rally attended by 85,000 Okinawans against the rape of a schoolgirl in 1995, then Governor Ota Masahide (of the first generation) delivered a powerful address in reference to the Battle of Okinawa and the U.S. military rule he experienced; then, a female high school student (of the third generation) complemented the governor's words by delivering a deeply moving speech that included a call for peace: "I would like us, the young generation, to get a new Okinawa started. . . . Please return Okinawa without the military, without the tragedy. Please return a peaceful island to us" (Nakamura 1995). In a way that took the intergenerational collaborations actualized in 1995 to new heights, the second generation led the movement to stop the construction of a new military facility in Henoko in 1997–98 and beyond by developing discourses of peace, the environment, and gender.

Transformation of the U.S. Military, Realignment of the U.S.-Japan Security Alliance: New Issues since the Mid-2000s

I completed the manuscript for the first edition of this book in 2006, covering the U.S. base problems up to that point. Since then, however, the situation in Henoko and Okinawa at large has continued to evolve.

As noted, since the reversion of Okinawa in 1972, the Japanese government has been injecting funds for infrastructure and economic development into Okinawa as political compensation for the continuing presence of the U.S. military there. The lack of large-scale anti-base mobilizations for the two decades after the Okinawa reversion demonstrates that money did, at least in part, displace Okinawa's frustration. However, this very money ironically became a constant reminder of the prolonged violence of the U.S. military presence, and ultimately helped Okinawans renew latent cultural sensibilities that were enmeshed with the pain of their collective historical experiences. The 1995 rape enabled Okinawans to express these cultural sensibilities in a vortex of protests.

In an attempt to conciliate Okinawa's anger, the U.S. and Japanese governments announced in April 1996 their intent to return the land occupied by Futenma Air Station to Okinawa within five to seven years. Futenma Air Station was (and is) a strategically vital U.S. Marine Corps base, seen by Okinawans as a symbol of the U.S. military presence because of its location in the congested residential area of central Okinawa and its size, 500 hectares (approximately 1,235 acres) of land. This return, however, was contingent upon a number of provisions. Chief among these was the construction of a replacement facility of Futenma *within* Okinawa. The original plan, announced toward the end of 1996 by the U.S. and Japanese governments, was to build a removable sea-based military facility across from Camp Schwab in Henoko. This original plan was unfulfilled, however, because of the success of Okinawan citizens' protests in 1997–98 and beyond.

After 1999, the plan was revised a number of times in complex negotiations and compromises among Washington, Tokyo, and Okinawa. It eventually transformed into the current plan, which was imposed by the U.S. and Japanese governments in 2005 and finalized in 2006. According to this plan, Futenma will be replaced with a new military airport with two runways, 1,800 meters (approximately 5,900 feet) each, to be created by "combin[ing] the shoreline areas of Camp Schwab and adjacent water areas" (Security Consultative Committee 2005). The new military airport will have added harbor and other functions that did not exist in Futenma. This new plan, which I call the *Camp Schwab fortification plan*, involves the return of the land used for Futenma to Okinawan control and is presented in parallel with other projects, such as:

1. transferring 9,000 (out of approximately 16,000) Marines, who account for approximately 60 percent of the U.S. forces in Okinawa, to Guam (4,000) and Hawaii (5,000), while also reassigning 1,000 Marines from the continental United States and Hawai'i to Guam;

2. utilizing Australia as a new site of rotational deployment of the Marine Corps;

3. considering places such as Guam and/or Northern Mariana Islands as a common training ground for the U.S. military and Japan's Self-Defense Forces (hereafter SDF) in the future; and

4. returning some of the U.S. military facilities located south of the Kadena Air Base to Okinawa (Ministry of Defense 2016, 1; Okinawaken Sōmubu Chiji Kōshitu Kichi Taisakushitu 2016, 10).

In the words of President Obama, "when our plans are complete, the Marine Corps presence in Okinawa will decrease by almost half, substantial land on Okinawa will be returned, and the military presence that remains will be concentrated in a less populated part of the island. Prime Minister Abe supports this plan, as do I" ("Obama Discusses Hiroshima Visit . . . " 2016).

When taking it at its face value, one might be indeed tempted to agree that this is a genuine project of the reduction and reorganization of the U.S. military for Okinawa. However, for reasons to be specified below, Okinawa has persistently been opposed to the Camp Schwab fortification plan, as evidenced by local movements in Henoko. Initiated in 1997, these direct, nonviolent protest movements have successfully blocked the construction work in and around Camp Schwab thus far. They continue to evolve today both on the land (i.e., in front of the gate of Camp Schwab) and on the sea (i.e., Henoko's sea surrounding Camp Schwab) in spite of police and governmental intervention, which is often violent. The movements are supported by Okinawa at large, where 70–80 percent—often more—of the population, including the current governor, have opposed the Camp Schwab fortification plan ("Opinion Poll . . . " 2015).

Two specific reasons for Okinawa's opposition have come to light through the resistance generated in and around Henoko over the past decade. First, Okinawa, against its will, would be permanently metamorphosed into a site of strategic significance for coping with novel threats and diversified contingencies in the Asia-Pacific region and beyond in the post-Cold War era—from terrorism and natural disasters to assistance in Iraq and engagement in "situations in areas surrounding Japan" (Security Consultative Committee 2005). Second, the new military airport in Camp Schwab is, after all, a replacement facility of Futenma; thus, the vast majority of U.S. bases—the burden of the U.S.-Japan security alliance that should be shared equally across Japanese prefectures—will continue to be imposed upon Okinawa.

The first issue—the transformation of Okinawa into a place of vital strategic significance in the post–Cold War Asia-Pacific region—can be clearly grasped if we place the Camp Schwab fortification plan in the context of the United States new security environment, which was characterized, particularly after 9/11, by "the unknown, the uncertain, the unseen, and the unexpected," to use the words of then Secretary of Defense Donald Rumsfeld (2002, 23). In the Cold War period, on the basis of its military and economic hegemony, the United States sought to establish peace and security in Asia, despite continuing bloodshed (e.g., the Korean War, the Vietnam War), by containing the threats of the clearly defined "enemy"— communism—through bilateral security arrangements with, for instance, South Korea, Taiwan, the Philippines, and Australia/New Zealand. Established in 1951 and revised in 1960, the United States–Japan security alliance was an important component of such overall arrangements. This alliance obliged the United States to defend postwar Japan—which was partially demilitarized during the U.S. occupation (1945–1952) before being redeveloped in the 1950s–60s as a locus of capitalist production and consumption in East Asia—in exchange for the bases and areas it provided.

Then, in the 1970s and 1980s, allies of the United States were invited to make deeper commitments and larger contributions to the Asia-Pacific security network, a process of "decentering" that went hand in hand with the shift of U.S. foreign policy "from operating within a bipolar or tripolar context to one taking into account an increasingly complicated and interdependent world" (Department of State, n.d.). Since the end of the Cold War, decentering has progressed as the "enemy" has transmuted into amorphous threats and diversified contingencies. For example, in the "coalition of the willing" formed for the Iraq War, the U.S. military incorporated a range of countries including Japan within a flexible and informal network of joint operations outside (though not necessarily in opposition to) permanent, formal institutions such as the United Nations and the North Atlantic Treaty Organization (Takahashi, Kawaguchi, and Yoneda 2009). In the process, the U.S. military has itself become a flexible and amorphous global network. The Camp Schwab fortification plan is one element of this new, broader project of transforming the U.S. military and realigning the U.S.-Japan alliance (and other security alliances) in the post–Cold War Asia-Pacific region.

For instance, in accordance with the Unit Deployment Program established in 1977, some Marines are already mobile, deployed for approximately six months away from a unit's home base in the continental United States or Hawai'i to duty stations around the world (Commandant of the Marine

Corps 2011, 1; Seigle 2013; Umebayashi 1994, 63–67). The Camp Schwab fortification plan, when combined with the array of related projects cited above, would make the U.S. Marines Corps even more mobile and flexible in deployment and operation, thereby accelerating the demise of its Cold War–era operational structure, characterized by total mobilization of amassed bodies against the "enemy" through a top-down chain of command. Remodeled Camp Schwab would also become a site of joint trainings and operations among the U.S. military, Japan's SDF, and other nations' militaries—a practice that has recently intensified in other bases in Okinawa, the Japanese mainland, and beyond—so that national boundaries would be increasingly undercut in the globally extended military network.

This networking process does not mean that the U.S. military has become somewhat benign; rather, the process has been grounded in the U.S. military's historical capacity for mass killing with nuclear, biological, and chemical weapons. For instance, the Henoko Ammunition Depot, adjacent to Camp Schwab, is one of the sites in Okinawa where a total of 1,300 nuclear bombs were once stored during the period of the U.S. military's direct control; and in the 1980s, the Henoko Ammunition Depot also stored materials that can be used for chemical weapons ("1962nen, Okinawa . . . " 2016, Umebayashi 1994, 129–146). These historical facts indicate that Camp Schwab, if upgraded, could potentially become a linchpin of advanced weaponry strategies of a new global military network.

Taken together, the Camp Schwab fortification plan would allow the U.S. military to get rid of outdated Futenma, along with other underused facilities sprinkled south of Kadena, while at the same time enabling it to obtain a new, upgraded military facility with additional port, weaponry, and other functions, all at the expense of the Japanese government.[1] This means that more bases would be removed from south-central Okinawa—where over 80 percent of Okinawa's population, or approximately 1.17 million people, reside (Okinawaken 2015b)—and consolidated in less populated northern Okinawa. The U.S. military, I suggest, expects that this process will result in fewer complaints about their presence from Okinawans and will allow them to use Okinawa more freely to achieve their strategic objectives in the new twenty-first century security environment.

This brings up the second issue: through the Camp Schwab fortification plan, the vast majority of U.S. bases in Japan would continue to be imposed on Okinawa. The murder of the twenty-year-old Okinawan woman in 2016 has highlighted this second issue in Okinawans' eyes. Indeed, the Camp Schwab fortification plan—with the new airport that is expected to last one hundred years—presupposes the continuing, or really permanent, U.S. military presence in Okinawa, the very situation that is responsible for this murder as well as other base-related crimes, incidents, and accidents that have happened over the past seventy plus years. This unfair situation persists because the Japanese government continues to use an outdated Cold War security paradigm (Takano 2008) in a manner that reinforces the policy of concentrating U.S. bases in Okinawa—even though this policy, like putting all the eggs in one basket, increases Japan's vulnerability to outside attacks (Nye 2014; Onaga 2015, 16–17). Okinawans argue that this policy is discriminatory because it is an extension and continuation of mainland Japan's sacrifice of Okinawa ever since (or even before) World War II (Medoruma 2005; Onaga 2015, 16).

The Japanese government's continued reliance on a Cold War paradigm was revealed, for instance, when Tokyo justified the construction of a Futenma replacement facility in Okinawa by saying that the continued presence of the U.S. Marine Corps in Okinawa functions as a "deterrent," i.e., a way to dissuade the enemy by displaying the capacity to retaliate (Takano 2008, 98–99). Such a justification is out-of-date: today, Japan's Air SDF serves as the deterrent through its capacity to master the air in or near Japan in case of emergency. The U.S. Air Force complements the Air SDF, but the Marine Corps does not really have any role to play here. In the meantime, the Marine Corps, while maintaining its tradition of being "first to fight," has redefined itself by actively engaging in humanitarian and peacekeeping operations with a capacity to "remove" (i.e., kill) those deemed a danger to others (Yara 2016a). Thus, contrary to what the Japanese government has argued, the presence of the U.S. Marine Corps in Okinawa should be understood not as a Cold War–style deterrent, but rather as a first responder to all kinds of emergencies—not just those caused by a clearly defined "enemy," but also natural disasters, refugee crises, terrorist attacks, and other amorphous contingencies. It follows that the Futenma replacement facility, a new facility for the U.S. Marine Corps, does not have to be built specifically in Okinawa.

Similarly, Tokyo's outdated logic concerning the geopolitical advantage of Okinawa breaks down because, for instance, the amphibious assault ship responsible for carrying the aviation units of Futenma Air Station to the site of conflict is stationed in Sasebo City in Kyushu, 800 kilometers (approximately 500 miles) north of Okinawa. While this arrangement helps enhance the networking capacity of the U.S. Marine Corps, it also raises a question: How can Tokyo argue that Okinawa has a geopolitical advantage when it takes four days for the ship in Sasebo to be put on alert, get ready, and actually come pick up the aviation units at Futenma? Clearly, the Futenma replacement facility could be located anywhere inside (or even outside) Japan, as long as it too could be reached from Sasebo within four days (Okinawaken 2015a, 29–37; "Special Feature . . . " 2016; Yara 2016b).

The Japanese government's outdated visions, intertwined with its discriminatory policies against Okinawa, are accompanied by a surge of nationalistic desire in Japan, which seeks to compensate for the decline of economic power with military presence. This desire, while often shaped by the central government, also has a large popular base of Japanese constituencies whose life and work have become increasingly precarious due to globalization, particularly the rise of China and other developing countries whose cheap laborers "steal" jobs from them. An irony here is that globalization also helps Japanese constituencies buy low-priced consumer goods produced by these laborers. As such, today's Japanese nationalism is sustained by the very globalization it opposes. In 2015, this nationalistic desire was manifested in the Japanese government's controversial "reinterpretation"—or abandonment, some would say—of Article 9 of the postwar Japanese constitution stipulating the renunciation of war. This reinterpretation, together with the transformation of the U.S. military and the realignment of the U.S.-Japan alliance, will allow the SDF to play an increasingly active role in coping with alleged threats in the Asia-Pacific region and beyond. For example, the SDF is expected to exercise collective self-defense with the U.S. military outside the territories of Japan. It would also be used to confront new security concerns, like North Korea's nuclear program or China's maritime expansion (Yara 2016a, 2016b). Against this background of security concerns, the Japanese government was also able to pass the controversial 2013 State Secrets Law, which potentially limits the public right of access to information concerning security in the name of national interest.

In short, even though the U.S. and Japanese governments present the Camp Schwab fortification plan as a benevolent gesture that will reduce the footprint of the U.S. military in Okinawa, what is actually happening in a broader context is the post–Cold War transformation of the U.S. military and realignment of the U.S.-Japan alliance, intertwined, somewhat paradoxically, with rising nationalism and the old Cold War security paradigm within Japan.

New Historical Circumstances, New Okinawan Identity:
A Hypothesis Concerning Empire and the Okinawan "Multitude"

I hypothesize that the transformation of the U.S. military and the realignment of the U.S.-Japan alliance are manifestations of a prolonged process of *decline* of a United States–centered order in the Asia-Pacific region. This decline began around 1970, a time marked by struggles and the eventual defeat of the United States militarily in Vietnam and economically via the collapse of the Bretton Woods system of monetary management. I further hypothesize that the end of this process goes hand in hand with the full and clear emergence of Empire, defined as "a *decentered* and *deterritorializing* apparatus of rule that progressively incorporates the entire global realm within its open, expanding frontiers" (Hardt and Negri 2000, xii, emphasis original). Indeed, unlike the United States–centered order established in the Asia-Pacific region after World War II on the basis of the hegemony of the U.S. military and the U.S. dollar, Empire, as a network power, sustains itself by expanding a system of interconnected synergies, where "*[t]he United States does not, and indeed no nation-state can today, form the center of an imperialist project*" (Hardt and Negri 2000, xiii–xiv; emphasis original).

One recent symptom of the transition from a United States–centered world order to Empire is Donald Trump's controversial foreign policy approach to the Asia-Pacific region, announced during his 2016 presidential campaign. Trump asserted that the withdrawal of U.S. forces from Japan and South Korea is inevitable without further financial support from these host nations, suggesting that the United States, with its astronomical national debts, no longer has the resources to continue to play the role of the world police as it did after World War II ("Highlights From Our Interview . . ." 2016). His announcement, though unpopular among strategic planners and governmental leaders in Asia (Ramzy 2016), has nonetheless revealed the plain fact that today, individual nations must assume a larger responsibility for actively participating in and jointly managing the global security network that the United States has built up since the World War II but can no longer sustain alone. In the age of Empire, each nation's peace and prosperity—or at least that of a particular privileged segment of the population—may be achieved only when this network is maintained. Even if Trump is not elected as the next U.S. president, such thinking may move the post–Cold War security paradigm toward Empire.

Under the paradigm of Empire, peace would be deprived and prosperity would be withheld at the level of everyday social life in Okinawa (and other politically vulnerable places), because Empire is a paradigmatic form of *biopower*—power over life—"that combines military might with social, economic, political, psychological, and ideological control" (Hardt and Negri 2004, 53).[2] The aforementioned governmental actions—the reinterpretation of Article 9 of the Japanese constitution and the introduction of the State Secrets Law—are good examples of effects of Empire as biopower on Japan as a whole. In Okinawa, Empire as biopower comes to bear in the form of the Camp Schwab fortification plan, which would destroy peaceful life in Okinawa and beyond. The plan involves offshore land reclamation to create 160 hectares (approximately 395 acres) adjacent to Camp Schwab from coastal waters known to be a migration route of the dugong, a manatee-like marine mammal under national and international protection (Okinawaken 2015a, 77–95). The plan would also continue to implicate Okinawa in the annihilation of human life, exemplified by the use of Okinawa to send U.S. troops to Iraq, Afghanistan, and other locations of bloodshed. Furthermore, it would also have a detrimental impact on Okinawa's already poor economic prospects, in a way that undermines the security of everyday life.

Unlike Okinawans of the 1990s, who benefited from growing job markets in affluent Okinawa, today's Okinawans are often without security in work and life. For instance, the number of non-full-time workers in Okinawa dramatically increased from 75,000 (17.1 percent of the employed labor force) in 1992 to 238,000 (43.0 percent) in 2012, highest among prefectures in the nation ("Hiseiki Koyōsha 3onende 2.7bai . . . " 2015). The poverty rate of children in Okinawa, an estimated 30 percent, is also the highest in the nation ("Shasetsu . . ." 2015). One reason for ordinary Okinawans' economic plight is that the majority (but not all[3]) of local industries, increasingly protected by government funds for Okinawan development, refuse to raise Okinawans' salaries and wages, thereby shutting down innovation, growth, and transformation in their business practices (Higuchi 2014). The Camp

Schwab fortification plan, as a manifestation of Empire as biopower, would reinforce this unhealthy economic condition: as Higuchi (2014) explains, if the plan is executed, the Japanese government would fulfill their promise to increase the subsidies for local industries as compensation. This would in turn maintain the status quo of Okinawa's conservative business and industrial structure, block the improvement of Okinawan productivity, and worsen the economic predicaments of ordinary Okinawans.

It is not surprising that Empire, as a form of biopower, attempts to ideologically control the depth of Okinawan cultural history and identity as well. In 2015, seventy years after the Battle of Okinawa, the majority, or approximately 53 percent of the population, fell into the third generation (who are forty-three years old or younger), while approximately 34 percent fell into the second generation (between forty-three and seventy years old) and 14 percent fell into the first generation (older than seventy) (Okinawaken 2015c). As a result, Okinawa's collective memory of the war and the alien rule has become increasingly difficult to maintain. Taking advantage of this intergenerational shift of the meaning of collective memory, the Japanese government has attempted to disavow, manipulate, and erode Okinawa's historical experiences, a crucial building material of an Okinawan identity of resistance. For instance, in 2007, the Japanese Ministry of Education, Culture, Sports, Science and Technology, responsible for annual screening and approval of all textbooks to be used in public school systems, instructed authors and publishers of high school history textbooks to modify and dilute descriptions about the atrocities that the Japanese Imperial Army perpetrated against Okinawans during the Battle of Okinawa ("Tokushū . . . " 2007). Relatedly, in one of the top-level meetings held between Okinawa prefecture and the Japanese government in 2015, Chief Cabinet Secretary Suga Yoshihide reportedly said to Governor Onaga: "I was born after the war, so it is difficult for me to understand Okinawan history. For me, the agreement [about the construction of a Futenma replacement facility in Henoko] made in the U.S-Japan joint meeting 19 years ago [in 1996] is the sole basis" upon which the Japanese government acts ("Onaga Chiji Kōen Yōshi . . . " 2015).

On the whole, Empire as a form of biopower is creating, at the level of everyday social life, an environment where once well-off Okinawan "citizens" have rapidly disintegrated into an aggregate of precarious lives deprived of peace, prosperity, and historical consciousness. This environment radically undermines the identity-making that was possible in the 1990s.

And yet, it is in this emerging social environment, I suggest, where new potentialities of Okinawa identity have also grown over the past decade. Specifically, Okinawa today has confronted the challenges posed by Empire through articulating a new identity, one increasingly shaped by the second generation and the third generation. In fact, the two issues presented above—(1) the metamorphosis of Okinawa into a site of strategic significance in the post-Cold War Asia-Pacific region and (2) the continued imposition of the vast majority of U.S. bases on Okinawa—are critically articulated mainly by those belonging to these two generations, including Okinawa Governor Onaga Takeshi, the staff of the Okinawa Prefectural Government, local media, scholars and critics, and participants of protest movements in Henoko. Of course, the aging first generation continues to be an integral part of Okinawan social life, political action, and public discourse. I call the collective agency emerging from this transgenerational structure—maintained primarily by the second and third generations and supplemented by the first generation—the Okinawan "multitude," signaling both the specificities of Okinawa and the universality of the multitude, defined by Hardt and Negri as "singularities that act in common" (2004, 105).

My participant-observations of protest activities in Henoko over the past decade, in particular the brief fieldwork in the summers of 2015 and 2016, indicate that in their shared efforts to block construction of a new military facility on Camp Schwab, the Okinawan "multitude" have constituted themselves as an open network of critical subjects. Internally, in a manner that reveals the specificity of local life, they have overcome the pro-base/anti-base divide that had been characteristic of politics in postwar Okinawa, while externally, in a manner that demonstrates the universality of the multitude, they have embraced outsiders (mainland Japanese and others) who share despair and antagonism against the larger system of power, Empire. In so doing, the Okinawan "multitude" powerfully rearticulate Okinawan identity, marshaling collective historical experiences not only as a way to remember the past but also as a method for shaping the future. This rearticulation of identity occurs through the explosive communication they produce not only in physical space (as Okinawan "people" of the 1950s–1960s and Okinawan "citizens" in the 1990s did) but also in new cyberspace of the twenty-first century.

Cyberspace is a particularly important site of struggle within and against Empire today. The Okinawan "multitude," like participants in the Arab

Spring (Stepanova 2011; Eltantawy and Wiest 2011) and the Occupy movement (Juris 2012; Milner 2013), have appropriated the advancement of information-communication technologies for mobilizing protests. For instance, the use of excessive force against protesters by the riot squad of the prefectural and national police in front of Camp Schwab and by officers of the Japan Coast Guard on Henoko's sea has been diligently captured by protesters through their cameras and disseminated across Japan and beyond, in real time, through blogs, YouTube, Facebook, Twitter, and other social networking platforms. Such activities help the Okinawan "multitude" *occupy* not only the physical space around Camp Schwab but also the virtual space dominated by the mainstream media, which tend to trivialize or completely ignore oppositional voices of Okinawa. In this struggle in both virtual and physical space, Okinawa presages, critiques, and reimagines its own future, or perhaps the future of Japan at large, by resisting Empire, the looming system of postmodern control.

In effect, I aim to theorize the development of Okinawan identity through a changing sequence of key social actors, i.e., the Okinawan "people" of the 1950s and 1960s, Okinawan "citizens" of the 1990s, and the Okinawan "multitude" of today. The continuing violence against women and children—exemplified by the 1955 Yumiko-chan incident, the 1995 rape of an Okinawan schoolgirl, and the 2016 murder of a young Okinawan woman—forms the foundation upon which this sequence is established. More specifically, my hypothesis is: (1) the Okinawan "people" of the 1950s and 1960s resisted the regime of *oppression* during the U.S. military rule of Okinawa in the age of the U.S.-centered world order; (2) Okinawan "citizens" of the 1990s challenged the regime of *discipline*, established after the 1972 Okinawa reversion, which sought to recreate Okinawans as docile subjects who would accept the U.S. military bases; and (3) the Okinawan "multitude" of today, in the age of Empire, critically engage in the regime of *biopower* that controls social life in its entirety by withdrawing peace, depriving prosperity, and regulating identity.

The first edition of this book fully articulates arguments (1) and (2) but only partially addresses argument (3). I have witnessed the development of the situation in Henoko from the mid-2000s to the mid-2010s, which enables me to discuss argument (3) more clearly and to present the sequence of the Okinawan "people"—"citizens"—"multitude" for the first time in this preface. It should be emphasized, however, that this sequence, particularly the last phase concerning the transformation of Okinawan identity by the

Okinawan "multitude" within and against Empire, remains a hypothesis. Additional ethnographic, historical, and theoretical exploration is necessary to fully substantiate this hypothesis. Meanwhile, this paperback edition of *Okinawa and the U.S. Military* continues to serve as an entry point into ongoing disputes over the U.S. bases in Okinawa from an informed anthropological and historical perspective.

Notes

With the help of Ms. Marguerite Floyd, I am able to correct in this paperback edition errors in grammar, typing, and fact that appeared in the first edition of *Okinawa and the U.S. Military*. I want to express my thankfulness to her for helping me accomplish this task. I also thank the Asia Library of the University of Michigan Library for providing Fukuchi (1983). Last but not least, I am grateful for the skillful and thoughtful copyediting performed by Ms. Marisa Lastres of Columbia University Press in helping me finalize this preface.

1. The Japanese government agreed to shoulder the entire cost of the Camp Schwab fortification plan, an estimated 1 trillion yen ($10 billion), when Japan's national budget is constantly in red (e.g., in 2016, the revenue is 57 trillion yen [$570 billion] while the expenditure is 96 trillion yen [$960 billion]) and the total of Japan's national debts is now reaching 1000 trillion yen ($10 trillion) (Kurashige 2016).

2. Hardt and Negri use the quoted line in order to explain what military theorists call "full spectrum domination," but Hardt and Negri (2004: 53) also add: "Military theorists have thus, in effect, discovered the concept of *biopower*" (emphasis mine).

3. A growing (though still relatively small) segment of local industries and business circles has begun to recognize that the U.S. bases in Okinawa, which neither conduct any economic activities nor produce any wealth, depress the full potential of Okinawa's economic and social development (Okinawaken 2015b); this segment often actively supports anti-base protests in Henoko and beyond.

References

"1962nen, Okinawa: 'Kakuheikiko' no Kadena" [Okinawa in 1962: Kadena as an armory of nuclear weapons]. 2016. *Mainichi Shimbun*, February 20. Accessed July 5, 2016. http://mainichi.jp/articles/20160220/dde/001/040/045000c.

Abe Takashi. 2016. "Saihatsu Bōshi Dokoroka Sabetsu Ishiki wo Kakudai, Kaiheitai no Shinjin Kenshū" [Recruit training programs in the U.S. Marine Corps: Not for preventing recurrence, but for reinforcing discrimination]. *Okinawa Times*, May 26. Accessed May 26, 2016. http://www.okinawatimes.co.jp/article .php?id=170024.

Agamben, Giorgio. 1998. *Homo Sacer: Sovereign Power and Bare Life*. Stanford, CA: Stanford University Press.

Arasaki Moriteru. 1995. *Okinawa Hansen Jinushi* [Okinawa's anti-military landlords]. Tokyo: Kōbunken.

Arashiro Toshiaki. 1994. *Ryukyu-Okinawa Shi* [History of the Ryukyus and Okinawa]. Okinawa: Okinawaken Rekishi Kyōiku Kenkyūkai.

Asato Eiko. 2000. "Beigunseika ni miru Kodomo to Josei no Jinken" [Human rights of children and women under the U.S. military rule]. *People's Plan Forum* 3(4) (September). Accessed July 5, 2016. http://www.jca.apc.org/ppsg/News/3–4 /F03-4-08.htm.

"'Bōkō Hakkaku Osore Satsugai' . . . Beigunzoku ga Kyōjyutsu" ['I killed the woman, fearing my crime would be brought to light' . . . former U.S. serviceman stated]. 2016. *Mainichi Shimbun*, May 22. Accessed May 22, 2016. http://mainichi .jp/articles/20160522/k00/00m/040/092000c.

Department of Defense. 1995. *United States Security Strategy for the East Asia-Pacific Region*. Washington, DC: Office of International Security Affairs.

Department of State. n.d. *1977–1981: The Presidency of Jimmy Carter*. Accessed July 10, 2016. https://history.state.gov/milestones/1977-1980/foreword.

Commandant of the Marine Corps. 2011. *Manpower Unit Deployment Program Standing Operating Procedures*. Marine Corps Order P3000.15B. Accessed August 15, 2016. http://www.marines.mil/Portals/59/Publications/MCO%20 P3000.15B.pdf.

Eltantawy, Nahed and Julie B. Wiest. 2011. "Social Media in the Egyptian Revolution: Reconsidering Resource Mobilization Theory." *International Journal of Communication* 5: 1207–1224. Accessed July 31, 2016. http://ijoc.org/index.php/ijoc/article /viewFile/1242/597&a=bi&pagenumber=1&w=100_1.

"Fukkimae Beihanzai Nen 1000ken, Gaimushōbunsho Kōkai" [Before reversion, 1000 crimes occurred annually on average, Ministry of Foreign Affairs documents opened to the public]. 2011. *Ryukyu Shimpo*, December 23. Accessed July 5, 2016. http://ryukyushimpo.jp/news/prentry-185512.html.

Fukuchi Hiroaki. 1983. "Yumiko-chan Jiken" [Yumiko-chan incident]. In *Okinawa Daihyakka Jiten*, vol. 3, 784. Okinawa: Okinawa Taimususha.

Hardt, Michael and Antonio Negri. 2000. *Empire*. Cambridge, MA: Harvard University Press.

———. 2004. *Multitude: War and Democracy in the Age of Empire*. New York: Penguin Press.

Higa Hiroshi. 2016. "Okinawa Josei Iki Yōgi Moto Beihei Taiho" [Former U.S. serviceman arrested for suspected abandonment of an Okinawan woman]. *Mainichi Shimbun*, May 20. Accessed May 20, 2016. http://mainichi.jp/articles /20160520/ddm/003/040/091000c.

"Highlights From Our Interview With Donald Trump on Foreign Policy." 2016. *New York Times*, March 26. Accessed March 26, 2016. http://www.nytimes .com/2016/03/27/us/politics/donald-trump-interview-highlights.html?ribbon -ad-idx=9&rref=politics&module=Ribbon&version=context&region=Header &action=click&contentCollection=Politics&pgtype=article&_r=0.

Higuchi Kōtarō. 2014. *Okinawakara Kichi ga Nakunaranai Hontō no Riyū* [The true reason for why U.S. bases stay in Okinawa]. *Politas*, December 14. Accessed on July 31, 2016. http://politas.jp/features/3/article/327.

"Hiseiki Koyōsha 30nende 2.7bai: Seikikyūjin, Izen Hikuku" [270 percent increase of non-full-time workers over 30 years: Demand for full-time workers remains low]. 2015. *Ryukyu Shimpo*, November 1. Accessed May 22, 2016. http://ryuky ushimpo.jp/news/entry-164213.html.

Juris, Jeffrey S. 2012. "Reflections on #Occupy Everywhere: Social media, public space, and emerging logics of aggregation." *American Ethnologist* 39 (2): 259–279. Accessed July 31, 2016. DOI: 10.1111/j.1548-1425.2012.01362.x.

Kurashige Atsurō. 2016. " 'Okinawa' 'Shōhizei' karamieta 'Hijiritsukoku Nihon' no Adabana" ['Futile Japan' revealed through 'Okinawa' and 'Consumption Tax']. *Sunday Mainichi*, June 12. Accessed June 15, 2016. http://mainichibooks.com /sundaymainichi/column/2016/06/12/post-905.html.

Kurima Yasuo. 1998. *Okinawa Keizai no Gensō to Genjitu* [Myths and realities of the Okinawan economy]. Tokyo: Nihon Keizaihyōronsha.

Medoruma, Shun. 2005. *Okinawa "Sengo" Zero-Nen* [Zero year "after the war" in Okinawa]. Tokyo: Nihon Hōsō Shuppan Kyōkai.

Milner, Ryan M. 2013. "Pop Polyvocality: Internet Memes, Public Participation, and the Occupy Wall Street Movement." *International Journal of Communication* 7: 2357–2390. Accessed July 31, 2016. http://ijoc.org/index.php/ijoc/article /view/1949/1015.

Ministry of Defense. 2016. *Zaioki Beikaiheitai no Guamu Iten no Keiigaiyō* [History and summary of Guam transfer of the U.S. Marine Corps in Okinawa]. Tokyo:

Ministry of Defense. Accessed July 5, 2016. http://www.mod.go.jp/j/approach /zaibeigun/saihen/iten_guam/pdf/gaiyo_160330.pdf.

Nakamura Sugako. 1995. "Kōkōsei Daihyō Aisatsu" [Address on behalf of high school students]. *Ryukyu Shimpo*, October 22.

Nakano Yoshio. 1969. *Sengo Shiryō Okiinawa* [Historical records of postwar Okinawa]. Tokyo: Nihon Hyōronsha.

Nichibenren. 2014. *Nichibei Chii Kyōtei no Kaitei wo Motomete: Nichibenren karano Teigen* [In search of revising the status of forces agreement: a proposal from the Japan Federation of Bar Associations]. Tokyo: Nichibenren. Accessed July 2, 2016. http://www.nichibenren.or.jp/library/ja/publication/booklet/data /nichibeichiikyoutei_201410.pdf.

Nye, Joseph. 2014. "Japan's Robust Self-Defense Is Good for Asia." *Huffington Post*, August 7. Accessed July 5, 2016. http://www.huffingtonpost.com/joseph-nye /japan-self-defense_b_5658883.html.

"Obama Discusses Hiroshima Visit, Nuke-Free Goal, Security in Asia." 2016. *Asahi Shimbun*, May 27. Accessed May 27, 2016. http://www.asahi.com/ajw/articles /AJ201605270001.html.

Okada Gen. 2016. "Onaga Chiji, Josei Iki Genba de Tsuitō: 'Mamorenakute Gomen'ne'" [Governor Onaga mourned for the woman at the site of abandonment: 'I am sorry that I could not protect you']. *Asahi Shimbun Digital*, June 2. Accessed June 2, 2016. http://www.asahi.com/articles/ASJ6167G8J61TIPE041.html?iref= comtop_photo.

Okinawaken. 2015a. *Dai2 Ikensho* [The Second Position Document (a document submitted to the Naha branch of Fukuoka High Court on October 21, 2015)]. Accessed July 5, 2016. http://www.pref.okinawa.lg.jp/site/chijiko/henoko/docu ments/ikensho02.pdf.

———. 2015b. *Chūryūgunyōchi Atochiriyō ni Tomonau Keizaihakyūkōka nado ni kansuru Kentōchōsa* [Results of an investigation on the economic and other effects of redeveloping returned land used as military bases]. Okinawa: Okinawaken. Accessed July 5, 2016. http://www.pref.okinawa.jp/site/kikaku/chosei /atochi/houkokusho/documents/150130chousakekkagaiyou2.pdf.

———. 2015c. *Heisei 27nen Jyūmin Kihon Daichō Nenreibetsu Jinkō* [Residents register 2015, population by age and sex]. Accessed July 5, 2016. http://www.pref .okinawa.jp/site/kikaku/shichoson/2422.html.

Okinawaken Kikakubu Tōkeika. 2016. *Heisei 7nen Kokusei Chōsa, Nenrei (Kakusai), Danjobetu Jinkō* [National census 1995, population by age and sex]. Accessed July 5, 2016. http://www.pref.okinawa.jp/toukeika/pc/pc_index.html.

Okinawaken Sōmubu Chiji Kōshitu Kichi Taisakushitu. 1998. *Okinawa no Beigunkichi Heisei 10nen 3gatsu* [The U.S. bases in Okinawa, March 1998]. Okinawa: Okinawaken Sōmubu Chiji Kōshitu Kichi Taisakushitu.

———. 2016. *Okinawa no Beigun oyobi Jieitaikichi (Shiryōtōkeishū) Heisei 28nen 3gatsu* [Bases of the U.S. military and Japan's self-defense forces in Okinawa, statistical materials, March 2016]. Okinawa: Okinawaken Sōmubi Chiji Kōshitu Kichi Taisakushitu. Accessed June 30, 2016. http://www.pref.okinawa.lg.jp/site /chijiko/kichitai/toukei.html.

Okinawa Prefectural Peace Memorial Museum (OPPMM). 2001. *Okinawaken Heiwakinen Shiryōkan Sōgōan'nai* [Okinawa Prefectural Peace Memorial Museum comprehensive guide]. Okinawa: Okinawan Prefectural Peace Memorial Museum.

"Onaga Chiji Kōen Yōshi: Chiji Kikoku Kōen" [Summary of Governor Onaga's address upon return from Geneva to Okinawa]. 2015. *Ryukyu Shimpo*, September 25. Accessed May 22, 2016. http://ryukyushimpo.jp/news/prentry-249409.html.

Onaga Takeshi. 2015. *Chinjyutusho* [Statement (delivered at the Naha branch of Fukuoka High Court on December 2, 2015)]. Accessed July 2, 2016. http://www .pref.okinawa.jp/site/chijiko/henoko/documents/chinjutusyo.pdf.

"Opinion Poll: 77% Support Canceling the Former Governor's Approval of Landfill Henoko." 2015. *Ryukyu Shimpo*, June 2. Accessed July 5, 2016. http://english .ryukyushimpo.jp/2015/06/06/18826/.

Rabson, Steve. 2012. *The Okinawan Diaspora in Japan: Crossing the Borders Within.* Honolulu: University of Hawai'i Press.

Ramzy, Austin. 2016. "Comments by Donald Trump Draw Fears of an Arms Race in Asia." *New York Times*, March 28. Accessed March 28, 2016. http://www .nytimes.com/2016/03/29/world/asia/donald-trump-arms-race.html?_r=0.

Rumsfeld, Donald. 2002. "Transforming the Military." *Foreign Affairs* 81(3) (May/ June 2002): 20–32.

Sato Taketsugu. 2016. "Ikiyougi no Motobeihei, Satsugai Honomekasu Kyōjyutsu: Okinawa no Joseifumei" [Former U.S. serviceman, hinting at killing of an Okinawan woman]. *Asahi Shimbun Digital*, May 20. Accessed May 20, 2016. http:// www.asahi.com/articles/ASJ5M5KC9J5MTIPE02S.html?iref=comtop_8_01.

Security Consultative Committee. 2005. *US-Japan Alliance: Transformation and Realignment for the Future.* Accessed May 21, 2016. http://www.mofa.go.jp /region/n-america/us/security/scc/doc0510.html.

Seigle, Monroe F. 2013. "Hawaii Marines rotate." *Marine Corps Base Hawaii*, April 18. Accessed on July 31, 2016. http://www.mcbhawaii.marines.mil/News /News-Article-Display/Article/538749/hawaii-marines-rotate/.

"Shasetsu: Kodomono Hinkon—Sōryoku Ageta Torikumi Isoge" [Editorial: Poverty of children—Necessary to hasten to implement measures by joining our forces]. 2015. *Ryukyu Shimpo*, August 1. Accessed May 22, 2016. http://ryukyushimpo.jp /editorial/prentry-246592.html.

Sōmushō Tōkeikyoku. 2011. *Showa 30nen Kokusei Chōsa: Nenrei Kakusai oyobi Danjobetsu Jinkō, Zen-Ryukyu* [National census 1955, population by age and by sex, all Ryukyus]. Accessed July 5, 2016. http://www.e-stat.go.jp/SG1/estat/GL08020103 .do?_toGL08020103_&tclassID=000001028029&cycleCode=0&requestSender= search.

"Special Feature: Okinawa Holds Mass Protest Rally Against US Base." 2016. *Ryukyu Shimpo*, June 19, 2016. Accessed July 5, 2016. http://english.ryukyushimpo.jp /special-feature-okinawa-holds-mass-protest-rally-against-us-base/.

Stepanova, Ekaterina. 2011. "The Role of Information Communication Technologies in the 'Arab Spring': Implications beyond the Region." *PONARS Eurasia Policy Memo* No. 159 (May 2011): 1–6. http://pircenter.org/kosdata/page_doc/p2594_2.pdf.

Takahashi Takeo, Kawaguchi Takahisa, and Yoneda Tomitaro. 2009. "Anzen Hoshō to Koarisshon: Kokusai Hōgaku, Gunjigaku, Kokusai Seijigaku no Shitenkara (2)" [International security and coalition of willingness: from the perspectives of international low, military studies, and international politics (2)]. *Chūōgakuin Daigaku Shaki Shisutemu Kenkyūjo Kiyō* [Chuogakuin University Journal of Social System Research], 103–128.

Takano Hajime. 2008. *Okinawa ni Kaiheitai ha Iranai!* [The U.S. Marine Corps is not needed in Okinawa]. Tokyo: Ningen Shuppan.

Tanaka Masakazu. 2015. "Guntai, Seibōryoku, Biashun: Fukki Zengo no Okinawa wo Chūshin'ni" [The military, sexual violence, and prostitution: Focusing on Okinawa around the time of reversion]. In *Guntai no Bunkajinruigaku* [Cultural anthropology of the military], edited by Tanaka Masakazu, 177–212. Tokyo: Fūkyōsha.

"Tokushū: Yugamerareru Okinawasen: Kōgi no Nami, Shimagurumi" [Special issue: Distortion of the truth of the battle of Okinawa: Waves of all-Okinawa protest]. 2007. *Ryukyu Shimpo*, September 29. Accessed July 31, 2016. http:// ryukyushimpo.jp/news/prentry-27637.html.

Umebayashi Hiromichi. 1994. *Jyōhō Kōkaihō de Toraeta Okinawa no Beigun* [The U.S. military in Okinawa revealed by the Furnishing of Information Act]. Tokyo: Kōbunken.

Yara Tomohiro. 2016a. "Okinawa Hatachi Josei no Shi wa, Nichibei Ryōseifuno Musakui no Tsumida" [The death of a 20-year-old Okinawan woman is the crime of the U.S. and Japanese government who have not done anything]. *Okinawa Times*, May 21. Accessed June 30, 2016. http://www.okinawatimes.co.jp/articles/-/50009.

———. 2016b. "Jimin wa Okinawa Renpai ni Manabe: Kaikensezuni Nihonga Ikirareru Michi" [LDP should learn from the consecutive defeats in Okinawa: The way Japan can survive without changing the constitution]. *Okinawa Times*, July 12. Accessed July 31, 2016. http://www.okinawatimes.co.jp/articles/-/49968.

Yomitan Village. 2008. "Yumiko-chan Jiken (1955/Ishikawashi)" [Yumiko-chan incident (1955/Ishikawa City)]. *Yomitan Bācharu Heiwa Shiryōkan*. Accessed July 5, 2016. http://heiwa.yomitan.jp/3/2674.html.

ACKNOWLEDGMENTS

Engaging in the U.S. base problems in Okinawa has been a daunting yet ultimately rewarding task which has taught me what anthropology can be about—skills and arts of subversive border-crossing in search of global solidarity. I would like to thank my teachers, friends, colleagues, and families in Okinawa, mainland Japan, the United States and elsewhere who have assisted me, over the years, to acquire, develop, and refine such skills and arts, of which this book is a product.

The members of my dissertation committee at the Department of Cultural Anthropology of Duke University—Anne Allison (chair), Orin Starn, Charlie Piot, Arif Dirlik (History), and Leo Ching (Asian and African Languages and Literature), together with Catherine Lutz joining from the Department of Anthropology, University of North Carolina at Chapel Hill—were paramount in shaping my anthropological and historical understandings of social movements, politics of identity and culture, and globalization. All of them have been critically compassionate teachers who have continuously inspired me even after I departed from Duke. Anne Allison and Orin Starn, particularly, kindly read each and every chapter of the earlier version of the manuscript and gave me invaluable suggestions and insights which are reflected in my arguments in this book.

My colleagues in the Japan Studies Program at the University of Kentucky—Doug Slaymaker, Kristin Stapleton, and Paul Karan—and friends and teachers in the Department of Modern and Classical Languages, Literatures and Cultures and across campus—Jerry Janecek, Susan Janecek, Suzanne Pucci, Ted Fiedler, Jane Phillips, Joanne Melish, Ron Bruzina, Anna Secor, Sue Roberts, Betsy Taylor, George Wilson, and Greg Epp—gave me thoughtful and insightful suggestions for the improvement of my text. Susan Janecek's editorial help, particularly, was indispensable for the preparation of the earlier version of the manuscript.

There are also other friends, colleagues, and critics who have helped, directly and indirectly, strengthen and improve my manuscript at various stages of its development: Mark Selden, James Roberson, Linda Angst, Michael Molasky, Gavan McCormack, Robin LeBlanc, Taira Koji, Medoruma Shun, Yakabi Osamu, Maetakenishi Kazuma, Ui Jyun, Arasaki Moriteru, Koshi'ishi Tadashi, Ota Yoshinobu, Tadatomo Keishi, Takahashi Meizen, Yoshimi Shunya, Ayse Gül Altinay, Ya-Chung Chuang, and Zhou Yongming.

I would like to extend my heartfelt appreciation to Editor Anne Routon of Columbia University Press, who has not only given me an opportunity to get Okinawan voices—my take of Okinawan voices—across the academy and beyond but also offered me skillful guidance on how best to produce this book. I am also grateful to Chris Nelson and Steve Rabson, two reviewers commissioned by the press, for their generous and perceptive responses to the earlier version of my manuscript, as well as their valuable suggestions for specific revisions, which have been thoroughly incorporated in the present version. I also would like to thank Leslie Bialler for his painstaking, careful, and skillful copyediting.

I also want to express my thankfulness to generous financial supports that have enabled me to conduct fieldwork in Okinawa in the summer of 1996 (Summer Research Award, Center for International Studies, Duke University and the Ford Foundation), between the summer of 1997 and the summer of 1998 (Foreign Language and Area Studies Fellowship, U.S. Department of Education), in the summer of 2000 (Summer Faculty Research Fellowship, University of Kentucky), in the summer of 2001 (Japan Studies Grant—Category: Short-Term Travel to Japan for Professional Purposes—Northeast Asia Council, Association for Asian Studies), and in October 2002, July 2003, March 2004, and July 2004 (Faculty Research Fellowship, Shibaura Institute of Technology in Japan).

Last, but not least, I want to express deepest gratitude to residents in Henoko and larger Nago City (including transient residents such as U.S. servicemen and Filipina hostesses). They kindly allowed my project to intersect with their everyday lives, as I had conversations with some in a village festival, was engaged in discussions with others in a political rally, shared with still others a couple of drinks in a local bar, and went out with still others to a beach for a little stroll. Because I want to maintain their anonymity, however, I can mention only a few names here: Kinjō Yūji, Kinjō Hatsuko, Miyagi Tamotsu, Tamaki Yoshikazu, Nakamura Zenkō, Miyagi Yasuhiro, Urashima Etsuko, Mashiki Tomi, Makishi Yoshikazu, and Ashitomi Hiroshi.

As my research progressed, I found myself constantly traversing local, national, and global dimensions of the problems of the U.S. military in Okinawa. While my border-crossing positionality may offend sensibilities of nationalists and patriots—in Japan, in the U.S., and elsewhere—I, together with other subversive hybrids in Okinawa and across the globe, prefer to see my positionality as a symptom of emerging global conditions whose merits must be reinforced to fight against the harms they have brought. My wife, Katie Clark, my mother, Maeda Teiko, and my late father, Inoue Kiyonori—themselves oppositional border-crossers in different ways—have known and lived such global conditions most skillfully. To them I would like to dedicate this book.

NOTE ON JAPANESE NAMES

AND TRANSLATIONS

Throughout this book, I follow the Japanese convention in which given names follow family names. In case of the Japanese authors who have published in English, however, I follow the English convention in which given names precede family names. Macrons indicate long vowels. However, macrons are omitted in the case of place names (e.g., Tokyo). In this study, while the names of political and public figures (e.g., Governor Ota, Prime Minister Hashimoto) are real, local informants' names are mostly altered to protect their privacy except where specified; the real name is provided if his/her name has been publicly known. Translations of Japanese and Okinawan "dialect" are mine throughout this book unless noted otherwise.

OKINAWA AND THE U.S. MILITARY

1

INTRODUCTION

 In the autumn of 1995, a twelve-year-old Okinawan school-girl was abducted and raped by three U.S. servicemen. The incident immediately set off a chain of protest activities by women's groups, teachers' associations, labor unions, reform-ist political parties, and various grass-roots organizations across Okinawa Prefecture. Shortly after, these activities culminated in an all-Okinawa pro-test rally attended by some 85,000 people from all walks of life, including business leaders and conservative politicians in Okinawa who had seldom raised their voices against the U.S. military presence. On stage, Governor Ota Masahide as much summarized as orchestrated Okinawa's exasperation by stating, "As the person granted responsibility for administering Okina-wa, I would like to apologize from the bottom of my heart that I could not protect the dignity of a child, which I must protect above all else" (*Ryukyu Shinpo*, October 22, 1995).

Although certain sectors of Okinawan society—such as the Military Land-lord Association, whose members had benefited economically from the pres-ence of the U.S. military—remained silent about the matter, the rape incident exposed what the U.S. and Japanese governments long wanted to hide—that Okinawa's prolonged sufferings derived from, among other things, the dis-proportionate concentration of the U.S. military facilities there. In fact, in its role as a strategic outpost for "stability and prosperity in the Asia-Pacific

=米軍人による少女暴行事件を糾弾し日米地位協定の見直しを要求する=

沖 縄 県 民 総 決 起 大 会

● 基地の整理縮小を促進せよ
● 米軍人の綱紀を粛正し犯罪を根絶せよ
● 日米地位協定を早急に見直せ
● 被害者に対する謝罪と完全補償を早急に実施せよ

FIGURE 1.1 85,000 Okinawans participated in a protest rally against the rape of an Okinawan schoolgirl by U.S. servicemen. Reprint from Okinawa Prefectural Government 1997: 9.

region" (U.S.-Japan Security Consultative Committee [1996] 1997: 26), this "remote,"[1] semi-tropical island prefecture (population 1.3 million), which makes up only 0.6 percent of Japan's total landmass, had been burdened with 75 percent of the U.S. military facilities and 65 percent (approximately 29,000[2]) of the 45,000 American troops in Japan.

Okinawa's collective will for the reorganization and reduction—if not the outright removal—of the U.S. bases took definite shape specifically when Governor Ota gave Tokyo a refusal to renew the lease of Okinawa's land for the use of the U.S. military. In doing so, Ota, as it were, attempted to redeem not only the dignity of the raped girl but also the pride of Okinawans that had long been infringed upon.

Okinawa, once known as the Ryukyu Kingdom, had flourished from the fourteenth through the sixteenth centuries by participating in China's trans-Asian trade network. In 1609, however, Satsuma, the southernmost feudal clan of the Tokugawa regime in mainland Japan, invaded the Kingdom in order to gain control of the profits made from that trade. For about 260 years following this invasion, the Kingdom, while keeping up its appearances as an independent state whose status was formally sanctioned by Ming and Qing China, was in actuality politically and economically subor-

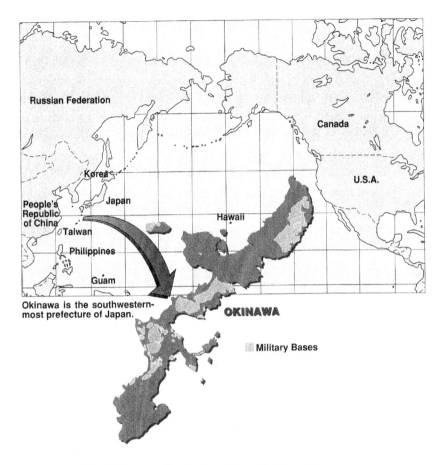

Russian Federation

Canada

Korea

U.S.A.

People's
Republic
of China

Japan

Taiwan

Hawaii

Philippines

Guam

Okinawa is the southwestern-
most prefecture of Japan.

OKINAWA

Military Bases

FIGURE 1.2 Map of Okinawa. Reprint from Okinawa Prefectural Government 1997: 2.

dinated to Satsuma, and by implication, Tokugawa Japan (Kerr 1958, Takara K. 1993, Arashiro 1994). In the late nineteenth century, the newly instituted Meiji government disposed of the Ryukyu Kingdom by way of the "Ryukyu Measures" (1872–1879) in order to turn it into a prefecture of Japan. From that moment on, Okinawan customs and manners became, in the eyes of Meiji government officials, the general public in Japan, and in some instances, Okinawan leaders themselves, a symbol of "backwardness" and an obstacle to making Okinawans genuine subjects of Imperial Japan. This view warranted the Meiji government's implementation of assimilation/Japanization programs for helping, or really making, Okinawans acquire "standard" Japanese, register with the conscription system, and show their allegiance to the emperor.

3

The image attached to Okinawans as the second-rate nationals eventually led Imperial Japan to use Okinawa as a strategic sacrifice to protect its mainland from U.S. military attack. In 1945 Okinawa became the site of the fierce ground battle known as the "typhoon of steel," in which approximately 150,000 lives—about a quarter of the prefectural population—were lost. The hardships of Okinawa did not cease with the war, however. In spite of the pretensions (or efforts, depending on the perspective) of the U.S. military government—named the United States Civil Administration of the Ryukyu Islands (USCAR) in 1950—to make Okinawa a showcase of democracy, violations of human rights were incessant during its period of control (1945–72). The requisition of Okinawa's land to construct military bases, the acquittal of U.S. servicemen who raped and/or murdered Okinawans, and the purge of the publicly elected mayor of Naha, Okinawa's capital city, who was critical of USCAR, are just a few examples of the inhumanity Okinawa experienced under USCAR's rule.

In response, in the 1960s, intense, island-wide reversion movements emerged, wherein the motherland, Japan, was imagined as the guardian of democracy and peace. Thus, Okinawa ironically submitted itself to an exploitative relationship even after the administration of Okinawa was transferred from the United States to Japan in 1972, because, by taking advantage of Okinawa's desire to escape alien rule, the "guardian," the Japanese government, agreed with Washington on the continued stationing of the U.S. military in Okinawa in order to counter the "communist threat" in the Far East and beyond. The end of the cold war did not stop the U.S.-Japan alliance from using Okinawa for the purpose of security. In 1995, the Pentagon declared—and Tokyo acknowledged—that "Asia remains an area of uncertainty, tension, and immense concentrations of military power" (Department of Defense 1995: 2), and reaffirmed its commitment to maintain a stable forward presence in the region (approximately 100,000 troops) into the foreseeable future.

The 1995 rape incident took place in the midst of this politico-military reaffirmation. In a way that undermined the security planning of Washington and Tokyo, the incident rekindled Okinawa's sedimented, smoldering sense of injustice, for which the apologies of President Bill Clinton, Ambassador to Japan Walter Mondale, Secretary of State Warren Christopher, and Secretary of Defense William Perry, and the promises of the Japanese government to reduce the burden on Okinawa, were like sprinkling water on parched soil. In November 1995 the U.S. and Japanese governments established the Special Action Committee on Okinawa (SACO) to deal with Okinawa's anger. In December 1996 SACO proposed that some of the major U.S. military facilities be returned to Okinawa by 2003 (Special Action Committee on Okinawa [1996] 1997). Among these was the 500-hectare (1,235-acre) Futenma Marine Corps Air Station,[3] a strategically vital U.S. military facility located in the congested residential area of central Okinawa.

It should be noted, however, that this proposal was only a part of an overall package that was designed more for the security goals of Washington and Tokyo than for the welfare of Okinawans. The main feature of the proposal was to establish and maintain a stable military presence in the region. Indeed, together with the return of Futenma, SACO also proposed the construction of a sea-based military base as its replacement facility off the waters of Camp

FIGURE 1.3 Futenma Air Station. Reprint from *Okinawaken Sōmubu Chiji Kōshitsu Kichi Taisakushitsu* 1998a: 19

FIGURE 1.4 Camp Schwab. Reprint from *Okinawaken Sōmubu Chiji Kōshitsu Kichi Taisaku-shitsu* 1998a: 6

Schwab in Henoko District (population: 1,400), a sparsely populated eastern coastal district of Nago City (population: 55,000). The Okinawans, however, viewed the idea of building a new base as an excuse to create a permanent U.S. military settlement and to strengthen its base functions. As a result, there was intense opposition from not only local residents but also from Okinawans everywhere. In 1998 Governor Ota declared that Okinawa was rejecting the proposal to construct the offshore base and, together with Okinawan citizens opposed to the base, demanded the unconditional return of Futenma. With this rejection, steps were to be steadfastly taken to reorganize and reduce the U.S. bases in Okinawa—or, so it appeared.

Io Jima Auxiliary Airfield

Northern Training Area

Okuma Rest Center
Yaedake Communication Site

Aha
Training Area

Nago
City

Nago Downtown

Gesaji Communication Site

Camp Schwab
Camp Hansen

Henoko Ordnance Ammunition Depot

Henoko District

Kadena Ammunition
Storage Area
Senaha
Communication Station
Yomitan Auxiliary Airfield
Sobe
Communication Site
Torli
Communication Station
Kadena Air Base
Army POL Depots
Camp Kuwae
Camp Zukeran
Futenma Air Station
Makiminato
Service Area
Naha Port

Gimbaru Training Area
Kin Blue Training Area
Kin Red Beach Training Area
Tengan Pier

Camp Courtney
Camp Mctureous
Camp Shields

Ukibaru-Jima Training Area
White Beach Area

Tsuken-Jima Training Area

Awase Communication Station

Deputy Division Engineer Office

Naha
(Capital of
Okinawa)

FIGURE 1.1 Map of Military Bases in Okinawa. Reprint from Okinawa Prefectural Government 1997: 4.

7

However, today, with the promised year of 2003 behind us, one finds that little change has come to Okinawa. Late in 1998, Governor Ota, the emblem of Okinawa's protest against the 1995 rape, was defeated in his bid for reelection. Originally, SACO had promised to return eleven military facilities to Okinawa, but only two have been restored thus far. The operations of Futenma Air Station have remained intact. In the community of Henoko in Nago City, preparations for the construction of the replacement facility of Futenma have been under way. U.S. servicemen raped Okinawan women even after the 1995 incident; the number of crimes committed by U.S. military personnel in Okinawa has tended to increase since 1997 (*Okinawa Taimusu*, June 3, 2004; Okinawaken Sōmubu Chiji Kōshitsu Kichi Taisakushitsu 2003).[4] Earsplitting daily jet noise and land pollution have also continued. Military accidents, too, continue to occur; in August 2004, for example, a U.S. Marine helicopter crashed into a university campus in central Okinawa.

Meanwhile, the functions of U.S. bases in Okinawa have been redefined as a forward presence to fight, no longer against "communist threats," but now, in the context of the post–cold war security environment, against "the unknown, the uncertain, the unseen, and the unexpected," to transplant the words of Secretary of Defense Donald Rumsfeld (2002: 23) from his discussion about "Transforming the Military." In alignment with this new strategic goal, Washington dispatched more than three thousand marines from Okinawa to the 2003 Iraq War, and now proposes to use not only Okinawa but Japan as a whole as a strategic foothold called "Power Projection Hub" (*Korea Times*, May 19, 2004; *Asahi.com*, September 22, 2004). In short, the sober reality is that Okinawa's protests in and since the mid-1990s have not helped restrain, let alone overthrow, the power of the U.S. and Japanese governments. Rather, power has paradoxically kept self-valorizing in spite of, and in the midst of, Okinawa's resistance.

Harvard sociologist Ezra Vogel (1999:11) approached this paradox by posing the question of why "Okinawans voted against Governor Ota and in favor of a man more willing to accept Tokyo's largesse and to keep a substantial U.S. military presence in Okinawa [?] " His conclusion: "In short, Okinawans were willing to provide facilities to U.S. troops to get economic aid from Tokyo." Challenging and complicating a reductionist economic view of this kind, my study, for its part, aims to give this paradox an anthropological—that is, ethnographic, historical, and theoretical—explanation by exploring the intricacies of Okinawan identity in the context of the nation-state and the larger processes of global history. Specifically, I conceptualize old cultural sensibilities of a uniformly poor and homogeneously oppressed Okinawan "people" in terms of a notion of totality, "we are Okinawans," and underscore how this totality—which had been shaped and reshaped by Okinawa's collective experiences of Japanese colonialism, the war, and U.S. military control—was, by the 1990s, increasingly rearticulated and sometimes disrupted by emerging internal differences. My intuition is that these internal differences have both renewed and dislodged Okinawa's unified front against the U.S.–Japan alliance, thereby helping us explain the puzzle of how and why power has multiplied in the midst of resistance. I will substantiate this intuition in three steps.

First, I introduce the general problematic of Okinawan modernity that has defined basic parameters of local identity (chapters 2 and 3). In chapter 2, the historical origin of Okinawa's oppositional sentiment will be discussed, together with how the affluence of contemporary Okinawan society—made possible by massive economic aid from Tokyo since the reversion of Okinawa in 1972—has acted as a background and vehicle of the unsettling transformation of this oppositional sentiment. The analysis of the unified protest against the 1995 rape specifically allows us to catch a glimpse of the larger historical process whereby the pan-Okinawan social consciousness of "we are Okinawans" has been articulated no longer in the sentiment as a poor, oppressed "people" but increasingly in the perspective of affluent "citizens" of diverse backgrounds awakened to globally disseminated ideas about ecology, women's equality, and peace.

Chapter 3 examines the same problematic of Okinawan modernity—Japanese domination, the war, U.S. rule, and the postreversion affluence—from the standpoint of the production of knowledge. Situating knowledge on Okinawa at a crossroads of local, national, and transnational circuits of intellectual discourse, this chapter specifically presents a critique of the body of "modern" Okinawan studies—three distinct but interrelated intellectual traditions concerning Okinawa that were developed between the 1920s and the 1980s in Japan, the U.S., and Okinawa, respectively.

My critique centers on their tendency to appeal to pure or original Okinawan-ness outside power and history by excluding the U.S. military and related social problems from their analyses. By delineating the contour of "modern" Okinawan studies, this chapter also wants to register and high-light the thrusts of new, critical, "postmodern" studies of Okinawa, within and against which this study is situated.

The second cluster of my study (chapters 4 and 5) ethnographically ex-amines, on the basis of the fieldwork I have been doing since the summer of 1997,[5] the politics of identity in a specific place in Okinawa—the com-munity of Henoko in Nago City. The readers will recognize that Henoko, as the proposed site for the relocation of Futenma Air Station, was and is the very center of the issue of military bases in Okinawa in spite of its small population and its marginal political status. In reference to the historical arrangement that had made this community in northern Okinawa home to a U.S. Marine Corps camp since 1957, I will highlight Henoko as a devel-opmental twilight zone which, while partially sharing in the affluence of postreversion Okinawa at large, has nonetheless been left behind as com-pared to more prospering south and central Okinawa. In the process, I will conceptualize the production of a sometimes reluctant and at other times enthusiastic pro-base[6] position in Henoko in reference to the idea "we are Okinawans but of a different kind." This idea specifically led Henoko's working-class residents to support, often against the grain, the U.S. military presence in exchange for jobs (chapter 4), while at the same time rousing the anti-base sentiment within this community among middle-class res-idents in reference to the enduring idea of pan-Okinawan unity, "we are Okinawans" (chapter 5).

In chapters 4 and 5 specifically, and in this study generally, the working class, a term that is admittedly somewhat awkward but useful, refers to "the socioeconomic class consisting of people who work for wages, especially low wages, including unskilled and semiskilled laborers and their families" (*The American Heritage Dictionary of the English Language*, fourth edition, s.v. "working class"; Cf. Williams 1983: 60–69). In Henoko, and by impli-cation Okinawa at large, they are, for example, construction workers, petty engineers responsible for maintaining equipment, delivery men, taxi driv-ers, employees in the food service industry, store clerks, and workers in the U.S. bases. The middle class in this study is defined as the socioeconomic class consisting of people who, while working for wages (like all workers), do so in more secure conditions with a greater degree of autonomy and comfort than workers of the working class. Within Henoko, and by impli-cation Okinawa at large, they are, for example, public employees, educators, health-care professionals, journalists, intellectuals, retirees with lifetime pensions, and their families.

Third, I will explore how the economic-cultural tension between middle-class totality ("we are Okinawans") and working-class difference ("we are Okinawans of a different kind) in Henoko entered into a city-wide (eventually island-wide) struggle over the construction of the offshore base that erupted in the late 1990s and has continued to unfold to date (chapters 6 and 7). Throughout, I highlight the politics of local identity as a product of and simultaneously a response to an age of globalization, which, while triggering increased traffic of capital, people, goods, technology, images, information, and—most importantly in the context of my argument—the *military*[7] across national borders, has not withered but rearticulated the functions of the modern nation-state (in this case, Japan) by soliciting its participation in today's U.S.-oriented, capitalist regime of power.

In opposition to the transnational form of power, the U.S-Japan security alliance, middle-class Henoko residents, together with Nago City citizens as a whole, brought the history of Okinawa's oppositional movements to a new height at one moment (chapter 6). They did so by forming, internally, a polycentric and horizontal movement organization and structuring, externally, a broader public sphere—an open realm of solidarity that emerges from among diverse perspectives (see below for the further definition of the public sphere). However, in the midst of the success of the anti-base mobilization, the collective agent of social transformation in Henoko/Nago, even though it at least partially bridged and encompassed age, gender, regional, and other differences in terms of the notion "we are Okinawans," came to be detached from, even offended, the local working-class ideology of "we are Okinawans but of a different kind." In other words, the anti-base sentiment and movement arising from Henoko/Nago in the late 1990s, in spite of its pan-Okinawan aspirations, often appears to have represented a rather exclusive, educated, middle-class position, while failing to acknowledge the fears of failure and underdevelopment rampant in the broader working-class sector of Okinawa that would accommodate and appropriate the U.S. military presence in Okinawa for the sake of livelihood. Eventually, assisted and abetted by the power of Japanese money, the assertion of "difference" prevailed in Henoko and spread like a ripple in a pond to Nago City at large, changing the tide of social movements and, ultimately, subverting and unsettling the unity of Okinawa (chapter 7).

With the Futenma relocation issue still pending for reasons I will enunciate, the third part of my study demonstrates that micro concerns of social life challenge as much as reinforce macro political processes of the Japanese nation, with global operations of the U.S. military as an overarching geopolitical influence.

After exploring Okinawan identity in these three steps, the concluding essay (chapter 8) will discuss, in a manner that summarizes and orchestrates findings of this study, the possibilities and responsibilities of anthropology in the age of globalization. I will accomplish this task by, first, exploring what can be called "radical appropriation," which suggests that Okinawa should (1) receive the "gifts" from Tokyo—development projects, rent, and subsidies—without giving up its land for the use of the U.S.–Japan alliance in return; and in so doing (2) radically redefine and reappropriate these gifts as rightful recompense for the historical violence of modernity—colonialism, the war, and the military—that Okinawa has experienced, not as political compensation for the new base and, by implication, the U.S. military presence in Okinawa in the future, as Tokyo and Washington would like to define them. In proposing radical appropriation, I pursue a democratic possibility of post-modernity in which to articulate a unity embracing anti-base and pro-base movements in Okinawa and beyond.

And in the process, secondly, I will critically examine my own position. In spite of—or, precisely because of—my direct involvement in the anti-base movement in Henoko and Nago City (see chapters 5, 6 and 7, specifically), the limits and paradoxes of intervention, together with the dangers in the idea of the anthropologist as someone who simply offers prescriptions for social change, must be taken up for discussion against the background of my border-crossing positionality: I am not quite American (I grew up and was educated in Tokyo), not quite Japanese (I was born, received graduate education, and have been teaching in the United States), and not quite Okinawan (I have been treated as an "outsider," sometimes an "intruder," in Okinawa in spite of my active and continued involvement in the U.S. base problems there). A critical examination of my own position will, ultimately, enable me to address how in the age of globalization, anthropology can contribute to "forging links between *different* knowledges that are possible from different locations [e.g., Okinawa, mainland Japan, and the U.S.] and tracing lines of possible alliance and common purpose between them [e.g., resistance] " (Gupta and Ferguson 1997: 39; emphasis in original).

Certainly, many of the issues raised in this study address my critical concerns for today's political milieu surrounding the military and security in the United States and in the world. Let me be clear at the outset: I do not reject the use of military power under all circumstances. For instance, measured use of military force might be justified for the clearly defined goals of constructing and keeping peace. Also, when an insurmountable power and economic imbalance exists between the dominating and the dominated, and the latter have been deprived by the former of any means of making their voices heard, the latter may be allowed to have recourse to violence.[8] Allow me to add that it is not my goal to denounce U.S. servicemen. Indeed, my sympathies go to the rank and file of the U.S. military, who, as will be partially explored in the course of this study, have been bought at the margin of the labor market to "[fight] for an institution whose principal beneficiaries were often excluded from service," to borrow from James Scott (1985: 31).

What I want to problematize is the U.S. military as a flexible global institution, which, composed of layers of local, national, and supranational-organizations, is not contained within Washington—it maintains bases in at least fifty-nine countries (Mertes 2003: 147; see also Gongora and von Rickhoff 2000)—and has an immense capacity to enter, influence, even structure local life in so many corners of the world. Although the critical treatment of the U.S. military in this study may be disturbing to those readers who hold the view of the military simply as a champion for freedom and peace, it is still important to bring historical experiences and marginalized voices of the Other (in this case, Okinawa) into discussion. This is important, not because I want to eliminate the U.S. military once and for all, which is neither realistic nor, perhaps, desirable. I want to accomplish this task because I hope to contribute to constructing an open, inclusive, and heterogeneous arena of discussion and action, a public sphere, within and against the global form of power which, in the U.S., Japan, Okinawa, and elsewhere, has now played on our fear to have us support the United States' controversial global war on terrorism and has encroached upon civil liberties under the name of security in our everyday lives. After all, persistent efforts to expand the public sphere might become the most effective force with which to constrain, influence, and suspend the dangerous logic of power, seek global management of the military, and thus extend the critical tradition of American and global civil society.

With the overall planning of this study thus laid out, the rest of this introduction will outline the key actors in a social drama that revolves around identity, power, and resistance. It will also specify the historical, ethnographic, and theoretical setting in which these actors operate.

Henoko, the Fieldwork Site

Passing a large sign that said (in Japanese) "*Yōkoso Henoko shakōgai e* (Welcome to the Henoko Entertainment Quarter)" and (in English) "WEL COME [sic] BAR st.," I drove into the Henoko district for the first time on a hot summer day in July 1997. Slowly moving forward, I saw bars and restaurants, rundown and long deserted, whose faded and peeling signs identified them in English as: "ALL THE WAY," "LIBERTY," "QUEEN" and so forth. Along the street, storefronts that had once contained a photo studio, an electric shop, a pawnshop, a barbershop, and a tailor shop stood shuttered; apparently they had gone out of business some time ago. These were the remnants of the time of Henoko's prosperity—during the Vietnam War period, this community had been a bustling and lively venue providing "recreation" and "entertainment" to the U.S. servicemen of Camp Schwab. In this mostly deserted commercial quarter, however, a dozen bars, together with a small number of restaurants, construction companies, grocery stores, and beauty parlors, still did business. Modest, air-conditioned concrete homes accompanied by decent cars could also be seen lining the streets of this small oceanside district. While the entertainment business had dwindled, the past affluence, along with the rent money Tokyo had been paying for Camp Schwab, helped residents cling to a relatively comfortable, consumeristic lifestyle.

Further down the road, there stood a tall concrete building decorated with a massive plastic hanging scroll that read "Henoko kasseka sokushin kyōgikai" (Henoko Council for Facilitating Economic Activities). The building was used by the pro-base group—made up of the owners and employees of local businesses—that saw the construction of the new base as an opportunity for the redevelopment of Henoko. An eye-catching, colorful poster titled "Mirai no Henoko (Henoko of the future)" hung next to the scroll, depicting a Japanese National Technology College (a "gift" from Tokyo, which was to be built along with the new base) and a casino complex with a yacht harbor named "Amerika mura (American village)."

FIGURE 1.6 Entrance to "Bar Street" (as seen from within Henoko).

Beyond this ambitious and somewhat deceptive poster of the Henoko Council for Facilitating Economic Activities, there was a road leading downhill to a residential area dotted with beautiful Okinawan (i.e., semi-tropical) trees. There, traditional wooden houses with Okinawan red tile roofs stood side by side with well-built American-style homes. On one side of this area was the administration building of the Henoko district, also known as *kōminkan* (literally, "meeting facility for the community"), which was attached to a hall that could accommodate as many as a thousand people. Previously a wooden structure (till 1968), now an air-conditioned concrete building, *kōminkan* had historically been owned and run by the community of Henoko, acting as the heart of its social, cultural, and political life (cf. Lanman 1998). Residents would come to *kōminkan* to attend meetings, perform rituals,[9] gossip about a resident's marriage, play with children, practice Okinawan drum dance for the village summer festival, eat and drink on social occasions, ask questions about the nationally administered welfare system, or simply say hello. As to the matter of the offshore base construction, the Henoko administration had publicly and somewhat ambiguously declared, "In principle, we are opposed to the new base," which sounded like "under exceptional circumstances, we may accept it." Indeed, as I learned later, this administration, while not necessarily hostile to the prevalent anti-base sentiment in Okinawa at large, represented a broader pro-base and working-class sentiment in the community of Henoko.

On the other side of the residential area, Henoko's semi-tropical, emerald-green sea extended to the horizon. The new sea-based military facility was to be constructed here. On the white-sand beach there was a barbed wire fence on which hung a sign saying both (in Japanese) "*Tachi'iri kinshi*" and (in English) "Off Limits." I looked into the distance and saw the barracks and buildings of the U.S. Marine Corps Camp Schwab[10] standing at the foot of an extensive mountain forest. The forest played a significant role in Henoko residents' life as a source of their subsistence before the war, as hideouts during the war, and as adjoining training areas for Camp Schwab that had generated massive amounts of rent after the war.

Turning my back on Camp Schwab, I saw a prefabricated structure just off the Henoko beach with a yellow banner sticking out, which read

FIGURE 1.7 Rundown Henoko bar/restaurant (1).

"*Inochi wo mamoru kai*" (Society for the Protection of Life). This cottage, called "*tōsō goya*" (the struggle hut), was built by a group of relatively affluent, older residents opposed to the construction of the planned base. I saw hand-made signboards tacked up here and there, which read, in bold characters, "*Henoko no Umi o Mamorō*" (Let's Protect Henoko's Sea), "*Kaijō Heripōto Hantai*" (We Oppose the Offshore Heliport), and "*Kane de Inochi wa Uranai*" (We Will Not Sell Our Lives for Money).

In brief, in this district of 1,400 residents (mostly living within a confined area of 0.3 square kilometers, or 74 acres) bounded by the vast Camp Schwab (21.84 square kilometers, or 5397 acres) and the surrounding forest, there was already a visible division between a rising anticipation of the new offshore base in the run-down commercial area on the hill on the one hand, and a sentiment against the new base in the established residential area near the sea on the other, with the Henoko administration loosely associated with the former without rejecting the latter.

During the first half of the twentieth century, Henoko was a relatively self-contained agricultural-forestry-fishing community of six hundred residents, but it also interacted with larger Okinawan history at various levels. For instance, many Henoko residents lost their lives during the battle of Okinawa. After the war, Henoko also accommodated some 29,000 people from northern Okinawa in a refugee camp set up on a hill facing the sea. Yet no Henoko-related events have had a more lasting impact on Okinawan history than this community's involvement in the land-acquisition dispute of the mid-1950s. In 1949, when war-ruined Okinawa was barely undergoing reconstruction, the U.S. government recognized the strategic significance of Okinawa in the cold war world, and started to turn the island into the center of its trans-Pacific base network. In the mid-1950s, U.S. bases—including part of the Futenma Air Station that is to be returned in exchange for a new base in Henoko—were built by means of the forced enclosure and expropriation of vast areas of Okinawa by the United States Civil Administration of the Ryukyu Islands (USCAR), which, in turn, provoked massive, desperate barefoot protests by Okinawans. In the midst of this chaos, Henoko District, after prolonged discussion among village leaders, finally gave in to USCAR's solicitation and pressure to accept an American base that came to be known as Camp Schwab. In a nutshell, this economically ill-fated community, while accused of being a "betrayer" by fellow Okinawans, chose to improve its own living conditions in exchange for the base construction, rather than lose everything by protesting in vain against the expropriation. This is precisely the moment (and thus a point of intervention in this study) when Henoko revealed and asserted its "difference"—"we are Okinawans but of a different kind"—which introduced fissures in Okinawa's unified front against USCAR. Indeed, after Henoko's compromise, other communities followed suit, and as a result, the island-wide protest eventually died down.

In 1957, while Camp Schwab was being constructed on the hill where the refugee camp had existed after the war, Henoko itself started to undergo an enormous social transformation at tremendous speed, and established its status as a closed "enclave" within Okinawa. The local administration hurriedly created an entertainment quarter by clearing communal fields on the hillside of Henoko, to which people from all over Okinawa came to look for jobs. In the 1960s in general, and at the height of the Vietnam War in particular, more than one hundred bars, restaurants, and brothels were built side by side along with other commercial enterprises. At this point, the population exceeded three thousand. In place of Okinawan toilets, in which residents traditionally raised pigs with human waste, American flush toilets, which became objects of envy among residents, were installed in the entertainment quarter according to the sanitary standards enforced by USCAR. The signboards were written in "real" English (as opposed to Okinawan "pidgin" English), although residents barely understood the language. Okinawan singers started to sing in English in Henoko bars and restaurants, which became a birthplace of Okinawan rock music. Meanwhile, dollar bills literally overflowed from cardboard boxes used as cash registers in the entertainment quarter. In the midst of this din and bustle, residents witnessed crimes committed by U.S. servicemen, including two murders—a bar hostess and a female bar owner in Henoko were murdered in 1961 and in 1974, respectively (Fukuchi 1995: 240-242; Okinawaken Sōmubu Chiji Kōshitsu Kichi Taisakushitsu 2003: 473).[11]

However, as the U.S. involvement in Vietnam came to an end, the once-booming Henoko sharply contracted and was virtually forgotten in Okinawa's social scene. In the late 1990s when I began fieldwork, there was hardly a trace left of the town's former prosperity in its decreased population of 1,400, among whom earnings differentials, which used to be concealed under the communal practice and ideology of coexistence and coprosperity with the base, could no longer be masked. To be sure, Henoko held together and maintained, if barely, its relatively comfortable living standard, owing to the massive annual rent for the communal military land paid by the national government—an estimated 140 million yen ($1.4 million[12]) in 1997 (Nago Shiyakusho 1996). Yet this yearly rent to the community can also be seen as a sedative that as much calmed as it aroused general discontent about the present and widespread anxiety about the future of Henoko. The governmental proposal to build a new offshore base in Henoko in 1996 created a context in which two competing views were articulated as the solutions to this communal discontent and anxiety.

On the one hand, in ways that extended Okinawa's collective memories of the war, the bases, and the servicemen, many Henoko residents—including, among others, residents from wealthy yet marginalized "native" Henoko descent groups, women who viewed nature and peace as critical to the welfare of their children, and senior citizens who had gone through the tragedies and atrocities of the battle of Okinawa—strongly opposed the construction of the offshore base. These residents, as a whole, represented an autonomous, middle-class citizen position; they tried to extend Okinawa's historical sense of unity against the U.S. military and the Japanese government in the idea that "we are Okinawans," while interweaving such an assertion with planetary citizenry discourses of ecology, peace, human rights, and women's issues. On the other hand, Camp Schwab had long induced a broader restructuring of the social ties of blood and place, transforming Henoko into a closed enclave within Okinawa consolidated by a particular pro-base community ideology and sentiment—also a working-class consciousness—of "we are Okinawans but of a different kind." Those who shared this ideology/sentiment tended to be from families of *kiryūmin* (or "out-of-towners") that had moved into Henoko during and after the 1960s, typically held insecure jobs and, while positioning themselves as the defenders of local culture and tradition, often participated in the Nago-citywide (eventually island-wide) pro-offshore base movement for financial reasons. Their pro-base sentiment was sanctioned by, as much as sanctioned, the position of the Henoko administration. In a word, when the offshore base dispute arose in the late 1990s, Henoko residents were divided by a deep social fissure between the middle-class, anti-base sentiment of Okinawan unity and the working-class, pro-base assertion of difference.

• • •

The brief ethnographic description of Henoko offered above should help concretize some of the ways in which Okinawan identity has unfolded by accommodating the existing political order at one level but also confronting it at another level. In order to structure my narrative on the ambiguous and paradoxical politics of identity in contexts cacophonously marked by power, history, and resistance, I critically use, explore, and engage three different fields of intellectual inquiry throughout this study: the new social movement literature, postmodern/colonial/structural anthropology, and modern Okinawan studies.

The New Social Movement Literature

The ethnographic sketch of Henoko involving the intractable dilemma of identity between unity ("we are Okinawans") and difference ("we are Okinawans but of a different kind") calls attention to what the so-called new social movement literature has dealt with, that is, the questions of culture, identity, and difference in contemporary struggles. This literature was first developed in the 1970s and 1980s and refined in the 1990s and beyond to explain the surge of "the civil rights movement, the anti-war movement, the women's movement, the peace, environment, anti-nuclear, and gay and lesbian movements [which] all fail to fit the paradigm of either traditional Marxism or conventional social science" (Epstein 1990: 35). Theorists of new social movements such as Inglehart (1977), Cohen (1985), Offe (1985), Tilly (1985), Melucci (1985, 1996a, 1996b) and Touraine (1985, 1988) announced that "old," large-scale collective insurrections by the "people" (e.g., the organized working class, aggregated colonized subjects, etc.) were essentially over. Joined and buttressed by the insights of social/cultural/literary critics such as Scott (1985), Gilroy (1987), Giddens (1991), Castells (1997), and Hardt and Negri (2000, 2004), the contemporary new social movement literature, broadly defined, has found "new," flexible, small-scale resistances and everyday subversions by autonomous "citizens" who were loosely networked—often even fragmented—not so much by ideologies of emancipation or causes for revolution as by desires for identity and culture.

Italian sociologist Alberto Melucci (1985: 795–96) specifically suggests that "social conflicts move from the traditional economic/industrial system to cultural grounds: they affect personal identity, the time and the space in everyday life, the motivation and the cultural patterns of individual action." In a manner not unlike that of Melucci, Anthony Giddens (1991) identifies a shift from "emancipatory politics" which is "concerned to reduce or eliminate *exploitation*, *inequality* and *oppression*" (211, emphasis in original) to "life politics" which is "a politics of self-actualization in a reflexively ordered environment, where that reflexivity links self and body to systems of global scope" (215). Drawing on the works of Melucci, Touraine, Castells and others, Paul Gilroy presents an analysis of contemporary black politics centering on identity, race, and difference that challenges the "ossified practices of corporatist class politics" (1987: 226).

The broader shift of the nature, mode, and form of social movements from class politics to identity/cultural/body/life politics has been explained as an effect of the passage of Western society from one that emphasizes material, industrial values and practices to one that highlights postmaterial, postindustrial, postmodern values and practices (Inglehart 1977, Offe 1985, Touraine 1988) revolving around, for instance, the information economy/technology (Castells 1997, 1998; Hardt and Negri 2000, 2004). From the 1990s on, as Morris-Suzuki (2000) has specifically pointed out, the rationales and premises of the Western new social movements have spilled into the projects of nongovernmental organizations (NGOs) that advocate human rights, environmental protections, health, citizenship, democracy, poverty, and women's issues in the third world and beyond.

I do not hesitate to acknowledge the contributions of new social movements (including activities of NGOs) to the local, national, and global political arenas. Yet I also want to note that these movements and the literature about them have often revealed a problematic tendency to suppress "old" questions that capitalism and, to some extents, colonialism have continuously posed—structural questions concerning class, the material conditions of life, and histories and memories of oppression and exploitation—by privileging "new" questions of identities, meanings, symbols, communities, networks, and self-actualizations.

For one thing, social conditions in Henoko—where the politics of identity ("we are Okinawans" vs. "we are Okinawans but of a different kind") is, simultaneously, a class struggle between the affluent and the poor—should already make one pause to be cautious about this tendency. As I will show, the working-class Okinawans have indeed reappeared, in the age of globalization, not as revolutionaries but as major reactionaries that would obstruct the middle-class citizens' movement. The exclusive focus of much of the new social movement literature on culture and identity, or *middle-class* culture and identity to be more precise, essentially masks this troubling phenomenon. A globally structural perspective is needed to examine the contemporary transformation of class relations, and to articulate a new perspective on social movements that can engage and include, not dismiss and exclude, the concerns and interests of the newly emerging poor.

In addition, much of the new social movement literature is not helpful for grasping the ways in which the "old" colonialist and imperialist regime, the territorially structured power of the nation-state, had exploited the local in the past and has transformed itself under new historical circumstances to reproduce oppressive social relations in the outside/periphery. In the specific context of my study, it may lead one to obscure Japan's colonial-national exploitation of and the U.S. imperial-global violence to Okinawa in the past, upon which its "new" politics of identity and culture has been founded.

In short, by focusing somewhat excessively on particularities in the symbolic/cultural/quotidian mode of existence in its critique of "the romance of resistance" (Abu-Lughod 1990), the new social movement literature may have not paid enough attention to the grand system of power and, in so doing, may have helped perpetuate such a system. In challenging the subtly opportunist act of inattention—as Enloe (2000: xii) has argued, "*In*attention is a political act" (emphasis in original)—this study, for its part, explicitly reclaims the *old* "romance of resistance" to the grand form of power through the analysis of the *new* everyday politics of identity, culture, and difference. In so doing, my study will articulate the emerging local reality lived by residents and citizens in Okinawa and many other corners of the world, the reality that has become both material *and* symbolic/cultural, structural *and* quotidian, colonial *and* postcolonial, old *and* new (Scott 1985, Escobar and Alvarez, eds. 1992, Ortner 1995, Abelmann 1995, 1997; Castells 1997, Foweraker 1995, Fox and Starn, eds. 1997, Alvarez, Dagnino and Escobar, eds. 1998, Starn 1999, Hardt and Negri 2004, Tsing 2005).

Self, Other, and the Third Person: Problems of
Post-Modern/Colonial/Structural Anthropology

On a related plane, the ethnographic scene of Henoko reveals the micropolitical practices of Okinawans as the Other, who actively and unexpectedly borrow, engage, and redefine—in short, "appropriate"[13]—the national and global power (the base, money, and U.S. servicemen) to produce specific local cultural forms and social practices. Inquiring further into the politics of Self and Other, this study challenges and complicates certain tenets of postmodern/colonial/structural anthropology, including its key trope of appropriation, without throwing away its theoretical and political advantages.

One way to begin thinking about the nature of postmodern/colonial/structural anthropology is to note its predecessor's—modern anthropology's—relationship with the questions of power. Spanning a period roughly between the 1920s and the 1980s, modern anthropology[14] largely treated the Other as a circumscribed, static, homogeneous crowd of faceless individuals for "the salvaging of distinct cultural forms of life from a process of apparent global [impacts] " (Marcus and Fischer 1986: 1), and in so doing, ironically contributed to reproducing the political status quo between Self (the West, individuals with history) and Other (the rest, the People without history) with which it intervened. However, shock waves sent across human sciences by postmodern/colonial/structural works including *Orientalism* (Said 1978) and *The History of Sexuality* (Foucault [1978] 1990) prompted anthropology in a fundamental way to interrogate its modernist paradigm of salvation, a paradigm that was complicit in the historical subordination of the Other. Theoretical texts produced in the 1980s such as *Writing Culture* (Clifford and Marcus, eds. 1986), *Anthropology as Cultural Critique* (Marcus and Fischer 1986), and *The Predicament of Culture* (Clifford 1988) can be seen as some of the fruits of serious efforts to decolonize and reinvent anthropology.

Going hand in hand with this theoretical endeavor was an attempt to ethnographically engage in and experiment with a variety of postmodern/colonial/structural thoughts. The idea of appropriation—along with the notions of mimicry (Bhabha 1994: especially 85–92), time-space compression (Harvey 1990), contact zone (Pratt 1992), diaspora (Gilroy 1993, Clifford 1994), the cultural logic of late capitalism (Jameson 1992) and others—has specifically helped anthropology reorient its ethnographic objectives from the essentialist/modernist/colonialist search for pure culture to the nuanced, grounded, and engaged understanding of the agency—hopes, fears, projects, calculations—of the Other within and against the constraining order of power. Analyses of the Kayapo Indians' appropriation of the commodity of video cameras to autonomously represent themselves (Turner 1991), of female Japanese part-time workers' appropriation of the ideology of a male-centered social order to create a sense of fulfillment and power as mothers, as erotic objects, and as caregivers in a Tokyo downtown workplace (Kondo 1990), and of India's appropriation of cricket, a privileged sport of the British Empire, in the process of the construction of its postcolonial national-cultural identity (Appadurai 1996: 89–113), to mention a few, are ones I see as exemplary of the emerging postmodern/colonial/structural anthropological paradigm of appropriation and agency. Put succinctly, this newly rising paradigm has exposed uncertainty and vulnerability of power in its constant struggles (or really failures) to obtain consent or submission of the dominated. In a way that, perhaps, redeemed modern anthropology's guilt feeling of having not explicitly addressed the political issues of justice and social change, these and other studies have enabled anthropology to align with traditional Marxist, nationalist, and feminist concerns[15] for exploitation, inequality, and oppression, even to the point of reshaping their understanding of power as always repressive. In so doing, anthropology has successfully repositioned and restaged itself as a driving force for constructing a vast, newly emerging field of critical yet nuanced studies of power and resistance.

However, anthropology's post-modern/colonial/structural turn, while being an effort well worthwhile, may also mask a number of political and theoretical dangers from our view, dangers that derive from the fact that the new paradigm still starts from and forever stays within the dichotomy and dialectic of Self and Other. The first problem arises because of its excessive attempts to revise a binary structure of opposition. Foucault ([1978] 1990: 45), for instance, talked about the dialectic "game" between Self and Other: "Capture and seduction, confrontation and mutual reinforcement: parents and children, adults and adolescents, educator[s] and students, doctors and patients, the psychiatrist with his hysteric and his perverts, all have played this game continually since the nineteenth century." Foucault ([1978] 1990: 45) designated this game as "*perpetual spirals of power and pleasure*" (emphasis in original). An enormous theoretical invention to redefine a rigid dichotomy of Self and Other notwithstanding, Foucault's model of power and resistance may dissolve analytically and politically meaningful contradictions along, for instance, the class, racial, and/or geographical lines of exploitation (between doctors and patients, teachers and students, etc.), while at the same time relentlessly decentering, refracting, and diffusing these contradictions to all levels of social life (Dirlik 1994a, 1994b). In terms reminiscent of Foucault's discourse on power and resistance, contemporary anthropology has been using the idea of appropriation (among others) at the higher register as one of the organizing theoretical tropes; in so doing, it may have reduced a series of very different struggles derived from distinct contradictions—the Kayapo Indians' movement, Japanese working-class women's protest, and postcolonial India's resistance—to the single plane of postmodern "games" of ambivalence and subversion, always enacted within the dialectic of Self and Other. As a result, the analyses often approach a level of generality at which historical, geographical, gender, class, race, and other specificities and differences tend to disappear.

The second and related problem is that while the practice of appropriation by the Other may help us discern previously unrecognized forms of resistance (Abu-Lughod 1990), it may also help, unwittingly, to multiply and reproduce power within the closed space of Self and Other. For instance, Kayapo Indians ironically invited the further penetration of commodity capitalism into their community in the very act of appropriating video cameras. Similarly, their agency to manipulate the male-centered workplace does not make Kondo's Japanese women innocent; it is their agency that may have helped reinforce the brutality of the broader capitalist system within which postwar Japanese society—both men and women, work and family, power and resistance—has been arranged. Appadurai's India, too, precisely because of its almost subliminal sense of "having hijacked the game [cricket] from its English habitus" (Appadurai 1996: 113), may also have subliminally presupposed and paradoxically perpetuated the imperial aura of Great Britain as the ultimate foundation and guardian of universal civilization. In short, while bringing small acts of the oppressed into sharper focus, the trope of appropriation may help power to manage and absorb resistance as it produces it. In other words, the trope of appropriation may have become indistinguishable from the new, postmodern operation and logic of power.

These two political and conceptual problems in the postmodern/colonial/structural idea of appropriation become evident as I try to apply it to my own study. In a manner that reminds us of Foucault's aforementioned statement about the dialectic "game" between Self and Other, my analysis will, indeed, show that in the post–World War II context, a similar game of mutual reinforcement has been enacted between the U.S./Self and Japan/Other with appropriation as a basic mechanism of "perpetual spirals": Japan has appropriated the power of the United States for its own national security and for the "miracle" of its postwar recovery, even to the point of challenging American economic hegemony in Asia and in the world, precisely as the United States has assimilated and subordinated Japan in a transnational military-political-economic system (the U.S.-Japan alliance). Historically, as will be elaborated in this study, financially insecure sectors of Okinawan society—such as the pro-base residents and the local administration as briefly described in the ethnographic sketch of Henoko—have also joined this game through the mechanism of appropriation. That is, they have appropriated the U.S.-Japan alliance for their own economic well-being, and in doing so, have ironically legitimized and perpetuated its violence they indeed detest. There, their agency ("we are Okinawans but of a different kind") has not been denied; it has been produced, mediated, and subordinated within a higher unity. Schematically, thus, this mode of appropriation, as well as our scholarly description of it if we end it here, may assist the global form of power—what Hardt and Negri (2000) call *Empire*—to incorporate Others within its open, expanding system of hierarchical positions (the second problem of the practice/idea of appropriation discussed above), while at the same time contributing to creating the world of atomized diversity without much radical political thrusts (the first problem).

In an attempt to overcome the problems of the Foucauldian/postmodern trope of Self and Other without, however, discarding its theoretical merits (attention to the agency of the Other and to the uncertainty and complexity of domination), I here want to invoke a segment—only a segment—of the thought of Emmanuel Levinas. Specifically, his critique of the "intimate society," together with his concept of the "third person," may help us open the space beyond the Foucauldian/postmodern model of appropriation.[16]

Levinas (1998: 30) states, "In fact, [an intimate society produced, for instance, by Foucault's "game" of pleasure and power] is dual, a society of me and you. We are just among ourselves. Third parties are excluded. A third man essentially disturbs this intimacy." Levinas identifies "love" enclosed in itself as a foundation of the intimate society: "The intersubjective relationship of love is not the beginning, but the negation of [plural] society" (p. 31) which "inevitably involves the existence of a third party" (p. 32); "If I recognize the wrong I did you, I can, even by my act of repentance [and love], injure the third person" (p. 30).

Incorporating Levinas' thought into my study, it becomes clear that the Foucauldian/postmodern model of power and resistance tends to not only trace and reproduce the intimate society of love—and, I should add, hate—between the United States and Japan (joined by financially insecure Okinawans), but also systematically suppress the critically transformative voices of Okinawa—the "third person" burdened with the U.S. military. I for one want to specify the democratic potentialities of "oppositional appropriation" by this third person, an excess that the Foucauldian/postmodern model of Self and Other will never be able to fully internalize.

Unlike Okinawans before the war or the reversion, today's Okinawans as a whole are no longer a poor "people" who feel that their way of life is something to be ashamed of. Rather, by appropriating the affluence of Okinawa made possible by Japanese money that has been offered as political compensation for the continuous U.S. military presence there, they assert confidence and pride in who they are/were, and express their autonomy within and against the intimate society. In other words, a large number of contemporary Okinawans, as an excess, as the third person, often challenge and undermine the very regime of power they have appropriated. Behind this oppositional appropriation lies the fact that financial aid from Tokyo—in spite of its goal of placating Okinawa's anti-base sentiment—has ironically become a constant reminder of the prolonged violence of power, the U.S. military presence, thereby helping Okinawa to renew cultural sensibilities that are enmeshed with the pain of local historical experiences—the war, the bases, the servicemen, and the rape. Oppositional Okinawans have specifically rearticulated such sensibilities as they have appropriated power/money in new historical circumstances, and in the process have constructed a hybrid global citizenship—grounded in locality, entangled in nationality, and involved in globality—with which to confront the U.S. base problem that is at once local, national, and global in scope.

Indeed, on the basis of their unified yet inclusive positioning of "we are Okinawans," critical citizens have formed a flexible, polycentric movement structure internally and triggered, externally, a spiraling sequence of resistance in Okinawa, Japan, and beyond in the wake of the rape incident in 1995. Seeking to render "Okinawa" sort of a universal metaphor—like "Hiroshima" and "Nagasaki"—that represents the ultimate violence of destruction and the foundational desire for peace, they have shaped "a configuration of [plural] wills" (Levinas 1998: 31), an ethical-political realm of hybridity, that does not fuse into a closed system of differences of the intimate society, although, I hasten to add, this configuration eventually broke down for reasons to be specified in the course of this study.

In this book, I will often employ the term "public sphere" to designate the ideal of hybridity derived from this oppositional, transformative form of appropriation. Specifically, drawing on Calhoun (1992), Fraser (1992, 2004), Saito (2000) and others who have critically refined Habermas' somewhat elitist and highly rationalist notion of public sphere (1989) [17] and its sociological/linguistic corollary, communicative action (1985, 1990, 2000),[18] I define the public sphere as an open, inclusive, and nonviolent realm of solidarity that emerges from among diverse perspectives of the third persons, a realm characterized by unrestrictedness with respect to who can participate, who can speak, and who can be heard. My conception of public sphere shares the globally democratic aspirations with Hardt and Negri's idea of the multitude (2000, 2004),[19] but I choose to use the "public sphere" in order to put emphasis on the grounded-ness of memory, sentiment, place, and language of the "lifeworld."[20] The idea of the public sphere as developed in this study, in other words, is more anthropological-ethnographic than that of the multitude and will critically complement a philosophical-theoretical nature of Hardt and Negri's project. The public sphere thus seeks the universal without being alienated from the local, by continuously renewing, reconfiguring, and expanding itself on the basis of a common concern—such as the problems of the U.S. military—but not of a common cultural attribute, history, or identity which would create atomized differences within the intimate society.

Okinawan Studies

Thus far, the ethnographic sketch of Henoko has allowed us to problematize both the new social movement literature that downplays the issues of class and the material conditions of life, and the postmodern/colonial/structural trope of appropriation that tends to ignore the voices of the third persons. From a slightly different angle, the ethnographic sketch of Henoko, which highlights Okinawan identity in the making, helps shed light on still another theoretical problem, that is, the essentialist tendency of modern Okinawan studies to appeal to pure or original Okinawan-ness outside power and history. One goal of this study is to overcome this tendency, which I will explain in Chapter 3 in detail. Here, allow me to establish a basic conceptual framework within which my analysis will be conducted there.

By "modern Okinawan studies," I refer to three distinct intellectual traditions concerning Okinawa that were developed between the 1920s and the 1980s in mainland Japan, the U.S., and Okinawa, respectively. Taking the 1920s as a starting point, mainland Japanese researchers (such as Yanagita Kunio) intellectually assimilated Okinawa into Japan by constituting the former as the storehouse of ancient Japan, while obscuring ongoing political tensions, conflicts, and differences between the two areas. In so doing, they claimed that "Okinawans were/are Japanese." Meanwhile, American anthropologists who conducted research in U.S.-occupied Okinawa in the 1950s and 1960s (such as Clarence Glacken, William Lebra, and Thomas Maretzki) were in a non-Japanese, outsider's position and exposed the tensions between Japan and Okinawa that Japanese scholars wanted to hide. In so doing, however, these American scholars, with their specific gaze fixed at pristine Okinawa, also reproduced the Orientalist binary of "us" (as the historical and political agency) and "them" (bereft of such an agency). Put differently, they asserted that "Okinawans are not Japanese, but not Americans either," thereby implicitly legitimizing the U.S. policy in the 1950s and 1960s of keeping Okinawa separate from Japan in order to use it for its own security purposes. For their part, Okinawan scholars—such as Iha Fuyū (active from the 1920s to the 1940s) and Nakamatsu Yashū (active from the 1960s to the 1980s)—sought Okinawa's irreducible particularities in its traditional cultural practices, while at the same time critiquing the violence of modernity (and by implication, of Japan and the U.S. which brought modernity) that, in their eyes, destroyed such particularities. In the process, however, they problematically fell into the nativist position, a position of seeking a pristine, bounded Okinawa untouched by power and history which may not have ever existed. In brief, they were trapped in their own assertion that "Okinawans were and are Okinawans and nothing else."

Thus, from the 1920s all the way up to the 1980s, scholars in Japan, the U.S., and Okinawa, for different political and intellectual reasons, uniformly discussed Okinawa in terms of immaculate traditions, implicitly and explicitly reducing Okinawa to an already established fact, a stand-alone museum of unchanging cultures. This tendency, while becoming an impetus for exploring as much as rescuing "what Okinawans really are/were," may also have given the researchers a convenient excuse to dismiss the question of the process, that is, "what Okinawans become" (cf. Hall [1990] 1994). As a result, modern Okinawan studies saw the U.S. military and related social practices (e.g., money-making activities, anti-base movements) as an impurity/noise in Okinawa that needed to be hidden and eradicated from their analyses. Informed by the ethnographic scene of Henoko, this study, for its part, prefers to see the U.S. military and related social practices as an integral part of Okinawa's "present" that needs to be exposed, explicated, and critiqued.

I here advisedly use "present" to convey three different, yet interrelated meanings. First, I employ the term to refer to Okinawa's temporal dimension, the present conditions in motion that are articulated by both restraining factors of the past and diverse desires for the future. Second, I use the term "present" to highlight Okinawa as a specific geopolitical site. That is, I want to make the questions of social protest in this place called Okinawa not absent and marginalized, but existent, visible, and thus present in the context of the national state and global politics. Taken together, I move across temporal (past, present, and future) and spatial (local, national, and global) dimensions in order to explore new Okinawan social consciousness. This post-Orientalist, postmodern move corresponds to the critical spirit of recent scholarship in Okinawa, in mainland Japan, and beyond. Chapter 3 discusses the ways in which some of the recent studies try to move toward a deeper understanding of the island prefecture and its history, culture, and identity.

Paradoxical as it may sound, however, I want to accomplish the task of overcoming the problems of essentialism without giving up the virtue of modern Okinawan studies, that is, their concern for the specificity of "place" (Gupta and Ferguson 1997, Dirlik 1999). Here, the third meaning of the term "present" makes its appearance. Borrowing from Sanjek, I employ this term to designate modern Okinawan studies as a gift: "*contra* anthropological post-modernism, there is much to salvage [and receive] from previous generations of fieldworkers" (Sanjek 1991: 620, emphasis in original). The actual content of the gift of modern Okinawan studies will be presented throughout this study. Suffice it to say that my study, guarding against slipping into a postmodern celebration of shifting positions and differences, investigates kinship, religion, and other themes of modern Okinawan studies on the basis of my intensive and extensive fieldwork, and that I do so because these can be a critical way to look at the particular forms that cultural meanings take in Okinawa, to bring politics into cultural/social analyses, and to commit to Okinawan identity and history in the making.

• • •

Critical engagement in the new social movement literature and the postmodern/colonial/structural discourses of appropriation, together with the critique of modern Okinawan studies, will help me articulate the ways in which the U.S.–Japan alliance, a global form of power composed of layers of local, national, and transnational institutions, is both oppressive, as exemplified by the prolonged U.S. military presence in Okinawa, *and* productive, as illustrated by the fact that the critical social consciousness has been generated in Okinawa against the background of its affluence. In doing so, this study will explore the nature and project of Okinawan identity that is inevitably complex, ambiguous, and uncertain, and will make a broad contribution to anthropological and cultural studies of identity, power, and resistance.

2

THE RAPE INCIDENT AND THE
PREDICAMENTS OF OKINAWAN IDENTITY

 No recent incident has caused such an intense public debate about the U.S. military presence in Okinawa as the rape of a twelve-year-old local schoolgirl by three U.S. servicemen in the fall of 1995. This chapter explores Okinawa's protest against the rape as an entry point into what I consider as two basic historical layers or modalities of contemporary Okinawan social consciousness. The first layer corresponds to Okinawa's experience of being attacked and then controlled by the U.S. military (1945–1972), which has been grafted onto and interacted with the second, broader historical layer corresponding to Okinawa's collective memory concerning the Japanese state violence since the late nineteenth century. In a word, I want to articulate the origin of Okinawa's contemporary oppositional sentiment directed both to Japan and the United States in terms of the general problematic of Okinawan modernity—Japanese colonialism, the war, the U.S. bases, and the servicemen.

Note, however, that my aim here is not so much to establish a direct causality between the problematic of Okinawan modernity and Okinawan protest in the age of globalization as to examine how the former has been profoundly reorganized and rearticulated in the context of the latter. The protest against the rape, in other words, is not to be read simply as a manifestation of Okinawa's sedimented anger against Japanese and American dominations. Rather, by taking the issues of political economy in post-reversion Okinawa seriously, I want to examine the protest against the rape as an expression of the fundamentally new and deeply ambivalent social consciousness in today's Okinawa—one that can be best characterized in terms of "citizenship"—that has complicated, dislocated, and reconfigured modern Okinawa's oppositional sentiment. Overall, with this chapter I begin thinking about how specific Okinawan identity made its appearance, in what ways its meanings have been transformed over time, and why, today, in this age of globalization, it provides so profound a political and emotional immediacy that is both liberating and problematic.

The Rape Incident

On the Labor Day holiday (September 4) of 1995, Marcus D. Gill, twenty-two, of the U.S. Navy proposed the rape to his fellow servicemen, Kendrick Maurice Ledet, twenty, and Rodrico Harp, twenty-one, both Marines, in a food court at Camp Hansen, located in Northern Okinawa.[1] All three servicemen were black Americans from poor regions of the American South.[2] Having failed to meet local women earlier on the day in Naha, the capital city of Okinawa, the two Marines wanted to hire prostitutes, but the Navy seaman said he had no money. There was another serviceman at the table, but he refused to participate.

The three men then left the base with their rental car, with Gill driving; while cruising, they looked for a female suitable for abduction and rape on the streets of Kin Town, adjacent to Camp Hansen. Ledet and Harp first attempted to abduct a woman who was walking on a narrow street, but she escaped by running into a building. Then, they found a girl on her way back home from shopping for a notebook at a local general store. It was now around 8:00 p.m. and already dark, the sun having set about seventy-five minutes earlier. While Gill waited inside the car, Ledet captured the girl from behind and Harp hit her in the face twice. After Ledet pulled her into the backseat of their rented car, Gill took off, while Ledet and Harp covered the girl's eyes and mouth with the duct tape Ledet had bought and tied her wrists and ankles before reaching a farm road near a deserted beach officially called Kin Blue Amphibious Training Area. There, Gill repeatedly beat the girl on the face and stomach with his fists so that she could no longer resist, and he and Harp raped her in the car one after another, inflicting physical injuries that required two weeks of medical treatment. Ledet did not rape her, noticing she was too young.

The victim's parents, infuriated, reported the crime to the Okinawa Prefecture Police (OPP) without delay. The United States Naval Criminal Investigative Service (NCIS), responding to OPP's request, arrested the rapists immediately. The girl, entreating the police to put them in jail until their death, courageously cooperated with the police while they inspected the scene of this unspeakable crime. In March 1996, Naha district court sentenced Gill and Harp to seven years in prison and Ledet to six and a half years.

• • •

There would appear to have been smooth coordination between Okinawa and the U.S. military in terms of the handling of the rape; under the surface, however, one notes a complex political process. On September 7, three days after the rape, OPP sought to detain the three suspects NCIS had taken into custody. Yet NCIS, while pledging full cooperation with the local police investigations, rejected the request on the basis of the Status of Forces Agreement (SOFA). This bilateral agreement, concluded in 1960, set forth the rights and privileges (and some responsibilities) of the U.S. military and its personnel in Japan's territory on such matters as the use, administration, and return of facilities and areas, criminal and civil jurisdiction, taxes, customs procedures, drivers' licenses, and air and sea traffic control, among others. Article 17 specifically stipulates procedures with regard to criminal jurisdiction, and provides that U.S. suspects can be transferred only after the Japanese authorities indict them. In the past, in order to escape legal punishment in Japan, suspects belonging to the U.S. military often manipulated this provision by taking refuge on base territory. When a serviceman raped a nineteen-year-old Okinawan woman in July 1993, he even managed to escaped to the United States (*Ryukyu Shinpo*, September 20, 1995).

Other treatments favorable to the U.S. military and its personnel arising from the provisions and interpretations of SOFA include: Within its facilities and areas, the U.S. military is situated essentially beyond the order of Japanese law (e.g., the Noise Control Law, the Environmental Pollution Control Law), because it may take "all" measures necessary for the establishment, operation, and safeguarding of the bases (Article 3); the United

States is not obliged, when it returns its facilities and areas to Japan, to restore them to their original condition (Article 4); and it is practically at the discretion of the U.S. military to make financial compensation for damages arising from crimes and accidents by U.S. servicemen off duty (Article 18). Okinawans had long deemed these SOFA provisions, as well as Article 17 on criminal jurisdiction, to be discriminatory, and, particularly after the rape incident, became immensely unsettled by them.

From the U.S. and Japanese governments' perspective, however, as Japanese Ministry of Defense Chief Etō Seijyūrō put it, "SOFA and the U.S.–Japan Security Treaty are two sides of the same coin" (*Ryukyu Shinpo*, September 25, 1995). That is, Washington and Tokyo both feared that any substantial changes to SOFA would lead to the revision of the framework of the security treaty itself, a framework that had made the stationing of the U.S. military in Okinawa possible in the first instance. Relatedly, the strategic planners in Washington were afraid that any revision of SOFA in Japan would trigger revisions of SOFA in other nations, which would in turn restrict U.S. military activities throughout the world. In fact, in the midst of apologies by U.S. leaders—President Bill Clinton (September 21), Ambassador to Japan Walter Mondale (September 21), Secretary of State Warren Christopher (September 26), and Secretary of Defense William Perry (September 27) as well as diplomatic requests from Tokyo that Washington implement new measures to prevent rape and other crimes, both governments deliberately dodged the SOFA issues altogether, so that there was no possibility of changing the agreement.[3] At the same time, the U.S. and Japanese governments did not forget to reassert the importance of the security treaty for the sake of the "peace and prosperity" of the Asia-Pacific region from which they had politically and economically benefited. As it turned out, however, this high-handed position of the two governments led not to the pacification and containment but to the intensification of Okinawa's indignation.

Governor Ota had already expressed his strong displeasure about the incident soon after it happened, stating that "words of apology [from the U.S. military] are not enough" (*Ryukyu Shinpo*, September 12, 1995). The governor's anger was soon echoed among other social and political circles in Okinawa. Officials of the Okinawa prefectural government reinforced the governor's view and said, "We have asked for the enforcement of discipline so many times" whenever this sort of incident happened in the past

(*Ryukyu Shinpo*, September 12, 1995). Over twenty-three years after the reversion of Okinawa in 1972 (see below), in fact, 4,784 crimes—including 22 murders, 356 robberies, and 110 rapes—had been committed by U.S. military personnel in Okinawa (Okinawaken Sōmubu Chiji Kōshitsu Kichi Taisakushitsu 2003: 471).[4] When the Okinawa Area Coordinator of the U.S. military, Major General Wayne E. Rollings, sent a message of apology to the prefecture, Ota even refused to accept it, because "the General should first have come in person to make the apology" (*Ryukyu Shinpo Weekly News*, September 19, 1995). The governor's attitudes toward the Japanese government were more bitter. In the emergency meeting in Okinawa on October 30, he stated to the officials sent from Tokyo, "You have always said that the security treaty is important for Japan [of which Okinawa is an essential part], but nobody in Japan has ever been willing to take responsibility by transferring the bases in Okinawa to mainland Japan" (*Ryukyu Shinpo*, October 31, 1995). Officials from the central government reportedly fell into silence. In the meantime, the prefectural board of education, the prefectural assembly, women's organizations just coming back from the 1995 Beijing Women's Conference, reformist political parties, labor unions, teachers' unions, peace organizations, and city and village assemblies, among others, organized gatherings, staged sit-ins, and released their statements of protest one after another.

The indignant voices of the Okinawans and their governor need to be understood in the depth of Okinawa's modernity, which will be discussed shortly. Here, I want to spend a couple of pages to underscore the significance of Okinawa's protest in more immediate historical terms, that is, in reference to the plight of post-reversion Okinawa's anti-base protests that had been lodged within and against changing relations of power among the local, the national, and the global.

• • •

Immediately after the "alien rule" of Okinawa by the U.S. military ended in 1972, the Japanese government made contracts with individual military landlords in Okinawa to pay the rent, thereby assisting the United States in maintaining a vast net of military bases there for its cold-war strategies to contain "communist threats." In addition, Japan's Self-Defense Forces, reminiscent of the Japanese Imperial Army responsible for atrocities committed upon Okinawans during World War II, made its appearance in

Okinawa for the first time, in order to take on part of defense responsibilities in East Asia and to maintain, in fact reinforce, the functions of this island prefecture as a strategic military stronghold.

In other words, contrary to the heartfelt plea of the majority of Okinawans, the reversion meant not the end, but a new beginning, of Okinawa's role as the foundation of the U.S.–Japan Security Treaty system.[5] In an attempt to resist the logic of power, a small number of landlords, called *hansen jinushi* (anti-military landlords) because of their explicit opposition to the use of their land for military purposes, refused to sign the contracts with the Japanese government. However, the number of such landlords was reduced from 3,000 (out of a total of approximately 27,000 military landlords in Okinawa in 1972) to 500 in 1977 and to 100 in 1982, because of such tactics of the Japanese government (Defense Facilities Agency) as intimidations, conciliations, the uneven and unfair distribution of the rent, arbitrary interpretations of the law, and "stirring up conflict between the landlords who accepted the contracts and those who refused them" (Arasaki 1998). For the small number of anti-military landlords who still refused to offer the U.S. military their land, the Japanese government enacted legislations to forcefully extend the contracts, which generated strong resentment among these landlords (Araski 1995).[6]

Under such political circumstances, the so-called one-*tsubo* anti-military landlords' campaign was initiated in 1982 by Okinawan intellectual and activist Arasaki Moriteru and others. With its slogan, "Change the military bases into places for life and production," the campaign sought (and still seeks) to support oppositional landlords, who in one sense carried the torch of the anti-base movement in post-reversion Okinawa, by buying and sharing one *tsubo* (a traditional Japanese measure equal to the size of two *tatami* mats, about 3.3 square meters or 35.52 square feet) or less of their land. It did not cost a lot of money to buy a small piece of military land, and this low-cost campaign helped citizens in Okinawa (and, often, even mainland Japan) join the movement and develop links of solidarity with struggling anti-military landlords. In the late 1980s, the number of anti-military landlords (including one-*tsubo* landlords) reached two thousand (Arasaki 1995, 1998).

In 1991, Ota—as the new governor after twelve years of a conservative, pro-Tokyo administration (1978–1990) led by Nishime Junji—acted, according to the law, as the proxy of some 570 anti-military landlords (including approximately 500 one-*tsubo* anti-military landlords and the city government of Naha) to give his consent to offer their land for the U.S. military (Arasaki 1995: 191–201). He did so with tremendous anguish, however, and on the condition that the Japanese government should swiftly take measures to reduce and reorganize the U.S. bases (Ota M. 1996a). Yet progress was at a snail's pace. In a period of transition away from the cold-war era, old strategies developed in terms of the clearly defined enemy, the Soviet Union, became irrelevant and useless, but a new organizing principle of the U.S. military activities in Okinawa and elsewhere was not yet clearly articulated (see, for instance, Department of Defense 1992; also see Gongora and von Rickhoff 2000: 15; Jablonsky 2001). In the meantime, age-old problems of U.S.-base-related crimes, pollution, noise, and accidents continued in Okinawa.

By 1995, however, against the background of "the increasing economic importance of Asia and the political and security uncertainties in the region in the wake of the Cold War," the United States repositioned itself as the only stabilizing power in the Asia-Pacific region by reaffirming "our commitment to maintain a stable forward presence in the region, at the existing level of about 100,000 troops, for the foreseeable future" (Department of Defense 1995: 5, ii). "100,000," a significant reduction in the number of troops from approximately 135,000 in 1990 (Department of Defense 1995: 23), signaled the ending of the cold-war security paradigm which aimed to eliminate and control the "communist threat" in the region; yet, this number also meant the permanent halting of previously planned troop reductions (Department of Defense 1995: ii), signaling the beginning of the post–cold-war strategic framework through which to incorporate the entire region within America's open and expanding political-economic-cultural boundaries.

Tokyo responded to the U.S.'s renewed commitment to the Asia-Pacific region by disclosing the view that global/American interests, rather than strictly national or local concerns, should take precedence. Thus, in August 1995, in anticipation of the expiration of the contracts with thirty-five anti-military landlords, Tokyo ordered Ota, once again, to give his consent to sign and renew the leases as their proxy in accordance with national policy (*Ryukyu Shinpo*, September 29, 1995; December 12, 1995; March 25, 1996).[7] This highhanded posture of the Japanese government concerning "national policy," however, was reminiscent of that of the past; in fact, the year 1995 marked the fiftieth anniversary of the end of the battle of Okinawa, a tragic battle taking the lives of 150,000 Okinawans which was executed also as a matter of national policy (see below). The governor had personally experienced this battle as a member of *Tekketsu Kin'nōtai* (Iron Blood Unit Dedicated to the Emperor) and, as a professor of the University of the Ryukyus, had extensively written about how the will of the nation-state crushed everyday life of Okinawans (Ota M. 1972).[8]

. . .

In sum, the mid-1990s were a crucial turning point of post-reversion Okinawan history, a moment of profound change of the functions of the U.S. military, which reconfigured the relationship among the global, the national, and the local. From the outset of the reversion of Okinawa in 1972, the global aspirations of the United States as the preeminent Pacific power and local desires for a life without the military had contradicted; this tension remained unresolved for twenty-plus years after the reversion and then became intensified in the mid-1990s as Japan more deeply participated in joint policing of the U.S-centered global order in a manner that extended its own colonialist violence over Okinawa (see below).

It was in this unique historical conjuncture that 1995 rape incident took place. In a way that represented a local resistance to the armed globalization from the above, Governor Ota, after some hesitation, made his stand by refusing to sign the land lease for the U.S. military with Tokyo. He explained, "In the past fifty years, Okinawa has always cooperated with the Japanese and U.S. governments, but they did not listen to Okinawan voices. This time, they should listen to us" (*Ryukyu Shinpo*, September 29, 1995). According to a news poll, an overwhelming 75 percent of Okinawans supported Governor Ota's decision (*Ryukyu Shinpo*, October 7, 1995).

Defense Facilities Agency Secretary Hōshuyama Noboru, frustrated with the magnitude of the upheaval, allegedly stated in mid-October, "The issue has got to the point where it is because Prime Minister[9] is dumb (*shushō no atamaga warui kara kō natta*)" (*Ryukyu Shinpo*, October 19, 1995). As a result, Hōshuyama was fired. In mid-November, the Commander of United States forces in the Pacific, Admiral Richard C. Macke, commented, "I think that it was absolutely stupid, I've said several times," adding that "for the price they paid to rent the car they could have had a girl" (*New York Times*, November 18, 1995). He was immediately forced to step down. With Washington anxiously watching from a distance, and Tokyo in a fluster trying to offend neither U.S. officials nor the Okinawan people, various protest activities were continuously being organized in Okinawa, culminating in an all-Okinawa protest rally attended by some 85,000 people from all walks of life. On stage, Governor Ota touched Okinawans' hearts by proclaiming, "As the person granted responsibility for administering Okinawa, I would like to apologize from the bottom of my heart that I could not protect the dignity of a child, which I must protect above all else" (*Ryukyu Shinpo*, October 22, 1995).

Ota's statement gives us an initial and important point of entry to the workings of contemporary Okinawan identity. The rape of the twelve-year-old girl merited every condemnation, which enabled Okinawa to represent the girl as *itaikena* (innocent), *kayowai* (helpless), and *kiyorakana* (pure) (all of which she was) in Okinawa's public discursive field. In the process, the raped girl may have been turned, metaphorically, into Okinawa's common property, prompting people with diverse backgrounds and interests who had never met each other to become united in this "imagined community" (Anderson [1983] 1991). With the totalizing ideas such as *Okinawa no ikari* (Okinawa's anger), *Okinawa no itami* (Okinawa's pain), and *Okinawa no kokoro* (Okinawa's heart), Okinawans homogenized themselves in opposition to the outside violence so as to discover, in its interior, the raped girl as a symbol of an innocent, helpless, and pure Okinawa.

As Angst (2003) has noted, the construction of homogeneous Okinawan identity also involves the process whereby the act of rape itself, and by implication the male violence against women in general, gradually faded from view. Indeed, Okinawans (Okinawan men, particularly) excluded from their discourses other raped and/or murdered hostesses and prostitutes who were not so "innocent, helpless, and pure"[10] as the twelve-year-old girl, and in this act of *in*attention ironically participated in perpetuating diverse forms of military violence. In addition, the construction of Okinawan homogeneity went hand in hand with the suppression of the question of race. Indeed, by constructing the U.S. military as a monolith without any internal differentiations in terms of race (as a function of class), Okinawan mass media did not clearly report the fact that the suspects were black Americans, nor showed pictures of them immediately after the rape incident (Ishikawa I. 1995), although people came to know their race by word of mouth. Needless to say, it never discussed complex race-class issues within the military, and within American society.

After all, Okinawan political leaders, in their desire to promote the cause of Okinawan resistance, framed the rape incident neither in terms of race nor gender. Instead they presented the case in nativist, masculine, political terms of the injustice of the U.S. military. That choice was a problematic one, because, as the Asia-Pacific region has been more thoroughly incorporated as a frontier of America's post–cold war project of capitalist, military, and cultural development, the politics of gender and race has become as pressing as ever and needs to be explicitly discussed and critiqued in the trans-Pacific public sphere. In other words, Okinawa's political leaders failed to approach the rape of the Okinawan girl as a structural problem of the "contact zone" (Pratt 1992) in the age of globalization, in which the weaker subjects of the two societies—Okinawans in Japan on the one hand, and black people in the U.S. on the other[11]—have been pitted against one another, and sexual violence has been waged against the weakest, the Okinawan girl, by the weaker, the black servicemen.

Below, in ways that complement perspectives of critical feminism and race studies, I want not so much to justify and rescue as to carefully historicize and explain, from ground level, Okinawa's problematic choice of creating an imagined community with the homogenized collective identity. What will emerge in the analysis below are the two basic historical modalities of contemporary Okinawan identity. On the one hand is the modality that corresponds to Okinawa's collective memories of the U.S. military—the humiliating experiences of U.S. rule after the war, and the continued U.S. military presence and violence after the reversion of Okinawa. On the other hand is the modality that involves the collective memories of Japan—its discrimination against Okinawa before the war, its "use" of Okinawa as a sacrifice to protect mainland Japan during the war, and its betrayal that has resulted in the continuous U.S. military presence after the reversion and the end of the cold war. Combined together, these two modalities had once helped Okinawan identity to be founded on the idea of a uniformly oppressed, poor "people"; this identity, however, has been in the midst of a significant and troubling transformation to one that is articulated through the idea and practice of autonomous, affluent "citizens" with confidence and pride. It is this Okinawan citizenship, I will suggest toward the end of this chapter, that was expressed in the form of the homogenized, collective identity in the wake of the rape incident.

The U.S. Military and Okinawans as a "People":
The First Modality of Okinawan Identity

Toward the end of World War II, the U.S. government had considered Okinawa for use as a launching base from which to attack mainland Japan, but the unconditional surrender of Japan in August 1945 left this idea not fully realized.[12] Then came a time of uncertainty (until mid-1949) over how to govern Okinawa (Nakano 1969: 1–35; Miyazato 1975, Shiels 1980, Miyagi 1982, Kano 1987, Eldridge 2001). On the one hand, the U.S. military was unwilling to give up Okinawa, a territory it had secured as a strategic stronghold on the Pacific by shedding the blood of more than twelve thousand of its servicemen. On the other hand, the State Department was reluctant to get involved in the task of governing Okinawa in part because of the Atlantic Charter (concluded in August 1941), wherein U.S. President Roosevelt and British Prime Minister Churchill agreed on opposing territorial expansion whether for themselves or for other countries. Owing to this divergence of views between the military and the State Department within the U.S. government, no systematic administrative action was taken in Okinawa; in its midst, the situation there became so aggravated that *Time* (November 28, 1949: 24) called Okinawa "a dumping ground for Army misfits and rejects from more comfortable posts." The same article stated, "More than 15,000 U.S. troops, whose morale and discipline are probably worse than that of any U.S. forces in the world, have policed 600,000 natives who live in hopeless poverty.… In the six months ending last September, U.S. soldiers committed an appalling number of crimes, 29 murders, 18 rape cases, 16 robberies, and 33 assaults."

The early uncertainty of the U.S. government over the administration of Okinawa was, however, doomed to be transfigured as the cold war intensified. Washington adopted a two-pronged strategy: while helping to redevelop occupied Japan in order to create a breakwater against the "communist threat," it separated Okinawa from postwar Japan so as to turn it into America's "keystone of the Pacific" (cf. Ogden 1954) by, for instance, appropriating fifty million dollars for the development of military facilities there in the 1950 fiscal year (Nakano 1969: 51).

The strategy—involving the politico-economic use of mainland Japan on the one hand and the military use of Okinawa on the other, for the sake of establishing hegemony in the post–World War II world—was reinforced in the San Francisco Peace Conference in September 1951. During this conference, in which Japan regained independence and was simultaneously subordinated by the U.S. power, President Truman's envoy and future secretary of state, John Foster Dulles, proclaimed the doctrine of Japan's "residual sovereignty" over Okinawa (Miyazato 1975, Shiels 1980, Eldridge 2001). This meant that while Japan maintained its nominal sovereignty, the United States would, in actuality, obtain all rights and powers to administer Okinawa for an indefinite period. As a result, Okinawa became suspended as a "stateless" land (Kano 1987: 105), wherein people were entitled neither to U.S. nor Japanese citizenship. Incidentally, in a manner that prefigured the idea of residual sovereignty (and also reinforced Japan's manipulation of Okinawa in the interest of the nation—see below), in 1947 Emperor Hirohito had delivered, without the knowledge of Okinawans, a message to the General Headquarters for the Allied Powers in Tokyo indicating in effect that the occupation of Okinawa by the U.S. forces—with sovereignty retained in Japan—for the period of twenty-five to fifty years or more was desirable, as it would help Japan to defend itself against the menace of the Soviet Union, which would in turn help maintain internal order in Japan (Shindo 1979).

The actual task of governing local Okinawans was carried out by the U.S. military in Okinawa, now named the United States Civil Administration of the Ryukyu Islands (USCAR), which was formally established in December 1950. One of USCAR's first assignments was to expropriate Okinawan land for base expansion and construction. While Imperial Japanese Army bases and a vast stretch of Okinawa's private land had been already confiscated and used by the U.S. military since 1945, USCAR's own expropriation started in the Naha area in 1950; after the promulgation of Ordinance 109 (that specified land-acquisition procedures[13]) in April 1953, it became especially systematic and atrocious. Okinawan intellectual and activist Kokuba Kōtarō described what he experienced on July 19, 1955, in the Isabama area in central Okinawa as follows (Kokuba 1973: 260–264, cited in Arasaki 1995: 63–65). The expropriation of the land started after midnight when most of the more than ten thousand protesters had gone back home:

> Around 3 A.M.,...I heard ominous noise coming from the military road right across the paddy fields. But I could not yet see what it was. When the noise approached, I looked hard, and found that trucks and bulldozers filled with armed soldiers were slowly coming one after another with their headlights

FIGURE 2.1 A house in Isabama is being destroyed. Reprint from *Okinawaken Chijikō-shitsu Kōhōka* 1996:18.

off. By dawn, the 40-hectare area of paddy fields was completely surrounded by the armed soldiers; then, the bulldozers rushed into the community of 32 families....

Things having come to this, the farmers could not do anything. They sat in the houses, now surrounded by barbed wires, to show their last resistance. After turning these farmers out of doors by pointing guns and pistols at them, U.S. soldiers started destroying the houses. First, a giant axe was driven into the roof of a variety store at the entrance of the community. The exposed crossbeam was then tied with a rope, which a bulldozer pulled, and the store fell down. Chopped wood was collected by bulldozers, put on trucks, and dumped on the nearby beach. In this way, all 32 houses were destroyed. Against such cruel treatment by the U.S. military, women protested with their hair disheveled. Watching all this happened, I could not stop something hot from welling in my eyes.[14]

This naked exercise of power, however, did not pacify but rather intensified the flames of anger among Okinawans, who formed their first organized protest, the so-called *shimagurumi tōsō* (the island-wide protest). In October 1955, the House of Representatives dispatched to Okinawa a Special Subcommittee of the Armed Services Committee chaired by Charles Melvin Price (D, IL); in June 1956, the Subcommittee submitted a report—so-called the "Price Report"—to the House of Representatives so as to (1) recommend that the U.S. acquire the fee title in the Okinawan properties now occupied by the military in exchange for the lump-sum payment of fair values and (2) authorize the acquisition of additional lands with the statement that such acquisition must be kept "to an absolute minimum" (Special Subcommittee of the Armed Services Committee, 1956).[15] Im-

FIGURE 2.2 More than 100,000 Okinawans participated in this rally, held in Naha on June 20, 1956, to protest the Price Committee's Report. Reprint from *Okinawaken Chijikōshitsu Kōhōka* 1996: 20.

mediately after the Price Report was issued, protest rallies were organized elsewhere in Okinawa; one meeting held in a schoolyard in Naha was attended by 100,000 people (June 1956). A quote from one newspaper article will convey the atmosphere:

> President of Okinawa Teachers Association Yara Chōbyō, whose passionate eloquence is well known, then rushed out of his seat to take the microphone…. The eloquence of President Yara, convincing and squared with reason, threw the whole audience into a state of feverish excitement. Dignified faces in the [nearby] amusement park, in the [adjacent] stadium, and on the rooftops of the school buildings shouted "yes!," "yes!," again arousing a storm of hand-clapping. [Meanwhile,] a housewife holding a baby, an old woman sitting on a bamboo mat without stirring an inch, a laborer who kept his worn-out cap on without wiping the beads from sweat on his brow, and a standing old man accompanied by his grand-daughter [all listened to and watched the stage attentively,] without fanning themselves in the stifling air of packed people.
>
> (*Ryukyu Shinpo*, June 26, 1956; cited in Nakano 1969: 192)

An important point to note is that the theme (emancipation from the oppressor), the mode (the large-scale collective protest), and the actors (subjugated residents, poor farmers and workers) of the desperate protest in Okinawa in the 1950s exhibited the basic characteristics of "old," organized social movements by the "people," called, in Japanese, *minshū*. In other words, the thrust of the island-wide protest in U.S.-ruled Okinawa can be adequately grasped less within the framework of the new social movement literature that addresses ecology, peace, women's issues, and so forth, than with that of the Marxist and nationalist literatures that emphasize structural conflicts between the dominating and the dominated to explain large-scale mobilizations. (See chapter 1 for the discussion of the shift of social movements from the old to the new.) In the midst of the island-wide protest, however, some local communities such as Henoko (see chapter 4) accepted the construction of the new American bases in exchange for higher bids, and by late 1958 the protest was put to an end due to the internal conflicts of the movement, wherein some insisted on an all-out confrontation with USCAR, others shifted their focus onto the methods and amounts of rent payment, and still others compromised outright with USCAR in light of the U.S–Okinawa "friendship." Nevertheless, throughout the 1950s, the structural conflicts clearly made their appearance in Okinawa in many other ways.

(1) Base-related crimes and accidents continued to occur in the 1950s. In 1951 a fuel tank fell from a flying fighter plane, hitting and destroying a house occupied by three families and killing six people. In 1955 a six-year-old girl was raped and killed by a sergeant. In 1956 a housewife was shot by two U.S. guards when she entered the vicinity of an ammunition depot; she was collecting scrap iron near this ammunition depot in order to help her family budget. In 1959 a fighter plane crashed into an elementary school, causing the death of seventeen students and injuries to more than one hundred. In the same year, a housewife was shot by a soldier who mistook her for a wild boar (Fukuchi 1995).

(2) Because the jurisdiction over the incidents involving U.S. servicemen remained in the hands of U.S. authorities, remedial measures for

FIGURE 2.3 On June 30, 1959, a U.S. fighter plane crashed into an elementary school, causing the death of seventeen students and the injury of more than 100 students. Reprint from *Okinawaken Chijikōshitsu Kōhōka* 1996: 26.

crimes and military accidents were virtually closed to Okinawans. For instance, no compensation was awarded to survivors of the family members
killed by the falling of the fuel tank in 1951 (Fukuchi 1995: 147), nor was any
awarded to the family of the woman who was shot near the ammunition
depot in 1956. She was judged to have been trying to "steal" the U.S. property (scrap iron) (Tengan 1999: 70). To the families whose children were
killed in the 1959 plane crash at the school, $2,525 was paid across the board
as against $19,906 requested by these families. Later, USCAR paid an ad-
ditional $2,000 (Nakano 1969: 333).

(3) Special Proclamation 28 in 1947 (Nakano 1969: 10–11) prohibited
marriage between Okinawans and Americans. However, only Okinawan
violators were to be punished. This proclamation was later canceled as the
number of mixed-blood children born between American GIs and Okinawan women increased, but many of these children, when abandoned by
their fathers, lost access to either American or Japanese citizenship.

(4) USCAR intervened against oppositional movements by, for instance,
instructing the University of the Ryukyus (which USCAR created) to ex-
pel student activists in 1954 and 1956, and by discharging Naha City Mayor
Senaga Kamejirō of the Okinawa's People's Party in 1957 on the basis that
he was a "communist" (Nakano 1969: 248–64).

(5) Passports, necessary for Okinawans to go to mainland Japan, and
visas, necessary for Japanese to come to Okinawa, were both controlled by
USCAR, and were often withheld from those with "communist" inclina-
tions (Nakano 1969: 95–97; Kano 1987: 200–62).[16] Needless to say, censorship was a common practice.

(6) In the early 1950s, strikes were waged against major Japanese construction companies (involved in base construction work in Okinawa), on
the basis of the wage discrimination against Okinawan workers[17] and their
extremely poor working conditions (Nakano 1969: 128–32). In 1953 USCAR
issued Ordinance 116, "Labor Relations and Labor Standards concerning
Ryukyuan Employees, for the purpose of suppressing labor movements
(Nakano 1969: 133–41).

In a manner not unlike that of large-scale peasant insurrections or revolutionary upheavals tied to the collective desire for the overthrow of the
power structure, diverse struggles in the 1950s cited above, when combined
with the island-wide protest against the expropriation of Okinawa's land,
provided a context in which the collective identity as the politically and

economically subjugated "people" (*minshū*)—the sense that "we are Oki-nawans"—took definite shape in U.S.-controlled Okinawa.

• • •

Without underestimating tensions between the dominating and the domi-nated, however, it is also important to note a variety of economic, political, and cultural projects USCAR introduced in the 1950s in an effort to foster a friendly attitude among Okinawans toward the United States. The analy-sis of these projects will help us understand the complexity of the political landscape of Okinawa in the 1950s on the one hand, and the ways in which these projects ironically stimulated the so-called reversion movement—Okinawan "people's" politico-cultural project in the 1960s that was staged in order to bring USCAR's rule of Okinawa to an end—on the other.

In the economic sphere, USCAR established the Bank of the Ryukyus (the central bank in Okinawa) in 1948, the Ryukyu Electric Public Corpo-ration in 1954, and the Ryukyu Water Public Corporation in 1958 so as to promote a stable economy. In 1958, furthermore, in place of the military currency called B-yen, which helped create an isolated, controlled econ-omy in Okinawa, the U.S. dollar was introduced as the currency in order to establish a "free" economy (i.e., the freedom of American companies to invest and conduct business in Okinawa, not vice versa) and economically reinforce American military rule in Okinawa (Makino 1996:10–57).

In the political sphere, USCAR established the Government of the Ryukyu Islands (GRI) in 1952, which, though ultimately required to obey the directives of USCAR, its overseer, was nevertheless run by Okinawans themselves (Nakano 1969: 165–171; Okinawa Prefectural Peace Memorial Museum [OPPMM] 2001: 114–19).

In the realm of culture, USCAR throughout the 1950s attempted to en-dorse Okinawa's pride and identity within the framework of U.S.-Okinawa friendship. For instance, USCAR created a fund to enhance cultural activities at the luxurious Ryukyu-U.S. Culture Centers (*Ryūbei Bunka Kaikan*) that were built in various parts of the Ryukyu Islands. It also funded programs for Okinawan youth to study in the United States and mainland Japan, and, in response to a grassroots movement to build Okinawa's first institution of higher learning, established the University of the Ryukyus (OPPMM 2001: 114). Furthermore, USCAR restored the war-ruined *Shureimon* gate of Shuri castle, the symbol of the Ryukyu Kingdom, and other culturally significant structures across Okinawa (Arashiro 1994: 286). In addition, Okinawan newspapers, radio stations, and TV stations were reestablished under the guidance and supervision of USCAR. The monthly official propaganda magazines of USCAR, named *Kon'nichi no Ryūkyū* (Ryukyu Today) and *Shurei no Hikari* (The Light of Courtesy), were two major print media sources for disseminating the idea of Ryukyu–U.S. "friendship" (Kano 1987: 161–99).[18]

Note that while introducing numerous economic, political, and cultural projects in the 1950s, USCAR constantly used "Ryukyu" but not "Okinawa," and in doing so subtly manipulated the very basis of cultural identity, one's name. "Ryukyu," the name used by the Sui dynasty in China in the seventh century, provokes a Chinese (i.e., a non-Japanese) connection, while "Okinawa," the name given by mainland Japan in the eighth century, conveys a Japanese connection. Meiji Japan disposed of the "Ryukyu" Kingdom in 1872–79 through the "Ryukyu" Measures, and then called it "Okinawa" prefecture in order to psychosocially detach Okinawa from China. The United States then reappropriated this historical process by "Ryukyuanizing" (i.e., "un-Japanizing") Okinawa, not in order to let China control Okinawa, but to detach Okinawa from Japan. They called inhabitants "Ryukyuans," and designated them so in their passports. An aborted attempt was even made to create the "Ryukyu" flag. It should be added that in prewar Okinawa, local culture was identified by Okinawan leaders (as well as the Meiji government) as something that had to be completely eradicated, something that signified Okinawa's backwardness vis-à-vis progressive mainland Japan (see below). The United States turned this same "culture" into a source of pride and identity of "Ryukyuans" (Kano 1987: 3–112).

In the 1960s, however, discontent among Okinawans could no longer be masked by the imposed language of pride, culture, and friendship. The lack of social equality and political autonomy was keenly felt. In 1957, on the basis of an Executive Order issued by President Eisenhower, the office of High Commissioner was created as "the locus of American military rule in Okinawa" (OPPMM 2001: 116). Until the reversion of Okinawa in 1972, the office was taken by a total of six Army lieutenant generals, who held ultimate administrative, legislative, judicial, and military authority in an all-encompassing way, and came to be called by Okinawans, with envy and awe, the "King" (Ota M. 1996b). The Chief Okinawan Executive was not elected by Okinawans but appointed by the "King." The Ryukyu Legislative Council declared that American military rule in Okinawa was

FIGURE 2.4 In 1965, a U.S. military trailer fell from a fighter airplane and crushed a local girl to death. Reprint from *Okinawaken Chijikōshitsu Kōhōka* 1996: 27.

not unlike colonial control in other parts of the world as defined by the United Nations.

In addition, Okinawa came to be used, against its will, by the U.S. military as a base, now fully equipped with nuclear weapons, B-52s, and poison gas, for dispatch, logistics, and training for the Vietnam War (Nakano 1969: 520–595, OPPMM 2001: 130–131). In the process, Okinawans witnessed in their everyday life continued and increased base-related crimes and accidents. For instance, in 1965 a military trailer fell from a fighter airplane and crushed a local girl to death; in 1966 a tanker airplane crushed and killed one local resident and ten servicemen, and a taxi driver was stabbed to death by a serviceman; in 1967 a hostess was strangled by a serviceman, a male high school student was killed in a military vehicle's hit-and-run, and a four-year-old girl was run over by a military trailer and died; in 1968, four Okinawans were injured and three hundred houses were damaged by an explosion of B-52 in Kadena Air Base; in 1969 poison gas leaked in a military facility and twenty-four servicemen were hospitalized, and a housewife was killed in a hit-and-run accident caused by a serviceman; and in

1970 a female high school student was stabbed by a serviceman on her way from school.

It is within this turbulent context of the 1960s that the so-called reversion movement gained momentum. While the island-wide protest in the 1950s represented "old" social movements of the politically and economically subjugated people, the reversion movement in the 1960s had an added dimension of "culture," and as such can be seen as a collective mobilization with a transitional character that presented features of both "old" and "new" social movements (and paved the way for the emergence of a "new" social protest, centering on citizenship, in the 1990s—see below). Put differently, in the 1960s a unitary conception of the Okinawan "people" was constituted at an intersection of the political, the economic, and the cultural. The cultural dimension of the reversion movement was underscored as Okinawans appropriated the very cultural pride USCAR had cultivated for their own ends. In a manner that disavowed the idea of the U.S.-Okinawa friendship (which reinforced the separation between Japan and Okinawa), indeed, Okinawans showed their pride by articulating the fervent desire to create "solidarity with the Homeland" and to "strengthen ethnic ties [with mainland Japan]" (Okinawaken Sokoku Fukki Kyōgikai 1960; cited in Arasaki 1969: 152).

Political, economic, and cultural energies for reversion found specific expression in the collective movement shaped and directed by the Council for the Reversion of Okinawa Prefecture to the Homeland, or *Fukkikyō* (the abbreviation of *Okinawaken Sokoku Fukki Kyōgikai*), an organization that was established in 1960 by the influential Okinawa Teachers Association, together with three reformist parties—the most radical Okinawa People's Party (OPP), the moderate Okinawa Socialist Masses Party (OSMP), and the class-conscious Okinawa Socialists Party (OSP)[19]—and other social organizations (Mi. Higa 1963, 1977).

On the political ground, "teachers are a key group in the moulding of public opinion and…any hostility they might feel against the United States as a result of a decline in status since the war [their status declined because of their low salaries, accompanied by the destruction of the imperial education system within which teachers had earned the esteem of the public] might easily be conveyed to" students and adults alike, so once predicted by Pitts, Lebra, and Suttles (1955: 219).[20] In a way that showed the accuracy of this prediction, *Fukkikyō*, with teachers as a central mobilizing force, demanded the public election of the Chief Executive, opposed the Vietnam

War, and insisted on the removal of B-52s, nuclear weapons, and poison gas; in so doing, it sought to achieve immediate and unconditional reversion of Okinawa to Japan, with the U.S. bases being all eliminated. On the economic ground, *Fukkikyō* expressed Okinawans' desire for a better life by incorporating the voices and movements of increasingly active labor unions—in spite of USCAR's obstruction, the number of labor unions increased from 4 in 1954 to 144 in 1967 (Nakano 1969: 774; Gabe 1975: 187; Cf. Uehara K. 1982). On the cultural ground, *Fukkikyō* mobilized the notion that the Okinawan and Japanese cultures and races come from the same root, the notion that had been (problematically) articulated by the Japanese native ethnology (e.g., Yanagita Kunio) and Okinawan scholars (e.g., Iha Fuyū) (see chapter 3).

In short, *Fukkikyō* attempted to "de-Americanize" Okinawa, i.e., to disconnect Okinawa from the United States politically, economically, and culturally, and in the process romantically imagined Japan as the homeland without oppression in spite of Okinawa's experiences of Japanese discriminations (see below). In the 1960s, reversion was the unified Okinawan voice—it became the preference of more than 90 percent of Okinawans over other options (e.g., independence or UN trusteeship) (Mi. Higa 1977).

What perhaps became obvious in the eyes of U.S. authorities in the 1960s was that the notion of Japan's "residual sovereignty" over Okinawa was a double-edged sword. That is, while this notion made it possible for the U.S. to monopolize all power in Okinawa, it also burdened the U.S. with the extremely difficult task of administering a frustrated and restless people, a task that was becoming virtually unbearable as dissent in Okinawa increased.

Yet, in the end, Washington got out of a predicament by doubly exploiting Okinawa's idealization of its "homeland," Japan, as a springboard to reinforcing its own hegemony in the Far East. On the one hand, by allowing Okinawa to return to Japan, the United States was relieved of a headache (i.e., of administering Okinawa). On the other hand, against the background of the ongoing cold war, the United States had Japan grant privileges and rights for continuous and unrestricted use of Okinawa's military base complex, and in so doing, implicated not only Okinawa but also its "homeland" more deeply into the global project of keeping out the "communist threat" from Asia.

After the basic scheme of the reversion—the administration of Okinawa would be transferred to Japan in 1972, but the U.S. military would continue to stay—became clear in 1969, the frustration of some Okinawans reached the absolute breaking point; this was expressed not only through organized demonstrations and rallies that culminated in two successful general strikes in May and November of 1971 (attended by more than 100,000 Okinawans respectively), but also in spontaneous resistance activities as exemplified by the legendary Koza "riot" (Isa 1996, Hirai 1998, Aldous 2003).

Around 11:00 P.M. on Saturday, December 20, 1970, a drunken Okinawan man was hit by an American car on the road near Okinawa's largest entertainment-sex industry frontier, Koza Town, adjacent to Kadena Air Force Base. The accident was not serious; after checking to see that the Okinawan man was OK (he walked away from the scene shortly), the four servicemen got back into the car to leave. Yet several taxi drivers who witnessed the accident approached the vehicle to accuse the servicemen, "Why are you guys leaving after hitting a man, huh?!," during which time a crowd of Okinawans started to gather at the scene. Then two military police cars came with earsplitting sirens and "rescued" the servicemen without attending to the "injured" Okinawan man, who in fact was asked by the taxi drivers to lie down on the road to reenact the scene of the accident.

When another American car that got through the checkpoints accidentally collided with an Okinawan car near the scene, "the crowd swelled to around 700, its mood now openly aggressive—attempts were made to turn the accident vehicle over and bottles, rocks and other objects were thrown at the military police" (Aldous 2003: 158). The MPs fired warning shots. This, however, only invited more protesters, including drunken customers, rock musicians, owners of bars and restaurants, hostesses, participants in daytime political demonstrations, and civilians inhabiting the area. Okinawans, now numbering five thousand, clashed with seven hundred MPs in pitch darkness, while breaking into, turning over, and burning seventy-odd cars, all owned by U.S. servicemen and/or the military, with instant handmade "fire bottles" (Molotov Cocktails), which Okinawan men created in the bars and hostesses carried from there. Out of excitement, some Okinawans danced traditional Okinawan dances while looking at the blazing fire. The MPs responded to the disturbance by using tear gas grenades. In the meantime, some protesters entered the gate of Kadena Air Base and continued to throw their fire bottles and rocks, so as to burn and destroy cars, windows of classroom buildings, a Santa Claus statue, a decorated Christmas tree, and other objects. The seven-hour "riot" was entirely spontaneous, prompted by Okinawa's discontent with the prospect that the U.S. bases—the main culprit behind the violation of basic human rights—would continue to stay even after the reversion, a discontent that was intensified by the fact that the U.S. serviceman who had killed a housewife in a hit-and-run accident (September 1970) had been tried and acquitted in court-martial two weeks earlier.

Evidently, in the midst of this "riot," an unspoken code came to be instantly formed and shared by all attending Okinawans. According to this code, women, children, and—most important in the context of my discussion—black servicemen should not be harmed. Pitts, Lebra, and Suttles (1955: 214) stated that "in observing the American Army's treatment of Negroes the Okinawans have seen segregation and some discrimination." This discrimination, in the context of Koza Town in the 1960s, was expressed,

FIGURE 2.5 70-odd American cars were burned in the Koza "riot" on December 20, 1970. Reprint from *Okinawaken Chijikōshitsu Kōhōka* 1996: 28.

54

among other things, as the segregation of the "white-men-only" bar street from the "black-men-only" bar street (Onga 1998: 28). Okinawan observation of white–black relations, when combined with their own experience of white servicemen who had often treated Okinawans as a sort of second-rate Orientals (Okinawa Shiyakusho 1994: 54), could have helped create a bond of sympathy between black servicemen and Okinawans against white servicemen. This bond, while not entirely neutralizing racial tensions between black *Americans* (the powerful) and Okinawans (the powerless), might have helped generate the code, "Don't hurt the weak, including black servicemen." The following day, a group of black servicemen in Kadena Air Base who were associated with the Black Panther Party released the statement, "We support the riot" (*Asahi Shinbun*, December 23, 1970, cited in Gabe 1975: 205). This was the moment at which broader solidarity between oppressed "peoples"—Okinawans, black servicemen, and others—was established, at least momentarily.

In sum, during the period of U.S. military control between 1945 and 1972, Okinawans were not only brutally oppressed but also actively made and remade its oppositionally collective consciousness as a *minshū*—a poor and subjugated "people" bound together in the idea that "we are Okinawans." Our historical understanding of the collective Okinawan consciousness, however, cannot be complete unless we take its second modality into consideration, a modality that corresponds to Okinawa's memories on the troubling relationship with modern Japan. Specifically, the analysis of a dialectic transformation of the social consciousness of Okinawans vis-à-vis Japan since the late nineteenth century, with the battle of Okinawa of 1945 as both the pinnacle and the demise of this dialectic, will help grasp a specific nature of Okinawan identity and the depth of its predicaments in a broader historical, politico-economic, and cultural perspective.

"Becoming" Japanese: The Second Modality of Okinawan Identity

In 1872, the newly instituted Meiji government initiated what were called the "Ryukyu Measures," which, over the next seven years, would transform the old Ryukyu Kingdom—long subjugated to both Tokugawa Japan and Qing China—into Okinawa Prefecture, and absorb the domain within Imperial Japan. Geopolitically, the establishment of Okinawa Prefecture can be seen as a manifestation, together with the control of the Kuril (Chishima) Islands in exchange for Sakhalin given to Russia (1875) and the possession of the Bonin (Ogasawara) Islands (1876), of the Meiji government's efforts to define clearly marked territory as a modern nation-state. Along with the dispatch of Japanese troops to Taiwan in 1874 and the forceful conclusion of a treaty of amity with Joseon (a Korean Kingdom) in 1876, the integration of Okinawa can also be seen as an incipient expression of Meiji Japan's desire to be able to stand up to the Western imperial centers, a desire that ultimately resulted in Japan's colonial expansion into Asia in the twentieth century. Politico-culturally, the same process came with the implementation of massive and forceful assimilation-cum-discrimination programs into Okinawa, of which language and culture—particularly "spirit"—became, under "modern" imperial eyes, identified as both signs of backwardness and points of intervention. In a word, these programs were informed by the idea that "*they* are Okinawans" (i.e., *they* are not Japanese enough), and aimed to remake them into authentic imperial subjects.

For instance, the Meiji government established the Conversation School (*Kaiwa Denshūjo*) for the purpose of training Okinawan teachers to speak "standard" Japanese. It also distributed copies of the Imperial Rescript on Education, along with photographs of the emperor, to the schools in Okinawa to develop loyalty to the emperor among teachers and students. The conscription system was swiftly implemented to produce soldiers endowed with the infallible spirit of Imperial Japan. Although the Meiji government used education and the military as two basic institutions with which to instill a sense of loyalty and duty (cf. Altinay 2004), it also deprived Okinawans of political rights and benefits as the national subjects. Indeed, the Okinawa prefectural government was controlled and monopolized by governors and officials sent from Tokyo, institutions of higher education were not created, financial support to develop industries other than sugar production was not provided, and the opportunity to represent Okinawan voices in the Diet via elections was denied in the early (sometimes well into late) Meiji period (1868–1912) (Arashiro 1994: 173–202, Beillevaire 1999).

Okinawa responded to the Japanese project of assimilation-cum-discrimination by actively internalizing, not rejecting, the idea that "*they* are Okinawans" (i.e., *they* are not Japanese enough)," in a way that produced the reverse notion that "*we* are Okinawans" (i.e., *we* are not Japanese enough; *we* are almost, but not yet quite, Japanese). In part abetted by the fear of exclusion from the realm of splendid monarchy, and in part motivated by the desire for discovering oneself in and devoting oneself to a higher unity (Hashikawa [1985] 2000: 1–225), Okinawa indeed ended up joining the dangerous game of "becoming" Japanese by initiating desperate efforts to collectively eradicate its own "deficits." For instance, Okinawa Prefecture introduced *fūzoku kaizen undō* (the culture improvement movement), whose objective was to change the "backward" Okinawan way of life into the "civilized" Japanese way of life. Programs for the culture improvement movement included the abolishment of the Okinawan hairstyle (1888), the tattoo practices of women (1899), and Okinawan holidays (1903) (Arashiro 1994: 183–84). Ota Chōfu, a respected native Okinawan leader and graduate of elite Keio University in Tokyo, even asserted in a lecture in 1900, "One of the most urgent tasks of today's Okinawa is to make everything look as it does in other prefectures of Japan. We should even sneeze the way people in other prefectures do" (Ota C. 1995: 58; cited in Oguma 1998: 281).

Okinawa's desire to be fully assimilated as subjects of Imperial Japan was perhaps most acutely and paradoxically expressed in the so-called "Pavilion of the Human Races" incident. During the 1903 Fifth Industrial Exhibition in Osaka, Korean, Ainu, Taiwanese-aboriginal, and Okinawan women were "displayed" in the "Pavilion of the Human Races" for visitors to appreciate the similarities and differences between "real" Japanese and some of the "primitive" Asian peoples within the expanding Japanese empire. Okinawan leaders, including Ota Chōfu mentioned above (1995: 211–16), fiercely protested to the officials, on the grounds that Okinawans were not as uncivilized and backward as Koreans, Ainu, and Taiwanese aborigines (cf. Ota M. 1976: 291). As Christy (1993: 617) points out, "the impetus [of Okinawans] to 'become' Japanese was propelled not simply by a desire to catch up to a progressive Japan, but also by a desire to gain some distance from the colonies and minority groups."

In the 1920s, the desire of the Okinawans to become Japanese unfolded in a specific political-economic context that was shaped by nationwide and worldwide relations of power and history. In the aftermath of World War I, the international market price of sugar sharply dropped because of an oversupply. The effect was devasting, because income from sugar had been constituting 80 percent of Okinawa's entire export income. By the mid-1920s, the economic situation became so aggravated that people reportedly had nothing to eat other than *sotetsu*, fern palms that grow in Okinawa (Arashiro 1994: 207–13).

The economic devastation triggered massive emigration from Okinawa to Hawaii, Peru, Brazil, Argentina, the Philippines, Saipan, and other regions and nations outside Japan. It is estimated that Okinawans constituted ten to twenty percent of overseas emigrants with Japanese nationality between 1923 and 1930 (Arashiro 1994: 211–212). The economic plights during this period also prompted many Okinawans to go to mainland Japan—particularly the Osaka area—to work as cheap laborers in the textile and other industries.

The emigration led not only to more contact with Okinawans, but also more discrimination against them, in Japan and abroad. Indeed, signs declaring "No Koreans or Ryukyuans allowed" were allegedly put up on the gates of Japanese factories (Tomiyama 1990). Taking this as evidence that the previous self-Japanization efforts had not been sufficient, Okinawan authorities became even further implicated into the project of remaking Okinawans into Japanese. For instance, the authorities initiated new campaigns to change "strange" Okinawan names into Japanese alternatives; they also urged individual communities to erect Japanese-style *shinto* gates and shrines in *utaki* (indigenous sacred groves) across Okinawa (OPPMM 2001: 34–35). The use of Okinawan toilets (used to raise pigs with human waste), as well as the practices of aerial sepulture, walking with bare feet, and local shamanism, was strongly discouraged to prevent the image of Okinawans as "unsanitary" and/or "backward" from spreading among mainland Japanese. With the use of *hōgenfuda* (a wooden placard to be hung, as punishment, around the neck of a student who uttered Okinawan "dialect") in schools, the eradication of the Okinawan "dialect" was well under way, while the acquisition of "standard" Japanese, together with the foreign idea of the respect for the emperor, continued to be enforced (Arashiro 1994: 232–33).

From the late 1930s onward, finally, Okinawans' desire to become Japanese came to be entangled with the empire's wartime efforts. While the government attempted to control and mobilize all human and material resources across the nation, Okinawans, for their part, appropriated wartime as an opportunity to erase the Japanese view of Okinawans as second class nationals insufficiently committed to military and other obligations. Okinawan children were involved in military drills at schools to demonstrate their patriotism and loyalty to the emperor. Men and women cheered the Imperial Japanese Navy when its warships arrived to carry out military exercises in Okinawa's sea. Military fervor rose to its highest pitch across Okinawa with the Japanese military's surprise attack on Pearl Harbor in December 1941, and with subsequent victories in the battles in Hong Kong, Singapore, Burma (present-day Myanmar), Indonesia, and the Philippines in 1941–42 (OPPMM 2001: 46–47; Henoko 1998: 525–74). Okinawans also enthusiastically received Prime Minister (also Army General) Tojo Hideki when he came to Okinawa in 1943 in order to "take important measures for constructing the Great East Asia Co-Prosperity Sphere and annihilating American and British troops," according to a newspaper at the time (cited in Okinawa Taimusu 1970: 172).

In actuality, however, the tide of the war already changed, as the U.S. military had won a decisive victory in the naval battle at Midway and then at Guadalcanal in 1942. Thereafter, they recaptured Saipan (1943), the Philippines (1944), and other territories that had been occupied by the Japanese military. The next target was Okinawa, which the United States forces intended to use as a launching base from which to attack mainland Japan. At the same time, Okinawa became, in the eyes of the executive staff of the Imperial Headquarters in Tokyo, simply a "rear area" to be sacrificed in order to buy time before U.S. military attacks. (After all, "they are Okinawans.") The 32nd Japanese Army (also called *Okinawa Shubitai* or the Okinawa Garrison Body) was dispatched from mainland Japan in March 1944 to defend Okinawa, but the strongest troops of this army were soon removed and redeployed to Taiwan in December 1944, right before the battle of Okinawa (Ota M. 1972: 34–35). *Bōei Tai* (the Defense Corps), which consisted of twenty-five thousand Okinawan men between the ages of seventeen and forty-five,[21] with no prior military experience whatsoever, was created in part to make up for this loss. Okinawan women, students, children, and horses were also mobilized to build airfields and fortifications across Okinawa. With eighty-six thousand Japanese soldiers and ten thousand sailors, the Okinawan *minshū* (people), politically, economically, and culturally subjugated, were made ready for the U.S. military attack that seemed imminent (Arashiro 1994: 222–39, OPPMM 2001: 41–49).

On October 10, 1944, a thousand U.S. fighter planes attacked Naha and surrounding areas from the air and reduced more than 90 percent of the city to ashes. In April 1945, with 1,500 warships and a total of 540,000 troops, the U.S. military executed Operation "Iceberg" to invade Okinawa. "Exploiting its material superiority, the U.S. military indiscriminately bombed

Okinawa from the air and barraged it from battleship cannons, firing enormous numbers of shells" (OPPMM 2001: 60). For its part, the Japanese Imperial Army was put to rout soon after it exhausted sixty thousand men (or 85 percent of the main military unit) in deadly fighting in central Okinawa in April and May. The Japanese Army abandoned their headquarters at Shuri (near Naha). Sick and wounded soldiers were deserted and disabled soldiers were poisoned with cyanide there, while others retreated south. As a result, however, frustrated Japanese soldiers were jumbled together with panicked inhabitants who had sought refuge in naturally formed limestone caves, ancestral tombs, and other places in the south. Some soldiers drove Okinawans away from these shelters in order to seize food and secure their own lives. Others ordered women to take the lives of their own babies and small children so that the enemy, the U.S. military, would not notice their presence. Still others treated Okinawans, whose "dialect" was not comprehensible, as spies for the U.S. military and killed them (Okinawa Taimusu [1950]1980; Ota M. 1972; Okinawaken Kyōiku Īnkai 1974a, 1974b; Arashiro 1994: 239–57; OPPMM 2001: 50–99).[22]

FIGURE 2.6. A U.S. battleship bombarding Okinawa. Reprint from *Okinawa Prefectural Government* 1997: 3.

FIGURE 2.7. An old man wandering through devastated Naha. Reprint from *Okinawaken Chijikōshitsu Kōhōka* 1996: 13.

I will discuss how Okinawans experienced the hell of the battle of Okinawa further in chapter 5, from the Henoko residents' perspective. Here, in exploring the historical modality of the Okinawa collective consciousness in the context of the Japan-Okinawa dialectic, I want to highlight their predicament in terms of what Norma Field describes as "compulsory group suicide" (1991: 61). More than 140 residents had taken refuge in a cave called *Chibichirigama* in Yomitan Village on the west coast of the island of Okinawa, which the U.S. military chose as the landing spot for its operation. Defying the U.S. military's urgings for them to surrender, a number of men charged the enemy's position with bamboo spears, only to find themselves fatally injured by U.S. grenades and machineguns. In spite of imminent danger from staying in the cave, however, villagers were unable to leave it, because their leaders ordered them not to surrender but to maintain their honor as the imperial subjects of Japan. In an attempt to extricate themselves from this impossible situation, eighty-plus villagers killed each other with knives, sickles, stones, and other items (Field 1991, Ōshiro 1995,

Yomitansonshi Henshūshitsu 2002), thereby as much demolishing (by their show of loyalty to Imperial Japan) as perpetuating (by the very necessity to show their loyalty) the view that they were not Japanese enough. In another location, Okinawans committed the compulsory group suicide for the same reason but on a larger scale: "One thousand residents were gathered at one place.... Finally, we were told to commit suicide [by the Japanese Army]. Some families formed circles and, with the grenades distributed by the military, killed themselves.... [In other circumstances,] husbands killed their wives, parents, children, brothers, and sisters by using sickles and razors to cut their wrists and necks, cudgels and stones to smash their heads, and cords to suffocate them.... I was sixteen-years-and-one-month old. When I, together with my brother, killed my mother who had given birth to us, I wept bitterly out of unbearable grief" (Kinjo Shigeaki, not dated; cited in Arashiro 1994: 243).

The battle of Okinawa, indeed, proved to be the historical conjuncture where Okinawans' desire to become Japanese was tragically completed and simultaneously shattered in the face of U.S. military power. By the end of the battle, the death toll among Okinawans reached 122,288, including 28,228 military personnel.[23] In addition, 65,908 Japanese soldiers and 12,520 American soldiers also lost their lives (Arashiro 1994: 253).

Transformation of Okinawan Identity from Minshū (People) to Shimin (Citizens)

In sum, the collective Okinawan consciousness of "we are Okinawans" was continuously articulated in the context of the Japanese nation-state and the larger processes of global history from the late nineteenth century on. This consciousness emerged from Okinawans' desperate attempt to become genuine subjects of Imperial Japan before and during the war, while unfolding as an oppositional consciousness of the politically and economically subjugated people against USCAR after the war. Finally it developed into a political-cultural identity grounded in the idea of ethnic ties between Japanese and Okinawans in the context of the reversion movement. In other words, we have identified the two historical modalities/layers of Okinawan identity, one related to Okinawa's encounter with the U.S. military and the other concerned with its experiences with the Japanese state, both of which were combined as well as grounded in the concept of the exclusive and unitary Okinawan "people" (*minshū*).

For two decades after the reversion of Okinawa to Japan in 1972, what was under way was not splendid large-scale social mobilizations against the U.S. military or the Japanese state, but a profound silent revolution on a deeper level against the background of a large number of localized and diversified protests.[24] Specifically, since the reversion, the two basic modalities of Okinawan identity have been reorganized as much as reproduced by new social actors, who, constituting the mainstream of post-reversion Okinawan society, have shaped and have been shaped by distinct cultural values and political styles under new historical circumstances.

In the case of South Korea, Nancy Abelmann (1997: 251) observes: "Many of the old activisms continue…. Nevertheless, the aesthetics of the age are certainly new. The dominant activist aesthetic of the 1980s—the *minjung* (people) imaginary [grounded in farmers' movements]—is by now a relic…. *Minjung*…was obsolete by the 1990s with its 'new generation,' 'civil society,' and 'civil movements.'" Similarly, the main actors of Okinawan society in and after the 1990s—in the post–cold-war era of globalization—have been no longer the subjugated *minshū* (people), but affluent, confident, and planetary yet grounded "citizens" with diverse backgrounds. In the wake of the 1995 rape incident, these new actors asserted Okinawan-ness in a manner that was fundamentally different from the Okinawan *minshū*. This chapter will end with an articulation of the historical and social significance of this change. To this end, I focus on the role the Japanese state has played in the post-reversion environment, while at the same time looking at both positive and negative sociocultural impacts of Japanese money on Okinawa in that environment.

JAPAN AS A MEDIATOR BETWEEN THE GLOBAL AND THE LOCAL

Throughout the 1970s and the 1980s, Japan functioned in the U.S.–Japan security alliance simulateously as its beneficiary and its benefactor. As a beneficiary, Japan skillfully manipulated the "peace constitution" (drafted by the U.S. after World War II to prevent Japan's remilitarization), which stipulates that "land, sea, and air forces, as well as other war potential, will never be maintained" in Japan (Article 9), for its own political-economic ends. That is, this constitution enabled postwar Japan to attain the security of the nation against the "communist threat" without using its scarce resources for its military (i.e., the security of Japan was maintained under the umbrella of the U.S. military) and simultaneously to enjoy miraculous economic growth by using these resources, even to the point of rivaling the status of its overseer, the United States. In return, as a benefactor, it assumed limited security responsibilities in the Asia-Pacific region by offering Japan's— in particular, Okinawa's—land to the U.S. military.

Yet, by the time the cold war was over, as Japan economically benefited more and more from the U.S-Japan security arrangement (e.g., Japan's "bubble economy" in the late 1980s), the United States increasingly pressed Japan to make greater contribution to regional and global stability. When this pressure became intertwined with Japan's (Japanese men's) century-old desire to become and behave like the powerful (Western white men), the premise of the "peace constitution" became difficult to maintain both internationally and domestically. Internationally, for instance, in the course of the 1990s Japan's Self-Defense Forces (SDF)—the military Japan is not supposed to maintain—become an essential part of a global form of power. The idea and practice of SDF making "international contributions" in Cambodia, Zaire, the Golan Heights, and East Timor in the 1990s[25] indeed helped Japan not only to discharge increasing security obligations the world (meaning, in Japanese eyes, the U.S.) has laid upon it, but also to tie Japanese subjects (men particularly)—increasingly atomized under global capitalism—into a bundle of national pride.

When assuming increased security responsibilities in the external political arena in the post–cold-war era of the 1990s, Japan's "peace constitution" has become a mere name at home as well, and in the process the burden on Okinawa has become specifically heavier. For instance, in response to Washington's request, Japan has been paying, under the name of the voluntary "consideration" (*omoiyari*) budget, part of the operating costs for the U.S. military presence in the country—which usually means "in Okinawa" because of the disproportionate concentration of the U.S. military facilities there (cf. Ui 1998).[26] The *omoiyari* budget increased from 6.2 billion yen ($62 million) in 1978 to 273.1 billion yen ($2.731 billion) in 1996 (Okinawa Taimusu 1997b: 69–73, Umebayashi 1994: 331–40), though it has declined lately. In the words of one U.S. official, "it [has been] cheaper to base the forces in Asia than in the United States. Japan [has paid] nearly all the yen-based costs of the 46,000 American forces, or nearly 70% of the troops' overall costs" (Nye 1995: 98). Effective in September 1997, responding to Washington's request, Tokyo also agreed to revise the old Guidelines for U.S.-Japan Defense Cooperation (first laid out in 1978) so that the U.S. forces could, in the case of emergencies (caused, presumably, by the aggression of North Korea and perhaps, of China), freely use not only the facilities of Japan's Self-Defense Forces but also civilian airports, seaports, hospitals, roads, and other facilities in Japan—which again usually means, "in Okinawa"—regardless of the consent of the local governments.[27]

While the sovereignty of Japan has become increasingly uncertain in the post–cold-war era of "armed globalization" (Hardt and Negri 2004: 231), Tokyo has also needed to carefully control the internal discontents of Japanese citizens, particularly the risk of aggravating Okinawa's deep-seated historical antipathy toward mainland Japan, in order to protect the very foundation upon which the whole system of the global military-economic alliance has operated. To this end, after the reversion of 1972 Tokyo has continuously transferred a massive amount of public funds to Okinawa under the banner of *hondonami* (catching up with the mainland) as political compensation for local discontent with the continuous U.S. military presence after the reversion.[28] With Manuel Castells, who states that "the fading away of the nation-states is a fallacy" (1997: 307), I suggest that in this age of globalization, the critical significance of the nation-state—in this case, Japan—lies not in its oppressive power over its subjects, but in the elusive, yet cunning "influence" via money that it can exert over them as a mediator between global interests and local concerns. To confuse globalization with the "postnational" (Appadurai 1996) is to conceal a new form of the operation of power, which has been manifested in the function of the nation-state as a rallying point of power in the globalized political, economic, and military network. Put differently, the nation-state and things global do not always conflict with each other but are often crystallized, reinforced, and transformed in relation to one another with the power of money as a common mediator.

After the reversion, the Japanese government's "influence" (the *hondonami* project) was exercised and felt in Okinawa, most notably through what was dubbed the "three-K economy"—consisting in *Kōkyō kōji* [public work], *Kankō* [tourism], and *Kichi* [bases] (Kawase 1998). Under the public work (*kōkyō kōji*) component, the *hondonami* project made it possible for new roads to be constructed all over Okinawa, though by the late 1990s the number of cars exploded beyond what these roads could accommodate, and traffic jams in Naha became as bad as those in New York. The *hondonami* project also helped develop tourism (*kankō*). While in 1972 only 440,000 tourists visited Okinawa, in the late 1990s 4.5 million tourists a year from mainland Japan and elsewhere stayed at splendid resort hotels that were built along the coastlines by Japanese money. Meanwhile, in the realm of base (*kichi*)-related money, the annual rent paid to the military landlord by the Japanese government increased by 600 percent immediately after the reversion, and by almost 400 percent in the following twenty-five years (Arasaki 1995, Okinawa Taimusu 1997a: 9, Kawase 1998).[29] The landlords' interests intertwined with the interests of banks and real estate brokers. To take the case of southern Okinawa as an example, the land of Naha military port was put up for sale, and it was purchased by banks and real estate brokers at a price twenty or thirty times as high as the publicly announced land price (Okinawa Taimusu 1997a). With these and other sorts of Japanese money, in the late 1990s Okinawa's per capita GDP exceeded that of some of the G8 nations, including Italy and Canada (Inoue 2002a).

Clearly, old images of Okinawa—the lack of electricity and water, walking with bare feet, sweet-potato–eating, thatched roof homes with "unsanitary" toilets, and muddy roads washed away by the typhoons, etc.—had been replaced with images showing a life of air-conditioned cars, fast food, and concrete homes and roads (McCormack 1999). The *hondonami* project contributed to a marked improvement in the overall material conditions of Okinawa, creating, for better or worse, the context for deeper changes of Okinawa's collective consciousness.

THE IMPACTS OF JAPANESE MONEY ON POST-REVERSION OKINAWAN IDENTITY

Ultimately, I see the dramatic rise of living standards in post-reversion Okinawa as a positive and productive consequence of the U.S. military presence of Okinawa; it has indeed induced and has been induced by the potentially liberating political consciousness across Okinawa, as will be shown shortly. But first, let me elaborate on the problems of depoliticization and fragmentation of Okinawa's social field triggered by the improvement of living standards in Okinawa, because it is only by engaging such problems that one can catch a glimpse of the potentiality of Okinawan identity as a new political project.

Depoliticization of post-reversion Okinawan social field was under way, first and foremost, because of the reversal of class relationship between the U.S. military and Okinawa. In other words, the *hondonami* project, initiated as compensation for the continuous U.S. military presence, caused the economic advantages that U.S servicemen enjoyed in Okinawa in the 1960s to completely disappear. In the late 1990s, their salaries—a Lance Corporal working for the Marine Corps for two years earns about $1,200 a month (Ishikawa, Kuniyoshi and Nagatomo 1996)—did not even allow them to buy more than one or two five-dollar bottles of beer a night in Okinawa. They could no longer hire Okinawans (women) as prostitutes; it was Okinawans (men) who hired Filipinas as prostitutes. Consequently, contact between Okinawans and U.S. servicemen decreased; and so did the number of crimes committed by the latter on the former (e.g., from 310 in 1973 to 39 in 1996; see Okinawaken Sōmubu Chiji Kōshitsu Kichi Taisakushitsu 2003: 471).

In the process, the U.S. military may have come to present itself, in the eyes of Okinawans, less as an oppressor against which they were to be politically unified than as a source of income (rent money and subsidies from Tokyo) which, although a nuisance, they would appropriate to articulate Okinawan pride and culture vis-a-vis mainland Japan. Unlike Okinawans before the war, inhabitants of post-reversion Okinawa, against the background of Okinawan affluence, no longer saw their culture as something to be ashamed of, let alone eradicated. In the 1980s and 1990s, specifically, along with a rosy picture of the post-reversion development, a celebratory view of local culture was on the rise. The era of the Ryukyu Kingdom was nostalgically evoked in a yearlong TV drama series called *Ryūkyū no Kaze* (The Wind of the Ryukyu Kingdom) broadcast all over Japan by the national TV station. Shuri Palace of the Ryukyu Kingdom, destroyed in the battle of Okinawa, was rebuilt to stand as a magnificent symbol of Okinawa's glory, while Okinawan "dialect," food, festivals, karate, fashion, music, pop stars, and the beauty of the semi-tropical archipelago, along with the easygoing "spirit" of its people (once seen as an obstacle to modernizing Okinawa), together came to constitute Okinawa's trademark. Note that these forms of Okinawan culture were thoroughly commodified in Japan's culture market, which while helping Okinawa to be included in the politico-economic system of the nation and beyond, may have also functioned to deflect its critical view of the U.S. military and related social problems onto the depoliticized plane of cultural pride. Okinawa might no longer be excluded from Japan, but it was forever subordinated within it.

In the midst of the depoliticization of Okinawa's social field as a whole, politico-economic fissures made their appearance within it. Take a south-north divide as an example: While Japanese money flooded south-central Okinawa (including the Naha area), the north (including the Nago area, the site of my fieldwork) was, relatively speaking, left underdeveloped in the two decades following the reversion. The fact that only cities, towns, and people with military land received massive subsidies and rent from Tokyo further contributed to the social disintegration of the island prefecture. Furthermore, political and economic fissures coincided with and were amplified by the continuous entry into Okinawan society of affluent generations born after the war (more than 70 percent of the entire population in the late 1990s) and after the reversion (more than 30 percent of the entire population in the late 1990s) who did not share the experiences of poverty, war, and oppression with the older generations.

In short, as an astute Okinawan critic already said in the early 1980s (Arasaki 1982: 162), Okinawa was transformed from "a poor yet equal society [in the period of U.S. rule] to an affluent yet unequal society [after the reversion]" in the process whereby Okinawa gained economic (if not political) advantages over the U.S. military. Unlike U.S.-ruled Okinawa before 1972, post-reversion Okinawa, with its affluence (which caused depoliticization) and its mosaic of social relations (which caused fragmentation), did not, and could not, wage any organized, unified protest against the U.S. military in spite of continuous problems with military accidents, crime, and noise.

To conclude this chapter, however, I also want to note a positive and productive aspect of Okinawa pride and culture unfolding in the midst of its affluence. That is, when a broader sector of diverse (and often fragmented) citizens critically appropriated the affluence of Okinawa, Okinawan culture turned into the common weapon of the weak, constructively providing them with an impetus for a new logic of social protest. This oppositional appropriation was made possible because the money from Tokyo—in spite of its goal of conciliating Okinawa's anti-base sentiment—ironically became a constant reminder of the prolonged violence of power (the U.S.

military presence), thereby helping Okinawa to renew cultural sensibilities enmeshed with the pain of local historical experiences—the war, the bases, the servicemen, and the rape—that had together constituted two "modalities/layers" of old Okinawan identity centering on the people's sense of "We are Okinawans." Placed against the background of the affluence of Okinawa, the protests against the rape in 1995, indeed, allowed us to catch a glimpse of Okinawa's efforts not to let Okinawa dissolved into depoliticized differences, but to ground the collective social consciousness in the new perspective of confident, affluent "citizens" of diverse backgrounds awakened to globally disseminated ideas about rights, women, and peace. Nakamura Sugako, an Okinawan high school student, perhaps best exemplified this process—the emergence of "new" social movements centering on citizenship—when she forcefully addressed an audience of 85,000 at the October of 1995 protest rally against the rape:

> It goes without saying that I am angry with the U.S. servicemen. Yet I also wonder if we really should protest, thus violating her feelings, her privacy. This small doubt still remains in my mind. But it is also true that, because of her courage and the courage of her family, this incident has been made public, now arousing a historic vortex. We could not possibly waste her courage.... I would like us, the young generation, to get a new Okinawa started.... Please return quiet Okinawa to us. Please return Okinawa without the military, without the tragedy. Return the peaceful island to us.
>
> (*Ryukyu Shinpo*, October 22, 1995)

The power of Japanese money—as Tokyo and Washington may have wished—closed off the mode of social protest anchored in the Okinawan *minshū* (people's) consciousness, which was best exemplified in the populist island-wide protest in the 1950s and the reversion movement before 1972. Yet, by creating a context from which a new collective consciousness emerged, the Japanese money ironically spawned, in the age of globalization, the potential for another mode of protest on the basis of grounded citizenship. Okinawa's oppositional sentiments to Japan and the U.S. have not disappeared, but been rearticulated and reorganized under new historical circumstances, as will be explored from chapter 4 onward.

3

REDUCED TO CULTURE WITHOUT
POLITICS AND HISTORY:

A Critique of Modern Okinawan Studies

This chapter examines the issues that I dealt with in the previous chapter—the problematic of Okinawan modernity—in light of the articulation of knowledge. In what can be called "modern" Okinawan studies, between the 1920s and the 1980s, Japanese, American, and Okinawan anthropologists, ethnologists, and folklorists typically reduced Okinawa to an island of pristine cultures untouched by power and history. In order to highlight this essentialist feature of modern Okinawan studies, and to elaborate on different political reasons behind it, I analyze several key texts produced in different locations in this period. Toward the end of this chapter, I discuss the subsequent analyses of Okinawa from the late 1980s which, in their emphasis on difference, power, and history, challenge the received notion of static, bounded, and homogeneous Okinawan culture. While generally endorsing this "postmodern" move, this chapter—or indeed this study as a whole—also proposes to underscore the specificity of the place (Gupta and Ferguson 1997, Dirlik 1999) by advancing, not discarding, the potentialities latent in "modern" Okinawan studies.

Yanagita Kunio and Japanese Native Ethnology

Yanagita Kunio (1875–1962) was a multifaceted scholar whose interests ranged from literature and linguistics to folklore, religion, mythology, art, agriculture, and urban sociology. I focus here on the ways in which he constructed the scholarly tradition of Japanese native ethnology with Okinawa as a foundational site. I want to do so by exploring how he declared "Okinawans are/were Japanese."

Although an image as the advocate of "new national learning," "one-nation folklore," "native ethnology," and the like is what Yanagita himself wanted to project to the public, and what his followers[1] have kept reproducing, he once was a highly regarded "poet of love" under the influence of European romantic literature (1895–1900, and possibly later), as well as an elitist bureaucrat-cum-intellectual who objectively dealt with the diversity of local cultural forms and their distinctive historical development (1900–1920) (Okaya 1991). In his earlier intellectual career, Yanagita's work was thus curiously both lyrical and truthful, as best exemplified by his highly regarded text, *Tōno Monogatari* (Tales of Tōno) published in 1910, a collection of 119 folktales from Tōno, a sparsely settled northern mountain village in mainland Japan (Ivy 1995, chapters 3 and 4; Morris-Suzuki 1998, chapter 4; Figal 2000, Harootunian 2000).

Not so much genuinely recording as skillfully rewriting the folktales of his native informant, Sasaki Kizen, Yanagita tried to both poetically and factually reconstruct the universe of these mountain people living at the margin of Japanese society, and to convey the vivid and often violent images of gods, spirits, nature, poverty, life, and death intrinsic to this universe. "May [the mountain people] speak these [numerous legends] to the people in the field to make them shudder" ([1910] 1968a: 5), wrote Yanagita. One might be tempted to read *Tōno Monogatari* as a manifesto of his commitment to and sympathy for the subordinated people in Japan. And yet, as Tanigawa (1975) has pointed out, Yanagita's sympathy for the subordinated was compounded by the power of his (and Imperial Japan's) observation and writing. In a different text titled *Yamabito Gaiden Shiryō* (Supplementary Materials on the Mountain People), he bluntly stated, "I believe mountain people are descendents of those natives who flourished in the past. Their civilizations declined. There has been no book written for them in the past 3000 years. Today, when their race seems to be almost extinct, I, one of their enemies, will write such a book" (Yanagita [1913] 1968a: 449; see also Tanigawa 1975: 119). Indeed, it seems that Yanagita rather nonchalantly subscribed to the then prevalent discourses about the ever-expanding, multiethnic, hybrid empire, Japan, with not only Japanese, but also Koreans, Taiwanese, Chinese, Ainus, Okinawans, and other "backward" peoples as its subjects. "That we, the present Japanese, are a mixture of various races does not seem to be completely proven, but my research considers this to be the already established theory, to be the starting point" (Yanagita [1917] 1968a: 172; see also Tanigawa 1975: 120 and Oguma 1995: 205–34). In *Tōno Monogatari*, Yanagita textually projected the lives of conquered and assimilated races onto the image of "mountain people."

Then, in the 1920s, Yanagita's interests in the mountain people/minority/non-Japanese disappeared and were replaced by newer interests in the common people (what he called *jōmin* = the majority Japanese), and in their origin, the southern islands—Okinawa (Tanigawa 1975, Murai 1992, Oguma 1995: 205–234, Harootunian 2000: 324–5). Oguma (1995) specifically relates the shift of Yanagita's interests to cultural trauma he experienced in the West.[2] After he resigned from his elite governmental position as the Chief Secretary of the House of Peers in 1919, the government sent Yanagita to the League of Nations in Geneva as a member of the Mandate Administration Committee, on which he served between 1921 and 1923.[3] There, as a representative of an ambiguous Japan—simultaneously an emerging power in the international political arena yet still a cultural third world—he felt utterly incompetent and alienated because of his language, culture, and race.

In terms of language, Yanagita ([1947] 1968b: 308) wrote, "while I have not been clearly aware of this, the speed at which we read European languages is very slow." Looking at representatives from European countries speak their own languages at ease, "I could not but seriously think that language is the fundamental problem" (Yanagita [1947] 1968b: 309). Concerning culture, Yanagita (p. 311) observed, "I was not aware of this until today, but the group mentality of the Japanese is [sadly] thrown into relief when abroad." Yanagita also faced the questions of race—the yellow peril discourses, more specifically—that Japan dealt with in the early twentieth century,[4] and in the process he himself became, as it were, like the threatened mountain people: "I here experienced for the first time the meaning of such words as rustic or bumpkin from the inside" (p. 307); "After the season of committee meetings was over, I rented a house in the upper town [of Geneva] and lived alone without any social intercourse" (p. 313); "Left in Geneva's winter, I was lonely"([1925] 1968d: 219). Before coming to Geneva, Yanagita was a subject whose positionality as a Japanese (man) was unquestionably and confidently constructed in relation to the "back-ward" minorities/mountain people in ever-expanding Imperial Japan; but in Geneva, the West took the position of subject, objectifying him as a Japanese (man)—a failure at once linguistically, culturally, and racially. He implored Tokyo to accept his resignation shortly after his arrival to Geneva (Iwamoto 1983: 49–77).

After the Geneva experience, Yanagita's intellectual retreat to "Japan" and desire to defensively constitute "Japan" in opposition to the West be-came highly visible on two fronts, in method and in theory (see below). He "became" Japanese after experiencing the West.[5] Yet, one should be made clear: Yanagita could not and did not become a narrow-minded anti-mod-ern cultural nationalist, because he knew all too well that Western material and cultural impacts had already made a mark on Japan in the early twen-tieth century to such an extent that naive restorative attempts to remove the negative aspects of such impacts would result in the destruction of modern Japan itself. In his highly regarded text titled *Meiji Taishō Shi Sesōhen* (Cul-tural History of the Meiji and Taisho Periods), Yanagita wrote, "I would like [people] to think about the beauty of the new that has been invented, and the significance of the old that has been lost" ([1936] 1974: 156), at the same time adding his criticism about those "who are constrained by old tastes, who even abhor what is newly born and developed" ([1936] 1974: 157). Framed this way, his task took on a character of what Stefan Tanaka identifies as the epistemological (and, I would add, existential) dilemma of modern Japan: "How to become modern [i.e., Western] while simul-taneously shedding the objective category of Oriental and yet not lose an identity" (Tanaka 1993: 3). Notably, Yanagita confronted this dilemma in order to define, both methodologically and theoretically, the scope and sig-nificance of Japanese native ethnology; his ethnology, in other words, was always already mediated by the global consciousness. Yanagita went on to argue that it is only by creating its own native scholarship that Japan could participate in the project of "world folklore" (Yanagita [1934] 1968c: 349) as a unified discipline of nation-bound scholarships across the globe.[6]

Methodologically, Yanagita insisted that ethnographic materials should be categorized into three domains (Yanagita [1934] 1968c, [1935] 1968c; Ito and Kamishima 1974, Tsurumi 1975, Morris-Suzuki 1998, chapter 4; Ha-rootunian 2000: 322–24). The first domain, *"seikatsu gaikei"* (outer forms of life) (Yanagita [1934] 1968c: 336), includes visible materials that appeal to the eyes of the observer, such as clothes, foods, dwellings, festivals, and other skills of life. The second domain, *"gengo geijutsu"* (art of language) (Yanagita [1935] 1968c: 297) or *"seikatsu kaisetsu"* (commentary on life) (Yanagita [1934] 1968c: 336), includes linguistic materials that can be comprehended through the eyes and ears of the observer, such as documents, dialects, proverbs, songs, etc. The third and most important realm, *"seikatsu ishiki"* (life consciousness) (p. 336), embraces all materials that cannot be understood by eyes or ears, but only by the subjective and sympathetic engagement of the researcher in such materials. Yanagita argued that the first two realms can be studied by outsiders (Westerners), but the third realm, which constituted for Yanagita the main objective of Japanese native ethnology, cannot. In a manner that disguised Japan's actual subordination to the West in the global politics of the 1920s and 1930s—his Geneva experience, the yellow peril discourses—Yanagita methodologically poised native ethnology as an arena wherein the epistemological-existential dilemma of modern Japan (i.e., how to reconcile Japan with the West) was worked through with the West not being excluded from it but being subsumed and controlled within it.

In the realm of theory, Yanagita was engaged in this epistemological-existential dilemma of modern Japan by developing a set of broad geocultural notions of territoriality, *shima* (the island, which signifies Japan[7]) and *tairiku* (the continent, which signifies, primarily, the West) (Oguma 1995, Morris-Suzuki 1998, chapter 4). More specifically, first, by contrasting the spiritual, gentle, harmonious *shima* (= Japan) with the progressive yet materialistic and discordant *tairiku* (= the West), Yanagita created a theoretical space in which to develop particular accounts of Japan's national history and culture. On the one hand, he stated: "Japanese, located at the margin of the northern Pacific, peacefully continued to live their lives" (Yanagita [1951] 1968d: 498); "Japan in the past calmly and in amity enjoyed the peace of one nation on these islands [of the Japanese archipelago] " (Yanagita [1928] 1968c: 90). On the other hand, the peacefulness of Japanese was thrown into relief by the nature of the Western men, which he described, for instance, as follows: "In the old 'Narrative of the Navigation of the Southern Shore of New Guinea,' there is a description about numerous natives gathering and dancing on the shore. The author of the book [a Western man] continues, 'We shot them with guns as a test and found them collapsed and dead one after another.' I have also read a travel account [by a Western man] which states, 'Negroes in West Africa are more difficult to tame than Chimpanzees. Although we took a child Negro with us after killing his mother, he died because he refused to eat' " (Yanagita [1928] 1968c: 93).

Second, after constructing peaceful Japanese on *shima* in relation to violent people from *tairiku*, Yanagita was able, within the category of *shima*, to "discover" Okinawa as the foundational site of his ethnology. "To our learning, the discovery of Okinawa is an epochal incident of great importance" (Yanagita [1935] 1968c: 316). The discovery was made possible by his visit to Okinawa in 1921 and by his interactions with Okinawan folklorists, including Iha Fuyū whom I will discuss shortly. Ironically (for reasons I specified in chapter 2), precisely when Yanagita established his Japanese ethnology in the 1920s, the Okinawan economy sank to rock bottom and Japanese discrimination against Okinawans as the second-class nationals deepened and widened. However, Yanagita's concerns did not lie with such concrete political, economic, and social issues. Rather, for him Okinawa was an allegory of Japan's ancient purity (Okinawa is "the place where ancient Japanese ways are being retained" (p. 317)) on the one hand, and of Japan's present misery ("the main reason for Okinawa's recent plights concerns social-economic failure [of national policies].... This is the nature of things all over Japan" (Yanagita [1928] 1968c: 160–62)) on the other. Put differently, while feeling a sense of closeness to Okinawa, Yanagita also saw it as the object to be distanced from and put to use for the political and intellectual ends of Japan and Japanese native ethnology: "In order to understand the grave weakness of this nation, we have attempted to study Okinawan life with great circumspection and sincere sympathy.... It was not necessarily our intention to study [Okinawa] for the sole purpose of the welfare of this region itself" (p. 166). The boundary between Okinawa and Japan collapsed within the category of *shima*, and Okinawa was at once included and subordinated as a foundation of Japan's/Yanagita's cultural-historical consciousness that confronted the distant, unfamiliar, foreign West. Yanagita declared: "Okinawans are/were Japanese."

The *shima–tairiku* dichotomy has yet another overlooked function, however. That is, Yanagita's focus on *shima* made it possible for him to hypothesize the origin of the Japanese people from the southern sea, while suppressing by default the issues related to Japan's colonization of another *tairiku*, i.e., the Asian continent to the north (northeastern China and Korea in particular). I contend that we need to examine Yanagita's post-

Geneva project of presenting the image of the peaceful, harmonious Japanese coming from the south not only by what he explicitly speaks about (Japan in reference to the West), but also by what he is systematically silent about (Japan in relation to Asia).

In a way that consolidated the recurrent idea of the archaic identity between Japanese and Okinawans as proposed by Torii Ryūzō ([1894a] 1976, [1894b] 1976), Tashiro Antei ([1894] 1977), Katō Sango ([1916] 1971) and others in light of comparative studies of race, language, myth, religion, and other domains of Okinawan and Japanese culture and society from the late nineteenth century onward, Yanagita first formulated his hypothesis of the southern origin of the Japanese race in 1921 in *Kainan Shōki* (Minor Travel Accounts of the Southern Sea) ([1925] 1968d) on the basis of his first trip to Okinawa. Later, he more explicitly presented this hypothesis in *Kaijō no Michi* (The Passage on the Sea) ([1961] 1968d) right before his death in 1962. Yanagita's hypothesis itself was not particularly popularized, but his idea of the Japanese as a homogeneous nation—with an emphasis on rice growing as the core of Japanese culture—enormously influenced the production of discourses on the uniqueness of the Japanese (*Nihonjinron*) in the 1960s–1980s (Oguma 1995: 234). It also set the broad standard against which Japanese ethnologists after Yanagita extended their analyses of Okinawa during and, in some cases, even after, that period (Ōgo 1962, Takemura 1965, Tsunemi 1965, Kyūgakkai Rengō Okinawa Chōsa Iinkai 1976, Watanabe 1971, 1990; Furuie 1994).

Yanagita argued that Miyako, an island located approximately 280 kilometers (174 miles) southwest of the main island of Okinawa, might be the place where people from the southern (but not northern) part of the Chinese continent first drifted away about two thousand years ago while searching for porcelain shells, a priceless item in ancient China. These people, according to Yanagita, gradually migrated to Japan proper from south to north, riding the ocean's *Kuroshio* (Black) Current, to become proto-Japanese. He supported his argument by tracing archaic Japanese culture in Okinawan religion, folktales, festivals, ceremonies, place names, and so forth. He claimed, for instance, that both in mainland Japan and in Okinawa, there exist various versions of a folktale about a traveler who has the ability to decide the sex of a newborn baby. Yanagita maintained that the content and structure of this folktale is diverse in the northern regions of mainland Japan, while it is almost identical across the Ryuku Islands, and that the southern version "is clearly the prototype, and our problem is to clarify how this folktale has spread as far as the Ōu area" [in northern Japan] (Yanagita [1961] 1968d: 49). He also underscored the central importance of rice, which was hypothesized as being transmitted from the south to the north by the proto-Japanese, in light of various rituals and beliefs observed in the Japanese archipelago. While Yanagita himself repeatedly and apologetically stated that his idea remained hypothetical and speculative, the southern islands/*shima* were nonetheless granted the privilege of becoming the storehouse of the original Japanese race and cultural forms. One should be clear here that Yanagita's interest in the southern islands is not to be attributed to his innocent fantasy. His theory is politically suspicious, curiously resonating with postwar Japan's collective amnesia about its own ideological contradiction and confusion over Asia—northeastern China and Korea in particular, but Okinawa also implicitly included as a "backward" place—during its prewar colonial era.

In the document titled *Draft of Basic Plan for Establishment of Greater East Asia Co-Prosperity Sphere*, the Total War Research Institute, "a body responsible to army and cabinet" (Tsunoda, de Bary, and Keene, eds. 1958: 294), stated in 1942 that the Japanese empire "strives but for the achievement of *Hakkō Ichiu* [different ethnic groups in Asia under one roof], the spirit of its founding.... It is necessary to foster the increased power of the empire, to cause East Asia to return to its original form of independence and co-prosperity by shaking off the yoke of Europe and America, and to let its countries and peoples develop their respective abilities in peaceful cooperation and secure livelihood" (cited in ibid., 294–95). Here, the project of *Hakkō Ichiu* was invoked as an allegory of power, benevolence, and morality of the "unique" Japanese race in the act of establishing the Greater East Asia Co-Prosperity Sphere, and was contrasted with the "yoke" of Western colonialism-cum-racism that implied exploitation, oppression, and materialism. But this colonial project, in spite of its rhetorical splendor, already contained a seed of an insurmountable ideological contradiction within it.

Imperial Japan needed to grant Okinawans, Koreans, Taiwanese, Chinese, and other "backward" subjects the same rights in suffrage, education, labor, and other dimensions of social life that were given to the Japanese,[8] if inclusive Japanese colonialism was really "peaceful" and "benevolent" unlike its Euro-American counterpart. However, granting such people the same political-social rights as the Japanese—and thus equating them with the Japanese, which implied the promotion of interracial (including sexual) interactions—potentially watered down and thus contradicted the idea of the unique Japanese race as the privileged leader of the Asiatic race fighting against the violence of white West. In short, Imperial Japan needed to defensively deploy the idea of the unique, bounded, homogeneous, pure Japanese race resisting to change when it constituted itself vis-à-vis the intrusive and threatening West, but at the same time, it also needed to assert the idea of inclusive, hybrid, and multiethnic Japan adapting to change as it defined itself as the leader of "backward" Asia (Okinawa included). The contradiction between homogeneity/purity and hybridity (spatially), between immutablity and change (temporally), of the Japanese race was never solved in the prewar discursive field; consequently, the Imperial Japanese government had to continuously devise tactics to keep these subjects deprived of full citizenship (to preserve purity and immutablity of Japan) while at the same time placating a mounting sense of injustice among them (to promote hybridity and change) (Sakai 1996a, 1996b, especially chapter 1; Oguma 1995, 1998).

Oguma (1995) identifies Yanagita as one of the key intellectuals who reworked and displaced this contradiction by shifting the focus of popular and intellectual discourses from the idea of the Japanese empire as an expanding multiethnic nation in the prewar period to the idea of an isolated, unique, homogeneous Japanese nation and people in the postwar period. Indeed, the image of the homogeneous Japanese peacefully and solitarily coming from the south/*shima* as presented in Yanagita's hypothesis has helped, first and foremost, suppress any smell of prewar and war violence, thereby assisting postwar Japan to obscure its colonial exploitation and oppression over Asia. Yanagita's hypothesis also helped postwar Japan to positively reconstitute its national identity as a forever unique, homogeneous, and peaceful nation with which to both resist and accommodate the U.S. occupation and hegemony. Along with this sleight of hand that displaced the prewar contradiction and dilemma, Yanagita's hypothesis, importantly, also helped postwar Japan to surreptitiously reposition Okinawa from the category of Asia (i.e., the second-class nationals) as in the case of prewar colonial discourses, to the category of *shima* as a storehouse of the proto-Japanese culture.

In sum, Yanagita's project of establishing Japanese native ethnology, incubated by a trauma he experienced in Geneva in the 1920s and completed in his hypothesis on the southern origin of the Japanese race in the 1960s, curiously resonated with the configuration and reconfiguration of modern Japan embedded in the global relations of power and history. Specifically, with the methodological claim of nativism and the theoretical invention of the *shima-tairiku* binary, Yanagita's ethnology contributed, since the 1920s generally, but particularly in postwar Japan's discursive context, to both critically constituting Japan in reference to the West (especially the United States) and conveniently suppressing the issues of power and history between Japan and Asia. Yanagita continuously used Okinawa as a methodological and theoretical foundation to accomplish both of the above, and, with a declaration that "Okinawans were and are Japanese," assimilated as much as subordinated Okinawa within modern Japan.

War and Social Control:
American Anthropology in Okinawa in the 1940s–1960s

One cannot adequately grasp the nature of modern anthropological investigations of Okinawa by American scholars between the 1940s and 1960s without taking into consideration the questions of war against and social control over the people they studied. To being with, the *Civil Affairs Handbook: Ryukyu (Loochoo) Islands* (U.S. Navy Department 1944) was prepared by Yale anthropologists George P. Murdock, John M. W. Whiting, and Clellan S. Ford for the restricted use of the commanders and officers of the U.S. military in anticipation of attacking and occupying Okinawa. Their 334-page *Handbook* covered geography, resources, history, people, customs, social groups, government, law and justice, public safety, public welfare, public health, education, transportation, industry, labor, finance, and so forth. It also contained maps, illustrations, and photos (including those of prostitutes, a native cemetery, and the gate of Shuri castle).

Significantly, the *Handbook* noted that in spite of official Japanese policy, "the Ryukyu islanders have not become wholly assimilated to the culture of the Japanese, by whom they are generally regarded as somewhat uncouth rustics" (U.S. Navy Department 1944: 69) because of the perceived differences in physical characteristics including their hairiness, habits of pork eating, and body odor. The *Handbook* also states, "the Luchuans who emigrate to Japan proper and other Japanese territories are generally poverty-stricken unskilled laborers, and are often treated in a manner similar to the Eta or outcast social stratum among the Japanese" (p. 69). In short, "the people of the archipelago are not regarded by the Japanese as their racial equals" (p. 43). The *Handbook* then continued: "Inherent in the relations between the Ryukyu people and the Japanese, therefore, are potential seeds of dissension out of which political capital might be made" (p. 43). In 1947, reiterating the view of the *Handbook*, General MacArthur justified the U.S. occupation of Okinawa by commenting that "Ryukyuans were not, ethnologically speaking, Japanese, and…Japan did not expect Okinawa to be returned to Japan" (*Okinawa Shinminpo*, July 15, 1947; cited in Nakano 1969: 4).

American anthropologists who worked in U.S.-ruled Okinawa in the 1950s and 1960s essentially extended and refined the view of the *Handbook* that Okinawans are not Japanese, thereby successfully countering the idea of sameness between Okinawans and Japanese that Japanese native ethnology assumed and promulgated. In spite of this positive role they played in the development of anthropological studies of Okinawa, however, American anthropologists who studied Okinawa in the 1950s and 1960s also inherited and exhibited the problems of Orientalism (Said 1978). In their analyses, Okinawa was typically separated from the realm of "our" culture and history, and in the process, the thesis that Okinawans are not American—in addition to the thesis that Okinawans are not Japanese—came forward. The double-sided thesis of American anthropological studies of Okinawa in this period was reflected in the problem of where American researchers stood. They clearly assumed the outsider's position so as to expose the differences and tensions between mainland Japan and Okinawa that Japanese native ethnology wanted to hide, but, simultaneously, they often implicitly and at other times explicitly contributed to the U.S. policy of keeping control of Okinawa as the insider of the power structure. The analyses of the works of Clarence Glacken, William Lebra, and Thomas Maretzki support the above argument.

In 1951, the Pacific Science Board of the National Research Council— of which aforementioned George Murdock was a member—inaugurated the "Scientific Investigations of the Ryukyu Islands" (SIRI) project under the authorization of the Department of Army (Kerr 1958, Maretzki 1962, Higa Ma. 1987) for "the dual purpose of advancing the broad anthropological horizon in the Orient and of providing information of administrative value to the civil administration of the islands" (Smith 1952: 1). Douglas

Haring (1952), Clarence Glacken (1955), William Burd (1952), and Allan Smith (1952) researched the social and cultural practices of the islands of Amami, Okinawa, Miyako, and Yaeyama (which are different islands in the Ryukyu archipelago from north to south), respectively.

Among them, the University of California Berkeley Geography Department-based Glacken published a monograph in 1955 based on his 1951–1952 SIRI fieldwork. His study, broadly articulated in terms of cultural geography, "is a glimpse, at a particular moment in time, of a culture which has been constantly changing, sometimes slowly, sometimes with great rapidity" (Glacken 1955: 5). In light of this research agenda, Glacken chose three villages in the northern and southern parts of the island of Okinawa according to the criteria of "what was typical" (p. vii) of Okinawa: "They are close to Naha [the capital of Okinawa], and yet distant from the main centers of American influence" (p. viii). In other words, Glacken faithfully juxtaposed the political goal of "providing information…to the civil administration of the islands" with the scholarly goal of "advancing the broad anthropological horizon in the Orient" (Smith 1952: 1), and in so doing, attempted to show how "Okinawans (Orientals) are not American (Occidental)." As he drew a line between the Occident and the Orient politically and conceptually, Glacken also moved on to examine the differences between Okinawa and Japan within the category of the Orientals so as to show how Okinawans are not Japanese. Specifically, in a way that underscored the nature of the distinctively Okinawan family system as compared to its Japanese counterpart, Glacken scrutinized ancestor worship, preservation of the family line, the household-order naming system, communal agricultural labor, mutual borrowing and lending of money, and so forth within confined local political contexts, and emphasized the central importance of the family system in these practices that took place in seemingly pristine and isolated Okinawan village life.

While Glacken's somewhat pastoral ethnographic descriptions of village life may reflect an Okinawa with a relatively peaceful social atmosphere, in 1953 (after his fieldwork), a major political uproar arose owing to the expropriation of Okinawan land by the United States Civil Administration of the Ryukyu Islands (USCAR) to expand and build the bases (see chapter 2). Against the background of changing political conditions in Okinawa, the Pacific Science Board of the National Research Council directed another anthropological project as part of the long-term SIRI program. William Lebra, together with Forrest Pitts and Wayne Suttles, undertook this project between September 1953 and June 1954. Their studies were brought together in a 1955 report entitled *Postwar Okinawa*, in which Pitts wrote on geography, agriculture, land use, food, and population problems; Lebra on language, traditional political institutions, and cultural changes in rural communities; Suttles on family, hygiene, and education; and Suttles and Lebra on the relationship between Okinawans and Americans.

Lebra keenly observed newly introduced complexities in U.S.-occupied Okinawa, and commented, for instance, that he "heard no sharp criticism of [Okinawan] men who were in military employment, yet many statements were heard about [Okinawan] women who were so employed. This dichotomy seems to stem from the widely held belief that the American employers have sexual access to these women, particularly the maids. Okinawan culture affords its males a high degree of sexual freedom, but not its females" (Pitts, Lebra, and Suttles 1955: 207).[9] In this somewhat vague language, Lebra was talking about the changing status of Okinawan women who, while being sexually exploited by U.S. servicemen, also appropriated their interracial relations for the sake of their own sexual autonomy vis-à-vis Okinawan men who used to dominate them.

In reference to the political goal to promote "a stable economy and a friendly attitude among the nearly 600,000 Okinawans toward the United States" (p. 217), Lebra, together with the co-authors, even critiqued the military administration in Okinawa, stating that "we have the distinct impression that a study of USCAR would reveal a strong tendency toward 'empire-building' on the part of some men who had no particular qualifications to begin with, but who have been allowed by time and circumstance to rise in the structure to the point where they are driven by their own insecurity to justify their positions by usurping numerous powers and functions that should be left to the Okinawans" (p. 220).

When Lebra wrote his *Okinawan Religion: Belief, Ritual, and Social Structure* (1966),[10] however, his engagement in the political/social actuality of Okinawa receded, and was replaced with his project to capture and rescue the immaculate elements of Okinawan culture. His focus on Okinawan "traits which appear to be purely local" (p. v) was motivated in part by his critique of Japanese ethnology, which showed only the similarities between Japanese and Okinawan religions; the problem, in his view, had been aggravated by the lack of detailed field research and an excess of subjective and speculative interpretation of Japanese native ethnologists. His focus on a pristine Okinawa seems to have been motivated also by his dismay (see, for instance, pp. 20, 123, and 206) at the subtle yet unmistakable process of Japanization in postwar Okinawa in the realms of education, pension/welfare, and politics, which, together with Okinawa's pro-Japanese sentiment, was ironically reinforced as a reaction to the violence of the U.S. occupation of Okinawa.

Lebra for his part approached Okinawa as an objective anthropologist (with an Okinawan "assistant") to highlight the differences between Okinawa and Japan. He described Okinawan concepts of the supernatural by meticulously transcribing the vocabulary of living informants instead of using the scholarly vocabulary established by Japanese ethnologists, discussed the legacy of the Ryukyu Kingdom including the parallelism between the men's political domain and the women's religious domain, which was not observed in mainland Japan, and explained uniquely Okinawan village-community religion, kin group religion, and household religion on the basis of the fieldwork of more than a hundred communities. Passing statements such as "the most notable phenotypic difference between the two people is in the relative degree of hairiness" (p. 7)[11] also helped give the reader the impression that Okinawans are different from Japanese, contrary to the thesis of Japanese native ethnology and to Okinawa's pro-Japanese sentiment.

However, his attempt to articulate the difference of Okinawa (i.e., to detach Okinawa from Japan) translated itself into a somewhat paternalistic view of the U.S. military occupation, and in the process Lebra failed to make any mention of the facts concerning its problems; consequently, Okinawa was represented as a self-contained island of religion with the violence of the U.S. military being eliminated as a noise from his analysis. He wrote, for instance:

At the present time [the 1960s], Okinawa enjoys an unprecedented economic expansion, and commercial development is proceeding apace. Nearly all Okinawans acknowledge being better fed and clothed than ever before, and the scars of war have been largely erased.... The new university [i.e., the University of the Ryukyus, created by USCAR] situated on the ruins of the royal castle symbolized an intent to modernize intellectually as well as materially.... With respect to technology and economic organization, they have largely caught up with the twentieth century [like us], but [because "the social distance separating the two people precludes significant interaction" (p. 20)] beliefs and patters of living have not altered so rapidly, leaving much to suggest the heritage of the Forgotten [Ryukyu] Kingdom.

(Lebra 1966: 20)

In the end, the persistence of Okinawan religion—the Otherness of Okinawa—was explained by the following psychologized view: "The absence of complexity in the system of belief may account for the unreceptiveness to more sophisticated belief systems, in that there seems to be an unwillingness or inability to digest or assimilate what is intellectually complex" (p. 204). In sum, in spite of his astute critique of Japanese native ethnology and valuable attempt to explore the specificity of Okinawa against the background of Japanization, Lebra's analysis in *Okinawan Religion* operated within the Orientalist framework of paternalistic Self and depoliticized Other, obscuring both the question of the violence of the U.S. military and the issue of agency of Okinawans for cultural and social change.

In 1961, in a way that orchestrated preceding studies on Okinawa of various kinds, the Tenth Pacific Science Congress of the Pacific Science Association summoned twelve researchers from the United States (including Haring, Suttles, and Lebra, who had joined the SIRI and/or Postwar Okinawa projects), Japan, and Okinawa to discuss diverse aspects of Okinawan history, culture, and society, although generally suppressing the questions of the U.S. military occupation of Okinawa. The presented papers were brought together in one volume entitled *Ryukyuan Culture and Society* (edited by Allan H. Smith, a member of the SIRI project) in 1964. In this edited volume, especially worth mentioning in the context of my argument is the paper written by Thomas W. Maretzki (1964), who initiated anthropological investigation of Okinawa in the mid-1950s outside the SIRI and Postwar Okinawa projects. In this paper, Maretzki discussed the personality characteristics of individual Okinawans within the theoretical framework of culture and personality. Psychological anthropology in general and theories of culture and personality in particular were a much popularized paradigm in the 1950s and 1960s in the United States because of the work of Margaret Mead (1935), Ruth Benedict (1934, 1946), Ralph Linton (1945), and Beatrice and John Whiting (1975), within which Maretzki's study was situated. (Maretzki was a student of the Whitings.)

Maretzki approached the question of the personality characteristics of Okinawans by exploring how Okinawans are not Japanese. Quoting a comparative insight by Charles Leavenworth, a missionary sent to Okinawa in the early twentieth century—"In character the Lochooans are gentle and docile, not as energetic as their Japanese rulers, but amiable and easily governed"—Maretzki (1964: 100) continued, "in the past seventeen years of military occupation and government, Americans came to similar conclusions when misunderstanding, frustration, and hurt of sentiments might have easily led to serious dissensions." Following the *Handbook*'s insights, Maretzki (p. 104), like Lebra, further noted differences between Okinawans and Japanese in terms of hairiness, skin color (Okinawans being darker), and language. Yet, the line of argument made in the *Handbook* (1944: 43)—"Inherent in the relations between the Ryukyu people and the Japanese, therefore, are potential seeds of dissension out of which political capital might be made"—was critically refined in the following way: "This fact [the Japanese disdain of Okinawans] has been used by American administrators to gain Okinawan support, but they failed to take into consideration the simultaneous positive feelings toward Japan" (Maretzki 1964: 103). Here, he unwittingly challenged one of the major theses of American anthropological studies of Okinawa—Okinawans are not Japanese.[12]

This challenge, however, became not simply intellectual but rather political against the background of Okinawa's mounting protest movements against USCAR in the 1950s and 1960s (see chapter 2). Perhaps for this reason, while stating that "One also has to see the mass demonstration of Okinawans in protest of some action or in response to some real or alleged injustice to appreciate the fact that the peaceful, 'nonaggressive' Okinawan can display a hostility which makes him more human" (Maretzki 1964: 109), Maretzki uneasily shifted his ground without exploring "human" dimensions of Okinawans, discussing instead the second, Orientalist thesis of American anthropological studies of Okinawa—Okinawans are not American.

He did so by textually salvaging pristine Okinawan culture from the impacts of urbanization, which was dissociated, of course, from the presence of the U.S. military. After all, for him Okinawa was "a laboratory setting which, in further research, could be put to good use" (Maretzki 1964: 99). Indeed, while acknowledging that "new complexities since World War II, especially urbanization, have modified the entire island more than any previous culture contacts" (p. 99), he nevertheless stated that "the urban veneer of most Okinawans is so thin that a slight scratch reveals a typical rural person whose adjustments to urban life, as yet, are quite superficial" (p. 100), and went on to cite "friendliness and pliability" (p. 100) as the basic personality traits of a "typical" Okinawan (man).

In extending his search for the typically, traditionally, and pristinely Okinawan, Maretzki published, with his Japanese wife Hatsumi Maretzki, a monograph aiming to explicate personality characteristics in terms of child-rearing practices in a northern Okinawan village (Maretzki and Maretzki, 1966). Their study was one of the cross-cultural studies of culture and personality directed by Beatrice and John Whiting (Harvard), Irwin Child (Yale) and William Lambert (Cornell), that were carried out in six different societies, namely, Khalapur in India, Juxtlahuaca in Santo Domingo, Orchard Town in the United States, Tarong in the Philippines, Nyansongo in Kenya, and Taira in Okinawa (cf. Whiting and Whiting 1975). In spite of its rich ethnographic data (collected in the mid-1950s), the study's theoretical paradigm of culture and personality does not help the Maretzkis pay attention to the agency of Okinawans in politics or the historical transformation of culture. Rather, adults, particularly mothers, are viewed as simply following culturally programmed child-rearing practices.

Overall, the studies of Glacken, Lebra, and Maretzki register, with varying degrees, the basic mode of American anthropological investigations of Okinawa in the 1950s and 1960s, which had a contradictory impetus within them. On one level, these studies operated outside the theoretical concerns of Japanese native ethnology, took a non-native, outsider's positionality in Okinawa, and successfully exposed the differences between Okinawa and Japan that Japanese native enthnology wanted to conceal. At another level, with their gaze directed specifically at "pristine" Okinawa, these studies reproduced the Orientalist binary of "us" (as the historical and political agency) and "them" (bereft of such agency), thereby leaving Okinawa suspended in a space that was neither American nor Japanese. The basic message that these studies conveyed was "Okinawans are not Japanese, but they are not Americans either," which curiously corresponded with the U.S. policy of separating Okinawa from mainland Japan and putting it to use for security purposes in the world dictated by actuality of the cold war.

Trapped into Essentialism: Okinawan Folklore Studies

With Yanagita studying Okinawa from a nativist positionality to assimilate it into Japan, and American anthropologists investigating Okinawa from an outsider's perspective to differentiate Okinawa from Japan (and the United States),[13] Japanese and American scholars may have mutually reinforced, in their very rivalry, the primordial binary between Japan (the national, the inside) and the United States (the metropolitan, the outside) with Okinawa as a normative hinge between the two. In contrast, Okinawan scholars, particularly folklorists, attempted to critique both the national/inside and the metropolitan/outside by establishing a specific regional scholarship in between by asserting "Okinawans were and are Okinawans and nothing else." The work of two prominent scholars, Nakamatsu Yashū and Iha Fuyū, reveals the thrust and limit of such scholarship.

Contemporary Okinawan folklorist Nakamatsu Yashū has long probed as much as romanticized the foundational essence of Okinawan primeval culture. He writes, for instance, "*kami* (gods), shrines, priests and so forth…have existed since ancient times [in Okinawa] with almost no changes" (Nakamatsu [1968] 1990: 10); "the Okinawan people's communal society was bound by love and trust, and nobody was controlled. What existed were *kusate* [social conditions in which the people completely depend on the ancestry gods] and *osoi* [social conditions in which the ancestry gods embrace the people]" (p. 271). It should be noted, however, that in his somewhat problematic idealization of an old Okinawa, Nakamatsu neither used Okinawa as the foundation of the homogeneous Japanese like Yanagita, nor appropriated it for obscuring the violence of U.S. rule like American anthropologists in the 1950s and 1960s. Rather, Nakamatsu, from within Okinawa, highlighted Okinawa's specificity against the background of what he saw as the disorder of modernity (urbanization, individualization, and industrialization, among others) introduced, in his view, from the outside throughout the twentieth century. His position is typically expressed by the following statement: "In Okinawa, *kami*'s villages still remain…. Yet, well-costumed devils called civilization have rushed into the islands of Okinawa" (Nakamatsu 1979: 83).

I will later problematize the essentialist-cum-anti-modernist position of this kind, a position widely shared by other Okinawan folklorists attempting to retrieve distinct cultural forms of local life that had (presumably) existed in the untainted past, but for the moment I want to discuss positive aspects of such an attempt in relation to the works of Iha Fuyū, the pioneer scholar of Okinawan studies in the early twentieth century. Indeed, in their problematic romanticization of Okinawa beyond power and history, Nakamatsu and other Okinawan scholars have inherited Iha's critical spirit of difference, which was expressed, for instance, in a lecture he delivered in 1907 to the Okinawan public (cited in Takara K. 1975: 860):

> It is of course important to show what Okinawans have in common with the Japanese race like I have just said, but it is also important to show how Okinawans differ. It is a bit misleading to say "how Okinawans differ," so I would restate this as, "what other people cannot imitate." I think that [the Okinawan race] has qualities that nobody can imitate.

Iha Fuyū was born in Naha in 1876 and died in Tokyo in 1947 (two years after the battle of Okinawa). He published more than three hundred articles and twenty books all about Okinawa, and has been praised in Okinawa and beyond as the founder of Okinawan studies, a figure whose influence has not diminished to date (Kinjo and Takara 1984). However, at the same time certain Okinawan critics have found him to be problematically reactionary for reasons that will be discussed below (Arakawa 1981a, 1981b). Iha's scholarship extended from linguistics (in which he was trained at the Tokyo Imperial University) to literature, folklore, ethnology, mythology, religion, political institutions, trade relations, and women's issues. The historical consciousness running through Iha's entire works centered on the predicaments of Okinawa that wanted to be part of, but was forever discriminated against by, Japan. In an attempt to save Okinawa from such predicaments, Iha in his earlier intellectual career (before ca. 1925) tried to theorize Okinawa as a genuine subject of expanding Imperial Japan in a way that was both dangerous and liberating.

A case in point is Iha's article "*Ryūkyū Shobun wa Isshu no Doreikaihō nari*" (The Ryukyu Measures are a Kind of Emancipation of Slaves) ([1914]

1974a), later renamed *"Ryūkyūjin no Kaihō"* (The Emancipation of the Ryukyuans). In this article, Iha contrasted the Japan–Okinawa relationship of the past with that of the present. Between the early seventeenth and the late nineteenth centuries, Iha argues, the Ryukyu Kingdom was dominated by Satsuma (the southernmost feudal clan of the Tokugawa regime) like its slave—in the sense of lack of self-autonomy. "The attitude of the Shimazu family [of Satsuma] to the Ryukyuans was that if we were imbued with Chinese thoughts and detached from the regime of *okunimoto* (the master), they warned us not to be so distant, while if we were imbued with Japanese ideas and assumed the slightest air of the master, they told us not to be too close [to the master]. In short, the Shimazu family [of Satsuma] wanted to leave the Ryukyuans suspended, forever ambiguous" (Iha [1914] 1974a: 491–92). He saw the slave mentality as having gradually penetrated not only the political institutions of the kingdom but also the psychology of the commoners during Satsuma's control. "Yet," he continued, "the times have changed; we have witnessed the [Meiji] restoration" (p. 492). Because of the Meiji Restoration, dating from 1868, Iha insisted, not only the old Tokugawa samurai regime (of which Satsuma was part) but also the similarly feudalistic Ryukyu Kingdom had been overthrown. Iha concluded, "I think that the Ryukyu Measures [in 1872–1879, during which the Meiji government turned the kingdom into a prefecture of modern Japan] are a kind of emancipation of the slaves.... As a result of the Ryukyu Measures, what is called the Ryukyu Kingdom was lost, but the Ryukyuan race was restored in Imperial Japan" (p. 493). Iha, at this point, saw the Meiji Restoration essentially as an opportunity for Okinawa to embrace so as to liberate itself from feudalism and enter the celebrated realm of modernity and progress.

Iha made his remarks on the basis of the theory of common ancestry between Japanese and Ryukyuan/Okinawan[14] people, a theory he advanced (before Yanagita Kunio) by borrowing from such pioneer researchers as above-mentioned Torii Ryūzō, Tashiro Antei, and Katō Sango. In one of his earliest articles,*"Ryūkyūjin no Sosen ni Tsuite"* (On the Ancestry of the Ryukyuans) ([1906] 1974a: 32), for instance, Iha stated: "The religious thoughts of today's Okinawa are rather complicated, but if one removes from them the elements of Confucianism, Buddhism, and Taoism, what remains is something that resembles Japanese Shinto." In the same article, he commented that Okinawan words are "examples of what became extinct in mainland Japan, and yet are still used in Okinawa.... Anyone would be surprised to hear that poor residents of Okinawa, who could not possibly read the ancient Japanese words contained in [such old texts as] *Kojiki* (The Record of Ancient Matters), *Nihon Shoki* (The Chronicles of Japan), and *Manyōshū* (The Collection of Myriad Leaves)[15] are actually using such words every day. I think these words are the remnants from the time when the ancestors of the Ryukyuan race parted from the *yamato* (Japanese) race to migrate south" (p. 23). Iha maintained that the proto-Japanese race, originating in the northern part of the Chinese continent, came via the Korean peninsula to Kyushu Island; and then two thousand years ago, a segment of this population migrated south to the Ryukyu Islands to become the Ryukyuan/Okinawan race and thus parted from the rest which became the *yamato* (Japanese) race. In the process, according to Iha, the Ainu people, who used to reside throughout the Japanese archipelago (including Okinawa), were conquered. In passing, I note that Iha's theory of the northern origin of the Japanese race was later appropriated by Yanagita Kunio, who, as I have stated, came to argue that a group of proto-Japanese people who had landed on the Ryukyu Islands gradually migrated to mainland Japan from south to north.[16]

After advancing the notion of the shared ancestry between Japanese and Okinawans on the one hand, and articulating the status of Okinawa as an integral part of Imperial Japan on the other, these two ideas were, in the early 1920s, dangerously synthesized and extended by Iha to justify the contemporary expansion of the Japanese empire. In *Koryūkyū no Seiji* (The Politics of the Ancient Ryukyus) ([1921] 1974a: 486), Iha deployed the then prevalent discourses about the ever-expanding, multiethnic, hybrid empire, Japan, by stating that "the Japanese [with Ryukyuan/Okinawan people included] have been a hybrid people," and went on to assert that "I think the reason the Japanese people were able to become a big nation lies in their integrity; and this integrity...has made it possible to assimilate the blood of various races, and to absorb various new thoughts in order to create a vigorous nation" (p. 486). Iha attempted to restore the commonality between Okinawans and Japanese—the commonality that had been lost two thousand years before—in the unified polity of the multiethnic nation, Japan, at present and in the future. In so doing, Iha hoped that Okinawa would be thoroughly assimilated into Japan, anti-Okinawan prejudice would disappear, and the welfare of Okinawans would be adequately promoted.

It should be noted, however, that Iha did not intend to completely dis-solve distinctive Okinawan ways of life into the imperial Japan's colonial project of establishing a multiethnic empire. The statement from his 1907 lecture, cited above, was one example in which Okinawa's irreducibleness was foregrounded. In other words, Iha, at least partially, resisted prewar Japan's colonial discourses by actively reshaping and modifying such dis-courses so as to speak about the difference—Okinawa's individuality and uniqueness—within and against Japan.

Framed this way, the problem of Iha's discourses before the mid-1920s lies not in the lack of his critical spirit but in the fact that the very criti-cal act of speaking about the difference may have ironically entangled the periphery, Okinawa/Iha, in an existing order of power. The irony was evi-denced in, for instance, Iha's statement ([1907] 1974a: 61) that "the stray child called the Ryukyuan race, even though he drifted on the China Sea for two thousand years, existed not as a people [without a state] like the Ainus and Taiwanese aborigines but as a nation [with a state]." Iha contin-ued: "Look at the Ainus. They joined the Japanese nation long before we did. But, my friends, what are the present conditions of the Ainus? They still exist only as a people, don't they? They still play sumou-wrestling with bears, don't they?" (p. 62). Iha's attempts to genuinely integrate Okinawa into Imperial Japan went hand in hand with his problematic desire to dif-ferentiate Okinawa from other "second-class" nationals, thereby paradoxi-cally reinforcing the very oppressive racial hierarchy of Imperial Japan Iha was challenging.

Then, roughly after 1925, issues of political actuality and urgency con-cerning the relationships between Okinawa and Japan disappeared from Iha's writing, as he turned to articulating the distinct features of older Oki-nawan social-cultural forms untouched by the power and history of Japan. His study on the political system of the Ryukyu Kingdom, a system that, unlike its Japanese counterpart, was composed of a religious hierarchy of women that paralleled a political hierarchy of men (e.g., [1938] 1973a, [1939] 1973b), can be seen as one example. Encouraged by Yanagita Kunio, Iha also conducted an in-depth study of *Omorosōshi* ([1938] 1973a, [1939] 1973b), a collection of divine poems compiled by the Ryukyu Kingdom in the sixteenth and seventeenth centuries. His research showed that old Okinawan poems were often sung on such grandiose topics as the sea and stars, topics which were absent from the Japanese classics, in which the dominant theme was the everyday beauty of nature (flowers, birds, winds, the moon, etc.).

As Hiyane (1981), Kinjo and Takara (1984), Kano (1993), and Tomiyama (1997, 2002) have demonstrated, Iha's intellectual shift was conditioned, at least in part, by Okinawa's bleak social reality in the 1920s. Far from being assimilated into Japan as genuine imperial subjects in the way he had earlier hoped and expected, Okinawa was economically broke and Okinawans remained on the periphery of Japan, continuously discriminated against by mainland Japanese in various ways (see chapter 2). Witnessing the misery of Okinawa as well as widespread and increasing anti-Okinawa prejudice, Iha gradually gave up, after the mid-1920s, his intellectual efforts to improve Okinawa's social status by integrating Okinawans into the Japanese mainstream. Instead, his writing after this period became directed by a desire not unlike what Franz Fanon, the Martiniquan-born psychiatrist and activist for the Algerian National Liberation Front, once called "the secret hope of discovering beyond the misery of today, beyond self-contempt, resignation and abjuration, some very beautiful and splendid era whose existence rehabilitates us both in regard to ourselves and in regard to others" (1963: 210).

In my view, it is Iha's "secret hope" of discovering a beautiful and splendid era of Okinawa that subsequent generations of Okinawan scholars, particularly folklorists including Nakamatsu Yashū discussed above, have inherited in their essentialist and antimodernist assertion, "Okinawans were, are, and should be Okinawans, and nothing else." Against the background of "the misery of today"—U.S. military control of Okinawa (1945–1972) and the continued stationing of the U.S. military there after the reversion of Okinawa to Japanese control (1972 to date)—Okinawan scholars have sought to discover a beautiful Okinawa in the idealized past. It is worthwhile to note here that they have often taken their essentialist search one step further by identifying northern Okinawa, the primary site of my own anthropological investigation, as the storehouse of original Okinawa (e.g., Shimabukuro [1927] 1977; Miyagi S. [1938] 1987; Tsuha 1978, 2001; Nagoshishi Hensan Ínkai 1988, 2001a, 2001b). Challenging the characterization (often shared by Japanese and Okinawans alike) of northern Okinawa as the underdeveloped place, Okinawa folklorists have tried to rearticulate and redefine the underdevelopment as a springboard to moving beyond "self-contempt, resignation and abjuration."

Note, however, that in their very attempt to move beyond the misery of the present, Okinawa scholars between the 1920s and the 1980s were trapped by the image of a self-contained Okinawa without social change, without politics, and without internal differentiation—the same image Japanese native ethnology and American anthropology produced during the same period for different political reasons—thereby contributing to reproducing the national and global system of knowledge that has obscured the concrete political problems such as Japanese colonialism, the war, and the U.S. military. At the national level, Okinawan scholars have, with their search for a pristine Okinawa beyond power and history, ironically assisted Japanese native ethnology in intellectually assimilating and subordinating Okinawa within modern Japan as the storehouse of untainted Japan. At the global level, Okinawan scholars' quest for a pure and isolated Okinawa without politics and social change reinforced the American Orientalist-cum-essentialist binary between "us" and "them" on the one hand, and the concomitant segregationist view that was used to administratively separate Okinawa from mainland Japan on the other.

In sum, in the solemn act of discovering authentic Okinawa beyond power and history, nativist Okinawan studies might have ironically served as a pivot around which the national/Japanese scholarship and the metropolitan/U.S. scholarship have spiraled and crystallized in relation to one another.

• • •

Allow me to insert a sequel to Iha's story in order to show how my own study will overcome the essentialist tendency of modern Okinawan studies in Japan, the United States, and Okinawa. In the midst of the intellectual crisis caused by the failure of his scholarly efforts (i.e., the failure to improve Okinawa's status by integrating it into Japan), Iha had a scandalous affair with a married Okinawan woman. They together left Okinawa for Tokyo in 1925 (Kinjo and Takara 1984: 49–52). There, as stated above, Iha tried to intellectually disconnect Okinawa/himself from Japan in order to textually rescue politico-economically ruined Okinawa. Yet he could go no farther from Imperial Japan than the southernmost border of its territory—Taiwan and, eventually, the Malay World—which became for him a romanticized space of "southern islands" untouched by power and history. Indeed, the distinction between Taiwanese aborigines (the colonized) and Okinawans (the colonizer as part of the Japanese empire) which he clearly made in his earlier writings (e.g., [1907] 1974a: 61) became blurred; both groups became included within the romanticized, and often sexualized, single category of *nantōjin* (southern islanders) that stretched even to include Malays (Tomiyama 1997, 2002). Iha could not have Okinawa be embraced by Japan when he had earlier attempted to do so, but he could not let Okinawa escape Japan while he was in Tokyo. He was never able to resolve this dilemma of Okinawa being unable to either attain or avoid the Japanese empire on his own. Rather, the dilemma resolved itself when the Japanese empire was destroyed by the battle of Okinawa and the A-bombs.

In Tokyo, right before his death, Iha published his last book, *Okinawa Rekishi Monogatari: Nippon no Shukuzu* (Okinawa Historical Story: A Microcosm of Japan) ([1947] 1974b). With Iha's earlier dream of Okinawa's integration into Japan now entirely gone, this book is filled with nostalgia for the Okinawa that was totally destroyed in the war. "Looking back, we should have retained the traditional land practices instead of giving them up under the name of [progress]" (p. 451). Looking forward, he concluded with the statement that can be read as an expression of despair or that of hope, or both:

> Where Okinawa belongs will be determined in the Peace Conference to be held in the near future; Okinawans must know that given the present world circumstances, we are not in a situation that would allow us to determine our own fate.... Anyhow, the question of under what kind of politics Okinawans could become happy is beyond the scope of Okinawan history and cannot be dealt with here.... I only want to add that when imperialism comes to an end on the globe, Okinawans will be liberated from the *nigayo* (bitter world) and will arrive at the *amayo* (sweet world) wherein they will be able to make use of their individualities so as to make a contribution to world culture.
>
> (p. 457)

Some fifty years after this anguished commentary, the collective consciousness of Okinawans came to be increasingly shaped by the changing political-social conditions of Okinawa and beyond, and in the process Iha's vision of Okinawans as global citizens beyond the confines of the island prefecture became no longer an unrealistic fantasy but a concrete political project. In a way that responds to the reconfiguration of Okinawa's political-social consciousness in the 1990s, a wave of new scholarship on

Okinawa has emerged in recent decades not only in Okinawa (Arakawa 1981a, 1981b, 2000; Miyagi E. 1982, Arasaki 1982, 1995; Hiyane 1996, Medoruma 1996, 2000; Yakabi 2000), but also in mainland Japan (Y. Ota 1997, 1998; Oguma 1995, 1998; Tomiyama 1990, 1995, 1996, 1997, 2002; Kano 1987, 1993; Miyamoto and Sasaki, eds. 2000) and beyond (Rabson, 1989, Christy 1993, Morris-Suzuki 1998, especially chapters 2 and 4; Molasky 1999, 2003; Johnson, ed. 1999, McCormack 1999, Eldridge 2001, Roberson 2001, Allen 2002, Hook and Siddle, eds. 2003, Nelson 2003, Hein and Selden, eds. 2003, Angst 2003). Collectively, this new wave of "postmodern" scholarship has attempted to go beyond the search for a pristine, bounded Okinawa that once characterized modern Okinawan studies, under new historical circumstances where the boundaries that might previously have justified narrow nation-bound scholarships are increasingly breaking down. Thus, for instance, Okinawan writer and critic Medoruma Shun (2000), in his novels and social commentaries, explores Okinawa's enduring collective memory of the war against the background of Japanese consumerism and global capitalism that has penetrated Okinawan society (cf. Inoue 2002a, Molasky 2003). Anthropologist Yoshinobu Ota (1997) examines subversive performances of an Okinawan theatrical group and sheds light on the ways in which specific subjectivity and agency has been constituted within and against the constraining order of contemporary power. Furthermore, the book edited by Hein and Selden (2003) extends Selden's (1974) pioneering project of critiquing American and Japanese power from an Okinawan perspective. Broadly interweaving the issues of politics, culture, and history surrounding Okinawa, contributors to this book throw into relief the thrusts of culture and memory in shaping and reshaping Okinawan identity in the nation-wide and world-wide relations of power and history.

This study aims to contribute to this new wave of scholarship by addressing the U.S. base problems as manifested in Henoko and Nago City. Indeed, an in-depth analysis of history, culture, and politics in Henoko and Nago, indispensable for understanding the magnitude, depth, and complexity of the U.S. base problems in Okinawa as a whole, has been long overdue. In a way that orchestrates previous efforts of my own (Inoue, Purves and Selden 1997; Inoue 1998, 1999, 2002a, 2002b, 2004a, 2004b), this study will specifically address questions that modern Okinawan studies ignored, questions of internal differentiation of Okinawa in terms of class, gender, place, and race; historical changes of Okinawa; relations of power and history among Okinawa, Japan, and the United States; and interactions and networks among these that would constitute an open arena of oppositional solidarity.

I am not proposing, however, to abandon the theses of modern Okinawan studies altogether. Quite the contrary. Certainly, bringing politics and history into cultural-social analyses will help us to overcome the essentialist tendency of modern Okinawan studies to appeal to pure or original Okinawan-ness. But if taken to extreme, this move may end up privileging the discursive production of differences, thereby slipping us into a questionable postmodern celebration of shifting positions.

Allen's (2002) otherwise informative, engaging study on Okinawan resistance and identity somewhat exhibits this problem. Explaining the thematic structure of his work, Allen (2002: 18) notes, "It seems a good idea to follow Sarup's statement about the evolving and dynamic nature of identity," and proceeds to cite Sarup: "Our identities are multiple and mobile. Though the process of change dissolves the fixed, stable, homogeneous identities of the past, it also opens the possibility of new articulations—the construction of new identities, the production of new subjects" (Sarup 1996: 57; cited in Allen 2002: 18). Drawing on Fuss (1989: 1–21), however, I suggest that the hasty attempt to pluralize Okinawa raises new questions about the politics of identity. First, it may lead us to disregard the problematics of Okinawan modernity in the context of globalization, that is, "old" but enduring Okinawan sentiment that is being expressed in opposition to Japan and the United States under new historical circumstances of the post–cold war era (see chapter 2). Second, fragmenting Okinawa into multiple identities does not necessarily solve the problem of essentialism if each fragmented identity still retains its own self-contained essence. Finally, contrasting the "fixed, stable, homogeneous identities of the past" with the "construction of new identities" is to accept essentialism in the very act of criticizing it, because it sounds as if the "fixed, stable, homogeneous identities of the past" had really exited without being subject to any historical change and redefinition.

It is in an effort to guard against sliding into the postmodern celebration of disaggregated, positional identities that my analysis wants to utilize the virtue of modern Okinawan studies, their concern for the specificity and totality of the "place" (Gupta and Ferguson 1997, Dirlik 1999). My task, then, is not so much to look back to the past to accomplish "the salvaging of distinct cultural forms of life from a process of apparent global [impacts]" (Marcus and Fischer 1986: 1), as it is to carefully examine who have been claiming, in spite of the "risk" of essentialism (cf. Fuss 1989), the specificity and totality of Okinawa, how it has been organized, why it has been utilized, and where its effects have been manifested at the particular historical moments.[17] In the chapters that follow, my readers will find the specific forms that cultural meanings and social identities take in this place, Henoko/Nago, by looking at complex interactions and negotiations between the essentialist assertion of totality-cum-unity ("we are Okinawans") and the postmodern claim of difference ("we are Okinawans but of a different kind").

4

"WE ARE OKINAWANS OF A DIFFERENT KIND":
Henoko History, Camp Schwab, and Working-Class Ideology of Difference

Chapters 4 and 5 will introduce readers to the history and culture of Henoko in order to explore the intractable Okinawan dilemma between peace and a better life, totality and difference, and anti-base and pro-base sentiments, a dilemma that would eventually enter the making and unmaking of social movements in the late 1990s and beyond. This chapter aims to clarify the origin and development of a communal, working-class sentiment in Henoko, "we are Okinawans but of a different kind," in light of its money-making activities, kinship and marriage, and related cultural practices. To this end, first, it will examine the process in which Henoko, since the late 1950s, has asserted itself as a "difference," as an enclave within Okinawa, by appropriating—not refusing—the potency of the U.S. military for its economic ends. Then, this chapter will ethnographically explore how Henoko has actively renewed and reinstituted Okinawa's "traditional" cultural practices in order to socialize, absorb, and control ever-diversifying residents into a closed, essentially pro-base life space. In chapter 5, we will look at the ways in which a renewed sense of totality and unity ("we are Okinawans") emerged from within Henoko's middle-class sector in opposition to its working-class ideology.

Henoko as a Difference

Henoko is a sparsely populated, somewhat obscure northeastern coastal district of Okinawa (population: 1,400), but it has always played a role in Okinawan and larger Japanese history at various levels.[1] In the 1920s, for instance, the depression in the Okinawan economy had an adverse effect on the lives of six hundred Henoko residents, the majority of whom made their living in agriculture, forestry, and fishery. Some residents had to sell their land, or worse, their children to fishermen's houses (in the case of boys) and teahouses (in the case of girls). Some migrated, together with other Okinawans, to thriving industrial cities and labor-intense agricultural towns on mainland Japan and beyond to work as cheap laborers (Henoko District 1998: 56–57, 159–96, 479–524).

Henoko, while situated outside the site of the hardest-fought battles (the central and southern parts of Okinawa), shared Okinawa's fate during the battle of Okinawa as well. Because of intense artillery fire and air raids, some residents hid in Henoko's mountain areas, others lost their homes, and still others were killed. For two years after the battle, the war-ravaged Henoko area created a foothold in larger Okinawan history as the site of one of the sixteen refugee camps built across the island of Okinawa and beyond by the U.S. military. Set up on a hill facing Henoko's sea, this camp was equipped with a jail, police station, school, and clinic, and accommodated some twenty-nine thousand Okinawans with nothing but the clothes on their backs, in the tents provided by the U.S. military (Henoko 1998: 552–59; Okinawa Shichōson 30 Nenshi Henshū Inkai 1982).

Yet no Henoko-related events have had a more lasting impact on Okinawan history than the region's involvement in the land-acquisition dispute of the mid-1950s, during which Okinawa staged its first island-wide protest in response to USCAR's expropriation of its land (see chapter 2). The following description was mostly based on the information provided to me by several Henoko men including Ōshiro Jirō, 71, and Yagaji Noriyuki, 73,[2] as well as newspaper articles in those days.

In January 1955, USCAR notified Kushi Village—the district of Henoko was within Kushi Village at that time; Kushi Village was dissolved in 1970 when it formed, together with three other neighboring villages/towns, Nago City—that the U.S. forces would use the mountainous sections of

Henoko as a training field for military exercises. Because the firewood collected from these mountain forests was a mainstay of the community, the Henoko administration petitioned against the plan immediately. Then, in the summer of 1955, USCAR notified Henoko of a plan of far greater significance: the expropriation of its land to develop a military base. In order to stop this outrageous proposal, Henoko leaders desperately worked with Kushi Village, which made its stand by refusing to cooperate with the preparatory topographical survey of Henoko that was being conducted by USCAR. Henoko village leaders also made a plea to the Government of the Ryukyu Islands (GRI, run by Okinawans within the limit of USCAR authorities—see chapter 2), which was the official agency that bargained with USCAR on land issues (*Okinawa Taimusu*, December 21, 1956). However, facing pressure from both USCAR, which was trying to expropriate plots of land across Okinawa, and a large number of Okinawans who were unified to oppose this expropriation, GRI had already been helpless and paralyzed, with virtually no political power to intervene in the situation. In a way that caught GRI off guard, USCAR then proceeded to deal directly with the landholders in Henoko and the mayor of Kushi Village so as to create and exploit a split within Okinawa.

In order to conciliate Henoko and Kushi leaders, USCAR offered higher bids than it had originally proposed (*Okinawa Taimusu*, December 21, 1956). By that time, tragic stories of other communities having their land forcefully expropriated with the use of bulldozers and bayonets and without enough compensation (see chapter 2) had reached Henoko. Fearful that the same fate would befall their community, the village leaders of Henoko reconsidered USCAR's proposal and eventually decided to accept the construction of the American base, with the conditions that USCAR not make Henoko residents evacuate their community; provide electricity and water to Henoko; preferentially employ Henoko residents in the base when completed; and allow residents to grow farm products in fields which the base would rent but not use. There was an unarticulated desire in this poor village for a modern, urban life with electricity and sanitary water to be provided by the new base. Many also hoped that the problem of depopulation—the youth had left Henoko to look for employment opportunities in central Okinawa where bases were being expanded and constructed—would be solved by accepting the base. The mayor of Kushi Village secretly contacted USCAR and agreed to proceed with the plan (*Okinawa Taimusu*, September 18, 1992).

On December 20, 1956, the contract was concluded between the representatives of Henoko and USCAR, and USCAR officials happily left the Henoko administration building wishing all a Merry Christmas. However, for Okinawans at large, it was not necessarily a merry day. Those involved in the island-wide struggle against the expropriation of Okinawan land would specifically accuse Kushi and Henoko of giving in to USCAR (*Okinawa Taimusu*, January 5, 1957). The mayor of Kushi Village apologetically said in a press conference that "I am prepared for the criticism against my decision to accept the construction when the military land issues have not yet been resolved today. [But,] Kushi village, which has been economically ill-fated, would not be able to attain economic transformation without the base building" (*Okinawa Taimusu*, December 21, 1956).[3] Indeed, while Henoko, together with Kushi Village, attempted to accommodate the power of the U.S. military so as to render social conditions manageable, this accommodation also introduced fissures into Okinawa's unified front against the violence of USCAR—a year after Henoko's acceptance of the construction of the American base, which was named Camp Schwab, another northern Okinawan community, Kin Town, just south of Henoko, followed suit by accepting the construction of Camp Hansen (Kinchō to Kichi Henshū Īnkai 1991), eventually bringing the island-wide protest to an end. In a word, Okinawa's problematic dilemma between peace and a better life, unity and difference, was acutely expressed through Henoko's acceptance of the American base.

In 1957, the construction of Camp Schwab began on the same Henoko hill where the U.S. refugee camp had existed after the war. From that moment on, Henoko underwent massive social transformation at a tremendous speed, a bit like the imaginary city of Macondo as described by García Márquez in *One Hundred Years of Solitude* ([1970] 1998). The Henoko administration hurriedly created an entertainment quarter by clearing communal fields and forests. Some leaders curried favor with the USCAR authorities and illegally appropriated their bulldozers and trucks for the development of the entertainment quarter, which ultimately got them arrested (*Okinawa Taimusu*, April 9, 1958). People from all over Okinawa flooded Henoko, where men became construction workers, and women worked for restaurants and bars.

After the completion of Camp Schwab in 1959, and especially during the Vietnam War era, Henoko came to be known in Okinawa as a thriving base town in front of vast Camp Schwab that occupied 21.84 square kilometers (5,387 acres) of land. In a small area of 0.3 square kilometers (74 acres) officially administered by the District of Henoko, more than 2,100 people[4] (Nagoshishi Hensan Īnkai 1988: 645)—or 3,000 if including transient workers—lived. The neon-lit entertainment quarter, called *Appuru Taun* [Apple Town] (after Major Apple of the Head of the Land Division of USCAR who was responsible for the acquisition of Henoko's land), now accommodated 100 plus bars-cum-restaurants (which also often functioned as brothels), as well as public baths, various shops, beauty parlors, and other enterprises. A man named Yagaji Ippan from a Henoko native descent group utilized his huge estate to establish a movie theater, a bank office, a radio station, a power plant, a rice mill, a tea garden, and an orange orchard, as well as several bars and restaurants within Henoko in the 1960s. Yagaji Ippan became something of a monarch of a communal dynasty, achieving island-wide fame in the world of entertainment business.

In the meantime, a bus terminal was constructed to accommodate commuters. A church was built to give residents sermons. In place of Okinawan toilets, in which residents used to raise their pigs with human waste, flush toilets (which became an object of envy among residents) were installed in bars and restaurants according to the sanitary standards enforced by USCAR (USCAR, not dated). The signboards in the district came to be written in "real" English (as opposed to Okinawan "pidgin" English) for the servicemen, although residents barely understood the language. A former bar owner told me that when she was asked by a serviceman to make a "screwdriver," she ended up giving him the actual tool, instead of the drink. Base authorities sometimes begged and sometimes threatened the hostesses to take medical examinations in order to control sexually transmitted diseases. Musicians also came to Henoko to entertain servicemen going to and coming back from Vietnam, turning this rural village into one of the birthplaces of Okinawan rock music. One vocalist—affectionately called Kacchan—in the legendary rock band Condition Green even had a try at killing a live chicken on stage by tearing its head off with his teeth. This performance, although it appalled the servicemen, created a great sensation among them as well, and became the band's forte (Okinawa Shiyakusho 1994).

Not surprisingly, the more Henoko thrived, the more dangerous, turbulent, and restless it became. An Okinawan newspaper, *Okinawa Taimusu*, dated July 4, 1961, for instance, somewhat routinely reported: "During the

nights of July 2 and 3, six incidents occurred in Henoko, Kushi Village,"
which included the theft of a whisky bottle by a group of three Marines at a
bar, the destruction of a restaurant's windows by another, and the violence
of a frustrated, drunken Marine who was rebuffed in his sexual advances by
a twenty-one-year-old hostess. In 1961, residents even witnessed the murder of a bar hostess by a U.S. serviceman.[5] While Henoko youth organized
a self-defense police unit called *jikeidan*, assaults, thefts, arsons, rapes,
and other crimes were continuously committed by members of Okinawan
gangs and drunken customers, as well as U.S servicemen.

In spite of (or perhaps precisely because of) disarrays of everyday life,
Henoko in the 1960s was seething with its excitement for money-making,
happiness, and a better life. Payments made by servicemen in a bar would
fill up, in a day, a big cardboard box used as a cash register, and the bar
owner would have to trample down the money just to keep it from flowing
out of the box. Policemen, who had been so poorly paid before the war that
Henoko residents had often provided them rice, were now high-handedly
sitting in the newly remodeled police station, saying to the owners of the
bars and restaurants that they did not intend to meddle in the prostitution business, but warned them to be careful so that it would not cause
legal troubles (Henoko District, not dated). Note that all this happened
in the 1960s when Okinawa, against the background of the escalation of
the Vietnam War, was unified in the reversion movement (see chapter 2).
With its multitude of money-making activities, Henoko asserted to fellow
Okinawans that its residents were "different."

However, as the Vietnam War came to an end, once-booming Henoko
sharply contracted as the number of U.S. servicemen in Camp Schwab decreased. By the late 1970s, hundreds of employees in Camp Schwab were
laid off, and the movie theater, radio station, bank office, bus terminal, and
other businesses were closed. The official population of Henoko continued
to decrease—it was approximately 1,900 in 1973, 1,700 in 1978, and 1,500 in
1983 (Nagoshishi Hensan Inkai 1988: 645)—and in the late 1980s, it leveled
off at 1,400.

During the 1990s, negative effects of Henoko's sluggish economy were
felt at various levels of social life. Most of the twenty-odd run-down bars
and restaurants in Henoko could seldom draw a full house. At least two-
thirds of the owners were not even running these bars and restaurants
themselves, but let their friends from outside communities do the business

FIGURE 4.1 Rundown Henoko bar/restaurant (2).

to earn a small amount of monthly rent (25,000 yen/$250) in return. Only about fifty residents were officially employed by the base (Henoko District 1997), while 25 percent of Henoko's working population (about six hundred) were insecurely absorbed into the construction and transportation industries and 55 percent into the service industry, working as, for example, cashiers of supermarkets, shop clerks at gas stations, and book store or pinball parlor employees in Henoko and in Nago City (Sōrifu 1995). In the midst of this, the economic disadvantages of non-native Henoko residents moving to Henoko in and after the 1960s and youth—they together constituted one-fourth of the estimated four hundred households in Henoko— were made apparent because they did not own military land and thus did not receive the rent from Tokyo, to which "native" residents, who owned land, had been entitled (see below).[6] Rumors of non-native residents and youth haphazardly borrowing massive amounts of money from loan sharks were not uncommon. In addition, most of the development projects were implemented on the populated west coast of Nago City (population 50,000), which left the east coast (population 5,000), including Henoko, lagging behind. Complaints such as "even sewage disposal has not been installed in Henoko" and "it would take ten years to get a road built in this district [Henoko], even if we put our hands together in supplication and begged Nago City authorities for help," were heard during my fieldwork in 1997–98.

And yet, for two reasons, the distinctive sense of "we are Okinawans but of a different kind" coupled with Henoko's fundamentally pro-base mentality seems to have remained intact even during the period of Henoko's deterioration (i.e., between the 1970s and 1990s). First, the economic difficulties were being offset by the massive rent paid (since 1972) by Tokyo for the continuous use of Henoko's land by U.S. troops. The payment in 1997 to the Henoko district was 140 million yen ($1.4 million), and an estimated average of 800,000 yen ($8,000) a year was paid out to the individual land holders (Nago Shiyakusho 1996).[7] The base-related money in general and the rent in particular became a drug that calmed—even as it constantly rekindled—general communal discontent about Henoko's present and anxieties about its future. Put differently, the deterioration of the communal economy, barely compensated by the rent money from Tokyo, remade Henoko into a peculiar twilight community of the new working class: By the end of the 1990s, Henoko residents had become well off as compared to nearby communities with no industry, but at the same time they could not quite emulate the middle-class Okinawans with secure jobs whose lives were established outside the economic influence of the U.S. military.

The second, and related, reason for the reproduction of the pro-base sentiment in Henoko derives from its specific deployment of Okinawan tradition—kinship and related cultural practices—as I will explicate below.

Kinship as Power

Across Okinawa, social and political relationships have long been structured by what Okinawans call *chien ketsuen*, nondiscursive ties of blood and place created around a particular kin system, which functioned as a basis for and indeed regulated public discussions, arguments, and negotiations. At the core of this system lies the *munchū*, which refers to a highly institutionalized patrilineal descent group composed of one main family and its branch families.[8] *Munchū* originated among the ruling class of the

Ryukyu Kingdom during the late eighteenth century, then spread among commoners after the kingdom's demise (1879); in spite of various changes in its form, principles, and rules, it has continued to exert considerable influence upon Okinawan social life. The foundation of the intricate rules of Okinawa's kinship is primogeniture—the rule of inheritance whereby the land and other fortunes of a *munchū* are passed down to the eldest son (Higa Ma. 1987).

In prewar days, Henoko village politics had been conducted on the basis of the balance of power among four major *munchū*s (*Yagaji*,[9] *Yamashiro*, *Iheya*, and *Furugen*). What Eric Wolf ([1982] 1997: 93) once remarked about kinship in world-wide relations of power and history aptly applied to Henoko: "In the escalation of kinship from a set of interpersonal relations to the political order, kinship becomes a governing ideological [and, I would add, material] element in the allocation of political power." And yet, as Wolf also suggested, no kinship system is immune to larger political and historical forces. Henoko kinship patterns, too, were disrupted because, for example, many firstborn sons, as well as a large number of their siblings, died in the war. Moreover, after the construction of Camp Schwab, marriage patterns changed drastically. While intercommunal marriages (small-scale exogamy) within northern Okinawa as well as intracommunal marriages (endogamy) had been the basic rules of marriage before the war, after the appearance of Camp Schwab quite a few Henoko women began marrying U.S. servicemen. Henoko residents also began marrying those from outside communities who came to Henoko to explore business and commercial opportunities. In short, owing to the influx of men (U.S. servicemen and others) and women into Henoko during its transformation period (ca. 1957–1972), and because of the permanent settlement of these men and women in Henoko, new affinal relations were necessarily formed, sub-lineages were created, and social-political relations became formidably complicated.

However, at a closer look, although the form of kin structure might have become complicated and, thus, somewhat damaged by Henoko's structural transformation, the substances of kinship remained intact. Among them were the high regard native *munchū*s receive for being the "originators" of Henoko, the importance of blood ties to these and other *munchū*s (which residents refer to as *shinseki*, a more generic term that signifies blood relatives), and the power ascribed to men (over women) and seniors (over the youth) as derived from primogeniture. In practice, after the establishment of Camp Schwab, kinship was restructured by Henoko as a primary social institution to absorb its ever diversifying residents without being hijacked by them.

Take, for example, Sueyoshi Kaoru, fifty-six (as of January 1998—see note 2), arguably the most powerful man in Henoko in the late 1990s. Sueyoshi considered himself a typical Henoko man, precisely because he is *not* a "genuine" native Henoko resident. In fact, his grandfather moved to Henoko before the war from an outside community and married a woman from *Iheya*, a major Henoko descent group. The blood relationship to *Iheya* provided a necessary (if not a sufficient) basis for him to enter the communal political structure.

Aggressive, bold, yet generous, Sueyoshi Kaoru first asserted his preeminence in the 1970s by becoming the leader of *jikeidan*, the self-defense police unit Henoko youth organized to protect the community from the everyday turmoil caused by U.S. servicemen, Okinawan organized gangs, and others. His talent was also evident in his successful engagement in and eventual monopolization of Henoko's beer-bottle collection business. Trusted by the elderly leaders of Henoko, in the 1980s Sueyoshi became a key member of the Henoko administration, and then, in the 1990s, the chair of the Henoko Executive Committee (HEC) within the Henoko administration. In the late 1990s, the HEC was composed of twelve relatively older male representatives[10] chosen from each of Henoko's twelve residential units called *han*. These men made decisions, usually behind closed doors, on such important community matters as budget, Camp Schwab, staff member changes, and the schedule of social events. Each HEC representative was tied to a circle of relatives (on the basis of kinship) and friends (on the basis of work and play), which helped the HEC constitute itself as the core of a densely meshed information-social-surveillance network. Until the year 2002, Sueyoshi was not only the chair of the HEC, but also a power in city-wide politics and beyond as chief of Nago City Fire Station. Today, retired from public life yet exerting enormous political influence within Henoko, Sueyoshi is deeply thankful for Henoko's openness to an out-of-towner like him, which (as he told me) "has helped a boisterous young brainless guy like me become a full-fledged adult."

Sueyoshi's life is only one example of Henoko's "openness." As of 1998, seven HEC representatives (less than 60 percent of the total number of

HEC representatives) were from Henoko's "native" descent groups, and the remaining five (more than 40 percent) were from newer households established after the installation of Camp Schwab. Aforementioned Ōshiro Jirō and Yagaji Noriyuki—both older, powerful leaders within Henoko who had worked under Yagaji Ippan, a communal monarch mentioned above, in the 1960s and who, by the end of the 1990s, came to have more symbolic than substantial authority vis-à-vis Sueyoshi and the HEC—were not "genuine" Henoko residents either. Just like Sueyoshi's ancestors, Ōshiro Jirō's and Yagaji Noriyuki's were originally from outside Henoko, and their access to the communal power structure was enabled by the marriage of their ancestors to women from dominant *munchū*s.

If anything, Sueyoshi marked Henoko as a product of the new blood of out-of-towners blended with the old blood of the major native descent groups. Since the 1960s, the kinship system continued to function as a millwheel, whereby out-of-towners were constantly incorporated, socialized, and assimilated into Henoko, its pro-base practices, and its working-class sentiment and ideology of difference. In other words, kinship opened up a social space in which a particular type of power manifested itself not through the conventional governing principle of exclusion and inhibition, but through a new principle of inclusion, socialization, diversification, and hybridization. The lasting significance of the kinship system and related cultural practices may become even clearer as we examine, below, the status of women, the youth (including mixed-blood children), and U.S. servicemen in Henoko.

Women in Kinship

The status of women in Okinawa is complex and the key to understanding it is primogeniture—a built-in mechanism of Okinawan kinship with three different dimensions: (1) The oldest son inherits land, fortunes, and other privileges of his *munchū* to create the main family; (2) younger sons, when they marry, create branch households under the authority of the main family and in doing so, collectively contribute to expansion of the *munchū* as a corporate unit; and (3) daughters, once married, are expected to produce male children to maintain and extend the lineage of their husband's descent group (similarly composed of one main family and many branch families).

My sense is that after the appearance of Camp Schwab in Henoko, the distinction between the oldest and younger sons lost its significance in the increasingly affluent community, because there was enough fortune to be evenly distributed to all male children. Ironically, this change was accompanied and complemented by a parallel process whereby women became increasingly bound and controlled in kinship.

For instance, when a woman from a major Henoko descent group marries a native Henoko man, she formally exits her own descent group (i.e., she usually takes the name of her husband) to enter her husband's descent group. But still, she is implicitly expected to introduce her husband into her own descent group through various social functions (e.g., weddings, funerals, festive events, and religious ceremonies). As a result, unless she chooses to leave Henoko with her husband to establish their own household somewhere else, her marriage often constitutes a field of contestation between her own kin group and her husband's kin group. Although her status as a wife is doubly secured, her autonomy as a woman is also doubly suppressed by the two descent groups to which she now relates.

The plight of the Henoko woman is exemplified by the experiences of the wife of one influential native Henoko man. Coming from one of the major *munchū*s in Henoko, this wife, then in her forties, was torn between the opinion of her husband who, following the line of thought of the HEC, endorsed the offshore base and the opinion of her own relatives in her *munchū*, who strongly opposed the base. When I tried to draw her out, she could only say to me, "It would be nicer if Henoko would be quiet." Examples of women immobilized in the web of kin relations are numerous. In the late 1990s, while households—including both the main and branch households—of the four native *munchū*s (*Yagaji, Yamashiro, Iheya,* and *Furugen*) added up to only (or as much as—depending on the perspective) one-fifth of the total number of Henoko's households (approximately four hundred), the influence of these descent groups was felt pervasively, because of the complex shadow work done by these women through marriage.

It should be noted, however, that the category of "woman" itself is not monolithic. For clarity, it will be useful to look at five situations of marriage and kinship that put women in different social positions: (1) A woman migrating to Henoko (whom I will call a "non-native woman") marrying a man born in Henoko (a "native Henoko man"); (2) a non-native woman marrying a non-native man; (3) a native Henoko woman marrying a non-native man; (4) a native Henoko woman marrying a native Henoko man; and (5) single women (native or non-native) living in Henoko.[11] I have just discussed Situation 4. Let us consider the remaining four situations, including some examples, which demonstrate that women have not been excluded from Henoko's social life, but subordinated within it through kinship and marriage.

One night before the Nago City referendum in December 1997—which asked Nago and Henoko residents if they would support or reject the construction of the offshore base (see chapters 5 and 6)—I was with anti-base activist and Henoko resident Kinjō Yōji,[12] who was walking throughout Henoko to persuade residents to vote against the offshore base. When we entered one of the houses, the housewife, a non-native woman in her forties married to a native Henoko man (Situation 1), started to desperately speak: "Yūji-san," she said, "I am really distressed. For several days, I have been just so depressed." While she definitely opposed the offshore base construction because of its obvious destructive impacts on the living conditions in Henoko, she was not able to express her opinion openly. First of all, as a non-Henoko woman, she was assimilated into the existing *munchū* in which she was, by definition of Okinawan kinship (i.e., primogeniture), deprived of power. In addition, she was stressed out by the fact that while her husband was against the new base, his brother, a man of influence in Henoko, was pro-base and put pressure on him. Furthermore, she felt uncomfortably restrained in her workplace, a local enterprise supporting the idea of the new base. All of these circumstances put her in an extremely difficult position.

For a non-native woman married to a non-native man (Situation 2), the dynamics of the communal kin structure work differently. Many non-native women came to Henoko because of the money-making opportunities opened up by the presence of Camp Schwab, and were married to non-native men who came to Henoko for similar reasons. Once married, the husbands of these women, as a vital economic force in the community, were often incorporated into the Henoko Executive Committee as its representatives or associates. Therefore, any negative opinions about the U.S. base expressed by these women would not only contradict the fact that they had financially benefited from the presence of the U.S. base, but also disturb the pro-base communal order enforced by the HEC. Consequently, many of the non-native women (e.g., hostesses, employees, and/or owners of bars and restaurants) married to non-native men were reluctant to talk about the offshore base construction altogether, and were ready to acquiesce to the plan.

However, this does not mean that these women did not have any emotions and thoughts about what they did. For instance, a non-native woman in her forties who ran a bar in Henoko with her husband (a non-native man, who supported the base) did express, though not openly, her opposition to the new base. "I don't like Marines. They are arrogant," she said, showing me numerous dollar bills with servicemen's scribbles on them that had been tacked up on the wall behind the bar's counter since the days of the Vietnam War. The bill she pointed out to me read, "The U.S. doesn't live in Okinawa, Okinawa lives in the U.S." She added, "If the new base is built, I will leave Henoko with my children."

The position of a Henoko woman married to a non-Henoko man (Situation 3) was more subtle, yet equally difficult. If she were to leave Henoko with her husband, she would be considered to be married out, and as such, the existing kin structure in Henoko would not be disturbed. And yet if she were to remain in Henoko, the pressure of kinship would fall back on her. This situation was most acutely revealed by those Henoko women married to U.S. serviceman now living in Henoko. A native woman in her fifties had been married to a U.S. serviceman. The couple had several children, some of whom had already been married and had their own children. When Kinjō Yūji visited their house to solicit signatures to oppose the base, the woman's mother (in her seventies) dropped in. The old woman expressed her opposition, on the grounds that she was protecting the well-being of her great-grand children. The wife of the U.S. serviceman said, however, "I myself am against the planned base; but I don't want to sign here because I don't know what other people in Henoko would say about me." To openly oppose the U.S. base, I gathered, would contradict who she was at many levels—by defying her husband (a U.S. serviceman), pro-base relatives, and therefore herself as a Henoko woman.

Allow me to conclude this section with a couple of episodes about single women (native or non-native) who lived at the margin of Henoko's communal life (Situation 5 above) in order to highlight some further predicaments of Okinawan women in kinship. The first episode concerns a single woman in her fifties. In a deserted, small bar in the upper commercial area where she worked, she told me that she was from a poor nearby village in northern Okinawa and had moved to Henoko in its heyday to work as a bar hostess. The oldest of five siblings (two younger brothers, two younger sisters, and herself), she needed to support her family by sending home $200 a month, as her mother was blind and her father had died at an early age. Time spent with her would cost a U.S. serviceman $5. The money she made enabled the family to remodel their thatch-roofed house and her sisters and brothers to attend and graduate from high school; she was very proud of the financial contributions she had made to her family. Nevertheless, one day, the elder of her two brothers during a quarrel disdainfully called her *panpan*, a derogative term meaning prostitute, which so chagrined her that she immediately grabbed a kitchen knife and shouted, "Say that word again! I will kill you!" As the privileged, protected oldest son (because of primogeniture in the Okinawan lineage system), "He would not understand how I felt when I had to sell myself," she said, half crying. "I would never forgive my brother, never."

The second episode concerns a single native Henoko woman in her mid-forties. Just before the Nago City referendum, she called the office of the anti-base Society for the Protection of Life in Henoko. She said, in paraphrase, "I consulted with my *shinseki* (a blood relative) on the offshore base issue because I am against it, but it turned out that this person was actually 'for' the construction. She will spread the word about my stance. I can no longer keep companionship here." In the midst of my fieldwork, her mental condition deteriorated, and she was briefly hospitalized. While the exact cause of the worsening of her mental condition was beyond the reach of my investigation, this incident was indicative of the amount of pressure kinship exercises on women.

Youth in Henoko:
Questions of Seniority Rule

One day in the winter of 1998, I was at a club located in Camp Schwab with several young Henoko men who were the key members of the Henoko Youth Association (HYA). When I asked what they thought of Camp Schwab, they proudly took me to this club, adding that they considered this base part of their community, their "playground."[13] Over beer, one of them mentioned the generation gap between the young and the old: "It's impossible for us to comprehend the feelings of grandpas and grandmas [who oppose the offshore base construction] because we didn't experience the war." Another jumped in, "Just because the offshore base is to be constructed doesn't mean that war will break out." In the minds of these young men, the functions of the base were detached from the actualities of war and killing, which led them to conclude that "we should view the offshore base construction not as a loss of Okinawan dignity [as some anti-base activists insisted] but as an opportunity. If we keep saying 'no' to the base, nothing [in this deserted community] will change." As to the existing base, one man stated, "Of course, it's true that we have been dependent on the base. But it makes us upset when servicemen commit crimes here in our community." However, overall, the beneficial aspects of the base were emphasized as he continued, "The Henoko mountain would be a barren forest that doesn't produce anything. By utilizing it as military land, we've made a living." Still another added, "If the U.S. military leaves Okinawa, Japan won't be able to defend itself. If this happens, we will be conscripted to defend Japan. I don't want to be conscripted."

I interpret the positive view of the U.S. military among HYA members, often remarkably pure and straightforward,[14] not as a genuine expression of their own thought. Rather, I see it as a reproduction of what adults kept talking to these youngsters during the formative years of their development as Henoko men. This interpretation derives from my observation concerning the shift of the points of application of primogeniture in Henoko from the material life to ideological grounds. More specifically, while primogeniture as a material rule of inheritance—whereby land and other fortunes of a kin group descend to the eldest son—largely dwindled after the establishment of Camp Schwab, from the 1960s on it continued to affect, as an ideological principle of male seniority rule, a system of thought and sentiment of Henoko's young people in such a way as to emphasize the financial benefits of the U.S. military. A case in point is Sueyoshi Kaoru's following comment.

Once, in the midst of the offshore base dispute in 1997–98, a special program about the Henoko-Camp Schwab relationship was broadcast all over Japan by Nihon Hōsō Kyōkai (or NHK; Japan Broadcasting Corporation) (NHK 1997).[15] On this program, Sueyoshi Kaoru forcefully declared, "We adults must think about the economic future of Henoko for the sake of the young people. If someone says that we do not need a base, I will say to them, 'get out of Henoko right away.'" In ways that substantiated Sueyoshi's declaration, Henoko male adults instilled the pro-base sentiment, together with the fear of exclusion from the community, into the consciousness of young residents. The Henoko Youth Association (HYA) served—or, "used to serve," to be more precise (see below)—as the locus of the intergenerational transmission and reproduction of this sentiment.

Historically, the HYA had assumed a variety of functions, including an economic function as the labor force in the fields, a social function as a police force responsible for enforcing communal regulations, and a cultural function involving preparations for festivals, funerals, and other formal events (Henoko 1998: 456–60). However, after the construction of Camp Schwab in Henoko, the basic functions of the HYA underwent dramatic changes. First, economically, through the HYA the Henoko administration (i.e., male adults) distributed to young people not jobs in the field, but jobs in and around Camp Schwab as construction workers and guards as well as jobs in the entertainment quarter of Henoko as cooks, waiters, and shop clerks. Second, socially, the Henoko administration relegated the responsibilities of protecting the community from the violence of outsiders (such as drunken U.S. servicemen and quarrelsome Okinawan gangsters) to HYA members, who in turn organized a self-defense police force called *jikendan*. Third, culturally, the HYA was held responsible for not only festivals, funerals, and other formal occasions inside the community, but also such events as the tug-of-war festival and the dragon-boat racing festival to which U.S. servicemen of Camp Schwab were invited. Actively participating in a range of Henoko's social life now structured around Camp Schwab, Henoko youth in the 1960s and 1970s endorsed, internalized, and reproduced the authority of pro-base Henoko male adults (i.e., the Henoko administration) even as they confronted, occasionally, this authority on budget and other administrative matters.

It should be noted, however, that in the late 1990s, the activities of the HYA, together with the ideological principle of male seniority rule embodied in them, met a serious obstacle because of the decline of the vitality of Henoko at large and its administration. Economically, the Henoko administration could no longer distribute jobs—construction- and entertainment-related jobs in Camp Schwab and/or in Henoko—to the youth in the way it had done twenty or thirty years before. (None of the HYA members I spoke with at the club in Camp Schwab in the winter of 1998 had a permanent job; all of them were desperately engaged in various kinds of part-time work, as cooks, carpenters, scaffolding men, and so forth.) Socially, the success of *jikendan* of the HYA was largely forgotten, as Henoko's deserted entertainment quarter had ceased to necessitate its police activities a long time ago. Culturally, while Henoko adults were individually involved in HYA activities by instructing children in *jūdō* and baseball, drinking and eating with young people on social occasions, and teaching them cultural traditions of Henoko (including a particular style of Okinawan drum dancing called *eisā*), one could hardly see any organized effort among Henoko adults to promote activities of young people in the community.

The decline of the importance of the HYA in the community is particularly clear if one takes its insurmountable membership problem into consideration. Until the 1970s, all young Henoko men were required to join and did join the HYA. In the late 1990s, however, only 30 men out of a total of 317 qualified residents (148 residents between 20 and 29 years of age and an additional 169 residents between 30 and 39 years of age[16]) were affiliated with the HYA, out of whom only ten or so were actively involved. With no rising generation of young leaders to take over, the HYA was run by those tied by blood to Henoko leaders such as Sueyoshi, Yagaji, and Ōshiro, and became essentially a puppet organization of the Henoko administration, to be used mainly as a work force on various social and festive occasions.[17] The majority of young residents in Henoko did not deny the value of the HYA, but did not actively support it either, and, upon graduating from high school, either looked for employment opportunities elsewhere or went on to college or vocational school outside Henoko.[18]

In sum, by the late 1990s the status of the HYA became quite shaky, if not completely ruined. The comment by Sueyoshi Kaoru ("we adults must think about the economic future of Henoko for the sake of the young people"), previously cited, can be seen not as an expression of power and confidence of Henoko adults and administration over the youth but as a manifestation of their uncertainty about the ideological principle of male seniority rule, which, together with the pro-base sentiment, used to be transmitted and reproduced through the HYA.

From a slightly different angle, mixed-blood children—those born of Okinawan mothers and American GIs—specifically spoke of the problematic hegemony of the Henoko administration. The number of mixed-blood children increased in Henoko—like other communities hemmed in by military installations—after it began interacting with Camp Schwab in the late 1950s; in the late 1990s, between twenty and thirty mixed-bloods were residing in Henoko, the oldest of whom were still in their twenties. Some of their fathers were Caucasians, some Mexican-Americans, and some black Americans. Although many of their fathers had abandoned them and their Okinawan mothers, some had settled in Henoko. While mixed-bloods, seen as "corrupt" hybrids bereft of pure Okinawan-ness, had often been discriminated against in Okinawa at large, they were generally well blended into Henoko and its youth culture because of Henoko's affinity with the American base. The president of the HYA in the late 1990s, in fact, was a mixed-blood.

Nonetheless, young mixed-bloods often revealed particularities that dislodged Henoko's attempts to assimilate, socialize, and ultimately control the youth via the male seniority rule principle. A half-American/half-Okinawan woman in her mid-twenties exemplified this. At one level, in a way that faithfully traced and reproduced the pro-base view of adult Henoko men, she showed an instinctive dislike of anti-base movements in Okinawa, saying, "If the U.S. military did not exist in Okinawa, who would protect Japan? Many Okinawans use Americans without thanking them." Nevertheless, her pro-base stance was complicated by the fact that she was not purely "Henokoan." As such, her anti-base sentiment like "When the anti-base people said, 'Yankees go home,' I was hurt because I felt like I was being discriminated against" was juxtaposed with her critique of pro-base Henoko men such as the core members of the Henoko Yoth Association: "In their early twenties, these men already develop beer bellies and become spiritless. Their world is so small, so confined within Henoko. I would never marry a man from Henoko." I take this dismissive statement as a subtle critique of the male seniority rule in Henoko which, after all, shaped the world of these HYA members, and as an expression of her desire to experience a larger world. Although she was embarrassed by the fact that she could not speak English, her racial-gender status as a half-American woman nevertheless enabled her to imagine the trajectory of her own life in a way that was different from many men enclosed in Henoko.

In sum, at one level the Okinawan kinship system structured by the rule of primogeniture manifested itself in the logic of seniority control, wherein the value of coexistence and coprosperity with the base (i.e., "we are Okinawans but of a different kind") was transmitted from one generation to the next, and in the process the youth were socialized as much as controlled within Henoko's social space. At another level, however, the rationale for seniority rule was rapidly dwindling because of the weakening socialization power of the Henoko administration. Young residents (including the mixed-bloods) often went beyond the confined boundaries of the communal life.

Lonely Marines

The governing principle of socialization, hybridization, and control that we have examined thus far—a principle based on nondiscursive social ties of kinship that enabled Henoko to assimilate out-of-towners, women, youth, and mixed-bloods—spilled over into the treatment of U.S. servicemen. This principle was, however, subtly modified by the specific trope of *shinzen* (friendship), which had long enabled Henoko not only to include this particular Other into Henoko's life world based on relations of blood and place, but also to carefully differentiate and forever separate him from it.

The crucial administrative interface that attempted to promote "harmony and friendship" between Henoko and Camp Schwab and to "solve any kind of problems or troubles that may occur among the military and [the] local [community]" (Henoko/Schwab Friendship Council 1998: 1) was the *Henoko-Shuwābu Shinzen Īnkai* (Henoko/Schwab Friendship Council). The 1998 council meeting—held on March 3 at the Henoko administration building—highlights the basic characteristics of the Henoko-Schwab "friendship."[19] The attendees were twenty-two officers (all men) from the Camp Schwab side (including the Commanding Officer), and twenty-two Henoko residents (all men, pro-base) from the Henoko side (including Henoko Executive Committee Chair Sueyoshi Kaoru, HEC representatives, as well as bar/restaurant owners, among others). First, the Camp Schwab Commanding Officer made opening remarks, followed by the Henoko district mayor (the intermediate authority working under the HEC), who replied with welcoming remarks. The Henoko mayor then proceeded to talk to the base authorities about such concerns as a recent robbery incident in Henoko, a theft incident in Okinawa City (located in central Okinawa), and an incident in which a serviceman spied on a local teenage girl in a bathroom of a Henoko house, all of which had been committed in

January 1998 by Camp Schwab Marines. To these concerns, Camp Schwab authorities answered with the same cliché that the Deputy Camp Commanding Officer once directed to me in an interview: "Being good neighbors, we shall prudently ensure that we take every measure to prevent any future incidents."

Following the council meeting, a gathering was held at which Okinawan food was served, a *kanpai* (cheers) toast was made, and attendees ate, drank, and talked with each other. Command of the Japanese language among U.S. military personnel was, however, less than minimal, and command of the English language among Henoko residents was no better, though some residents rattled off such words as "party [pārī]," "water [wārā]," "fuck you [fackku yū]" and so forth which, sounding like English, amused the servicemen. Because of continuous interactions with Camp Schwab over a forty-year span, Henoko residents had acquired American accents for these and other words without ever learning how to construct more complex sentences necessary for meaningful communication. A few short conversations and some "baby talk" thus took place here and there in English, while the Okinawan interpreter—a Camp Schwab public relations officer—was busy translating many conversations back and forth. But then the interpreter became too busy, and as a result servicemen simply started to talk with the interpreter or amongst themselves in English, while Henoko residents spoke to each other in their own language. The gathering ended relatively early because the Marines had training the following day. The Henoko men, on the other hand, stayed up late drinking amongst themselves in the houses and bars in their district.

The above description reveals three different yet interrelated functions of "friendship." First, the idea of friendship enabled Henoko to rearticulate and redefine the unequal political relationship from the perspective of the weak. Originally, in 1957, Camp Schwab had taken the initiative in establishing the Henoko/Schwab Friendship Council in the midst of the base construction (Henoko 1998: 623) so as to cover up, essentially, the power differential between Henoko and the U.S. military. In the late 1990s, however, Henoko actively appropriated "friendship" so as to connect "us" and "them" (e.g., by holding a gathering with the U.S. military), while at the same time distancing "them" as someone who did not belong to "our" world (e.g., by avoiding drinking with them). Second, in the process, the notion of friendship also defined basic parameters of a particular gender politics in favor of Henoko. That is, "friendship" helped Henoko men establish homo-social bonds with the U.S. servicemen (note that no women attended the Henoko/Schwab Friendship Council), generating a de-sexualized context of intercultural communication in which making advances on local women would violate the principles of "friendship." In other words, the U.S. military found itself being welcomed and simultaneously monitored and controlled in an inclusive/exclusive world of friendship, devoid of women. Third, in spite of Henoko's intent to assert itself vis-à-vis the U.S. military, friendship nonetheless perpetuated Henoko's economic dependence on Camp Schwab. That is, Henoko's various friendship activities (e.g., festivals, meetings, and parties with U.S. servicemen) would not have been possible without the rent money Henoko acquired from Camp Schwab. In other words, Henoko depended on "them" even as it constructed "we-ness." In these ways, "friendship" effected complex, mutual (but not equal) appropriations, negotiations, and compromises between Self and Other.

On August 3, 1997, when *ōzunahiki*, the great tug-of-war festival, was held, the excitement and enthusiasm of the festival once more revealed the complexities of friendship. This festival, seen as a timeless, "exotic" local cultural practice by U.S. servicemen, had not even taken place for the first seventeen or eighteen years after the battle of Okinawa. In the mid-1970s, then, it was reinvented by the Henoko administration as a promising way to revitalize the economically declining community after the Vietnam War. The local administration had put a great deal of effort into this special event, which took place once every three years, in order to reinforce the ties between Henoko and Camp Schwab. It so happened that the 1997 *ōzunahiki* was held in the midst of the offshore base dispute to be discussed in chapters 5 and 6, and the festival became an ideal opportunity for Henoko to publicize to the outside world its intimacy with the existing base and to lay the groundwork for accepting the new one. Virtually all households in Henoko were mobilized and held responsible for hand-weaving a 50 cm (19.68 in.) segment of a small rope (to be used as a handle) that would be attached to a giant main rope which was as long as 150 meters (492 ft.).

On the day of the festival, the entire community was filled with excitement. In the morning, men came out to twist and twine the rope. Once finished, they carried it over to the major intersection of the entertainment quarter, where members of the Henoko Youth Association were busy setting up a stage and tents. By late afternoon, Henoko residents, Marines, and others had gathered around the stage for live performances of rock music by Henoko youth, band music by Marines dressed in their uniforms, Okinawa's traditional *eisā* drum dance, the fire dance, and swordplay, among other events. Everybody looked pleased. One resident proudly told me, "Okinawa is large, but no place in Okinawa has gotten along better with the U.S. servicemen than Henoko."

Later in the evening, the giant rope was finally placed in front of the spectators, now numbering two thousand or more. With intense anticipation for the tug-of-war to begin, Marines and Okinawans, men and women, young and old, divided themselves up into two groups, and on the whistle cue, finally, began pulling on opposite ends of the rope with all their might against the background of massive cheers. When witnessing such an event, one may be tempted to celebrate it as a beautiful moment of multiculturalism, wherein different cultures, genders, and ages embraced one another, even to the point of appreciating the U.S. military presence in Okinawa, which had made such wonderful "friendship" possible in the first instance.

Notably, included in the audience were the bureaucrats of the Japanese government's Defense Facilities Agency who were taking pictures of seemingly happy residents and servicemen mingling together during the event. One such picture was used in a pamphlet (Futenma Hikōjō Isetsu Taisaku Honbu 1997) distributed by the Japanese government in its promotion of the offshore base construction. What is more, images of Henoko residents getting along with the base and its servicemen—along with Sueyoshi's statement, cited earlier, concerning the economic future of Henoko—were also broadcast by NHK (1997) and viewed by the entire nation.

Whatever the intentions of NHK and the Japanese government may have been, however, this festive event also revealed that in truth, there were no substantial, meaningful, or lasting interactions between Henoko residents and the U.S. Marines. Yes, they did engage in a playful tug-of-war together, but the boundaries between the world of Okinawan civilians and that of U.S. Marines were maintained, even reinforced, because of the overall absence of communication between the two. After the festival, Marines and residents simply scattered in different directions, often without exchanging parting remarks or farewells, while the former went back to Camp Schwab and the latter drank and chatted until late at night in their community. I found that the young Marines felt happy because they were allowed to participate in this "exotic" Okinawan cultural practice under the name of "friendship." However, at the same time they also felt somewhat frustrated and alienated because, also under the name of "friendship," they were not included as equals but enshrined as distant guests. They were isolated and lonely.

Young Marines' sense of isolation and loneliness was reinforced by harsh training programs to which they submitted and a specific class position in which they were put. One of my military informants was a twenty-year-old white single mother, who belonged to a unit composed of four female and seventy-four male Marines. Part of her duty consisted of driving military trucks for twenty-four straight hours. She had joined the Marine Corps in order to pay the medical bills and other expenses for her two-year-old daughter, who lived in Pennsylvania with her mother. Another white Marine in his early twenties from Colorado joined the Marine Corps because he wanted to have "a respected career," and because "I needed to work." He underwent training programs that included diving into a muddy pond 10 meters (33 ft.) deep and gripping a rope suspended from a helicopter. From a slightly different perspective, another serviceman, a black sergeant from California, told me that he suffered from the racism that was prevalent in the military, but that he continued to serve because he needed the GI Bill to pay back the student loans that he had taken out in order to attend college.

Indeed, I found that most of the enlisted Marines, if not officers, joined the military not necessarily out of patriotism and a sense of duty, but often out of financial need; the U.S. military provided them one of but a few social avenues for moving upward (cf. Moskos and Wood, eds. 1988). For this reason, many Marines did not intend to make the Corps their career. Bought at the margin of the labor market, they went through years of harsh training and active duty, which were conducted in complete isolation from the civilian society, while solitarily dreaming about the day they would exit the military and get the money they deserved.

Loneliness afflicted not only young enlisted men, but also some officers. While the former in many cases did not know the political conditions and histories of Okinawa (several of them said, "We are doing what the U.S. government told us to do"), officers were commonly aware of the tensions their presence had generated in Okinawa as well as the pressure to downsize the Marine Corps there, particularly after the rape incident. One officer in Camp Schwab expressed to me the fragile self-confidence. Although the

Air Force is more popular than the Marine Corps because of the image associated with, say, Tom Cruise in *Top Gun*, "They have been around only fifty years. We have been around since the United States has been around, so we have a lot of traditions." He wanted to say, perhaps, "We are better than the Air Force. But people do not appreciate the Marine Corps." Another officer complemented this thought with the unsentimental comment to the effect that "if Okinawan people do not want us to stay here, we should pack up and leave."

Camp Schwab tried to relieve Marines' (both enlisted men's and officers') stress by providing an "American style" environment. There was a movie theater complex, a gym, a bowling alley, a swimming pool, a food court, a bank, a post office, a laundromat, two clubs, several beach volleyball courts, and other recreational facilities in Camp Schwab. At one level, such a compassionate arrangement may have helped alleviate the stress on young Marines. At another level, however, when combined with the disappearance of the economic advantages U.S. servicemen had enjoyed in Okinawa in the 1960s and the tightening of Marine Corps discipline after the 1995 rape incident, the "American style" environment may have aggravated their isolation and alienation. As to money, in the 1960s Marines certainly had enormous economic advantages over Okinawans, because women and other forms of "entertainment" had been "cheap," but such advantages had disappeared as Okinawa's living standards became ever higher. As I stated in chapter 2, in the late 1990s, U.S. military salaries—a Lance Corporal in the Marine Corps after two years of service earned about $1,200 a month— did not even allow them to buy more than a couple of bottles of beer a night in Okinawa (one bottle of beer would cost at least $5), let alone a woman.

Tightened discipline also confined Marines into the "American style" environment more and more. For instance, those Marines who were scheduled to stay in Okinawa less than six months did not, practically speaking, have the freedom of movement because they were prohibited from driving in Okinawa owing to the growing criticism from Okinawans about traffic accidents involving young, uninsured Marines (Camp Schwab Public Relations Officer 1998).[20] Curfew orders were often issued by the military authorities in response to Okinawans' complaints about crimes and misbehaviors of Marines. In addition, enlisted men were expected to attend more and more "educational programs" (lectures, videos, etc.) on the history of Okinawa and the feelings of Okinawans about the military, which were provided by the Japanese ministry of Foreign Affairs (*Ryukyu Shinpo*, October 3, 1995). Exhausted by training, monitored by officers, Japanese officials, and Okinawans both within and outside the base, and without much money, young "service members feel oppressed, and suffer from frustration due to differences in culture and life-style"[21] (*Ryukyu Shinpo Weekly News*, October 17, 1995).

As a last resort, Marines were encouraged to actively seek "friendship" with Henoko residents. However, the irony here is that if Marines stayed on the base, they felt lonely, but leaving the base made them feel even lonelier, because in this so-called "friendship," American servicemen were connected to but still very much alienated from, Henoko residents. I felt an unexpected, bitter dimension inherent in Henoko's idea of "friendship" specifically when several pro-base residents stated, "I don't want my daughter to marry an American," or "When the money is gone, the friendship will also be gone."

Predicaments of the Henoko Administration

In summary, Henoko actively mediated, appropriated, and absorbed the profound social impacts of Camp Schwab for the transformation of its own economic-political-cultural structure. Henoko did not try to overthrow the U.S. military; rather, it tried to make do within, and come to terms with, the emerging social order (or really disorder) that the base had triggered. In the process, Henoko reinvented kinship and related cultural practices—marriage and male seniority rule, especially—which, operating as an internal social mechanism through which to assimilate out-of-towners, women, the youth, and mix-bloods, functioned to diversify and expand nondiscursive ties of blood and place in the community. The same cultural practices also functioned, externally, as a buffer against the imposed impact from the base, enabling Henoko to exclude U.S. servicemen from the ties of blood and place at one level, but also to recycle and contain them into the community through the cultural practices of "friendship" at another. The fundamentally pro-base, working-class sentiment of "we are Okinawans but of a different kind" is a historical product of Henoko's internal and external adaptation process to the American base. In the late 1990s, this sentiment came to be re-inscribed by the Henoko administration as Tokyo and Washington announced the planned construction of the new base off the waters of Camp Schwab.

The Henoko administration stated that in principle it was opposed to the new base while claiming, in addition, that more time was needed in order to listen to the diverse voices of Henoko residents—implying that under exceptional circumstances the base would be accepted. There were three reasons for this ambiguous, although ultimately pro-base, attitude, which together highlight Henoko's complex position of being "different" from the rest of Okinawa.

First, the ambiguity of the Henoko administration about the matter of the new base went hand in hand with its implicit and calculated desire to make a deal with the Japanese government on the Henoko administration's own terms, if it really needed to accept the base. In other words, the moment Henoko would make a gesture toward accepting the base, the nuisance facility that only a handful of Okinawans wanted, it would lose its bargaining power and political upper hand vis-à-vis the national government. Thus, before saying "yes" to the government, Henoko needed to secure as much financial compensation as possible. Therefore, the Henoko administration had to indefinitely defer its decision to accept the planned base without actually rejecting the plan. Ideally for the Henoko administration, it would be Nago City, Okinawa Prefecture, and the Japanese government, but not the Henoko administration itself, that decided that Henoko must make the "anguished decision" (*kujyū no ketsudan*, the Okinawan/Japanese cliché meaning to accept the unacceptable). That way, the Henoko administration could mask its desire to receive economic compensation.

Second, by its double-sided tactic of opposing the base in principle and accepting it under exceptional circumstances, the Henoko administration kept the increasing pro-base voice at bay, while allowing itself to dodge opposing voices, who were already posing a latent threat to the communal political order. In effect, by leaving its position slippery, the administration intended to let conventional nondiscursive ties of kinship and place stifle public discussions about the U.S. military, thereby continuously maintaining communal harmony and enveloping the majority of residents in the pro-base, working-class ideology of difference. It should be added, however, that because public discussions about the new base were suppressed, the atmosphere of Henoko was made palpably tense, uneasy, and nervous when it became the topic of heated discussions outside Henoko—

in Okinawa, mainland Japan, and beyond. Eventually, the communal nervousness reached an absolute breaking point at which anti-base arguments started to take specific shape.

Third, the ambiguity of the Henoko administration about the matter of the new base needs to be understood in reference to its own *ryōshin no kashaku* (qualms of conscience). In fact, the local administration was very aware of the ethical problems of outright utilitarianism—ceding Okinawa's autonomy in exchange for money—the problems that were thrown into relief against the background of the pervasive anti-base sentiment in the rest of Okinawa after the 1995 rape incident. Indeed, most of the representatives in the pro-base Henoko Executive Committee shared anger at the rape of an Okinawan girl and worried about the potential deterioration of Henoko's environment with the construction of the new base. One of the representatives, who was active in inviting the base, told me with a sigh, "Inoue-san, if we had jobs, we would not invite the base, such a noisy thing." Another representative hesitantly commented, "I still think it better to keep the quiet community as is" (Ishikawa M. 1998: 27). To be sure, representatives of the Henoko administration often apologetically said, "Most of the residents against the offshore base are financially secure civil servants. But we do not have jobs. In order to make a living, we need the new base." Nonetheless, their attitudes toward the offshore base were not straightforward, but fundamentally ambiguous and uncertain because of the qualms of conscience.

It is this conscience—obscured by economic concerns of poor Henoko residents—that the anti-base movements articulated, expanded, and reinforced, as will be shown in the chapters that follow. It is also this shared conscience that will help us envision—in the final chapter of my book—the possibilities of unity between anti-base movements and pro-base sentiments in Okinawa in spite of their apparent contradictions.

5

"WE ARE OKINAWANS":

Local Identity in a Global Perspective

 While the Henoko administration appropriated the U.S. military presence for the economic ends of Henoko, and in so doing absorbed diverse residents into the working-class, communal ideology of "We are Okinawans but of a different kind," this process involved suppressing latent feelings of opposition against the local administration and, by implication, against the U.S. military. Seizing the political opportunity opened up by the offshore base dispute, some middle-class Henoko residents—including those from native and wealthy yet marginalized descent groups, women who viewed nature and peace as critical to the welfare of their children, and senior citizens who had gone through the tragedy and atrocity of the battle of Okinawa—organized *Inochi Wo Mamoru Kai* (the Society for the Protection of Life) to consolidate Henoko's anti-administration and anti-base energies. In this chapter, we will explore, in reference to complex negotiations across local, national, and global levels, the ways in which Henoko became entangled in the offshore base dispute—whether or not Okinawa should accept a replacement base of Futenma in Henoko. We will then see how from various perspectives Henoko residents articulated and politicized Okinawa's collective experiences of war, subjugation, and gender oppression with the assertion of unity: "We are Okinawans."

"We Are Okinawans"

The Offshore Base Dispute in Global Perspective

PREDICAMENTS OF GOVERNOR OTA

In April 1996, in order to relieve the political stress in Okinawa caused by the 1995 rape incident, the U.S. and Japanese governments announced the return of Futenma Air Station, a strategically significant United States Marine Corps base, to Okinawan control. The original form of Futenma was created out of the U.S. military's expropriation of land immediately after the battle of Okinawa in 1945 and, because of its size (500 hectares; 1,235 acres) and location (in the congested residential area of central Okinawa), had been a symbol of U.S. military presence in Okinawa. With a compromise that included the return of Futenma, something the Okinawa prefectural government had been requesting since the 1980s in light of the welfare and safety of the residents living in the area, Washington and Tokyo hoped to appease Okinawa's anger after the rape incident.

In truth, however, this compromise was also a rejection of the basic principle underlying Okinawa's protest—the reorganization and reduction of U.S. bases—for two reasons. First, with the subtle but unmistakable aid of the pro-government judicial power—the district court (in Naha; March 1996) and the Supreme Court (in Tokyo; August 1996) dismissed Ota's objection to the renewal of the land contracts for the U.S. military[1]—Tokyo finally forced Ota to give his approval for these contracts in September 1996, while at the same time beginning to prepare a special bill that would forever transfer power to sign the land lease for the U.S. military from Okinawa governor to Tokyo.[2] In addition, the U.S. and Japanese governments cleverly made the return of Futenma conditional on the construction of a substitute facility to be built in Okinawa—Washington was to give up one base, but get a replacement in return. On December 2, 1996, approximately eight months after the initial announcement, Washington and Tokyo formalized their proposal by having the Special Action Committee on Okinawa (SACO) announce its final report, which stated that the substitute facility would be constructed "off the east coast of the main island of Okinawa" (SACO [1996] 1997: 36). In more explicit geopolitical terms, this meant that the new facility would be built in the sea of Henoko, Nago City, where Camp Schwab is located.

In response to the Futenma replacement plan, which showed not so much the benevolence of the U.S.-Japan alliance as its cunning manipulation of Okinawa's protest, Governor Ota, however, evasively stated that "the issue is to be settled between the Japanese government and Nago City" (*Ryukyu Shinpo*, December 3, 1996). Ota's statement made a stark and curious contrast with his adamant opposition to the U.S. military presence in Okinawa, which he had earlier made clear in the wake of the rape incident. What happened to him? His statement and position, in fact, expressed the predicaments of Okinawan resistance within and against the nation-state and global power in their purest form.

Back in January 1996—after the 1995 rape incident, with evolving anti-base sentiments in Okinawa behind it—the Ota administration proposed *Kichi Henkan Akushion Puroguramu* (the Base Return Action Program), aiming for the return of Futenma by 2001 and the phased removal of all U.S. military bases by 2015. In November 1996, the Ota administration expanded the Action Program by issuing *Kokusai Toshi Keisei Kōsō* (the Grand Conception for Creating an International City). The basic assumption underlying the two proposals in general, and the Grand Conception in particular, was that the 20 percent of land mass on the island of Okinawa used by the U.S. military had long prevented Okinawa's economic development. These proposals further asserted that Okinawa would be able to transform itself into a hub of high-tech and other industries by removing the U.S. bases and redeveloping the vacant lots to Okinawa's benefit. Okinawa would gain, according to Ota's design, both peace and economic development once the U.S. bases were returned (Okinawaken Sōmubu Chiji Kōshitsu Kichi Taisakushitsu 1998a). Ota was, perhaps, in his heyday when he forcefully announced the Grand Conception.

SACO's final report on the conditional return of Futenma came in December 1996, after the announcement of the Base Return Action Program and the Grand Conception. With the report, the global form of power effectively reappropriated the thrust of Ota's grand design for its political ends and cleverly trapped him in a no-win situation. On the one hand, if Ota rejected the offshore base as proposed by SACO, Futenma would remain. This would mean, politically, that Okinawa would lose a chance to reduce the U.S. military presence on its soil[3] and, economically, that the massive subsidy money from Tokyo, to be provided in exchange for accepting the new base, would be withheld. Yet, on the other hand, accepting the new base might simply perpetuate the U.S. military presence, and thus undermine the very foundation of Ota's/Okinawa's anti-base protest after the rape incident. The governor was now put in the position in which he could neither reject nor accept the conditional return of Futenma that the U.S. and Japanese governments proposed.

In order to extricate Okinawa, and himself, from this no-win situation, Governor Ota needed to become a pragmatic politician in addition to being a peace idealist. His ambiguous statement that the issue of the offshore base construction was "to be settled between the Japanese government and Nago City" made this tactic possible. At one level, by shifting the burden of the offshore base issues onto the shoulders of peripheral northern Okinawa (Nago City), he subtly watered down and modified his explicit anti-base position, thereby implicitly accommodating the Japanese government's scheme to cooperate with U.S. global strategies. At another level, this repositioning, theoretically at least, should enable Ota to seek both peace (i.e., the return of Futenma) and economic development (i.e., the subsidy from Tokyo) for Okinawa at large; to satisfy the greatest number of people (both anti-base and pro-base Okinawans); and thereby to maintain and extend Okinawa's unity in negotiating with Tokyo. Governor Ota was thus trying to please everybody by simultaneously getting Futenma back, accepting the offshore base, and receiving money from Tokyo in return. However, his acrobatic attempt to solve Okinawa's predicaments resulted, ironically, in the breakdown of the Okinawan unity that Ota himself had created after the rape incident. This, in turn, triggered the Japanese government's intervention to exploit the split within Okinawa.

THE NAGO CITY MAYOR'S RESPONSE AND
THE CRISIS OF OKINAWA'S UNITY

The split within Okinawa became immediately apparent with Nago City's response to Governor Ota's statement that the offshore base construction issue was "to be settled between the Japanese government and Nago City." Expressing both helplessness and pride as the leader of marginalized northern Okinawa, Mayor Higa Tetsuya of Nago City condemned Ota, saying that "the northern region is not a trash-bin of military bases" (*Ryukyu Shinpo*, January 22, 1997). Speaking for Nago inhabitants at large, 72 percent of whom felt that there was an economic inequality between the poorer northern and the wealthier south-central parts of Okinawa (*Okinawa Taimusu*, December 9, 1997), the mayor further insisted that ever since the age of the Ryukyu Kingdom, south-central Okinawa had continuously dominated northern Okinawa by taking from the latter firewood (the mountainous north had long provided firewood before electricity became available in Okinawa), water (several dams in the north sent water all over Okinawa), and people (because of the lack of employment opportunities in the north, residents, particularly the youth, continuously moved into more prosperous central and southern Okinawa), without giving anything in return. Now the Ota administration was trying to put another U.S. military base, a nuisance facility no one wanted, in the north, when 70 percent of the U.S. bases in Okinawa were already concentrated in the northern part of the island. In July 1996, that is, after the conditional return of Futenma was announced (April 1996) and before the Futenma/offshore-base trade-off proposal had elicited Governor Ota's equivocal response (December 1996), Higa had organized a rally with his constituencies to declare that Nago would reject any new facilities within its boundaries and stated, "We are inflamed with anger to hear that the base will simply be moved around within Okinawa.... As the mayor, I swear I am determined to lead and take action against the strengthening of base functions in Okinawa" (*Ryukyu Shinpo*, July 11, 1996).

In spite of the mayor's adamant political rhetoric, however, many residents of Nago, Henoko residents included, felt that Ota's statement—"the issue is to be settled between the Japanese government and Nago City"—could give conservative Mayor Higa, in power for the past eleven years, a convenient excuse for accepting the new base. That is, by accusing Ota of being a selfish and evil power broker willing to sacrifice Nago for the interests of south-central Okinawa where Futenma was located, the mayor could pose himself as a righteous martyr forced to accept the offshore base while masking his desire to receive massive financial compensation from Tokyo in return. One rumor went that Nago City might accept the new base in order to wipe out the huge debts that had accumulated from several large-scale development projects, including the opening of a four-year college in the city in 1994. Another rumor went that in exchange for accepting the new base, Nago City would receive financial aid from Tokyo that would help redevelop the commercial district of Nago City (where the mayor's old supermarket happened to be located), an area that had been rapidly deteriorating owing to the recent establishment of several modern supermarkets in the newly developed areas outside downtown Nago.

In the fall of 1996, Henoko's needy construction companies, bars, and restaurants were already showing interest in the offshore base construction plan, and the Henoko administration, in not explicitly opposing the plan, implicitly endorsed it. Once the plan was officially announced in December 1996, the influential Northern Okinawa Construction Industry Association, which consisted in 260 construction companies all located in northern Okinawa and whose members were political supporters for Mayor Higa, decided to actively invite the planned base. At the prefectural level, the pro-base Liberal Democratic Party of Okinawa, which had backed Mayor Higa (as well as other conservative mayors in Okinawa), also supported the offshore base plan in order to secure a massive subsidy to be provided by Tokyo (*Ryukyu Shinpo*, December 8, 1996). There were voices of resignation, too; as one Henoko resident told me, "it is of no use trying to oppose the government. They will do it if they want to do it no matter what we say." Among the communities on Nago City's eastern coast, there was also an unarticulated sentiment that the new base might help solve the depopulation problem that they had been experiencing since the 1972 reversion (*Ryukyu Shinpo*, November 30, 1997). In Kayō, one of the thirteen communities located in the east, for example, 44 percent of the population was older than sixty-five years of age (Sōrifu 1995).

In brief, Mayor Higa's insistence on the ideal of an Okinawa without the U.S. military was already being undermined by the reality of the economic, historical, and political lag of northern Okinawa. Meanwhile, the Japanese and U.S. governments now found the fissures by which to transform Okinawa's unified opposition to the U.S–Japan alliance into internal conflicts within Okinawa. And the targeted site for the cultivation of such internal conflicts was the politically weak and economically needy Nago City, of which Henoko, the construction site of the new base, was part.

At the beginning of January 1997, the officials of Nago City and the Japanese government held a closed-door meeting in order to jointly map out a plan for the mayor's acceptance of the offshore base (*Okinawa Taimusu*, April 5, 1997). After that meeting, Mayor Higa's voice was clearly toned down. In his own words, "in principle, we oppose the offshore base" (*Okinawa Taimusu*, April 6, 1997), which implied that under exceptional circumstances, Nago

City would accept the base. At around the same time, the Henoko admin-istration also contrived to duplicate this ambiguous statement, giving itself and Nago City a convenient excuse for not intervening in the situation (see chapter 4), which was gradually moving toward to the base construction. In early April 1997, Mayor Higa formally accepted Tokyo's request to conduct the preparatory topographical survey of Henoko's sea, saying, "This does not mean that the new base will be built. It is just a preliminary survey" (*Ryukyu Shinpo*, April 19, 1997). Prime Minister Hashimoto (April 10), Director Gen-eral of the Defense Agency Kyuma (April 18), and Director General of the Defense Facilities Agency Morotomi (April 18)—who all belonged to the ruling Liberal Democratic Party—commented in Tokyo, "*arigatai* (we are very thankful to the mayor)."

THE CONSTRUCTION OF THE "INTIMATE SOCIETY" ACROSS THE PACIFIC

When the volatile political situation surrounding Okinawa came to be reoriented toward reinforcing the U.S.–Japan security alliance in a way specified above, the Pentagon, for its part, asserted and justified its "com-mitment" to the Asia-Pacific region, and in doing so, proceeded with the project of reinforcing the "intimate society" across the Pacific. The "inti-mate society," as defined in chapter 1, refers to the process by which the global form of power ("I") flexibly produces and controls Others ("you") by including them into a closed society of differential positions. Notably, "such a society is dual, a society of me and you. We are just among our-selves. Third parties are excluded" (Levinas 1998: 30). Indeed, in the 1990s U.S. strategic planners economically, militarily, and ideologically executed something of a program of planetary governance, not by oppressing the Asia-Pacific region with force but by soliciting its participation in today's U.S.-oriented, capitalist "intimate society."

At the economic level, America's goal of national prosperity became in-fused with its transnational project of reinforcing market capitalism in the Asia-Pacific region. The Pentagon acknowledged that "United States trade with the Asia-Pacific region in 1993 totaled over $374 billion and accounted for 2.8 million United State jobs" and that "the Pacific Rim today is col-lectively the United States' largest trading partner." The significance of the Asia-Pacific region—a key market for the success of the U.S. economy—

would increase, the Pentagon argued, because it would "account for about one-third of the world's economic activity at the start of the [21st] century." In short, "the stability and prosperity of the Asia-Pacific region is a matter of vital national interest affecting the well-being of all Americans" (Department of Defense 1995: 2, 6, 6, 7).

According to the Pentagon, at the security level, it is the U.S. military that must play a pivotal role in attaining prosperity of the Asia-Pacific region by maintaining its stability (Department of Defense 1995, 1998; SACO [1996] 1997). Indeed, the Pentagon insisted that the Asia-Pacific region remained, even after the end of the cold war, "an area of uncertainty, tension, and immense concentrations of military power"; this rhetoric was then juxtaposed with the Pentagon's typically comfortable view of itself, asserting that the U.S. military had been "viewed by almost every country in the region as a stabilizing force" (Department of Defense 1995: 2).

Needless to say, such a view, even if true, must be complemented and complicated by the observation that the U.S. military presence also caused many uncertainties and tensions within the region it claimed to reduce. For instance, for China, the U.S. military was indeed a stabilizer insofar as it curbed the remilitarization of Japan; but it was also a threat, because it placed China in a position somewhere between friend and enemy to the U.S. The increasing role of Japan's Self-Defense Forces, thoroughly integrated in the U.S. global strategies by the late 1990s, also provoked vigilant caution in South Korea, where, as was evidenced by the much publicized comfort women's issues (Yoshimi 1995), the scar of Japanese militarism was deeply felt. Furthermore, the monopoly of nuclear weapons by the U.S. and other industrialized Western nations triggered—not discouraged—the testing of such weapons by India in 1998, which provoked a counter test by Pakistan, thus intensifying the tension between the two nations. Meanwhile, North Korea remained unyielding in spite of—or, precisely because of—the political-military pressure of the U.S. and its allies. In short, the U.S. military was a cause, as much as a result, of "uncertainty, tension, and immense concentrations of military power" in the Asia-Pacific region.

In the meantime, at the ideological level, in response to the continuing presence of the U.S. military and to the deeper penetration of Asian markets by multinational corporations—Euro-American and Japanese, predominantly—cultural nationalism flourished in the 1990s in various forms within China, Singapore, and Malaysia.[4] There it rejected calls for (American) models of "democracy" and "human rights," or the "global (American) standard" and so forth (Dirlik 1996). In actuality, this anti-U.S. sentiment may have done little to frustrate the U.S. global actions, because such sentiment, if translated as "uncertainty" and "tension," served to justify the presence of the U.S. military in the first place. Asian cultural nationalism thus ironically fed on America's simultaneously economic, military, and ideological strategy to expand its capitalist project in the post–cold war Asia-Pacific region. In the words of the Pentagon, "United States interests in the region are mutually-reinforcing: security is necessary for economic growth, security and growth make it more likely that human rights will be honored and democracy will emerge, and democratization makes international conflict less likely" (Department of Defense 1995: 3).

> Of the selfishness of our motives we readily admit that we sought commercial intercourse with Japan, because we supposed it would be advantageous.... But it is quite possible to believe that benefit to *both* nations [the U.S. and Japan] may result from the intercourse we would establish, and such benefit may be honestly desired [by Japan], even while we seek our own interest. This is not selfishness. (emphasis in original)

So once said Commodore Matthew Calbraith Perry (1857: 93) when he led an American Navy squadron to the China seas and Japan.[5] In the age of globalization, extending and reorienting Perry's reasoning of "selfishness" (which he simultaneously said was not selfishness, but "mutual benefit"), the Department of Defense (1995: 2) states that "the stability brought about by United States military presence provides a sound foundation for economic growth in the Asia-Pacific region, *benefiting Asians and Americans alike*" (emphasis mine). In this reasoning, "I" (the U.S.) socialized "you" (Asia) into "my" basic values such as prosperity, stability, and democracy in a way that "my" interests and "your" interests infinitely blurred; and in the process, an "intimate society" came to be constructed, at once economically, militarily, and ideologically, across the broader Asia-Pacific region.

Okinawa occupied a distinct position of directly experiencing the workings of this intimate society in terms of what a local newspaper called the "burden shifting" of the U.S. bases (*Ryukyu Shinpo*, April 11, 1997). That is, the U.S. government ("I") shunted military responsibilities onto the shoulders of the Japanese government ("you") while at the same time providing "you" with the conditions for "prosperity, security, and democracy" (i.e., benefit). Then, the Japanese government ("I") took the U.S. bases and passed them onto the shoulders of Okinawa ("you") while rendering "you" financial aids. Within Okinawa, in turn, the relatively powerful southern and central Okinawa ("I," or Governor Ota) shifted the burden onto the shoulders of marginalized northern Okinawa, Nago City ("you"), and in so doing, provided "you" with the opportunities for economic development. And finally, the relatively prosperous west coast of Nago City ("I": population 50,000) was now attempting to pass the U.S. military base onto the shoulders of the sparsely populated east coast of Nago, Henoko and its vicinity at a distance ("you": population 5,000). After all, as far as promising to invest a portion of the money "I" would receive from Tokyo in "you," the great majority (90 percent) of Nago residents would not only avoid the problems of base-related noise, accidents, pollution, and so forth, but also obtain the bulk of developmental money for themselves.

In short, together with the promise of "mutual benefit" involving money, development, and a better life, the U.S. bases had been constantly displaced and transferred in an oppressive chain of global burden shifting by means of which a closed system of intimate society was expanded. With the regime of power being thus decentered, the relations of subordination and appropriation between "you" and "me" were endlessly renewed, absorbed, and recycled in a unified planetary political space with the United States as the overarching authority. In other words, the U.S. alliance with Japan can be seen as an expression of what Hardt and Negri (2000: xii) calls Empire: "It is a *decentered* and *deterritorializing* apparatus of rule that progressively incorporates the entire global realm within its open, expanding frontiers" (emphasis in original).

I note that Hardt and Negri (2000) often obscure the enormous political-economic-military-cultural-racial power of the U.S. as a mega nation-state in the postmodern world.[6] They write: "*The United States does not, and indeed no nation-state can today, form the center of an imperialist project*" (xiv, emphasis in original); "It might appear as if the United States were the new Rome, or a cluster of new Romes: Washington (the bomb [i.e., the center of military power]), New York (money [i.e., the center of financial power]), and Los Angeles (ether [i.e., the center of communication industry]). Any such territorial conception of imperial space, however, is continuously destabilized by the fundamental flexibility, mobility, and deterritorialization at the core of the imperial apparatus" (347). These statements, while allowing us to shift our attention to the global sphere of power of which the United States is only a part, also masks the tremendous violence that the United States has exerted on that sphere. In the words of Tom Mertes (2003: 147):

> The actually existing United States constantly threatens to emerge from the pages of *Empire* like the face in a nightmare, and has to be perpetually repressed.... "Empire," we are continually assured, "has no Rome"—despite the fact that US defense spending is more than that of the next twenty-five governments combined. It has bases in at least fifty-nine countries.

While agreeing with Mertes' reading of *Empire*, I also suggest that Hardt and Negri's model of power nonetheless helps us understand the nature of the postmodern "intimate society," the contemporary nexus of global relations among the U.S., Japan, and Okinawa, better than the conventional understanding of American military imperialism as always oppressive. In a way that extends this conventional understanding of power, Chalmers Johnson (1999: 110), for instance, writes, "East Asia is no longer underdeveloped, the Cold War has ended, the USSR has imploded, the United States has become the world's leading debtor nation, Mao Zedong has died, and elected presidents rule in Seoul and Taipei—but nothing has changed in Okinawa." Yet statements such as "nothing has changed in Okinawa," while perhaps true at some level, does not help us fully grasp the paradoxical nature of the emerging intimate society/Empire which was revealed in, for instance, the following episode.

The Japanese government kept emphasizing that the matter of the construction of the offshore base had been settled by, in the words of several cabinet members, *hanashiai* (dialogue; mutual consent) with the local people. The idea of "dialogue," when combined with the glitter emitted from money given from Tokyo to Okinawa/Nago/Henoko, helped stage the intimacy between the center and the marginal when in actuality they were not equal in their standing. Meanwhile, the U.S. government declared, while watching the "dialogue" off stage, "this is an internal affair of Japan" (*Ryukyu Shinpo*, November 26, 1996). In so saying, they conveniently forgot their own statement, cited above, that "the stability and prosperity of the Asia-Pacific region [made possible by Okinawa] is a matter of vital national interest affecting the well-being of all Americans" (Department of Defense

1995: 7). The transnational form of power reinforced itself not by oppressing others but by systematically erasing the traces of its own oppressiveness.

RESISTING THE INTIMATE SOCIETY FROM THE POSITION
OF THE THIRD PERSON

Critical residents in Henoko and Nago City, however, did not pass over the matter in silence, but actively responded to the oppressive chain of the global intimate society from the position of the third person. In fact, after Ota retreated into a noncommittal position by declaring that "the issue is to be settled between the Japanese government and Nago City," and after Tokyo ("I") attempted to directly co-opt Nago ("you") into the intimate society with the lure of Japanese money behind it, it was ordinary residents of Henoko/Nago City—a marginalized region within Okinawa—who came to enact resistance for the sake of Okinawa at large.

Specifically, Nago City inhabitants—members of oppositional political parties, labor unions, and teachers' associations—became active, perhaps more active than Henoko residents, in launching the campaign against the construction of the offshore base. Some saw it as a critical struggle in the context of postwar Okinawan history; they came to Henoko to build a picket line near the waterfront upon the initiation of the preliminary topographical survey of Henoko's sea in early May 1997. Others brought a giant tent to Henoko in order to help some of the residents there who started to voice their opposition to the offshore base plan. The tent, originally pitched in front of Henoko's fishing port, was later replaced in July 1997 with a prefabricated structure that came to be known as *tōsō goya* (struggle hut). Activities of "vanguards" in Nago City struck a responsive chord in the hearts of Okinawans, particularly when they started to form a citywide coalition to stop the construction of the offshore base. In the summer of 1997, in attempt to insert oppositional voices of ordinary Nago residents in the political process, they proceeded to propose a citywide referendum that would ask eligible voters if they would support or reject the construction plan.

In postwar Japan, the American idea of "democracy," an idea through which to prevent Japan's remilitarization and to develop its economy as a "breakwater" of capitalism, was appropriated and rearticulated at various social levels. In the 1960s, for instance, students, workers, women, intellectuals, and others constituted what came to be collectively called

FIGURE 5.1 The "Struggle Hut" of the Society for the Protection of Life. The hut was built by local residents who opposed the offshore base.

the *shimin*/citizen to participate in new forms of democratic movements; they did so in order to resist the hegemony of the United States—the very authority that introduced democracy in postwar Japan—in the Far East as well as Japanese politicians and bureaucrats who supported and benefitted from American hegemony (Oguma 2002). In the 1970s and 1980s, however, when people's passion for social movements came to be subsumed by a national pursuit for happiness and a better life, the critical standpoints for ecology, women's issues, and social justice were largely suppressed and marginalized as a minority perspective—often under the same banner of democracy (i.e., majority rule). In the meantime, the majority were typically co-opted by the dream of development mayors and other leaders fostered at the city/village level, who were in turn controlled by governors and other leaders at the prefectural level, who were ultimately controlled through the nationwide subsidy distribution machine handled by elite bureaucrats and national assemblymen of the Liberal Democratic Party in power.

Yet in the aftermath of Japan's economic glory of the 1980s, the ideology of happiness and a better life could no longer completely cover up ever-escalating social, economic, and environmental problems and damages, and critical citizens started to express their democratic aspirations through the referendum, a form of direct democracy, as a way to shake up the ossified pyramid-like bureaucratic-political system (Imai 1997). Indeed, from the late 1980s on, local residents at odds with the system requested referendums and registered their objections to various state-initiated projects, including land reclamation work on Lake Shinji and Nakakai (Yonago City, Tottori Prefecture, 1988), the construction of a nuclear power plant (Maki Town, Nīgata Prefecture, 1996), and the creation of an industrial waste site (Mitake Town, Gifu Prefecture, 1996). In September 1996, the Ota administration also conducted a referendum; more than 540,000 Okinawans came to the polls, and 89 percent of them (which meant a majority of the eligible voters in entire Okinawa Prefecture) expressed their wish to reduce and reorganize the U.S. bases in Okinawa and to revise the (discriminatory) Status of Forces Agreement (SOFA).[7] In part extending and appropriating the tradition of democratic, oppositional movements in mainland Japan, while at the same time redirecting and deepening postwar struggles within Okinawa under new historical circumstances, Nago citizens had recourse to the constitutionally granted principle of local autonomy to counter global power. The profound irony is that through the very principle (local autonomy, of which the referendum is an expression) the United States had introduced to postwar Japan, Okinawans inherited the spirit of American democracy and mobilized the anti-American-base movement.

When the referendum was first proposed, however, the oppositional movement in Henoko was still at its early stage, and Henoko residents against the offshore base—numbering less than twenty—were rather hesitant about this idea of direct democracy. As a leader of the movement told me, "I wonder if people on the west coast of Nago will really understand our predicaments and help us out." He continued that if the west coast, where fifty thousand people resided, became blinded by the lure of money and let the oppositional group lose in the referendum, the population of Henoko and its vicinity, about five thousand, would immediately be cornered to accept the base in the very name of democracy (majority vote). Yet, it was also apparent that a protest confined and isolated within Henoko and delinked from a larger realm of Okinawan citizenship had its own limits. That is to say, without the support of a large number of Okinawans, Henoko residents would be unable to sustain themselves against the formidable power of Tokyo and Washington. In June 1997, oppositional Henoko residents finally agreed to join the citywide movement body, named *Nagoshimintōhyō Suinshin Kyōgikai* (the Coalition for Realizing a Nago City Referendum), together with more than twenty political, labor, and social organizations. This became an impetus to expand and strengthen the anti-base movement in Henoko itself as will be examined shortly.

The sole task of the citywide coalition in the summer of 1997 was to collect as many signatures as possible from eligible voters to request that the Nago city council and mayor approve the referendum. This task was not an easy one: the Nago city council was dominated by eighteen conservative assemblymen, who opposed the referendum (one of whom was an assemblyman from Henoko), while reformist assemblymen, who were in favor of the referendum, numbered only eleven. In order to overcome this obstacle, the coalition aimed to collect signatures from a third of the 38,176 eligible voters in Nago City. To everyone's surprise, the coalition, toiling under the scorching sun of an Okinawan summer, ended up collecting 19,734 signatures. (The Election Administration Commission would in the end approve 17,539 of them.) The members of the coalition were jubilant, while the mayor and the conservative assemblymen were left reeling. In August 1997, the coalition formally requested the reluctant Nago city council to pass the local ordinance for a referendum. The proceedings, which commenced in September, turned out to be stormy ones, as will be seen in the next chapter.

Constructing Okinawa's Point of View in Henoko

Separately, but parallel with the referendum campaign by Nago constituencies during the first half of 1997, the oppositional consciousness in Henoko also started to take specific form. Instrumental in this process was the Society for the Protection of Life, with its radical platform "oppose the base, democratize the Henoko administration."

As noted earlier in this chapter, toward the end of 1996 Nago City Mayor Higa Tetsuya had showed his readiness to accept the offshore base. When this happened, the Japanese Communist Party in Okinawa organized a meeting in Henoko, giving some fifty residents one of their first opportunities to raise critical questions about the new base (*Ryukyu Shinpo*, January 16, 1997). Given Henoko district's widespread aversion to the Communist Party, which

FIGURE 5.2 Members of the Society for the Protection of Life discussing strategies to oppose the offshore base construction.

had long proposed immediate withdrawal of the U.S. military from Japan's (and Okinawa's) soil and which residents had often disdainfully referred to as "*aka* [red]," as if the party were a contagious disease, the number of participants was notable. Communist Party member and Nago City assemblyman Ōshiro Yoshitami proved to be a vital agent in this process. In the meeting in Henoko, he openly critiqued the offshore base construction in light of the deterioration of the living environment. In so doing, he successfully brought the "outside" discourse on ecology into Henoko's closed life-space, where oppositional voices against the U.S. military had long been silenced by the pro-base, working-class ideology. Notably, Ōshiro expressed his critique through impeccable northern Okinawan "dialect" (not "standard" Japanese which would sound formal but distant) which helped his message reach the depths of the consciousness of Henoko residents. It was Ōshiro's engagement with the issue that stimulated talk among Henoko residents about organizing a local oppositional movement. Not long after, on January 27, 1997, some twenty men and women instituted the Society for the Protection of Life.

Unlike many working-class Henoko residents in favor of the offshore base, members of the society were well off. Indeed, my interactions with these members revealed that as sons, daughters, or wives of major Henoko descent groups, as widows who had inherited the fortunes of their deceased husbands, as individuals who had benefited from the entertainment business by running bars or by becoming hostesses, or as former maids, petty engineers, and sweepers in and around Camp Schwab who were now receiving the fruits of hard work, men and women in the society had attained financial—and thus political—autonomy from the Henoko administration.

In its anti-base mobilization, the middle-class Society for the Protection of Life challenged the ways in which nondiscursive ties of blood and place regulated, often stifled, public discussions about the U.S. military, while subsuming this challenge under Okinawa's collective memory, culture, and consciousness in light of the idea that "we are Okinawans." Within Okinawa, there existed a popular and scholarly view that northern Okinawa was less developed and thus backward as compared to the more modernized and urbanized southern and central Okinawa (see chapter 3). With confidence as affluent citizens behind them, members of the society redefined, as it were, their own "backwardness" as an essence of Okinawa that had not been contaminated by the process of urbanization, Japanization, and militarization, and in so doing, set up the relation of Self (a pristine Okinawa unified in its resistance) and Other (the U.S.-Japan alliance) in a binary structure of opposition. Instrumental in this process were their experiences of three major forms of oppression in Okinawa, centering on kinship, the war, and gender.

CONSANGUINITY AND THE OPPOSITIONAL CONSCIOUSNESS

First, the important role consanguinity (kinship) played in the construction of the oppositional consciousness in the Society for the Protection of Life is indicated by the fact that many (if not all) of its members were related to "native" Henoko descent groups long relegated to the fringe of the communal power structure. Early on in my fieldwork, I heard residents who had joined the society constantly talking about who was related to whom, while articulating the increasingly fine line between "genuine" Henoko residents and "out-of-towners" in Henoko. When I listened to these stories, it almost sounded as if out-of-towners, who had exerted enormous influences on Henoko's prospering entertainment business in the 1960s and beyond and who had joined the Henoko administration thereafter, wanted the offshore base because they did not share Okinawa's collective memories of war, the bases, and the servicemen, while genuine natives did share those memories and, consequently, did not and should not want the new base. Put differently, in the realm of consanguinity, the "native/Henokonian" (i.e., genuine, righteous) point of view was being constructed in opposition to the "corrupt" out-of-towners, while it was also being conflated with a more general, and authentic, Okinawan perspective ("we are Okinawans") that was combating the "immoral," even "evil," power of Tokyo and Washington.

One of the central figures of the society—a seventy-eight-year-old man affectionately called Grandpa Iheya—asserted such genuine nativeness and, by implication, "Okinawan" conscience as well. He somewhat proudly told me, while holding a thick family tree book of fifteen generations in his hand, that he was descended from one of the (lower ranked) official families that served the Ryukyu Kingdom. Other residents also told me that Grandpa Iheya's descent group, although it had been mostly eliminated from the Henoko administration since the 1970s, had produced distinguished figures in larger Okinawan politics, business, and education. Familial ties to the kingdom, reduced as they may have been, were nostalgically evoked through Grandpa Iheya, who assumed an aura of being distinct from the descendants of the subjugated peasant class that now populated Henoko and "contaminated" authentic Henokoness as intertwined with the essence of timeless, pristine Okinawa.

Another leader of the Society for the Protection of Life, fifty-three-year-old Haebaru Kenji, also brings the questions of consanguinity to the fore. The Haebaru *munchū*, a native Henoko descent group which is related to Grandpa Iheya's *munchū*, is composed of three sublineages that launched into various domains of Henoko social life.[8] Haebaru told me that he started the anti-offshore-base movement, like Grandpa Iheya, out of pride as a genuine Henokonian and antagonism against the out-of-towners such as Sueyoshi Kaoru who had dominated Henoko in general, and the Henoko administration in particular (see chapter 2).

It should be noted, however, that Haebaru originally made a resolute proposal to the local administration about actively *inviting* the offshore base to Henoko on the grounds that it would revitalize Henoko's economy. As he openly acknowledged, politically Haebaru was on the side of the conservative establishment, deeply involved in the activities of Japan's ruling Liberal Democratic Party in Okinawa. He also told me that in the early

1970s he had once been employed as a guard for Camp Schwab, at which time he had carried a shotgun over his shoulder in order to obstruct (not help) Okinawan workers' struggles against personnel reduction of base employees, which were a part of the reversion movement.

One basic reason for the drastic shift of his position from a hard-core conservative to the leader of a radical movement was that he had long been marginalized in community politics. For instance, Sueyoshi Kaoru, Haebaru's friend, held the titles of Nago City Fire Marshal and Chair of the Henoko Executive Committee, among others, while Haebaru had none. His antagonism toward the Henoko administration intensified especially when it rejected his proposal to invite the offshore base. Generous, aggressive, but often inconsistent, Haebaru was persuaded by Grandpa Iheya (his uncle) and his followers, and joined the Society for the Protection of Life in order to organize a movement of "genuine" Henoko natives (including himself) to oppose—and, if possible, replace—the "corrupt" Henoko administration. Soon after, Haebaru was elected president of the society, and found himself situated in the larger political arena beyond communal politics. The offshore base dispute had transformed his status as a mere conservative resident into an exemplary anti-base Okinawan.

EXPERIENCES OF THE WAR
AND OTHER HARDSHIPS

The second way in which the Society for the Protection of Life constructed Okinawa's oppositional collective consciousness ("we are Okinawans") originates in the historical issue of subjugation. Indeed, the name *Inochi Wo Mamoru Kai* (Society for the Protection of Life) itself evoked the Okinawan folk notion "*Nuchi du takara*" (Life is Treasure)[9] together with the collective memory of the battle of Okinawa, in which more than 150,000 lives had been lost. The organization's name also inherited and embodied the spirit of Okinawan resistance in the 1950s, when many grass-roots organizations had used *inochi* (life), *mamoru* (to protect), and/or *kai* (group) as part of their names. For instance, in 1956 the *Okinawa Kodomo wo Mamoru Kai* (Okinawan Society to Protect Children) waged protests against a murder, in which a housewife, who had three children, was shot by two U.S. guards when she was collecting scrap iron near an ammunition depot (Nakano 1969: 127; Tengan 1999: 70; see chapter 2). Yet at issue was not only the name, but also the actual experiences of the members of the Society for the Protection of Life. Importantly, the society was composed of, mostly, senior men and women who had experienced hardships before, during, and after the battle of Okinawa. These experiences, together with these senior residents' "nativeness," constituted the core of their oppositional sentiment. Below, I will describe several stories told by these men and women in a way that would reinforce and expand my description of Okinawan experiences of the World War II battle (see chapter 2) from the perspective of Henoko residents.

In 1944 men and women of Henoko (together with residents of the entire northern Okinawa area) were forced by the Imperial Headquarters in Tokyo to fill their quota of labor for the construction of an airfield on Ie Island, off the coast of the Motobu peninsula of northwestern Okinawa. Iheya Haruko, a native Henoko woman in her early seventies and member of the society, told me about the harshness and cruelty of the labor. She had to work from dawn to 11 p.m. The food was poor, and she was allowed to take a bath—whose water had already been used to wash the horses employed for the construction—only once during the three-week labor period. When she came back from Ie Island, she was, in her own words, "as thin as a needle." Back in the Henoko community, the Japanese Army had also constructed various military facilities, such as a port, a bridge, and underground air raid shelters. As Iheya Haruko told me, Henoko men and women were ordered to cooperate in this task daily, by providing food, sawing lumber, and assembling the structures.

After Naha (capital of Okinawa) was heavily bombarded in the U.S. air raid of October 10, 1944, Okinawans from the southern and central regions fled to what was considered safer northern Okinawa, by walking and/or using horses and carts. Yamashiro Tae, another native Henoko woman in her early seventies who had joined the society, told me that houses in Henoko immediately became full; one house accommodated as many as six families. By early 1945, air strikes began in northern Okinawa as well. According to Yamashiro Tae, Henoko residents, along with evacuees, started to work on building straw huts in the mountain areas. She said that they hid together in the mountain forests during the day, and came down to collect food and cook at night. Food grew scarce, however, and confrontations between evacuees and Henoko residents often occurred as the former, out of hunger, stole potatoes, rice, and other items from the latter's fields.

The U.S. military landed on the island of Okinawa on April 1, 1945, and reached Henoko by April 6, after easily destroying the hastily constructed military facilities of the Japanese Army (Henoko District 1998: 525–74). The U.S. troops also used flamethrowers to burn the houses of the community. They also burned the forests to force the people—Henoko residents and evacuees mixed up with defeated Japanese soldiers—down the mountain slopes, while disseminating messages to the effect that "the American military is the friend of all" (Military Government Headquarters, not dated; cited in Okinawakenritsu Toshokan Shiryō Henshūshitu 1996: 233).

In the meantime, several rumors spread among Henoko residents and evacuees hiding in the mountain, helping them to construct as much as distort reality. According to Yamashiro Tae, one rumor claimed that, once captured, men would be torn into pieces and women would be raped and murdered by U.S. soldiers. In response to this, she put black Japan ink on her face to pretend, naively, that she was a boy (who tended to have a darker skin than a girl). Furugen Haruko, another native Henoko woman in her early seventies who joined the Society for the Protection of Life, told me that there was a rumor that U.S. soldiers had goat-like eyes (*hījā mē*), which could not see things at night. Therefore, she said, many believed that as long as one hid in the mountain during the day, one would be safe. According to her, there was still another rumor that U.S. soldiers were so tall that they would not notice things low to the ground. Apparently, some Henoko residents believed that one should simply squat down when encountering the soldiers in order to escape capture.

These rumors were appropriated and reinforced by the Japanese soldiers still in the forests. They saw the surrender and capture of Okinawans as a matter of great disgrace, and ordered hiding Henoko residents and evacuees not to give up, telling women, for instance, "You will be raped if you are captured" (Yamashiro Tae's information). Yet Henoko residents and evacuees could see before them armed American soldiers, alive and real, demanding surrender. When attempting to decide whether to surrender or not, one old woman evacuee was burnt to death by a U.S. flamethrower. Another woman was killed when she mistakenly stepped upon a bomb. Two residents died of illness; nine others were bombarded and killed in the mountain forests (Henoko District 1998: 525–74).

Yamashrio Ei, still another native Henoko woman in her early seventies and member of the society, told me the story of one U.S. soldier who pointed

FIGURE 5.3 Local "Tower of Peace" standing against the background of Henoko's sea.

a gun at her mother. "Though I feared my mother would be killed, she did not surrender. Perhaps she was so frightened that she could not move." And at that point, Yamashiro Ei continued, "Another soldier interfered and yelled (to the soldier pointing the gun), '*pīpō, pīpō* (people, people) [i.e., this person is a civilian],' and this stopped him from shooting my mom." After paying a heavy price in the form of blood and property loss, Henoko residents and evacuees gradually surrendered and came down the mountain, or were eventually captured between April and the end of July.

Outside Henoko as well, some residents experienced the senselessness of war and the inhumanity it inevitably brings about. For instance, more than forty Henoko men were killed in battle in various parts of Okinawa and beyond (Henoko District 1998: 569–74). Yamashiro Fumi—a member of the Society for the Protection of Life in her early seventies who grew up in the south—told me, while showing me the scars on her arm, that bombs from U.S. naval warships fell like rain. She continued that dead bodies were piled on top of one another, and a woman with a headless baby strapped to her back was running around, half mad. Meanwhile, the *Himeyuri Butai* (Lily Corps), composed of students of the Okinawa Female Normal School and Okinawa First Girls' High School and their teachers, treated soldiers in the battlefields (Nakasone [1982] 1995). One survivor of the Lily Corps was Yagaji Kiyoko, a Henoko woman opposing the offshore base construction.[10] During an interview at a bar she ran in Henoko, she told me that as a student, she had been assigned to an operating room in a limestone cave in southern Okinawa to which wounded soldiers were carried. The maggots that hatched in the open wounds of soldiers emitted an offensive smell. When the doctor cut off the limb of a wounded soldier without anesthesia, she fainted away. Unlike soldiers outside the cave, however, she was ordered to stay and work in the operating room of the cave, and thus survived what Okinawans call the "typhoon of steel."

Another of the key activists of the society, Kinjō Yūji, age sixty-two, also embodied the plights of Okinawa before, during, and after the war. A likable man, Kinjō was the child of an Okinawan man from Henoko and a woman from northern Japan, and grew up in an area which was once called the "Okinawa slum" in Osaka, to which many Okinawans emigrated from the 1920s onward to work as cheap laborers. During the war he had been in Osaka, which was reduced to ashes. Later, as a young adult, he helped with his father's transportation business. In 1972, Kinjō moved with his Japanese wife and children from Osaka to Henoko to take care of the estate and fortune of his descent group. His *munchū* was once powerful; for example, Ōshiro Jirō, one of two older leaders who still exerted influence in local Henoko politics in the late 1990s (see chapter 4), was from a poor family that had come to Henoko three generations ago to "serve" Kinjō's *munchū*. Although Kinjō's life experiences in mainland Japan helped him escape a stifling web of local social relations, he still maintained status as a "native" Henoko man because of his family's estate and blood ties. This liminal status, when combined with his experiences of discrimination against Okinawans by Japanese in Osaka, and his wisdom as a former unionist in an Okinawan bus company, had made Kinjō Yūji a deeply grounded yet brilliantly informed citizen, and enabled him to keep raising an oppositional voice against the Henoko administration, the Nago City mayor, and the Japanese government all together. Throughout the offshore base dispute in 1997–98 (and today), Kinjō usually came to the "struggle hut" first early in the morning and left it last late at night.

He was (and is) the one who at the hut welcomed visitors from Okinawa, mainland Japan, and beyond, talked to them about the violence of the U.S. and Japanese governments over Okinawa, and articulated why the offshore base should not be built in Henoko. He was liked and trusted by many, because he was not only tough but also sincere, kind, and warm. I developed a deeply emotional bond with him during (and after) the field-work, who often treated me as his own son.

Finally, the life history of one member of the Society for the Protection of Life, Higashikawa Yūtoku (in his early sixties), throws into relief Oki-nawa's collective experiences of the war and other hardships in a global perspective. One autumn day, while swatting flies with a newspaper in the "struggle hut," Higashikawa Yūtoku said out of boredom, "Oh, it's such a dull day. Nobody has come. The only guests we have had so far are flies." It was on such "dull" days, indeed, that I came to know more about the lives of Henoko residents such as him.

Higashikawa Yūtoku's parents emigrated to Saipan in the early 1920s to work for *Nanyō Kōhatsu* (the South Seas Development Corporation), a sugar manufacturing company instituted on Saipan (which was then put under a Japanese trusteeship[11]) in 1921, closely working with Imperial Japan's South Seas Agency. The number of emigrants from Okinawa to Saipan continued to rise through the 1920s and the 1930s because of the former's severe depression, and in 1940 it reached fifty-six thousand, which surpassed the local indigenous population and constituted more than 70 percent of all immigrants with Japanese nationality. In addition to producing sugar, emigrants engaged in raising coconuts, mining phosphate, and fishing (Akamine 1983: 97–98, Okinawa Prefectural Peace Memorial Museum [OPPMM] 2001: 31). Higashikawa Yūtoku was born in Saipan in 1935 during this major social change, and he would soon come to be implicated in an even larger historical transformation.

In June and July 1944, in the midst of the U.S. military's counteroffensive campaigns against the Japanese military in Asia and the Pacific, Saipan be-came one of the battlegrounds. Higashikawa, together with a total of some twenty Koreans, Japanese, and Okinawans (including his own family), hid in an air-raid shelter, but the U.S. forces easily bombed and destroyed it. He recalled the moment of attack: "I could not open my eyes amidst the cloud of dust in the shelter. I was sure that I would be killed, while hearing a wounded girl of my age crying, 'Mother, mother.' A Korean man, whose throat was cut, also groaned, 'Give me water, give me water.' My father was fatally injured, but was still alive. I knew that the enemy was still outside the shelter, so I decided that I would save my father when they were gone. And then, I somehow fell into sleep, and woke up the next day. The shelter was pitch black, but I could tell that the twenty other people, including my father, were all dead. Tears did not flow at all. Why? I don't know."

After the war, Higashikawa was sent from Saipan to Okinawa together with other Okinawans. He was first put in a refugee camp created by the U.S. military in central Okinawa. There, he witnessed the sufferings of Okinawans, including, for instance, the travail of a former schoolteacher, who had become insane. She would bow down to a gasoline drum can. Before long, Higashikawa was taken in by a relative, and he began to work in the fields without going to school.[12] When he was nineteen, he suffered from meningitis and became lame in one leg. Meanwhile, he continued to work not only in the paddy fields, but also sometimes as a pimp and sometimes as a petty engineer responsible for maintaining equipment in the military bases across Okinawa. In 1973, Higashikawa moved to Henoko to start working for Camp Schwab. He then married, had a child, and bought a small but cozy house in the district. Eventually, he retired from the base a number of years before I met him.

Throughout the offshore base dispute, short and skinny Higashikawa Yūtoku, always walking with a slight limp, worked in the background of the oppositional movement, cleaning and fixing the "struggle hut," riding in the campaign car, not to make eloquent speeches, but to distribute flyers to pedestrians, collecting signatures at night, planting flowers in front of the hut, etc. He kept saying to me, "We don't need any more American bases here."

Higashikawa Yūtoku's multidimensional life encapsulates an important aspect of Okinawa's collective memory (involving the emigration, the war, the bases), which, as I see it, became the basis of the strong attitude against power and authority that was shared by oppositional Henoko residents and many other Okinawans. It should be added that memories of the war and subjugation had been largely set aside (if not completely forgotten) in these residents' minds amidst the excitement that permeated Henoko in the 1960s and beyond when the entertainment business flourished. During the offshore base dispute in the late 1990s, these memories resurfaced to form the basic element of their oppositional consciousness, and they were connected to newly emerging middle-class confidence and Okinawan pride in a way that would reconstitute Okinawa's collective anti-military sentiment and consciousness, "we are Okinawans."

THE POLITICS OF GENDER

The third and last, but not least important, realm in which Okinawa's unified point of view was articulated in Henoko involves the politics of gender as intertwined with the questions of consanguinity and subjugation. Specifically, it is important to examine the ways in which the marginalization of the native Henoko women's realm of life conditioned the construction of a specific and critical Okinawan perspective.

Generally speaking, because of the influx of women into Henoko from outside districts after the construction of Camp Schwab, the native women's influence in Henoko shrank from the 1960s onward. For instance, the Henoko Women's Association, active before the war, became increasingly

FIGURE 5.4 Henoko priestesses perform a local ritual commemorating the spirits of ancestors.

represented by non-Henoko women (Henoko District 1998: 464), and was thereby restructured as a puppet organization of the Henoko administration to promote "harmony"—both racial and sexual—between the servicemen and the district.

Compounded with this process in which non-native women gained an advantage over native women was the intervention of the Henoko administration (consisting of both natives and out-of-towners, all men) into native women's cultural practices. Historically, Henoko women, like women in other parts of Okinawa, once independently and collectively presided over religious functions, and in doing so long complemented and even curbed the men's political domain (Iha [1938]1973a, [1939]1973b; Mabuchi 1964, Lebra 1966, Henoko District 1998, Sered 1994, 1995, 1999). Writing about Henza, the Okinawan community in which she conducted her fieldwork, Israeli anthropologist Susan Sered (1999: 6) notes that even in the context of the 1990s, "Many Henza rituals strive toward social and cosmic harmony, toward smoothing out or clearing up rough spots, and toward dramatizing themes of complementarity and balance [between men and women]." In the case of Henoko, however, after the construction of Camp Schwab, the historically prescribed, autonomous women's practices became an ever-shrinking cultural domain that no longer checked but rather authorized and reinforced male domination over them.

First of all, farming, which used to define and regulate the religious/women's functions of the community, was made to virtually disappear, because paddy fields had been expropriated and turned into Camp Schwab by men (Henoko leaders and the U.S. military). In addition, although before the construction of Camp Schwab individual households voluntarily made financial contributions to religious events, after the late 1950s, expenses related to such events came to be paid and thus controlled exclusively by the Henoko administration (Henoko District 1998: 299). Similarly, in the 1960s communal shrines (*utaki*) and the communal structure for religious/festive services (*kami ashage*) were remodeled by the Henoko administration with revenue from the entertainment quarter (Henoko District 1998: 301). Furthermore, in the 1970s and 1980s, the Japanese government helped to enhance the power of men (Henoko leaders and the U.S. military) by paying the rent. In brief, in the 1960s, 1970s, and 1980s, the Henoko administration (men) appropriated the presence of the American base (men) maintained by Tokyo (men) as a way to rearticulate an Okinawan tradition, through which to preserve the religious sphere of native women and simultaneously deprive them of their political autonomy and economic independence.

In the social environment of the 1990s, finally, the women's religious sphere became a mere name: Younger generations were less interested in religion than they were in fashion and pop music; it became increasingly difficult for Henoko native women to find successors to the *kaminchu* (priestess) positions;[13] the compensation paid to *kaminchu* women by the Henoko administration was reduced; and religious ceremonies lost the sense of seriousness and solemnity that Henoko women wanted to maintain, because men often drank, chatted, and laughed in the midst of rituals.

Operating within a feminist, comparative and (still) structural-functionalist line of thought,[14] aforementioned Susan Sered argues that women find in their religious functions ways in which to release, resolve, and contain their frustration: "In many cultures, it is precisely within the realm of religion that many women find avenues for ... acceptable outlets for their frustration with subordination" (Sered 1994: 4). However, in the midst of the offshore base dispute, the women's religious realm, hitherto minimally retained within the communal power structure, ironically expanded its influence beyond the prescribed limit, and finally started to undermine and challenge the male political domain. Indeed, against the background of the manifold marginalization of native Henoko women's realm of life, the offshore base dispute provided them, for the first time in decades, a context in which to confront a broader institution of masculinity consisting of the Henoko administration, the Japanese government, and the U.S. military. Building on, yet departing from, a feminist structural-functionalist view like Sered's, I here want to argue that tensions and fissures, which religious activities were supposed to dissolve, were rather amplified by some (if not all) of the women in Henoko during the offshore base dispute.

In fact, *kaminchu* women and a few dozen of their friends, together with Grandpa Iheya, joined the Society for the Protection of Life, explicitly mobilizing themselves in order to stop the construction of the offshore base. The Henoko administration could not intervene in these women's mobilization, because of the "tradition" of keeping the political/men's sphere and the religious/women's sphere separate, which the administration itself had reinforced. The idea that senior citizens must be respected—resulting from the seniority rule principle of primogeniture (see chapter 4)—also functioned to the older women's advantage. The influence of this women's group at one point became so pervasive that they, along with two hundred other concerned women living in northern Okinawa, young and old, met with Okinawa Governor Ota Masahide. After the emotionally touching meeting, Governor Ota decided to officially declare his opposition to the planned base (see chapters 6 and 7).

In the meantime, while it was often difficult to openly express their opinion because of the nondiscursive pressure of blood and place to conform to the pro-base community ideology, many women in their thirties and forties residing in Henoko with children (particularly daughters) informally expressed strong sympathy with the activities of the Society for the Protection of Life. For instance, one woman said to me, "Our children will not be able to sleep because of the noise." Still another said, "I would be worried about our daughters if the base is built." She was alluding to the 1995 rape incident. While I was somewhat hesitantly—because of my position as a researcher[15]—distributing a flyer from the anti-base group to the houses in Henoko the night before the referendum, I ran into a middle-aged woman at the entrance of her house. She told me, "Thank you for doing this. I also worry about the children. I will vote to oppose the base." In short, the older women's critical spirit—if not their religious passion itself—filtered down into their daughters' and granddaughters' generations, and helped them create a space to explore their own views and opinions about the future of Henoko.

Two Aspects of Contemporary Okinawan Identity

At this juncture, it would be useful to review and summarize the analyses in chapters 4 and 5, in order to highlight two moments that articulate a particular contour of contemporary Okinawan identity. On the one hand, as this chapter has shown, the prolonged coexistence with Camp Schwab helped Henoko to incubate a group of critical middle-class residents within it, who organized the Society for the Protection of Life in the wake of the announcement of the construction of the new offshore base. Using Okinawa's historical and cultural experiences of consanguinity, the war, and gender as points of reference, these residents forcefully constructed the category of Okinawa—"we are Okinawans"—in opposition to Japan (the national) and the U.S. military (the global) in a manner that began to extend as well as transform the identity of an Okinawan "people" (*minshū*) that I have elaborated in chapter 2. In this move, these residents appropriated economic opportunities opened up by the presence of Camp Schwab as a foundation of their middle-class political autonomy, turning this autonomy against the very source of economic opportunities, the intimate society.

On the other hand, as demonstrated in chapter 4, the prolonged coexistence with Camp Schwab also helped a large number of Henoko residents to differentiate themselves from the rest of Okinawa by proclaiming what they saw as the often problematic, but more or less peaceful, sociocultural and historical interdependence of the U.S. base and Henoko. Importantly, most of them were financially insecure working-class residents in fear of failure, decline, and underdevelopment; while offsetting their fear with a cultural pride of "difference," as expressed in various festive activities (e.g., the great tug-of-war festival), they tended to reluctantly support the U.S. base in exchange for rent money and jobs the Japanese government provided. Thus appropriating the national (money) and the global (the U.S. base) within their consciousness and everyday practices, these residents destabilized the totalizing category of Okinawa, while constructing a closed enclave in which the particular pro-base ideology, "we are Okinawans but of a different kind," permeated.

Taking Henoko as a paradigmatic example, I see Okinawan identity of the late 1990s as the manifestation of the historical tension between the plane of totality ("we are Okinawans") and the realm of difference ("we are Okinawans but of a different kind"). In the next two chapters, I will discuss, in reference to the offshore base dispute, the ways in which the plane of totality, initially forcefully extended by middle-class Okinawans in reference to the anti-base ideal of peace, the environment, and women's issues, came to be challenged and undermined by the logic of difference, articulated by working-class Okinawans through their pro-base desires for development, happiness, and a better life. Then, in the final chapter of this book, I will formulate the crisis of Okinawan identity as an opening for new possibilities of inclusive citizenship that transcends and mediates the tension between totality and difference in the realm of the global public sphere. I would like to conclude this chapter by describing one way in which Henoko catalyzed this citizenship.

In September 1997, the Society for the Protection of Life organized an open forum at the Henoko *kōminkan* (the auditorium attached to the Henoko administration building) in order to discuss the offshore base construction plan. One of the presenters, Pastor Shimada Zenji (his real name), then fifty-six, started his talk by having the audience listen, via an amplifier, to the ear-splitting noise of aircraft that he had recorded at Futenma Air Station. Silence fell over the *kōminkan* after this demonstration, and the pastor, with a perfect mixture of Okinawan dialect and standard Japanese that helped him capture the hearts of the audience, started to address the 370 Henoko residents in the hall.

The pastor, who had been living in the Futenma area for eighteen years before, said that he had started the movement against Futenma Air Station because, soon after moving into their new house, his newborn child stopped taking mother's milk owing to, they concluded, the daily jet noise. He continued that, near Futenma Air Station, some people had gotten rich from the revenue they received for renting their land to the U.S. military. However, he claimed, their children's morality had been corrupted precisely because of this money and "they are no longer willing to work hard." He added, "Yes, as the pro-base people are saying, we need to invigorate the community. But when the money is gone, the friendship [between the government and Okinawa] will also be gone.[16] . . . The invigoration is not to be realized by passively waiting for money, which will only ruin people, but by actively bringing up the youth under our own care and responsibility." His forty-minute talk ended amidst a thunderous applause, as he concluded, "I think we should criticize and reconsider the governmental plan to relocate the base within Okinawa. We have to raise our voices. People who remain silent will be ruined." His presentation became an impetus for Henoko residents to leave the confined lifeworld of Henoko structured by ties of blood and place and to enter the larger public sphere of discussions and arguments about the U.S. military.

6

NAGO CITY REFERENDUM:

Constructing Okinawan Citizenship

 This chapter examines the complex process whereby Okinawans, in spite of governmental threats, conciliations, and manipulations, democratically expressed their opposition to the construction of a new U.S. base in Henoko in a referendum held in Nago City on December 21, 1997. I will first talk about the ways in which the pro-base group in Henoko and Nago appropriated the power of the Japanese state to position themselves as the defender of "difference" ("we are Okinawans but of a different kind") in the language that appealed to the class-cultural consciousness of the region. I will then focus on the ways in which anti-base voters—including Henoko residents—confronted the pro-base movement embraced by Tokyo and brought the history of Okinawa's social movements to a new height by forming, internally, a polycentric and horizontal movement organization and structuring, externally, a broader public sphere of discussion about the U.S. military. Attention will be paid to the status of Okinawa's collective consciousness, which was articulated not so much in the perspective of a poor, oppressed "people," as in that of confident, affluent "citizens" of diverse backgrounds awakened to globally disseminated ideas about ecology, women's issues, and peace.

Reinforcing Cooperation Between the State and Local Subjects

In September 1997 the Coalition for Realizing a Nago City Referendum pressed reluctant Mayor Higa Tetsuya and eighteen pro-Tokyo, pro-base assemblymen in the city council who supported the mayor to pass the ordinance calling for the referendum. The coalition insisted that the 17,539 signatures they had collected had come from a diverse body of residents who, regardless of their positions on the offshore base issue, wanted to decide on the matter according to the democratic procedure of a referendum. The coalition went on to argue that it would recall the mayor and pro-base assemblymen if its request for the referendum were rejected. Of course, the mayor and pro-base assemblymen wanted to avoid the disgraceful prospect of a recall, yet they did not want to conduct the referendum either, because, while it was not binding, the referendum might expose the fact that a majority of Nago inhabitants indeed opposed the construction of the new base in Henoko—the fact the Japanese government and Mayor Higa and the majority of the city assemblymen wanted to hide.[1] Behind the scenes, Tokyo was strongly pressing the mayor to make sure the referendum would not come to a vote (*Okinawa Taimusu*, October 4, 1997).

To get around this dilemma of being unable to either conduct or avoid the referendum, the mayor proposed to change the original proposal submitted by the coalition. In the proposal as revised by the mayor, voters were now asked to decide not between the two choices of rejecting or approving the base but among four choices: (1) approve; (2) approve if the construction is done with appropriate measures for protecting the environment, and has positive economic effects; (3) oppose; (4) oppose if the construction is not done with appropriate measures for protecting the environment, and does not have positive economic effects. The modification was necessary because, in Mayor Higa's words at the session of the city council held on September 25, 1997, the city administration "needs to know diverse, intermediate opinions that cannot be grasped by the approve/oppose votes." But choice 2 of the proposed four-choice referendum would cunningly lead voters to the position of "conditional approval." That is, many Nago residents, Higa apparently thought, might oppose the new base in principle, but would tolerate and approve it on the condition of financial compensation. After all, the new base was to be constructed in Henoko—i.e., on the sparsely popu-

lated east coast of Nago (population 5,000)—away from the city's downtown (population 50,000), and thereby would not pose the problems of
base-related noise, accidents, pollution, and so forth to the majority of
Nago residents. The mayor in fact stated to one of the cabinet members
of the Japanese government who visited Okinawa in September 1997, "We
will definitely win the referendum if more development projects are provided for downtown Nago" (*Okinawa Taimusu*, December 31, 1997). In
short, the mayor decided to hold the referendum in order to create a justification for building the base in Henoko and receiving the much-needed
financial aid for downtown Nago from Tokyo. With pro-base municipal
assemblymen voting for it, the revised ordinance received a majority of
votes in the Nago city council at midnight on October 2, 1997, in the
midst of angry roars by members of the coalition, one of whom shouted
to the mayor, "You are the thief!!" Mayor Higa had indeed stolen and
manipulated the democratic idea of Nago/Henoko residents for his own
political purpose.

Yet it should be emphasized that the revision of the original proposal
did not entirely invalidate the historical significance of the efforts of the
citywide coalition, because Okinawa now obtained an opportunity to express, for the first time in its history, an opinion on whether to endorse or
reject the construction of a U.S. base.[2] Governor Ota was expected to take
certain actions based on its result. The Japanese government kept saying,
nervously, "We will not build the base against the will of local residents" so
that it would not provoke Nago/Henoko voters. More than anybody else,
perhaps, U.S. officials became anxious because the result of the referendum
could affect the broader military-political-economic planning in the Asia-
Pacific region in the twenty-first century. In short, the referendum to be
conducted in the marginalized region in Okinawa was to carry significant
political weight not only at the level of Henoko and Nago City, but also at
the prefectural, national, and even global levels. For the mayor, the referendum was a major gamble with his political life; if he won he could get what
he wanted—money, development projects, and fame—but if he lost, he
might have to resign and live the rest of his political life in humiliating
obscurity. Eventually, he scheduled the referendum for December 21, 1997.

Meanwhile, in order to consolidate broader voices for the "conditional approval" of the new base, the *Nagoshi Kasseika Sokushin Shimin no Kai* (Nago
Citizens' Society for Facilitating [Economic] Invigoration) was created. The

Invigoration Society, as I shall call it here, mobilized the traditional social ties of blood and place across Nago City, while at the same time connecting them with extensive local commercial and business networks. Included on the list of supporters were the Nago Women's Association, Nago Youth Association, Nago Commerce and Business Association, Nago Military Landlords Association, Northern Okinawa branch of the Okinawa Prefecture Construction Industry Association, Northern Okinawa Taxi Business Association, Nago Tourist Hotels Association, Nago Entertainment Business Association, along with twenty or so other key organizations in Nago City. The Henoko Council for Facilitating Economic Activities—which dreamed of creating a casino establishment called *Amerika mura* (American Village) in Henoko (see chapter 1)—was of course a vital agent of the pro-base Invigoration Society. All district mayors on the west coast of Nago City (comprising forty-two of the city's fifty-five districts) also joined this organization, if only unofficially, by expressing their "conditional approval." These supporting groups and individuals were organized into a pyramid-like mobilization structure with President Arakaki Seifuku—also the president of the largest construction/real estate enterprise in Nago City—and the eighteen conservative municipal assemblymen at the top. National assemblyman Kakazu Chiken of Japan's ruling Liberal Democratic Party,[3] who was elected from the Nago area, acted as an adviser and a pipeline between the Invigoration Society and the Japanese government.

I attended the Invigoration Society's kickoff campaign on September 19, 1997, in the Nago City Athletic Hall along with a massive crowd of more than six thousand people. The President of the Invigoration Society stepped onto stage and, while surveying the audience, insisted that the offshore base construction was a "once-in-a-life-time chance" to bring development projects to long-economically-abandoned northern Okinawa.

Significantly, although he was supposed to remain impartial as a holder of public office, Mayor Higa Tetsuya was also on stage. With his perfect command of northern Okinawan dialect, he skillfully used Nago's famous commercial activities of catching whales and dolphins (which, though now obsolete, had thrived until the late 1960s) as a metaphorical starting point to invoke the sentiments of "locality and belonging" (Lovell 1998:1). Taking the microphone, Higa exclaimed: "Together we will corner whales and dolphins [which are a metaphor of development projects from Tokyo] into Nago Bay, together catch them, and together eat them. This is

Okinawan heart! This is the Nago people's heart!!" There, Higa militantly pronounced a desire for a better life by positioning himself as a person embodying pure Nago-ness (synonymous with pure Okinawan-ness) untouched by power and history, against what he saw as an idealistic, experience-distant, infatuated, middle-class anti-base movement represented, in his mind, perhaps, by Governor Ota. The sentiments of locality and belonging were then reinforced in his rhetoric of the misery of today's Nago—once the number two city following Naha, but now economically lagging behind several south-central Okinawan cities. This rhetoric also paved the way for declaring the developmental projects as an opportunity to restore pure Nago-ness bounded by blood and place: "It is now or never. Let us create a region where three generations—grandparents, parents, and children—can live together happily [by creating jobs for the Nago youth who will otherwise move to south-central Okinawa]!" A storm of applause followed.

In a manner that reinforced the sense of solidarity of Nago that Higa invoked, representatives of various social, commercial, and business organizations then unanimously and somewhat monotonously juxtaposed their dream of a better life—to be actualized with the new Community Center, the new Youth Center, the new Elderly People's Center, etc.—with the crisis of high unemployment rate in Nago which had reached 10 percent overall and 20 percent among youth. Asato Susumu, the leader of the pro-base municipal assemblymen, concluded the meeting by exclaiming, "Are we idly waiting for our region to become deserted and without industry?! Do we simply want to protect natural resources [as the anti-base group would insist] only to end up being depopulated and de-industrialized with just the elderly and children in town?!" Throughout this kickoff meeting, notably, speakers focused on the issues of Nago's economic development in conjunction with the pride in and love of their hometown while simultaneously suppressing any mention of the larger structural problem of the U.S. military in Okinawa—the very problem that made their talk about development possible in the first instance.

Shortly thereafter, the Invigoration Society built up its movement by extending the discursive strategy they used in the kickoff meeting, that is, by emphasizing local economic issues and bypassing the structural U.S. base issues. In other words, to a problem that was global in scope, they posed a solution that was rigidly local. Positioning themselves as

FIGURE 6.1 Posters and signboards of both the anti-base and pro-base camps hang side by side in Nago Downtown.

the defender of the local Nago ways of life, its culture and tradition, its difference, they tried to delink Nago from the rest of Okinawa and shelter itself by fixed boundaries.

Numerous posters and signboards of various sizes were thus put up across Nago City including Henoko, asking constituencies to vote for the conditional approval in order to realize their parochial *yume* (dream), which now included the construction of the Women's Center, the Entertainment Hall, the Sports Center, and a new baseball field. Other signboards stated that by using the money given in exchange for the offshore base, Nago City—and only Nago City—would be able to equip schools with musical instruments and swimming pools, reduce the water rate and tax, remodel the old Nago port, and construct a new hospital, to mention just a few. Wearing green headbands and white polyester jackets with the word *yume* on them, men—apparently employed by local construction companies and small businesses—distributed, on foot, flyers, posters, and pamphlets for the cause of conditional approval. Sometimes, the language became less than dreamy, when used to attack the anti-base movement, which was starting to gain momentum within and beyond Henoko and Nago City. Some of the flyers written by the pro-base group read, for instance, "Watch out! Nago City is now being hijacked by Extremists and Communists!!" and "Nago City is now being contaminated by outsiders!"

Note, however, that by fashioning a specific form of localized, pro-base discourses around the keyword "dream," the Invigoration Society was actually signaling precisely what it had to anxiously repress—its feelings of frustration and guilt over accepting the military and giving up on Okinawa's collective memory of the war, the U.S. bases, and servicemen in exchange for money. One Henoko resident unwittingly disclosed a fragment of these feelings by telling me, "Inoue-san, if we had jobs, we would not invite the base, such a noisy thing" (see chapter 4).

It is notable that participants in the pro-base movement included construction workers, taxi drivers, unemployed youngsters, and pachinko-parlor clerks, among others; in short, like this Henoko resident, they were

FIGURE 6.2 The "dream" jacket worn by pro-base residents. The association that created this jacket advocated economic invigoration for Nago by supporting the offshore base.

mostly financially unstable working-class Okinawans. In my view, Nago/ Henoko workers had immersed themselves in the localized, pro-base discourses of "dream" not only because they believed in it but also because they wanted to suppress their uncomfortable feelings arising from receiving money. The irony here was that the more they talked about their dream, the more deeply they were gripped by the very feelings of frustration and guilt they were attempting to escape, because the discourses around dream had been made possible in the first place by the massive amount of money from the Japanese government and other sources (e.g., the construction and related industries in mainland Japan) that had already flooded Nago in the form of campaign expenditures. At the discursive level, the Invigoration Society tried to shelter itself by setting up fixed boundaries. Yet at the material level, it was already being dictated to by the global form of power that would, with the lure of money, absorb Okinawa into the "intimate society."

The Japanese money (campaign expenditures) was used, for instance, to hire Nago and Henoko youngsters at the unusually high rate of 800 yen ($8)[4] an hour to have them distribute flyers and set up signboards all over the city. When I asked how he ended up participating in the pro-base movement, a young Nago worker who was setting up a signboard on the street said in a feeble voice, "Well, my boss told me to do so." The money was also spent to recruit other young Nago and Henoko residents at the high rate of 8,000 yen ($80) a day, whose job was to drive campaign cars throughout the city in the case of men, and to smile and wave at pedestrians from these cars in the case of women, together with pro-base activists who screamed for conditional approval of the new base. Apparently, the money from Tokyo was also spent by dubious ultra-right organizations (e.g., *Shin-Nihon Kyōkai* [the New Japan Society]) that drove giant loudspeaker trucks decorated with the rising-sun flag around in the city. Rumors of bribery by the Invigoration Society were incessant. One person said, for instance, "each member [of my family] received 50,000 yen ($500); the entire family received a couple of hundred thousand yen (a couple of thousand dollars)" (*Mainichi Shinbun*, December 11, 1997: cited in Nago Shimin Tōhyō Hōkokushū Kankō Īnkai 1999: 128). In fact, since Japanese election laws did not apply to the referendum, virtually anything could be done to get votes. In one meeting, the local pro-base group spent the campaign expenditures to offer food and drinks to a hundred residents gathered in an old bar run by a Henoko Executive Committee representative. In still another gathering outside Henoko, a pro-base municipal assemblyman butchered a cow in order to treat local constituencies to beef soup, a treat for special occasions in Okinawa.

While in September 60 percent of Nago constituencies opposed and 21 percent approved (*Okinawa Taimusu*, September 23, 1997), the Japanese government, at first, seems to have optimistically believed in the effectiveness of their strategy of flooding Nago with money to realize its political goal. In early November 1997, Tokyo thus still kept saying that it would not enforce the plan against the will of Nago and Henoko residents. However, to Tokyo's dismay, Nago voters as a whole remained opposed to the offshore base in spite of the massive amount of money it provided. Some seem to have spent the campaign funds by failing to recognize the intention of the government, while others seem to have resisted the temptation of money and messages of "dream" by being true to their feelings of guilt over getting money in exchange for accepting the new base. Thus, for instance, a public survey jointly conducted by the Japanese government and Liberal Democratic Party in late November still showed that 60 percent of Nago constituencies opposed the offshore base construction while only 30 percent approved it (*Okinawa Taimusu*, November 25, 1997). As the date for the referendum drew near, Tokyo became increasingly anxious and desperate, because, for the sake of its own national interests and survival in the global political arena, it needed to expeditiously fulfill its diplomatic obligation to the United States by relocating Futenma Air Station to Henoko.

In December, reflecting the sense of its anxiety and desperation, Tokyo, in addition to providing Nago and Henoko with ample campaign expenditures, began to apply the carrot and the stick treatment. As far as the carrots were concerned, Tokyo took pains to explain that the construction of the base would "benefit" Okinawa in general and Nago City in particular for two reasons. First, Tokyo insisted, the risk of military accidents would be significantly reduced when base functions were transferred from the land (Futenma) to the sea (Henoko). Second, balanced economic growth would be realized within Okinawa by redeveloping the 500-hectare (1,235-acre) area of Futenma Air Station as the core of south-central Okinawa on the one hand, and by pumping money into Nago, the center of northern Okinawa, in exchange for the offshore base on the other. The arrival of several cabinet members, including Prime Minister Hashimoto himself in November 1997,[5] to Okinawa/ Nago—a peripheral region in Japan no national politicians would care about if it did not have bearing upon the question of the U.S. bases—specifically created an impression that the construction of the new base would be of great benefit to the region. For instance, Chief Cabinet Secretary Muraoka Kenzō visited Nago in December 1997, at which time he presented the Northern Regional Promotion Policy to the mayors of the northern region. That same month, the Director General of the Okinawa Development Agency, Suzuki Muneo, came to Nago, saying that the government was determined to get actively involved in the reinvigoration project of the much-deteriorated Nago downtown.[6] Along the same lines, Hashimoto Seiko, a bronze medalist in women's speed-skating in the 1992 Olympics and now a member of the House of Councilors, was invited to the "Meeting for Facilitating the Building of the Women's Center" sponsored by the Invigoration Society. A colorfully illustrated pamphlet published by the Defense Facilities Agency explained the benefits of the offshore base almost as if it were an amusement park or playground (Futenma Hikōjō Isetsu Taisaku Honbu 1997).

Of course, the carrots would never be so sweet unless there were sticks. Tokyo thus occasionally let its tyrannical dimension be seen by Nago and Henoko residents. For instance, the previously mentioned Suzuki Muneo came to the Northern Okinawa Road Construction Office and intimidated the leaders of the construction industry by saying, "Some of your employees are not committed enough to the [pro-base] movement" (*Okinawa Taimusu*, December 14, 1997). The pamphlet mentioned above threateningly stated, "The return of Futenma has been requested by the Okinawan people [you]" (Futenma Hikōjō Isetsu Taisaku Honbu 1997: 1), as if Nago [you] was responsible for accepting the offshore base so that the request could be met. After all, Tokyo was promising those financial carrots *for future* on condition that Nago City and Henoko accepted the offshore base.

Tokyo's carrots and sticks, when fused with the pro-base group's desire to revitalize the local economy, slowly but steadily permeated from the top to the bottom of Nago's pyramid-like pro-base mobilization structure that the Invigoration Society had created. On top of the pyramid, there emerged an unarticulated sense of burden and obligation, because the more commitments Tokyo made to Nago, the larger the responsibilities of the Invigoration Society to repay the favor and compensate for its indebtedness by winning the referendum became. Prefectural assemblyman Nishida Kenjirō of the Liberal Democratic Party of Okinawa said in a banquet attended by more than a thousand supporters, "If we Nago citizens abuse the national government's compassion, the governmental logic [that it is of no use being compassionate and offering development projects to Nago] will fall back upon us. We must be aware of the terrible power the state has over this small town" (*Okinawa Taimusu*, December 17, 1997). In stirring the fear among Nago and Henoko residents that Tokyo would not only abandon them but also actively retaliate against them should they fail to get the base approval, Nishida was trying to make them overcome their reluctance to accept it.

At the bottom of the pro-base campaign structure, the will of the global-national form of power was also manifested in the utilization of the absentee ballot system, whereby employees of construction companies and other small businesses across Nago City were asked—if not ordered—by their bosses (rumor had it that money had been provided) to go to the voting booth together before the official voting date. There, they were forced to mutually check and look at which choice they circled on the ballot sheet; they were given only two of the four choices: outright approval or conditional approval. Over the days between the official announcement of the referendum (December 11) and the actual voting date (December 21), as many as 19 percent of eligible voters were mobilized in this way. One anti-base activist began weeping when seeing this, adding, "The spirit of the referendum and democracy has been entirely ruined."

While public opinion polls consistently showed that the majority of residents still objected to the planned base, the margin between approval and objection was shrinking. While in November (as stated earlier) 60 percent opposed and 30 percent approved, by early December 54 percent opposed and 33 percent approved (*Okinawa Taimusu*, December 9, 1997). The December polls showed, specifically, that the higher percentage of opposition (67 percent) vis-à-vis approval (22 percent) in the depopulated east coast (population: 5,000) was offset by the lower percentage of opposition in the more populated west coast (population: 50,000)—in Yabu, one of the regions on the west coast, 41 percent opposed and 35 percent approved. What is more, the rumor had it that in one area (actual location unknown), the vote was evenly split (*Okinawa Taimusu*, December 19, 1997). In its midst, the Invigoration Society announced that it had collected signatures from 15,987 Nago voters a week before the referendum and more than 20,000, or the majority of Nago constituencies, right before it. The day before the referendum, 2,000 supporters and associates of the Invigoration Society, all wearing green headbands, gathered in downtown Nago. Leaders were standing on a campaign truck, and they bowed and exclaimed amidst the sound of drums and whistles, "For the sake of the development of Nago, please do us this favor (and vote for conditional approval)!" (*Okinawa Taimusu*, December 21, 1997).

Shimin *as Hybrid Global Citizens*

As the date for the referendum drew near, the intimate society, dictated by the global logic of the U.S. military and mediated by the national logic of Japanese money, increasingly engulfed Nago City. However, to reiterate Levinas (1998: 30), "such a society is dual, a society of me and you. We are just among ourselves. Third parties [broader anti-base voices of Okinawa] are excluded." In a way that countered the surge of the intimate society, the citywide coalition—which had made strenuous efforts to realize the referendum—now renamed itself *Kaijyō Herikichi Kensetsu Hantai: Heiwa to Nago Shisei Minshuka wo Motomeru Kyōgikai* (the Coalition for Opposing the Construction of the Offshore Helicopter Base and Seeking Democratization of the Nago City Administration) in order to consolidate and orchestrate a broad anti-base sentiment in Nago City and beyond. In so doing, the coalition, in place of Governor Ota, started to represent Okinawa as the "third person" unified in its resistance to the transnational intimate society.

The power of the third person was expressed through discourses structured around *shimin,* a term which conveyed two sociopolitical meanings simultaneously. On the one hand, *shimin* signified autonomous "citizens" with an educated, middle-class perspective and global aspirations, and on the other hand, ordinary, living "residents" grounded in a specific place—in this case, Nago. In addition, as will be elaborated below, the two meanings concerning globality and locality were mediated and fused by a critical language against the nation-state of Japan. In this way, *shimin* became a metaphor for hybrid citizenship that was simultaneously grounded in locality, entangled in nationality, and involved in globality.

In its first sense, the term referred to Nago *shimin*—citizens who were no longer a uniformly poor, oppressed "people." Indeed, unlike Okinawans before the war or before the reversion, Nago *shimin*—citizens of the late 1990s—did not believe that their culture, their way of life, was something to be ashamed of. Rather, while appropriating the affluence of Okinawa made

FIGURE 6.3 An Okinawan *shimin* (citizen/resident) delivers a speech opposing the off-shore base in front of a small campaign car belonging to the Society for the Protection of Life.

possible by the post-reversion Japanese money, they expressed confidence in who they were, and in the process successfully consolidated newly appearing internal differences along the axes of gender, age, and locality into a fresh sense of totality and unity ("we are Okinawans") against the U.S. military in light of the globalized citizenship discourses centering on human rights, democracy, peace, ecology, and women's issues.

Yet *shimin* not only referred to global "citizens" but in its second meaning also signified ordinary, living "residents" grounded in the history and culture of this specific place, Nago City. In the context of the offshore base dispute, Nago *shimin* as residents, precisely because of the image that they fell behind south-central Okinawa with development and urbanization (see chapter 3), came to represent pure, uncontaminated, and original Okinawan-ness, both culturally and politically.

Sometimes implicitly and sometimes explicitly inserted in the double signification of *shimin* as global citizen and local resident was the sense of *shimin* as an ordinary yet critical Japanese, the sense derived from leftist movements in the 1960s in mainland Japan. To reiterate what I have discussed in chapter 5, *shimin* was an originally mainland Japanese sociopolitical term put to use in this period; various forms of new social movements converged under the category of inclusive and expansive *shimin*; they challenged the central government that attempted to situate postwar Japan in the system of U.S. military-political-economic hegemony in Asia. As we will see, Nago *shimin* actively re-created and extended the leftist spirit of democracy in mainland Japan by speaking as critical Japanese also known as Okinawans.

In sum, confident and affluent Nago *shimin* traversed the local, national, and global realms of power and history; they recast the old style of social movement by the "people" into a new form of resistance in the age of globalization without giving up the specificity of Okinawa, while at the same time they joined a critical political genealogy of postwar Japan. The moral fiber of *shimin* as a hybrid global citizen was, for instance, well personified in the relatively young president of the anti-base coalition, thirty-nine-year-old Miyagi Yasuhiro, affectionately known as *hige no ojisan*—the man with a beard. On the one hand, Miyagi's civic language of democracy, rights, sovereignty, and peace[7] was forceful and new in Nago and Henoko, certainly different from conventional local values centering on social ties of blood and place. He acquired his stance while living in Tokyo, the nation's capital, for twelve years, during which time he joined a progressive theatrical group as an actor, and read Deleuze and Guattari, political theories, postcolonial criticism, and so forth. On the other hand, Miyagi's planetary-national citizenship was simultaneously grounded in his "Nago-ness": He was born and grew up in Nago City, and graduated from Nago High School. Without these basic qualifications, no one would be allowed to enter the political arena of Nago City.

Three stories below will highlight the thrust of the mobilization by *shimin*, which I observed and often participated in during the referendum campaign. The first story involves looking at an informational meeting about the new base that the Japanese government conducted in the Henoko area. The second concerns the dugong, a marine mammal under international and national protection, as an icon of the anti-base movement. The third focuses on women's autonomous mobilization. Each account addresses the issues of justice, peace, the environment, sovereignty, and democracy from different, yet interrelated perspectives. Woven together, these episodes show the ways in which confident, educated, middle-class *shimin* as the critical third person collectively framed the local sensibilities concerning the war, the bases, and the servicemen in the language of global citizenship, with the sedimented sense of injustice of the national government as an indispensable emotional component of that language.

The presence of *shimin* did not mean, of course, the absence in the offshore base dispute of the labor unions and political parties which had mobilized the Okinawan "people" in various social movements in the 1950s–1970s (e.g., the island-wide protest in the 1950s and the reversion movement before 1972; see chapter 2). During the referendum campaign, numerous flyers were written by members of the Japanese Communist Party in Okinawa. Dedicated unionist Miyagi Tamotsu (his real name) drafted the ordinance for the referendum. Furthermore, from the very beginning, members of labor unions were actively involved in background mobilization efforts, such as collecting signatures, distributing flyers, and setting up stages at rallies. Nonetheless, the participation of union and party activists was soon subsumed by that of ordinary, increasingly affluent, *shimin*. This made it possible for the movement to reach deeper and wider social strata beyond the shrinking electoral basis of unions and parties.[8]

The Governmental Explanation Meeting

The Japanese government's Defense Facilities Agency held informational meetings about the offshore base in six places across Nago City during the time leading up to the referendum. One of them was held on the evening of November 12, 1997, in the Athletic Hall of Kushi District (a district adjacent to Henoko) for residents living in Henoko and its vicinity. In the afternoon before the meeting, I was driving a campaign car belonging to the Society for the Protection of Life with activist Kinjō Yūji. The small blue car was equipped with a loudspeaker on its roof, through which Kinjō summoned residents in the Henoko area to the meeting with the words, "Let's disclose the lies and contradictions of the government's construction plan for the new base!" Our car then came to a stop at the Kushi Athletic Hall, in front of which some Defense Facilities Agency officials in gray suits were busy preparing for the meeting. From inside the car, Kinjō joyously spoke to them, "Hang in there!" The officials looked perplexed, staring at the car, which was decorated with a signboard (handwritten by Kinjō) that said, "We Will Not Sell Our Lives for Money!"

Tension was high in the meeting from the very beginning. The governmental officials were enforcing a strict entrance check in order to let in only the residents of the Henoko area, for fear that the meeting would be disrupted by outside "activists," "instigators," and "communists" (like myself). Looking like anything but an Okinawan, I nevertheless passed through the entrance by calling out to Haebaru Kenji, then the president of the Society for the Protection of Life, "Hey, dad!" A total of 270 residents came to the athletic hall by twos and threes and sat on the floor. Many of them (more than 80 percent) were men and women who had already let others know their position against the new base, but some Henoko leaders for the new base as well as their followers also showed up. Considering that eligible voters in Henoko and its vicinity added up to 1,800, the number of attendees was rather small. As one of the residents explained to me, "Coming here shows that you are against the base and attracts a lot of attention. Fearing what other villagers might say later on, many people cannot come." Watchful eyes in Henoko's lifeworld were ubiquitous, cast like a dragnet over various aspects of community life.

To the left side of the stage sat several Defense Facilities Agency officials, and to the right several Nago City officials. The meeting started shortly after 7:00 p.m. The opening remarks were made by the head of the Defense Facilities Department, who repeated the official governmental line as if the return of Futenma was a sign of compassion on the part of Tokyo: "Given the strong request of Governor Ota, the Japanese government, with the cooperation of the U.S. government, decided to fully return Futenma Air Station to Okinawa!" On the huge screen set up on stage appeared a picture of Governor Ota and Prime Minister Hashimoto smiling and shaking hands. This official continued that the government had conducted a careful preliminary survey of Henoko's sea and decided that it was the appropriate construction site in light of safety and ecology. He added that Nago City, including the Henoko area, would economically benefit from the base construction as it would receive subsidies of various kinds.

Then another official came before the audience and began to discuss the distribution of corals and algae in the Henoko's sea, after which he proceeded to explain the structure of the offshore base. Showing computer-simulated pictures of the base, the official stated that (1) the new "facility"[9] would be 1,500 by 600 meters (1,640 by 656 yards), or one-fifth of the area of Futenma Air Station; (2) the facility would be designed in such a way as to protect the environment; (3) the facility would be built at least 1,500 meters (1,640 yards) away from Henoko's shore in order to minimize the noise level; (4) safety would be ensured by prohibiting helicopters from flying above residential areas; and (5) this offshore structure would be removed when it was no longer needed.

A few listeners gave a small round of applause at the end, and a torrent of questions followed. Opponents of the base construction had, in fact, carefully studied the government plan in advance under the guidance of several Okinawan scientists and architects so as to determine what questions to ask. One of the questions was: "Have you conducted preliminary surveys in other seas as well? No? Then, how do you know that Henoko's sea is the most appropriate construction site?" Answer: "Taking into consideration the operations of the U.S. forces, and the busy activities on the west coast of Nago City, it was decided that east of Camp Schwab was ideal." (The floor jeered, "Are you saying that you don't care what happens to people living on the east coast?!")

Another question: "You said that the helicopters would not fly above the residential areas. Then show us where they will fly." Answer: "We will discuss the matter with the U.S. forces, and try to ensure that they fly above school and residential areas as little as possible." ("Give us a break!!") The hall became increasingly filled with booing and angry roars from the floor.

Another question: "Vertical take-off aircraft called Osprey will soon be deployed worldwide. Will they come to the offshore base? If so, when?" Answer: "We have not heard from the U.S. military on that regard." ("Don't cover up!!")

Another question: "Okinawa is, as you know, a Mecca for typhoons. What kind of safety measures against typhoons will be taken? Also, what measures will be taken to prevent the new base from being damaged by the ocean salt when typhoons come?" Answer: "We will carefully design the facility so that no problems would be caused by typhoons." ("Answer the question!!")

Another question: "When a military accident occurs, what will you do?" Answer: "We will take every possible measure to ensure safety, which always comes first. But should an accident happen, we will assume every responsibility." ("That means the offshore base is not safe, contrary to what you have said!!")

Following this outburst, a Henoko male resident in his mid-sixties, who had joined the Society for the Protection of Life for a while but dropped out owing to personal conflicts with some of the members, questioned, and accused, the officials from his wheel-chair. "You guys are liars!" he said, "I don't trust you! I've been diving in this sea to catch fish ever since I was little. But you guys don't know anything about this sea, because you just let some survey companies do a survey of the sea. You guys are liars! And Prime Minister Hashimoto, your boss, is the big liar!!" A storm of praise was heard from the floor. For his part, the governmental official, who had so far been calm in spite of the jeering and heckling, became noticeably agitated by being called a "liar," and replied, "We deeply regret that our proposal was misunderstood. We have honestly disclosed and will continue to disclose all information available in the interests of this area."

After only thirty minutes of questions and answers, the emcee, a government official, ended the meeting, saying, "We are running out of time." He then let the head of the Defense Facilities Department make concluding remarks. Anger intensified in the hall as people began to shout, "We haven't finished our questions at all!" and "Are you going to run away?!" Society for the Protection of Life president Haebaru Kenji stood up with glaring eyes, approached the table at the front of the hall, and started to yell at the government officials. The head of the Defense Facilities Department hastily continued to read the "concluding remarks," which had to be done, I gathered, in order to preserve appearances at the meeting. When Haebaru Kenji, infuriated, began pounding the table, Ōshiro Jirō, an older Henoko leader, shoved him, which triggered a fight between the two. The meeting ended in utter confusion. The government's attempt to create a pretext for constructing the offshore base had been completely subverted by a strong anti-Japanese sentiment present in Henoko (just as in elsewhere in Okinawa) that was articulated through the globalized notions of citizenship such as peace, democracy, and ecology.

In other words, reading their prepared answers, the officials were incapable of hiding from the residents the fact that the new base would be built not for the sake of Okinawa, but for the interests of the U.S. military.

It is quite possible that the officials from Tokyo were not fully convinced by their own logic of the safety, quietness, and environmental-friendliness of the offshore base. After all, no one in the world had ever built a sea-based facility of this scale before. It is also possible that they themselves might not have known the details of the offshore base, because, as has been pointed out (see chapter 2), the U.S. military, not the Japanese government, was the one who had administered the bases in Japan (including Okinawa) under the Status of Forces Agreement (SOFA). After the governmental meeting, suspicions even spread among residents who were for the planned base. One of them told me dismissively, "The government's plan is a fake. Everybody knows that."

Following the meeting, critical voices did indeed start to be heard within Henoko—voices that were always running like underground water beneath the power of the Henoko administration—in a way that tore up the close-meshed net of community life. In my conversation with one male high school student, he cynically criticized the attitudes of pro-base Henoko residents/adults who would not openly discuss the offshore base issues. As the date of the referendum drew near, junior high school students wrote a composition that explained that their opposition to the planned base was for ecological reasons, and they distributed this composition around the community on foot. Henoko children scribbled with pencils on the signboards set up by the pro-base group to change the original appeal "vote for the planned base" into a new message saying "no to the offshore base."

The citywide anti-base coalition, for its part, was quick to highlight the problems of the U.S. military in general and the offshore base in particular that became obvious after the governmental meetings in Henoko and elsewhere in Nago City. Some of the coalition's flyers invoked the memory of continuing lies told to Okinawa by the Japanese state: Just as the central government betrayed us during the war (by sacrificing Okinawa for the defense of mainland Japan) and in the reversion of Okinawa (by allowing the U.S. military to be continuously stationed in Okinawa), "the U.S. Marine Corps has no bearing upon the defense of Japan [although the Japanese government wants us to believe otherwise]. It is a special unit whose task is to storm in, attack, and raid other countries. The offshore base is to be built to dispatch such Marines.... Contrary to the 'reorganization and reduction' [of the U.S. bases in Okinawa], a dangerous base will

stay for many, many years to come." In addition, the anti-Japanese sentiment was blended with and transformed into the critical messages about
the violence of the U.S. military: "Please do not forget the rape incident
[committed by U.S. servicemen in 1995]"; "An MV-22 Osprey flies twice
as fast, carries three times as much, and travels five times as far as an old
helicopter.... When MV-22s are deployed to the offshore base, the noise
will become unbearable"; and "Once the base is built, the U.S. forces will
be given a free hand in operating it."

In one booklet made and distributed by the citywide coalition, the critical positioning of oppositional Okinawans as *shimin*—grounded in locality, engaged in nation-statehood, and linked to globality—was visually
represented by a picture on the front page of a young Okinawan mother
holding her child. At one level, the picture of the grounded motherhood
was supplemented by the detailed descriptions in the booklet of how the
Japanese government tried to deceive Okinawans in order to build the
offshore base. At another level, this picture was juxtaposed by another picture of Marines in a battlefield, which helped to present her as the local
guardian of peace and democracy against the violence of the global military. The binary between good, righteous Okinawa and the evil, violent
Japanese-American power was, understandably but perhaps also somewhat problematically, reinforced.

Instituting the Logic of the Protection of the Environment

The second story that highlights the thrust of the hybrid global citizens'
mobilization concerns the social issue of environmental protection, which
became tied to Okinawa's traditional cultural sensibilities. Specifically, this
story pertains to the dugong, a marine mammal related to the Atlantic-
inhabiting manatee. The dugong, between seven and nine feet long at ma-
turity, is "distributed west in the Red Sea, the Indian ocean and east in the
Pacific as far as the Solomon and Marshal Islands; it ranges south along the
coast of northern Queensland, Austr., and north into the East China Sea"
(*Encyclopedia Britannica*, 15th edition, s.v. "dugong"). The northern limit of
its range is the sea around Okinawa. In the age of the Ryukyu Kingdom,
the dugong was called *jan* or *zan*, and, because of the belief that its flesh,
an esteemed delicacy, was the elixir of life, it was presented to the King

when captured. In Europe, it was taken for a mermaid in the seventeenth and eighteenth centuries by seafarers (Takara K. 1984: 44–51). Because of its taste, the commercial value of its oil, and its gentle character, the dugong was caught to excess, and in recent years has been placed under international and national protection.

The possibility that this medium-sized marine mammal might be frequenting Henoko's sea was brought up early in the anti-base movement by the Japanese Communist Party in Okinawa (*Okinawa Taimusu*, August 22, 1997). Responding to their call, several divers dived off the east coast of Nago City and reported that there were remains of submarine pastures of algae and seaweed that the dugong might have eaten. This initiated a search for the dugong. The Japanese Scientists' Association, the World Wide Fund for Nature (WWF)-Japan, local and mainland Japanese TV stations, environmental NGOs, and divers (both professional and amateur) came to Henoko's sea to look for the dugong. Dugong T-shirts and badges were made as a source of revenue for the Henoko Society for the Protection of Life as well as the citywide coalition. In the process, the dugong became a symbol of the anti-base campaign, and the basis upon which the logic of protecting the environment was built. Some of the flyers, pamphlets, and posters of the anti-base group, often adorned with pictures and drawings of the dugong, read, "Money disappears in a moment, but nature, if protected, lasts forever"; "The rich nature of northern Okinawa is Okinawa's treasure"; and "On the beautiful sea and beautiful island that cultivates life, we do not need the offshore base.… Let's hand down these [treasures] to our children and grandchildren." An animated cartoon of the dugong, which holds a flag in its fin that says "No," also appeared on a hand-made signboard of the Society for the Protection of Life.

Finally, on January 13, 1998 (after the referendum that I will discuss shortly), an Okinawan TV crew flying in a helicopter found and videotaped a dugong basking on the surface of Henoko's sea. Grandpa Iheya exclaimed, "Here comes the messenger of our Gods from *niraikanai* [i.e., the paradise from across the sea where Okinawan ancestors (gods) are believed to live]!" Grandpa Iheya's words, indeed, showed the ways in which *shimin*, as a grounded citizen, anchored the often experience-distant, imported language of ecology in locally informed Okinawan sensibilities through the local spiritual vocabulary of *niraikanai*. The global-citizenship and local-residentship of Okinawan *shimin* also took on a critical national/Japanese character when its icon—the photographic image of the dugong—was distributed to mainland Japan via national news media.

Women as Shimin

In October 1997, two months before the referendum, a new organization was instituted in order to represent the anti-base voices of the ten districts north of Henoko, so as to make an alliance with the Henoko Society for the Protection of Life and get involved in the evolving anti-base movement across Nago City led by the citywide coalition. The new organization was made independent from the Society for the Protection of Life because these ten districts and the Henoko area, while geographically close, had long maintained a subtle psychological distance. This distance had been created mainly because, unlike Henoko and its vicinity, these districts had very few economic and political ties to Camp Schwab and thus experienced quite a different social history from the Henoko area. The new group was named *Herikichi Iranai Futami Ihoku 10ku no Kai* (the Association of the Ten Districts [north of Henoko] Not Wanting the Offshore Base).

It is notable that the association's activities, although initially led by men, were supplemented and then, toward the end of the referendum campaign, taken over by women. There were two main reasons for the men's retreat. One was job-related. Many of the districts' men made their living by working for pro-base construction companies and small businesses across Nago, and the pressure from their workplace often became too great. The second and related reason was that the older leaders (men) had long been supporters of the conservative Nago City mayor, Higa Tetsuya, and did/could not actively lead an anti-base movement for fear of possible retaliation from the Nago City administration. The association's women therefore filled in the oppositional political space that the men evacuated. They did so with an acute sense of urgency, believing that the offshore base would be built if they did not raise their voices now. In the process, the women asserted themselves as *shimin*, grounded in locality on the one hand and connected with the trans-local values and practices of ecology, democracy, and active agency on the other, with the broader anti-Tokyo sentiment as the common denominator.

The women, most of whom were employed, and often along with their children, visited houses after work and attended, often organized, base-related meetings in order to express their opposition. Their activities were flexible, decentered, and characterized by the absence of a rigid chain of command. For instance, they did not spend much time doing *nemawashi* (preparatory negotiations aimed at reaching a consensus, which are to be done behind the scenes), which was very common and frequent among male-dominated groups. As leader Mashiki Tomi (her real name) told me, women "do not need to rely on an organization [be it a company, a school, a labor union, or a political party] to speak up. We do not shoulder the burden of an organization." Rather, the basic principle of action among these women was a kind of controlled and thoughtful spontaneity. That is, each person did whatever she could do whenever she could do it, contributing to creating a loosely organized movement body. Thus, some wrote essays for public speeches, some read/translated these essays into Okinawan dialect; others drew posters, animated cartoons, flyers, and signboards; still others sometimes cooked and sometimes performed traditional Okinawan dance in demonstrations.

In part because of the flexibility of their organization, creative ideas sprang from within the women's group. For instance, they wittily nicknamed their group[10] *Jan'nu Kai*, which meant simultaneously the Society for the Dugong and the Society of Joan of Arc. Their consciousness as grounded Okinawan mothers, wives, and homemakers was expressed, both implicitly and explicitly, in their activities, as was exemplified in their slogan, "We oppose the base, for the sake of our children and grandchildren." This was not to be taken as a nativist statement, one should be clear, because as entering the planetary terrain of ecology as *shimin*, these women developed critical stances that were national and global in scope. For instance, when I interviewed activist Urashima Etsuko (her real name) in 1998, she said, "We may be deceived into believing that the government thinks and cares about our region in issuing those development projects. But these are projects that are imposed upon us. We would like to think about a different form of development that is compatible with our environment, which we can devise and implement by ourselves." In the aftermath of the referendum, indeed, several women (and men) in the ten districts instituted a project to promote eco-tourism in order to help people from mainland Japan experience the natural richness and beauty of the northern region, which faces both the sea and the mountains. Mashiki Tomi explained to me this project in her usual nonimposing voice: "Maybe we should reexamine the foundations of our own life relying too much on technology. Do we really need to be richer and wealthier than we are? If so, why?"

The women's group's synthesis of grounded womanhood, critical nationhood, and global citizenship was perhaps most dramatically revealed when they first organized a demonstration of, for, and by women. Three days before the referendum, realizing that the pro-base group had massively built up its movement, several core members of *Jan'nu Kai* had an emergency nighttime meeting to discuss what they could do. They decided on a demonstration to be held under the name of *Onna tachi no michi junei* (The Women's Walking). *Michi junei* refers to a traditional religious-festive activity, from the age of the Ryukyu Kingdom, of walking to demarcate the territory of a community. The women appropriated this traditional activity and added a new political meaning to it. In a departure from the conventional demonstrations organized by political parties and labor unions, they decided not to use flags

FIGURE 6.4 The Women's Walk. The sign reads, "Vote against the offshore base. Let the voices of the women touch your heart."

and banners of any organization, and not to chant slogans. Instead, they appealed to women to attend the demonstration as autonomous individuals, to bring drawings, posters, and anything of their own making, and to express whatever they wanted to say in their own words, not only during the demonstration but also in an open forum held before the demonstration.

The women, however, were not aware that they needed to get a permit from the Nago Police. The day after the meeting, they found that the Nago Police would normally issue a permit only a week to ten days in advance of a planned demonstration. However, the women did not have that much time, so they rushed into the police station, and, with fake tears, persuaded the policemen to give them the permit by saying, "Please forgive us, please. Women just don't know anything!" The day before the referendum, some five hundred women from all over Okinawa (including the elderly women from Henoko) and even some from mainland Japan[11] walked resolutely through Nago, declaring, "We want to pass down not the military base, but this environment, to our children and grandchildren," and "Please do not sacrifice the east coast for the development of Nago." They proceeded undaunted even after the pro-base group splashed them with water. While witnessing the power of these ordinary women, or *shimin* in the exact sense of the term, one male supporter exclaimed to me in excitement, "I was thinking that the pro-base group had the upper hand in this campaign. Now for the first time ever, I feel we are winning the referendum!" As one woman told me, "If you decide you cannot do anything, you really cannot. It is after you start doing something that you realize that you can actually do whatever you want."

• • •

In summary, *shimin* as hybrid citizens replenished the global discourses on peace (the first story), ecology (the second story), and women's issues (the third story) with specific local sensibilities informed by Okinawa's collective culture and identity, while at the same time appropriating and extending the tradition of democratic, oppositional movements in mainland Japan as critical participants in the national political sphere. Even though Nago *shimin* were diverse in generation, gender, occupation, geographic positioning, what they had in common, the desire for a life and a world without the military, enabled them to act together as a "multitude," to use Hardt and Negri's (2004) term. In short, by confidently declaring "We are Okinawans,"

Nago *shimin* accentuated the unity and specificity of Okinawa against the background of national-global power without erasing internal differences.

Notably, as the hybrid citizenship was constructed in this way, its multitude also spilled outside the local context. That is to say, *shimin* in Nago and Henoko constructed and extended what Sonia E. Alvarez calls "social movement webs," characterized by polycentricness, expansiveness, and horizontality, by "the intricacy and precariousness of the manifold imbrications of and ties established among movement organizations, individual participants, and other actions in civil and political society and the state" (Alvarez 1997: 87, 90). From mainland Japan, for example, major newspapers and TV stations came to Nago and Henoko, and, upon returning to mainland Japan, circulated critical information about the planned offshore base construction. Intellectuals, activists, students, and members of labor unions, political parties, peace organizations, environmental groups, and women's groups also came in large numbers from mainland Japan to listen to what Nago and Henoko residents had to say about the war, the bases, and the servicemen, to donate money, and/or to help and support the movements as volunteers.

Beyond the boundaries of Japan, there always existed a question of the power of global English; because of the insurmountable problem of the language barrier, *shimin* did not, and indeed could not, formally participate in any organized global networks of the anti-base movement. Risking a shameless self-promotion, however, owing in part to a letter I wrote, translated, and distributed in English through mail and e-mail at the behest of Miyagi Yasuhiro (President of the citywide anti-base coalition) and Haebaru Kenji (President of the Society for the Protection of Life in Henoko), the movement was connected, if loosely, to a larger global circuit of oppositional movements and sentiments. For instance, several organizations outside Japan, such as the City of Berkeley, Peace Council of Aotearoa New Zealand, Friends of the Filipino People, and the Japan Policy Research Institute in California, as well as students and intellectuals in Asia and in the United States, expressed solidarity in the name of peace, democracy, and ecology. Some of them even visited Henoko and Nago.

Ultimately, the spread and densification of the social movement webs gave the public sphere in Okinawa a specific universal character, at least at the discursive level. For this was not only a Hebermasian domain of public discussion, argument, and deliberation regulated by the Euro-American model of liberal rationality and civility (Habermas 1989), but also a realm of sentiments, beliefs, and practices grounded in local culture, memory, and history connected with the war, the bases, and servicemen (cf. Hirschkind 2001). Put differently, mediated by a smoldering sense of injustice against the Japanese state, the Okinawan public sphere became an arena wherein the local sentiments and practices were externalized in the global language of citizenship while simultaneously the global language of citizenship was framed, interpreted, and practiced in Okinawa's historical sensibilities. While residents in favor of the planned base tended to view Nago and Henoko as an isolated enclave/lifeworld regulated by the single logic of blood and place, Nago and Henoko *shimin*, as the third person, lodged the multilayered collective agent of social transformation, embracing the diversity within and beyond Okinawa in a fundamentally renewed sense of totality—"We are Okinawans."

Victory

On the day of the referendum, December 21, 1997, the simple act of voting became for many people in Nago City and Henoko sort of an existential matter revolving around the predicaments of being Okinawan, because their votes to accept or reject the offshore base could determine not only the future of Henoko, Nago City, and Okinawa at large, but also that of the Japanese state and the U.S.–Japan alliance. On that day, I was at the voting place in Henoko. One voter, after a long deliberation, left the voting station without voting, explaining, "I just couldn't decide" (Taira 1997). A few older voters, whose literacy was somewhat questionable, were asking their friends in the voting booths if they were circling the correct item on the ballot sheet. Anti-base residents finished voting by twos and threes with an anxious look. Leaders of Henoko in favor of the new base also came to the voting place, looking confident and certain. A group of junior high school students ran out of their school gate for physical exercise, timed to their shouts of " 'no' to the base, 'no' to the base" which were directed toward the line of people standing in front of them at the poll.

The voting ended at 6:00 p.m. By the time the ballot counting started about an hour and a half later, I was at the "struggle hut" of the Henoko Society for the Protection of Life, which was already packed with supporters as well as TV and newspaper reporters and photographers from both

Okinawa and mainland Japan.[12] I heard later that the offices of the citywide anti-base coalition in downtown Nago, the Association of the Ten Districts [north of Henoko] Not Wanting the Offshore Base, and the pro-base groups in Nago and Henoko were similarly crowded.

At around 10:30 p.m., as Henoko residents were anxiously awaiting the news about the referendum results, a TV station in the struggle hut broadcast a short message on the screen, which read that "the anti-base group is likely to gain the majority." Before 11:00 p.m., the victory of the anti-base group became certain. People burst into joy. Leaders of the society held a press conference inside the struggle hut to thank all supporters in Okinawa and beyond for the victory. Kinjō Hatsuko, wife of Kinjō Yūji, was so overwhelmed with tears of joy that she could barely express the words, "my husband, my husband [made this happen]." Grandpa Iheya started to

FIGURE 6.5 The Society for the Protection of Life holding a press conference inside the struggle hut to declare its victory in the referendum.

dance to Okinawan music, followed by Henoko older women and other residents and supporters of the society. Leaders of the citywide anti-base coalition came to the struggle hut to celebrate. Victory banquets lasted well beyond midnight in Henoko—as well as in other places in Nago City.

Only a few hundred meters away, in the commercial district of Henoko, pro-base residents could not help showing a deep sense of disappointment and loss (*Okinawa Taimusu*, December 22, 1997). The atmosphere of the pro-base Nago Citizens' Society for Facilitating Invigoration office in downtown Nago was similarly heavy. President Arakaki Seifuku weakly commented on TV, "We started from nothing. This number of votes (see below) indicates our victory. We will not end our efforts." Nago City Mayor Higa Tetsuya held a 4-minute press conference, read a prepared statement that said, "I will carefully handle the matter by taking into consideration the votes both for and against the base construction," and immediately left the city hall (*Okinawa Taimusu*, December 22, 1997). Cabinet members of the Japanese government were also disappointed and frustrated, saying that "we would like to carefully observe the situation of Nago City and the prefecture." Needless to say, the U.S. government also communicated to Tokyo its displeasure with the results of the referendum (Ogata 1997).

The breakdown of votes in the referendum was as follows:

1. I approve—2,562 votes (8.13 percent)

2. I approve if the construction is done with appropriate measures for protecting the environment and has positive economic effects—11,705 votes (37.18 percent)

3. I oppose—16,254 votes (51.63 percent)

4. I oppose if the construction is not done with appropriate measures for protecting the environment and does not have positive economic effects—385 votes (1.22 percent)

5. Spoiled ballots, no preference selected, etc.—571 votes (1.82 percent)

Total votes—31,477 (82.45 percent of eligible voters)

In short, 52.8 percent of voters opposed the offshore base, while 45.3 percent favored it. The margin (7.5 percent, or 2,372 votes) showed the "conscience of *shimin*" in the words of the president of the citywide coalition, Miyagi Yasuhiro (*Okinawa Taimusu*, December 22, 1997). This was, indeed, the moment when new collective agents of social transformation, *shimin*, emerged from the depth of postwar Okinawan history.

7

THE NAGO CITY MAYORAL ELECTION AND THE CHANGING TIDE OF OKINAWAN RESISTANCE

 Nago *shimin* as grounded citizens successfully extended Okinawa's historical anti-military and anti-Tokyo sentiment into the globalized language of democracy, peace, women's issues, and the environment, so as to bring diverse constituents within Nago, Okinawa, and beyond together into an inclusive, heterogeneous public sphere of discussion about the U.S. military. The success of the anti-base movement paradoxically spelled its own defeat, however, because the totalizing oppositional idea of "we are Okinawans," though effectively encompassing age, gender, regional, and other differences, failed to acknowledge the fear of failure and underdevelopment of a broader sector of Okinawa's working-class residents. In other words, in their emphasis on the middle-class, citizenry values of ecology, women's issues, and peace, the anti-base movement might have "gone global" to such an extent that it became detached from and even offended the experiences and cultural sensibilities of financially insecure local residents.

In an attempt to compensate for this centrifugal tendency, the anti-base movement then "went local" perhaps too much by negating its own accomplishments, including a flexible, mobile, polycentric movement web that ended up being replaced with a somewhat anachronistic male-and-seniority-centered hierarchical organization with a rigid chain of command. In the process of swinging between the global and the local, the sense of the unity of Okinawa that the anti-base movement had created fell apart. By recycling the fragments of the anti-base movement in Nago, the pro-base movement for its part then successfully consolidated the local with the ideology of a class-regional difference, "we are Okinawans but of a different kind." This chapter will articulate the ways in which this "difference" surfaced in Henoko and spread like a ripple in a pond to Nago City at large, changing the tide of social movements and, ultimately, subverting the unity of Okinawa.

Tensions Within the Anti-Base Movement

As the date of the referendum drew near, numerous citizens—unionists, party activists, intellectuals, teachers, students, concerned *shimin*s, journalists, and so forth from various parts of Okinawa, mainland Japan, and beyond—swarmed to the struggle hut with cars and tour buses in order to support the movement of the Henoko Society for the Protection of Life. Members of the society hosted these visitors (numbering twenty to three hundred a day) by serving tea, delivering lectures on the current situation in detail, and distributing handmade pamphlets. According to the society's records, the total number of visitors before the referendum eventually reached ten thousand. The more successful the movement became, however, the more seriously the society faced the question of how to relate to the world outside Henoko without being uprooted from its own soil.

On the positive side, the visitors were a tremendous help in spreading the society's message to the outside world. TV cameras captured activities and statements of Haebaru Kenji, Kinjō Yūji, and other core members. Articles featuring interviews with society members appeared in Tokyo newspapers and magazines. A documentary about Haebaru Kenji was filmed and broadcast all over Japan. The president of the Japanese Communist Party, executive members of the Social Democratic Party, and other well-known leftist national politicians visited Henoko in order to show their solidarity, and members of the society, in return, often went all the way to mainland Japan to deliver lectures on the current base struggle. Furthermore, foreign correspondents, students, and researchers from South Korea, the Philippines, the U.S., and France, among others, came to the struggle hut in order to learn about the movement and inform the world of Henoko's predicaments.

On such occasions, I was asked by the society to act as interpreter, and I assumed that role (On the question of my positionality, see chapter 8). It should be added that visitors helped increase the society's budget by buying its original T-shirts, badges, pamphlets, and so forth and by donating substantial amounts of money. In the midst of all, Henoko took on a "divine" character representing various oppositional movements in Okinawa and beyond.

On the negative side, however, the visitors' support also often offended the cultural sensibilities of pro-base Henoko residents enmeshed with the prolonged presence of the U.S. military (Camp Schwab). When certain environmental and peace organizations came to the struggle hut with the slogan "Save the Dugong," irritation rose especially high among these residents, some of whom told me, "Our life is more important than the dugong's. Without jobs [i.e., the base, new and/or old], we can't live." Specifically, they were disturbed by the ways in which ecology and peace activists, always situated in a safe, infallible, ethical realm, denounced the U.S. military from above without understanding the complex local sentiments and histories about it (as explored in chapter 4). Visitors' good intentions—sometimes self-satisfactions—often ended up generating resentment among local Henoko residents, leading them to vent their anger upon the Society for the Protection of Life that hosted these visitors. In other words, to the eyes of local residents, the orientation of the society became too global, middle-class, and experience-distant.

The tension between the society's global aspirations and Henoko's local sensibilities was manifested most clearly in the plights of residents, which ultimately translated themselves in the society's membership problem. Before the referendum, pro-base residents no longer even said hello to anti-base residents on the street, in the village festivals, or in other social functions such as funerals and weddings. This tendency became even more obvious after the referendum. "I feel like I have to hold my breath. The air of Henoko has gotten so suffocating," one anti-base resident told me. For this reason, one man serving the pro-base Henoko administration who was also related to anti-base Grandpa Iheya of the society, disappeared from Henoko with a letter to his family behind him stating, "Don't worry about me," to be found eventually in his car in Kagoshima Prefecture in Kyushu some 700 kilometers (435 miles) away. He stated in retrospect that "I understood both anti-base and pro-base perspectives. Pressured by residents from both sides, I became panicked" (*Asahi.com maitaun Okinawa*, January 12, 2006). The president of the Association of the Ten Districts [north of Henoko] Not Wanting the Offshore Base (see chapter 6), a man in his fifties, attempted suicide by hanging himself for the same reason (he escaped death; *Asahi.com maitaun Okinawa*, January 12, 2006).

Often unable to bear the pressure, and often discouraged by their own relatives and family members who opposed the new base but did not want to attract attention in the community, original members of the Society for the Protection of Life one after another dropped out of the movement. At one moment before the referendum, the number of members had dwindled to three, which left a heavy burden on their shoulders when, for instance, receiving three hundred visitors a day. President Haebaru Kenji, who essentially sacrificed his job as a plumber to organize the movement, said to me, "I want to quit the movement but I can't." He became understandably irritable, which only drove Henoko residents (even sympathizers of the society) further away. The other two members, Kinjō Yūji and Higashikawa Yūtoku, worked to the limit of their capacity, and as a result, became literally exhausted. Transgressing my role as a researcher, I helped them out by writing signboards, setting them up, and driving through Henoko and beyond to make announcements about meetings and demonstrations. Otherwise, perhaps, the society would not have functioned at all.

In order to overcome the membership problem, after the referendum the society chose to focus its movement more specifically on local matters. In their discussion of labor movements, Piven and Cloward (1977: 20; cited in Scott 1985: 43) once argued that workers "experience the factory, the speeding rhythm of the assembly line, the foremen, the spies, the guards, the owner, and the paycheck. They do not experience monopoly capitalism." In a way that extended Piven and Cloward's insight, I found that Henoko residents experience the noise of military helicopters, the English spoken by servicemen, the rent paid by Tokyo, the bosses of the community, the friends, and the relatives; they do not experience the U.S.–Japan security alliance. In an attempt to maintain close compliance with the sensibilities of these locally grounded residents and their essentially pro-base sentiment, some leaders of the society prohibited, after the referendum, members from being interviewed by TV and newspaper reporters, and forbid "outsiders" (except this writer) to enter the struggle hut without permission. Members were even told not to discuss the U.S.–Japan Security Treaty and related issues of global politics because they were "too political." In a word, the anti-base movement in Henoko tried to reorient what came to be seen as its excessive global/outward tendency by going to another extreme, the local/parochial.

In fairness to the Society for the Protection of Life, this reorientation was not entirely inapposite; members now aggressively and rightfully addressed local everyday life issues, such as the potential deterioration of the living environment after the construction of the new base, the questionable accounting practices of the Henoko administration, and the monopoly of administrative power held by a few bosses. They emphasized, "We are fighting for the sake of Henoko residents." Yet, it is also true that the shift of the movement orientation from the translocal/outward to the parochial/inward also watered down the critical edge of the anti-base movement of the society which was, originally, global in scope and aspiration. This shift prompted even Henoko Executive Committee Chair Sueyoshi Kaoru, the most powerful pro-base boss in the community, to tell me that he "appreciated" the movement of the society which, now being operated within the limits of local sensibilities, no longer posed a threat to the communal order.

The reorientation of the movement may have solved one problem the society faced, that is, its isolation and alienation from local Henoko residents, but this also caused a number of new ones. The first problem had its genesis in the way the society was structured and run. Precisely because of their efforts to organize a movement firmly grounded in local cultural sensibilities, the society after the referendum, somewhat ironically, rapidly produced a replica of the traditional, male-and-seniority-centered power structure akin to the Henoko administration (see chapter 4) that belied its progressive platform "oppose the base, democratize the administration." Henoko youth even before the referendum had shunned the society in part because of the domineering attitudes of some of its adult members. Henoko women—particularly old women—joined the society, but their role was always restricted to preparing food for male activists, answering telephones, serving tea to visitors, and carrying out other minor functions. One Henoko woman sympathetic to the society nevertheless once commented, "There is something about the society that keeps women away." Yagaji Kiyoko, a survivor of the *Himeyuri Butai* (Lily Corps) during the battle of Okinawa (see chapter 5), and her followers gradually moved to act outside the society. Moreover, as the society after the referendum tried to be grounded in locality and parochiality, the assumed hegemony of the native residents over the nonnative ones made an appearance within the society itself, arousing internal conflicts among the members. In short, the society's activities became, particularly after the referendum, somewhat inflexible, centralized, and narrow, characterized by a rigid channel of command that was structured along the axes of gender, age, and nativity. The polycentric, horizontal, and inclusive tendency of the society, manifested earlier in its movement structure and spirit, rapidly disappeared.

Second, the society's return to the local/parochial sensibilities caused conflicts with the anti-base coalition in Nago City, which sought citizen movements in the larger public sphere. The relationship between the two organizations had already become problematic before the referendum. The citywide coalition found it difficult to "take the local" out of the Henoko Society for the Protection of Life, while the society was frustrated with the way in which the coalition led and even dominated the movement under the notions of *shimin*, women, democracy, peace, and the environment. Yet, at the same time, the two needed each other. Without the Society for the Protection of Life in Henoko, the site of the new base construction, the coalition would lose the very cause of its mobilization. In turn, the society could not win the referendum without the mobilizing power of the coalition. The love-hate relationship between them was somewhat masked until the referendum was over. In fact, in a heated closed-door discussion in October 1997 (before the referendum), which I was allowed to attend, President Haebaru in frustration declared the withdrawal of the society from the unified front established by the citywide coalition, although he was dissuaded by Kinjō Yūji as well as by the president of the coalition. However, after the referendum the tension could no longer be contained.

In sum, the society lost its decentered organizational character internally and simultaneously, faced the insurmountable problem in engaging in the larger global public sphere externally, both of which contributed to isolating the society from the social movement web in Nago and beyond. The society's move for isolation was symbolically captured in the day before the referendum, December 20, 1997. On this particular day, an Okinawan newspaper reported that the Henoko Executive Committee decided to accept the base in exchange for local development projects. Kinjō Yūji was furious. He immediately jumped into the campaign car and drove around Henoko, denouncing the Henoko administration at full volume through a half-broken public address system. Then, some thirty members of the society went to *kōminkan*, the Henoko administration building, to protest. When confronted by these residents, the Henoko District mayor, whose face flushed with frustration about the leak of the information (i.e., apparently, the Henoko administration communicated its "conditional approval" to the Nago City mayor around the time of the referendum), responded, "There is no such fact that the Henoko administration decided to accept the base." Behind the flustered district mayor, Henoko Executive Committee Chair Sueyoshi Kaoru was sitting, quietly watching the situation develop.

In retrospect, members of the society could have exploited this opportunity to directly confront and accuse Sueyoshi Kaoru, not the district mayor, who worked under Sueyoshi, of disregarding the wishes of the residents against the new base. Yet, they did not and could not do this at least in part because of the conventional control mechanism within Henoko of the rule of seniority (see chapter 4). Most male members present were younger than Sueyoshi Kaoru and senior to the district mayor, which meant that they were supposed to direct no accusation toward Sueyoshi, though granted the privilege of having a junior official like the district mayor obey (or at least listen to) them. In a word, the social-cultural sensibilities that members had long acquired as residents of Henoko frustrated the goal ("oppose the base, democratize the local administration") they had set up themselves. Tied up in self-contradiction, President Haebaru Kenji, among others, gradually lost his passion for the movement, particularly after the referendum. In his words, "I just do not feel like doing this any more. My heart no longer burns." He eventually dropped out of the movement entirely. In this and other ways, the relatively fragile unity between locally grounded residentship (represented by the Henoko Society for the Protection of Life) on the one hand, and global citizenship (represented by the Nago citywide coalition) on the other, the unity made possible by the oppositional notion of *shimin* that captured Okinawa's sedimented anti-base sentiments, decisively crumbled into fragments.

Meanwhile, as will be shown below, Mayor Higa Tetsuya of Nago City reconstructed the Nago "residentship" from these fragments and multiplied it along the regional-class line within Okinawa. In doing so, he shattered the unity of Okinawa while making internal conflicts reappear on its political landscape. The Japanese government, for its part, exploited the internal split for its own political ends—to force Okinawa to bear the burden of the U.S. bases.

The Mayor's Political Acrobatics

At one moment after the referendum, Mayor Higa decided to abandon, once and for all, the plan to build the new offshore base in Henoko/Nago (*Okinawa Taimusu*, December 23, 1997). On December 24, however, there was a huge turn of events, apparently owing to the uproar from local pro-base leaders as well as the pressure from Tokyo. The mayor went to Tokyo to see Prime Minister Hashimoto Ryūtaro, after which he actually accepted the base—declaring that the base construction in Henoko/Nago would be "a step toward the reduction of the U.S. military presence in Okinawa" (*Okinawa Taimusu*, December 25, 1997). At the same time he stepped down from his position as mayor "to take responsibility for the disorder of city administration" (*Okinawa Taimusu*, December 25, 1997). Higa cited the fact that the Henoko administration had decided to conditionally accept the new base as the main reason for his decision. Prime Minister Hashimoto reportedly shed tears out of happiness. Higa's behavior certainly constituted a betrayal of the will of Nago *shimin*, who had just said no to the new base in the referendum.

At Christmastime in 1956, in the midst of the land acquisition dispute, Henoko had signed the contract to accept the construction of Camp Schwab, which the mayor of Kushi Village (the forerunner of Nago City) had endorsed in order to transform this economically ill-fated village into a thriving town. In doing so, northern Okinawa triggered the collapse of Okinawa's unified protest against the U.S. military in the 1950s (see chapter 4). Forty-one years later, in the midst of the offshore base dispute, the Henoko administration similarly decided to accept the new base in return for money, which the mayor of Nago City reinforced by securing the prime minister's "solemn promise" to develop northern Okinawa at large. Once again, the unified front was destroyed.

It would, however, be an oversimplification to merely denounce the mayor as a person under the thumb of Tokyo. Higa's acceptance of the new base, for example, went hand in hand with his resignation against the wishes of, and despite pressure from, the Japanese government, which would have preferred him to remain in office. Presumably, the Japanese government was afraid that the mayor's decision to accept the base and then resign would incite Nago constituencies' anger and lead them to vote for the anti-base candidate in the following mayoral election. If Higa were replaced by an anti-base mayor, his acceptance of the offshore base would come to nothing. Nevertheless, Higa perceived that he had no choice other than to resign as mayor upon his acceptance of the new base, because the anti-base group was sure to recall him if he stayed in office, which, to this dignified man, would have been an unbearable disgrace.

Higa therefore dislodged and paralyzed both the premise of the anti-base movement and the logic of the Japanese government. He managed to carve out a peculiar third space at the closest point of contact between domination (the Japanese government) and resistance (the anti-base movement) whereby he expressed a specific identity that was both broadly Okinawan and parochially "Nago-ish." On the one hand, in his peculiar resistance to the Japanese government that tried to patronize him as its puppet, Higa asserted that "I am an Okinawan" by dramatically enacting his resignation in Tokyo, capital of the nation. His Okinawan-ness was also revealed by the letter he wrote and submitted upon his resignation to the Japanese government wherein he cited the words of Tei Junsoku (1663–1734), a legendary magistrate of Nago in the age of the Ryukyu Kingdom, to call for the restoration of harmony in Okinawa. On the other hand, in Tokyo Higa also expressed the peculiarity of Nago—"I am an Okinawan but of a different kind"—by stating to the press that "for the sake of the development of my hometown, I have decided to sacrifice my own political life [i.e., resign my post]" (*Okinawa Taimusu*, December 25, 1997). Enveloped in this statement was unarticulated resentment shared broadly by Nago residents against middle-class citizens residing mainly in south-central Okinawa. Many Nago residents felt, I found, that middle-class citizens not only trivialized the specific economic needs of northern Okinawa but also obscured the actuality that the governmental subsidies had provided these citizens the very foundation for their pan-Okinawan discourses on peace, democracy, and ecology. And perhaps it is this particular sentiment of Nago residents, when articulated as a class-regional difference within Okinawa, that changed the political tide in Nago, probably beyond what Mayor Higa intended. Indeed, in the Nago City mayoral election campaign that followed,

FIGURE 7.1 The pro-base candidate, together with Nago City leaders, standing on a campaign truck to initiate the mayoral election campaign.

the "Okinawan" (vis-à-vis Japanese) aspect of Higa's message receded into the background, while the sentiment of Nago-ness in his message became the force that created a class-regional split within Okinawa.

The Mayoral Election

During the mayoral election campaign, Nago's pro-base group, given a second chance, modified its campaign strategy. It moved the Japanese government's intrusive presence and ostentatious voice—which had annoyed Nago voters, including many pro-base voters, during the referendum campaign—to the background, while framing the offshore base dispute thoroughly in the parochial language of local economy, tradition, and culture. The "solemn promise" of the Japanese government was no longer talked about; it was simply assumed as a given. On the basis of this promise, the pro-base group rallied behind the politics of the local, Nago City, and in doing so, intertwined the working-class pride with the love of hometown so as to constitute the sentimental identity of locality and belonging, "we are Okinawans but of a different kind."

For instance, pro-base candidate Kishimoto Tateo aggressively underscored the local economic issues, such as the 20 percent unemployment rate among Nago youth, while avoiding the offshore base issue altogether by declaring that he would follow the prefectural governor's decision. Local sentiment and longing for the community bounded by love and pride were heightened also by small-scale meetings in every one of Nago City's fifty-five districts (including Henoko), a total of 230 gatherings in a single month (January 1998). In one such meeting in a northwest district of Nago, which I attended, the pro-base group well coordinated the speeches of Kishimoto Tateo, former Mayor Higa Tetsuya, national assemblyman Kakazu Chiken, Kishimoto Tateo's wife, and the president of Kishimoto's campaign club, so as to conciliate, intimidate, move, patronize, and glorify local residents. This set up a stark contrast with the mantras of peace, democracy, and the environment used by the leaders of leftist political parties supporting the anti-base candidate, Tamaki Yoshikazu (on him see below). Furthermore, the pro-base group emphasized the fact that Kishimoto Tateo was born and raised in Nago, while anti-base candidate Tamaki was not (he had been born and raised in Izumi Town, adjacent to Nago City). Implicit in this message was that no "outsider" should govern Nago. A Nago City assemblyman, elected from Henoko, epitomized the pro-base group's strategy to highlight locality and belonging when he raised his voice there: "In the referendum campaign, I was criticized by the pro-base group on the grounds that I was not explicit enough about inviting the base, and simultaneously by the anti-base group on the grounds that I was not explicit enough about rejecting the base. I had no room to move because of various pressures, as you know. But we have to win the mayoral election. This is a campaign to protect Nago from communism and socialism, not about the offshore base!"

It should be noted that Kishimoto came from a rather leftist background. He graduated from the highly ranked Waseda University, known for its critical traditions, with a major in political science. He had once worked with Tamaki Yoshikazu (the anti-base candidate), and had even been actively involved in the anti-military movement before the reversion of Okinawa. But from the mid-1980s on, he worked under nativist Mayor Higa Tetsuya as vice mayor of Nago City, gradually shifting his stance from leftist idealism to conservative realism. Kishimoto's complex, if somewhat inconsistent, position was well expressed in the statement he made during the mayoral election. He declared, "I am not for the new base," while adding, "I am not against the new base either." The pro-base group, in one sense, capitalized on Kishimoto's ambiguous political background, which, when combined with his genuine Nago-ness, would help gain support from a broader range of Nago voters, including anti-base voters.

In the course of the pro-base campaign, the anti-base group's previous denunciation of Higa Tetsuya as a betrayer of the wishes of *shimin* was rapidly overshadowed and replaced by the growing volume of voices coming from traditional social ties of blood and place in Nago and Henoko as enmeshed with its local commercial and business networks. These nativist/working-class voices now praised Higa as a selfless martyr, who had resigned for the sake of the development of their hometown. When the issue became framed in a rigidly local idiom, the global language of citizenship became ineffective. Anti-base candidate Tamaki Yoshikazu, who had to face the rapid upsurge of the pro-base argument intertwined with sentimental Nago parochialism, said to me in retrospect, "The more I talked about the offshore base, the more distant I felt from Nago." President of the citywide coalition Miyagi Yasuhiro, who supported Tamaki's campaign, similarly told me, "I have run out of language with which to speak to Nago voters." In short, the pro-base group recycled the offshore base dispute—which was global in scope—into the normal political channel of the local election of Nago City, thereby dispersing and displacing the binary between the resisting (good) *shimin* and the domineering (evil) power, in terms of which the anti-base group had built up its momentum during the referendum campaign.

Needless to say, the anti-base coalition did not stand by idly. In January 1998, *Jan'nu Kai* (see chapter 6 on this group) coordinated voices of some two hundred women from Nago and beyond in organizing a rally at the Okinawa Prefecture Hall (which I could not attend) in order to request that Governor Ota not accept the offshore base. Before the rally, the women's group had been notified that Vice Governor Tōmon Mitsuko, a woman, and not Governor Ota, would meet the women's group due to the governor's busy schedule. However, Ota himself unexpectedly showed up at the last minute. Upon his arrival, the hall was filled with excitement and cheers, causing some of the women to break down into tears. Perhaps this Okinawan governor was perceived not simply as an elected governor as was the case in other prefectures of Japan. He was seen more as a king of the nation called Okinawa, and, with his dignified attitude, may have evoked the popular imagination concerning the glory of the Ryukyu Kingdom.

Notably, what was different from the age of the Ryukyu Kingdom was that the commoners (i.e., women) were no longer passive and obedient subjects, but were asserting themselves as informed citizens in front of the king. The agency of these women was specifically evident when the women's group gave the governor a washtub full of letters. The use of the washtub (the idea of *Jan'nu Kai*) referred to the Japanese word *taraimawashi*, which literally means "spinning the wash tub." The intended message was, "please do not simply spin the washtub" (i.e., "do not hold things by rotation," or more specifically, "do not rotate the base within Okinawa"). Apparently, Governor Ota had taken encouragement from the women's rally to clarify his position on the matter of the offshore base; in February 1998 he formally rejected the offshore base—after several months of having ambiguously stated, "the matter is to be settled between the Japanese government and Nago City."

However, the women's efforts also intensified, ironically, ongoing gender tensions, which overlapped with tensions between *shimin* ("new" social movement actors) and parties/unions ("old" social movement actors), within the context of local mobilization. After the Nago mayor's abrupt resignation, a special committee for choosing the anti-base candidate was established within the citywide coalition. In January 1998, the committee announced that prefectural assemblyman Tamaki Yoshikazu would be their mayoral candidate, and also chose Miyagi Yasuhiro, president of the coalition, as their candidate for the local by-election, to be conducted on the same day as the mayoral election, to fill a vacancy in the Nago City Council. Tamaki was a strong candidate and was seen as a man of sincerity by many people. For instance, the morning after being elected as prefectural assemblyman, he had stood at a crossroads in downtown Nago and bowed to cars and pedestrians, saying "Thank you for your support." The choice of Tamaki, however, was also a carefully calculated strategy with which the committee was attempting to cope with emerging tensions within the coalition.

In addition to the tension between the citywide coalition and Henoko's Society for the Protection of Life (see above), the conflict between the old political force (political parties and labor unions) and the new political force (*shimin* and women) had already been in place during the referendum campaign. In fact, the leftist political parties and unions (led by male activists), while themselves an integral part of the coalition, became somewhat envious of the coalition's sweeping popularity and wary of what they saw as the self-righteousness of its president, Miyagi Yasuhiro, and women who supported him. By choosing Tamaki as the candidate for mayor and relegating Miyagi to the less significant position of candidate for the Nago City Council, the selection committee suppressed and deflected the wish of *shimin* (particularly women's) groups to pick Miyagi Yasuhiro as the mayoral candidate, and thereby tried to curb the influence of the *shimin* women who were now overriding their (male) control.[1]

Women's group leader Mashiki Tomi (see chapter 6 for her critical and refined political discourse) specifically commented on the position of the women on the selection committee. As she summarized it to me, "Women became somewhat like tokens with little say in the matter of choosing the candidate." In the aftermath of the political turmoil in Nago, Kyoda Kiyoka, who was unofficially and symbolically designated a cute "mascot" of the anti-base movement, amplified Mashiki Tomi's comment when she wrote somewhat controversially in *Sekai* (The World), an influential leftist journal in Japan, about her experience of being gradually removed from the center of the movement. Although her account presents only one possible interpretation of the motives at work, it does exemplify the emerging conflicts within the anti-base movement. She wrote:

> Existing forces [i.e., leftist political parties and labor unions] were afraid of new forces, and unable to accept them. Rather, they trashed such new forces. While [giving lip service to women by] saying that "we would like to listen to and incorporate your fresh opinions…" they in fact sneered at such opinions. Middle-aged men do not want change. Their ideas about the reformation of society do not keep up with the times.… I would like to suggest that they themselves reform first.
>
> (Kyoda 1998: 316)[2]

As this and other complications indicate, the knot that had bound the political parties, labor unions, and women's/*shimin*'s groups in the referendum came loose. More than anything else, the anti-base group was already physically and mentally exhausted from a year of strenuous nonstop efforts.

Ironically, Governor Ota himself reinforced the process by which the anti-base movement fell apart. As was noted in chapter 5, after December 1996, when he was caught between the powerful cross pressures of anti-base advocates in Okinawa and government officials in Tokyo, Governor Ota did not (and could not) intervene in the offshore base dispute while declaring that "the matter is to be settled between the national government and Nago City." During the mayoral election campaign, some of anti-base voters started to openly criticize Ota by echoing the pro-base camp's view of him as an authority without compassion. Some of them even claimed that Ota was ready to abandon northern Okinawa in order to get Futenma (located in south-central Okinawa) back together with money for Okinawa development. Tamaki's campaign club asked the governor to reassure Nago voters of his opposition to the new offshore base, which he eventually did toward the end of the mayoral election campaign—that is, right after his meeting with the women's group at the Okinawa Prefectural Hall. However, the governor's decision backfired; many in Nago and Henoko criticized him for doing too little, too late.

An opinion poll conducted by a local newspaper three days before the election showed that Tamaki was leading the campaign (*Ryukyu Shinpo*, February 5, 1998). Tamaki's campaign office, now dominated by male activists from political parties and unions, was optimistic (perhaps too much so) about the results, owing to the anti-base group's previous victory in the referendum. However, one of the leaders in pro-base candidate Kishimoto's campaign office, who apparently misidentified me as a newspaper reporter, approached me and confidently told me during a rally (in which three thousand supporters participated) on the day before the mayoral election, "A miracle will happen tomorrow." And so it did. Successfully setting up Nago's regional-class identity ("we are Okinawans but of a different kind") against the anti-base group's idea of totalized Okinawan citizenship ("we are Okinawans"), the pro-base group won the mayoral election on February 8, 1998, by a razor-thin margin—51.5 percent favored the pro-base candidate and 48.5 percent favored the anti-base candidate (Total votes—31,567 (including 167 spoiled ballots), or 82.35 percent of the 38,335 eligible voters).

After the votes were counted, residents belonging to the pro-base group in Henoko put their arms around each other's shoulders and cried for joy. In contrast, the anti-base struggle hut of the Henoko Society for the Protection of Life was in a state of shock. One older woman, who had usually happily acceded to the requests of newspaper photographers during the referendum campaign, angrily yelled at one photographer, "Don't take any more pictures!!"

The Crisis of Okinawan Resistance

In summary, in the 1998 mayoral election, the key site of contestation shifted from the one revolving around a binary between Okinawa and Tokyo/Washington to the one centered on a split within Okinawa. The synthesis of residentship, anti-Tokyo sentiment, and global citizenship, which was momentarily actualized by informed, middle-class *shimin* in the 1997 Nago City referendum, rapidly broke down. In the mayoral election, the pro-base group successfully recaptured the local cultural sensibilities of the residents of Nago and Henoko, which the anti-base group had offended; in doing so, the pro-base group, with the indirect support of the Japanese government, reconstructed the vision of the local as a bounded, homogeneous, working-class community bonded by the nondiscursive ties of blood and place. In the process, the anti-base coalition in Nago lost sight of a clearly defined "enemy" (the Japanese and U.S. governments), and as a result its internal contradictions surfaced to an extent that it could no longer maintain itself as a coherent movement.

The defeat of anti-base candidate Tamaki Yoshikazu in the 1998 Nago City mayoral election made a great impact on Okinawan politics at large, because it also implied that Governor Ota, who had endorsed Tamaki, was not given a vote of confidence. Indeed, by the time the gubernatorial election was conducted in November 1998, it became clear that Governor Ota's program for gaining both peace (the return of Futenma) and economic development (money from Tokyo) for Okinawa at large had come to a dead end, because of his explicit statement during the Nago City mayoral election that Okinawa would not accept the offshore base, when its acceptance had been the basic condition for gaining both peace and development in the first instance. In the election, Ota lost his position to Inamine Kei'ichi, who, as the president of the influential Okinawa Business Owners Association, represented the economic interests of Okinawa.

Governor Inamine's platform was not entirely different from Ota's. Like Ota, he promised to achieve both peace and economic development for Okinawa at large. Yet Inamine proposed to attain these goals by a different means. That is, during the gubernatorial election, he proposed replacing the plan for a facility of 1,500 by 600 meters (1,640 by 656 yards) offshore of Henoko with a new plan to build a bifunctional military-commercial "airport"—which was just another way Inamine, and then Tokyo, referred to the military base so that residents in Henoko and Nago City would be more willing to accept it—of an even larger scale (2,500 by 700 meters—2,734 by 765 yards) in the same location, so that a hub of business activity compatible with south-central Okinawa would be created in northern Okinawa. Toward this end, Inamine pledged to work with (not against, as Ota had done) the Japanese government. While Ota's and Inamine's platforms were similar, Inamine's watered down significantly the critical, oppositional spirit that had been found in Ota's.

Before Inamine officially cut a deal with the Japanese government concerning the new "airport" in November 1999, Tokyo increased its public works spending across Okinawa, and especially in Nago and its vicinity. Also, Tokyo responded to the proposals made by the so-called Shimada Committee—the ad-hoc committee that had been led, in accordance with the central government's desire, by Keio University Professor Shimada Haruo, in order to deal with the economic problems of the cities/towns/villages in Okinawa that had been hosting the U.S. military—by distributing a total of 10 billion yen ($100 million) to Okinawa, including Nago City, over seven years from 1997. In addition, Tokyo created the Northern Okinawa Development Fund, from which Nago City and its vicinity has received and is likely to continue to receive a total of 10 billion yen ($100 million) over ten years from 2000 (Miyamoto 2006). As a result, new community centers and clinics were built across Nago and beyond, the meat processing facility in downtown Nago was renovated, and the construction of a brand-new Telephone Operators Center, Multi-Media Center, International Oceanographic Center, National Technology College, and other facilities began (or were set to begin) in the Henoko area. With all of these efforts Tokyo indirectly pressured Okinawans—Nago and Henoko residents, in particular—to endorse, once and for all, the Inamine-Tokyo collaboration to build a new facility in Henoko. The results of these tactics were significant. For instance, in 1999 various business and commercial organizations as well as branches of the Military Landlords Association across Okinawa issued pleas to relocate Futenma. In the same year, middle-of-the-road and conservative candidates, who would tolerate (if not actively support) the U.S. military, came to be repeatedly elected as mayors elsewhere in Okinawa. In November 1999, by which time an anti-base mood receded considerably, Governor Inamine finally and officially struck a deal with Tokyo to construct a military-commercial "airport" in Henoko. Nago City Mayor Kishimoto Tateo followed suit in December 1999 and agreed to the construction. The Cabinet in Tokyo swiftly authorized and endorsed this "airport" plan in the same month.

In the meantime, Tokyo chose Nago (together with Naha, Okinawa's capital) as the venue for the 2000 G-8 Summit in the spirit of suppressing Okinawa's anti-base feelings with the "dreams" of development, happiness, and a better life. After a splendid convention center was built by Japanese money along Nago's coastlines, the G-8 Summit specifically dramatized Okinawa's cooperation with—not its resistance to—Tokyo in the eyes of world leaders. Female dancers performed the traditional welcome dance at Shuri Palace, and an Okinawan pop singer (female) sang at the dinner table. An Okinawan high school student (once again, female) gave flowers to President Clinton at the Cornerstone of Peace, which former Governor Ota had built to honor all the war dead regardless of nationality (see chapter 2, note 8). There, the U.S. President delivered a speech that emphasized the strategic importance of Okinawa in maintaining the "peace and security" of the Asia-Pacific region. Okinawa's will for peace and democracy was completely stolen by the global form of power.

In the summer of 2002, governmental representatives from Tokyo, Okinawa, and Nago City, who had continued closed-door deliberations since the end of 1999 with occasional breaks, finally drew up a basic plan of the new bifunctional military-commercial "airport." Instead of pursuing an offshore base construction plan, they decided to build this airport by filling in an area of water (Henoko's sea) with landfill. The landfill plan was chosen because Tokyo wanted to reduce the cost of construction; building an offshore base as was originally proposed by the final report of the Special Action Committee on Okinawa ([1996] 1997) would cost 1 trillion yen ($10 billion), but the construction costs for the bifunctional "airport" were estimated to be 330 billion yen ($3.3 billion) (*Okinawa Taimusu*, September 2, 1997; July 29, 2002). In addition, the governmental representatives claimed that the new "airport" would have another merit. That is, it would not violate the will of Nago and Henoko *shimin* who opposed the "offshore" base in the 1997 Nago City referendum, because the new airport would not be an offshore base but a ground facility.

By this time, paralyzing cynicism permeated Okinawa. Okinawan resistance seems to have been over. Is it true, after all, that Okinawans were "willing to provide facilities to U.S. troops to get economic aid from Tokyo" as Harvard sociologist Ezra Vogel (1999: 11) once said?

The chain of events in Henoko, Nago, and Okinawa from 1999 till today has suggested, to the contrary, that the very U.S. military that has brought money to Okinawa has also conditioned and continually renewed a collectivity of cultural sensibilities enmeshed with the pain of local historical experiences—Japanese colonialism, the war, the U.S. bases, and the rape—which the politicoeconomic system of the U.S-Japan alliance would never be able to completely internalize. Pain, whose "resistance to language is not simply one of its incidental or accidental attributes but is essential to what it is" (Scarry 1985:5), has thus constituted the absolute limit of the system's own mechanism. The existence of such a limit on the reach of power has been evidenced on a number of different occasions over the past several years. I discuss some of these below.

(1) In October 1999, in anticipation of the 2000 G-8 Summit in Okinawa, it was widely publicized that the Inamine administration, with the help of revisionist Okinawan historians, was attempting to rewrite the history of the battle of Okinawa by erasing virtually all references to the atrocities committed by the Japanese soldiers on Okinawans (see chapter 2) from the exhibition of the soon-to-be-remodeled Okinawa Prefectural Peace Memorial Museum. The motivation behind this act was complex. For its part, the Japanese government was anxious, because if it let Okinawa's anti-Tokyo sentiment be revealed in the form of museum exhibition, this would certainly taint its credentials, in front of the U.S. president and other world leaders, as an able player in the transnational alliance. At the same time, the Inamine administration wanted to accommodate to Tokyo's wishes in order to keep the aid flowing from Tokyo. This collaboration between Tokyo and Okinawa, however, provoked intense protests from many different walks of life within Okinawa, and the Inamine administration ended up making apologies to Okinawan constituencies for what it had planned to do. The Peace Memorial Museum incident is a testimony to the presence of Okinawa's collective memory and historical pain concerning the war, the military, and the bases.

(2) This collective memory has run through the island prefecture like underground water, and it has been maintained by a variety of public activities—among them, a prefectural project of gathering the remains of the war dead still left unburied; school teachers' efforts to teach the battle of Okinawa and the U.S. control of Okinawa; and artists' involvement in the production of the critical films on the U.S. military in Okinawa. In addition, the historical pain has been passed down from one generation to another through the everyday conversations taking place at dinner tables, bars, festivals, and other sites of Okinawan social life. Indeed, in the aftermath of the attack on America on September 11, 2001, while Okinawa acquiesced in the retaliatory operations of the U.S. military in Afghanistan, and then military attack on Iraq, the pain of assisting the U.S. military to destroy local life, as well as the fear that this might make Okinawa the target of a future "terrorist" attack—just as it became the target of the U.S. military attack in the battle of Okinawa—has been addressed not only from the older but also from the younger generations in Nago and Henoko when I visited there in the summer of 2003. In the summer of 2004, in a way that expressed such pain and fear of military violence, I saw that young members and supporters of the Society for the Protection of Life staged sit-ins on Henoko's beach in order to prevent the Defense Facilities Agency from conducting a geological survey of Henoko's sea for building the new "airport." At the time of this writing, the sit-ins are continuing.

(3) Since the late 1990s, Okinawa's anti-base movements have made strenuous efforts to learn from and act with a broader coalition beyond the confines of the island prefecture and the nation-state. For instance, in the summer of 2000, the International Environmental NGO Forum[3] was held in Okinawa, and participants brought up the negative environmental impact of many U.S. military activities—the medical problems caused by depleted uranium weapons the U.S. military used in the Gulf War and elsewhere, birth defects caused by herbicides sprayed during wartime by the U.S. military in Vietnam, and problems of crimes, pollution, and military accidents caused by the U.S. military in South Korea and Okinawa. Extending such grass-roots efforts, American, Japanese, and Okinawan environmentalists, together with the dugong (as the legal plaintiff), the Society for the Protection of Life in Henoko, and other local anti-base movement bodies, sued the Pentagon in September 2003 at the U.S. District Court in

Oakland, California, in order to prevent it from constructing the "airport" in Henoko.[4] They specifically pointed out that the destruction of precious natural resources such as the coral reef and feeding places for dugongs would be likely to go far beyond the limit stipulated by Japanese law. At the time of this writing, the trial is continuing. In the meantime, the struggle hut of the Society for the Protection of Life in Henoko has continued to be visited by activists, intellectuals, students, and the like from the mainland Japan and beyond. These and other activities have indicated the survival and extension of an anti-base message in the trans-Okinawan context.

(4) In the process, oppositional residents and critics in Okinawa and beyond have continuously exposed serious defects of the "airport" plan before and after its construction was officially confirmed in the summer of 2002. First, unlike the offshore base originally proposed, the military-commercial "airport" must be built within the coral reef of Henoko's sea across from the residential area of Henoko. This would cause, residents and critics have pointed out, not only environmental destructions but also unbearable noise problems in Henoko and its vicinity. Relatedly, in an attempt to underscore the obvious fact that the "airport" would be built not to benefit Okinawa per se but to meet and promote global strategic interests, they revealed that the commercial portion of the new "airport" would be no more than 5.4 percent while the rest (94.6 percent) would be used by the U.S. military (*Asahi.com*, April 28, 2004). Finally, critics showed that it would take no less than twelve years to complete the construction of the new "airport" (*Asahi.com* April 28, 2004), which meant that the return of Futenma would not happen before the year 2016. The obvious question, from an Okinawan perspective, is, Can this really be called the "return" of Futenma as was proposed by the Japanese and U.S. governments back in 1996 after the rape incident? Or is it just another pretext for perpetuating the U.S. military presence in Okinawa?

(5) Both Governor Inamine and Nago City Mayor Kishimoto faithfully assisted the Japanese government in relocating Futenma to the Henoko area in exchange for its aid. At the same time, however, Inamine and Kishimoto also needed to take measures to prevent what Inamine called the "magma [of Okinawa's deep and pervasive anti-base sentiment]" from gushing through its volatile political bedrock. To this end, Inamine and Kishimoto made their acceptance of the new military-commercial "airport" conditional on the conclusion of an agreement between Tokyo and

Washington concerning the restriction of its use to fifteen years. Washington rejected this proposal outright, but the Japanese government could not say "no" to Inamine and Kishimoto because it did not want to risk ruining the "airport" plan by offending Okinawans at large. In fact, to ruin the "airport" plan would be Tokyo's worst nightmare, because that would not only deny all of the tremendous efforts it had invested since the 1995 rape incident in its various negotiations with the local authorities of Henoko, Nago, and Okinawa, but also lead Washington to question its credentials as a reliable partner. Caught between local demands and global interests, the Japanese government simply evaded the issue of restricting the use of the "airport" by repeatedly saying to Nago/Okinawa, "We will discuss the matter with the U.S. government," while it never did. In short, the "magma" of Okinawa's anti-base sentiment prompted the governor/mayor to show their partial resistance to Tokyo (in spite of their pro-Tokyo position). Put differently, disclosing the vulnerability of the Japanese government, the governor and mayor ended up frustrating the planned relocation of Futenma in their very act of promoting it.

In brief, while the construction of the bifunctional military-commercial "airport" in Henoko was agreed upon locally, nationally, and globally, more concrete questions of how, where, and when to construct it remained unsettled. This peculiar situation—which irritated Secretary of Defense Donald Rumsfeld, along with Commander of the U.S. forces in the Pacific and others in the Pentagon, so much that they, over the course of 2004, expressed one after another complaints about the stubbornness of Okinawans and incompetence of Tokyo—can be seen as a manifestation of persistent and resilient Okinawan resistance, contrary to Vogel's (1999) hasty conclusion that Okinawan resistance was over. In other words, the fate of Okinawa's military base problems is uncertain, still wide open to conjecture. This made anthropological commitment to the present of Okinawa a critically pressing issue, both politically and intellectually. The final chapter will propose a specific strategy with which to revitalize the anti-base movement of Okinawa in the public sphere, while exploring the possibilities and responsibilities of the anthropologist as the "third person" (Levinas) in this age of globalization.

8

CONCLUSION:

Anthropologists as the Third Person,
Anthropology in the Global Public Sphere

 Tracing the larger chronicle of colonialism, the war, the U.S. bases, and the servicemen in the local social context, this study has explored the intricacies of Okinawan identity against the background of the nation-state (Japan) and the larger processes of global history. Social movements and sentiments after the 1995 rape of an Okinawan school girl by U.S. servicemen have been ethnographically examined as a point of entry into the profound transformation of Okinawa's collective consciousness. I have conceptualized this transformation as a shift in the modality of local identity from the one grounded in the perspective of a uniformly poor and oppressed "people" to the one articulated in the perspective of confident and affluent "citizens" of diverse backgrounds awakened to globally disseminated ideas about democracy, human rights, ecology, women's issues, and peace. My study has assessed both potentialities and limits of this identity shift by engaging one of the most important issues of our time—social movements in the age of globalization—and in so doing, has aimed to explain a paradox of power and resistance: Why have Okinawa's protests since the 1995 rape incident not helped restrain, let alone overthrow, the power of the U.S. and Japanese governments?

The primary site of fieldwork at which I have undertaken this task— since the summer of 1997 to date—is Henoko, an eastern coastal district of Nago City in northern Okinawa. Although small in size (population: 1,400), Henoko has had a significant impact on Okinawa's political landscape, because it has been home to the U.S. Marine Corps' Camp Schwab since 1957, and because the U.S. and Japanese governments since 1997 have been trying to execute the plan to construct a sea-based military base off the waters of Camp Schwab as the replacement facility for Futenma Air Station. Indeed, these historical and political circumstances have made Henoko a privileged site at which to explore the question of potentialities and limits of Okinawa's identity shift, in specific reference to two different, complementary forms of "appropriation" (see chapter 1)—one being exercised oppositionally yet somewhat exclusively by middle-class Okinawans and the other being employed by financially vulnerable working-class Okinawans in a manner that accommodates and reinforces the existing relations of power.

The potentialities of new Okinawan identity have been expressed by middle-class citizens. They have successfully appropriated the affluence of Okinawa for the construction of their economic independence and political autonomy against the very source of this affluence—the Japanese government that has flooded Okinawa with money as political compensation for the U.S. military presence there. Rearticulating and reworking the older anti-Japanese and anti-base/American sentiment once shared by the Okinawan *minshū* (people), the middle-class *shimin* (citizens/residents) in Henoko and Nago launched a citywide/island-wide anti-base movement with the pan-Okinawan identity of "we are Okinawans."

However, the potentialities of the new citizenry identity have revealed its own limitations when it has offended cultural and historical sensibilities of working-class Okinawans who have employed a different form of appropriation. Camp Schwab (and by implication, the U.S. military in Okinawa at large) has long induced, since the late 1950s, a broader restructuring of the social ties of blood and place in Henoko, generating and regenerating economic opportunities for its working-class residents. Because of fears of failure and underdevelopment, they have sometimes reluctantly and at other times enthusiastically appropriated as much as accommodated the U.S. military presence in exchange for jobs with the idea of "we are Okinawans but of a different kind." It is this *difference* that, as manifested in the 1998 Nago City mayoral election and beyond, eventually subverted—at least momentarily—the call for the pan-Okinawan identity that had once unified the resistance; and it is this *difference* that explains, at least partially, the paradox of power and resistance that I have posed: Power kept self-valorizing in spite of, and in the midst of, Okinawa's resistance by exploiting its identity divide across class lines. Indeed, taking advantage of this difference, Tokyo has assisted the U.S. global strategies of instituting something of a system of planetary governance, the "intimate society" (Levinas 1998), which has progressively expanded itself not by oppressing the Asia-Pacific region with force but by soliciting its full participation and cooperation in today's U.S.-oriented, capitalist order. This study has thus demonstrated that micro concerns of social life challenge as much as reinforce macro political processes of the Japanese nation, with global operations of the U.S. military as an overarching geopolitical influence.

Radical Appropriation and the Public Sphere: A New Opening

I now propose what can be called "radical appropriation," whose distinctiveness lies in its capacity to reconstruct a subversive and oppositional public sphere in Okinawa and beyond, in such a way as to mediate and transcend the tension between two complementary forms of appropriation that I have discussed throughout this study. I propose this idea not because I want to eliminate the military from the earth once and for all, which is neither realistic, nor, perhaps, desirable,[1] but because I hope to formulate what has been happening in the ethnographic actuality of Henoko, Nago, and Okinawa as a more general theoretical and political possibility, or really necessity, that the military is to be globally managed by the production of an open, inclusive, and heterogeneous arena of discourse and action within and against power. Persistent everyday efforts to maintain and expand the public sphere—efforts to articulate and rearticulate the issue (e.g., "terrorism") from different positions and perspectives in a way that would infinitely delay military actions intended to hastily "resolve" that issue—might indeed be the basis of the most effective force to constrain, influence, and suspend what I see as the dangerously native, and increasingly influential and popularized, view of the U.S. military as simply a champion for freedom and peace.

My proposal specifically avoids the two types of arguments that have repeatedly appeared in scholarly as well as larger public discourses about how to deal with Okinawa problems, one duplicating the logic of the middle-class appropriation and the other reproducing the rationale for working-class appropriation. Indeed, in my view, they do not necessarily help reconstruct the public sphere, but may inadvertently contribute to fragmenting it and thus reinforcing the production of the "intimate society." The first type of argument is oppositional and conscientious, but somewhat idealistic. It seeks to constitute a collective identity of Okinawa against and outside the violence of national and global powers on the basis of the educated, middle-class logic of appropriation that excludes the working-class perspective. For instance, Okinawan critics (Nakamatsu [1968] 1990, 1979; Hiyane 1996; Arakawa 2000) have often enunciated the ideal of a timeless and irreducible Okinawa as the basis for countering incursions of Japanese and American money, culture, and military into Okinawa's modernity. Extending this logic, some Okinawan critics have proposed the independence of Okinawa from the Japanese state (Takara B. 1996). Scholars residing in Japan and elsewhere have similarly addressed visions of resistance in terms of Okinawa's collective memory and culture (Tanigawa 1972, 1996; Shimao 1992; Johnson 1999), while others have linked such visions with the potentialities of the peace constitution of Japan (Umebayashi 1994, 2002), ecological movements (Ōnishi 2001), autonomous regional development (Kurima 1998), democratic diplomacy (Ota M. 1999), and the international feminist coalition (Spencer 2002). These analyses are certainly helpful in extending the leftist ideal of peace, freedom, and self-determination in the age of globalization. What they generally refuse to see, however, is the complex contemporary reality of diversification and fragmentation of the category of "Okinawa" itself; this refusal makes it difficult for us to imagine the inclusive public sphere in which diverse voices, including voices and interests of working-class Okinawans who reluctantly support the U.S. military, should be heard and expressed.

The second type of argument may be realistic but is often reactionary, legitimizing—under the pretense of "analyzing"—the power grid of the U.S.-Japan alliance in which Okinawa has been embedded. Typically, in its appropriation of the working-class accommodation to power, this argument subtly calls for the subordination of Okinawa to the post–cold war global order, which is often concealed by a euphoric language concerning the development of Okinawa, the prosperity of Japan, the security of the Asia-Pacific region, and so forth. For instance, *Yomiuri Shinbun*, Japan's largest newspaper with a daily circulation reaching 10 million copies, has endorsed the present policy of the Japanese government, which promises the development of Okinawa to compensate for (and thus to perpetuate) the burden of the U.S. bases.[2] From within Okinawa, accomplished historian Takara Kurayoshi et al. (2000) sanctioned the U.S. military presence in Okinawa while promoting native cultural pride, suggesting that a self-assured Okinawa, as an active member of the nation of Japan, should take the "initiative" in protecting and promoting the peace and prosperity of the Asia-Pacific region (Inoue 2002a). The previously mentioned article by Vogel (1999: 11), which declared that "in short, Okinawans were willing to provide facilities to U.S. troops to get economic aid from Tokyo," also falls into this second type of argument. Overall, this position assumes an air of realism by highlighting the actuality of harsh international relations and the sluggish local economy, which the oppositional, romanticized discourses (the first position) often fail to acknowledge. Yet, in doing so, this realist yet reactionary position also dissolves the long-standing ideal of an Okinawa unified in its resistance. Put differently, it fragments Okinawa into atomized, depoliticized consumer/cultural identities by uncritically embracing the capitalist dream of happiness and a better life. As such, this position does not help us build a public sphere either—a critical sphere of discussion, communication, and deliberation about and against the U.S. military.

What I propose by way of "radical appropriation" is a third possibility. It intervenes in the interface of Okinawa's historical unity (the first position reproducing the logic of middle-class appropriation/resistance) and contemporary diversity (the second position replicating the rationale for working-class appropriation/accommodation), while at the same time seeking to provide an alternative to this binary. By being oppositional, and even romantic, yet informed by the realism of the global military and political economy, "radical appropriation" also hopes to interrogate a basic premise that is shared by the two positions above. In fact, in their proposals to be *either* "outside" (the first position) *or* "inside" (the second position) the system of the Japanese state subsumed under the U.S.-Japan security alliance, they similarly reinforce the premise of modernity that the nation-state is a basic unit of the global order. I for one want to articulate a position that is within and simultaneously against such an order not by making Okinawa look like just another nation-state but by resituating Okinawa in the global public sphere.

Succinctly put, "radical appropriation" suggests that Henoko and Nago, and by implication, Okinawa at large, receive the "gifts" from Tokyo—development projects, rent money, and subsidies—without giving up its land for the use of the U.S.-Japan alliance in return. In so doing, Okinawa should radically redefine and appropriate these gifts as rightful compensation for the historical and continuing violence of the war and the military in Okinawa, not as political justification for the new base and the U.S. military presence in Okinawa in the future as Tokyo and Washington wants to define them.

On the one hand, in its premise of accepting the "gifts" from Tokyo, radical appropriation will help the anti-base movement in Henoko/Nago and in Okinawa at large to take more seriously the economic concerns for happiness and a better life among financially insecure working-class residents (the second position). This, in turn, will help reground and reframe the universalistic, idealistic, middle-class aspirations of the anti-base movement in locally specific historical-cultural-economic realities enmeshed with the sixty-year presence of the U.S. bases in Okinawa. This would also provide a context in which middle-class and working-class Okinawans work together for Okinawa's future, by helping them to deal with the problem that has confronted all of Okinawa—how should it construct the autonomous regional economy that does not forever depend on the Japanese government or the U.S. military? Finally, the working-class desire for happiness and a better life, if taken seriously, can be transformed into a common, universal ground upon which fragments of the anti-base movement (unions, political parties, women's groups, *shimin* groups, etc.) would be reconsolidated in such a way as to actualize the multitude within its own mobilization structure.

On the other hand, radical appropriation, in its straightforward logic of rejecting the new base, will help pro-base sentiments of various kinds in Henoko/Nago/Okinawa to be regrafted onto the soil of Okinawa's oppositional memory concerning Japanese colonialism, the war, the U.S. military, and servicemen. In other words, the idea of radical appropriation is proposed to help support a collective desire in Okinawa for a world without military violence, fear, and pain (the first position).

In sum, radical appropriation will become a means to initiating interactions of the two antagonistic social positions in Okinawa's political scene, the anti-base and the pro-base positions. It is in these interactions that I would like to see the possibility of reconstructing Okinawa's public sphere, an open, inclusive, and heterogeneous realm of solidarity.

It is important to note that the idea of radical appropriation is not an abstract postmodern fantasy, but a perspective and practice anchored in the ethnographic reality of Henoko. I found over and over again in recent years that the official agreement to build the bifunctional, military-commercial "airport" in Henoko (see chapter 7 for the "airport" plan)—the agreement that was reached across the local/Okinawan, national/Japanese, and global/American *governmental* levels—clearly exposed, rather than suppressed, uncertainty and vulnerability of power in its constant struggles (or really failures) to obtain consent or submission of ordinary Okinawans. As was shown in chapter 7, the Peace Memorial Museum incident (1999), a suit against the Pentagon (2003–present), and sit-ins on Henoko's beach (2004–present), among others, have revealed deep resentment among ordinary Okinawan citizens against the imposition of the U.S. bases on their lifeworld. In addition, the ethnographic reality in Henoko was that its residents, including those who once indicated their willingness to tolerate the offshore base in exchange for money, were increasingly ambivalent about the "airport" plan because of the potential noise, environmental, and other problems. As Sueyoshi Kaoru, the most powerful man in today's Henoko (see chapter 4) told me in the summer of 2001, should the Japanese government decide to execute this plan, these residents might join the Society for the Protection of Life to mobilize the anti-construction movement. It is in order to prevent this from happening that the anxious Japanese government has continuously increased its public works spending. By proposing radical appropriation—Henoko and Nago should take the development projects, rent, and subsidy while simultaneously rejecting the new military-commercial "airport"—I am suggesting that they appropriate the anxiety of Tokyo in order to restore the unity and totality of Okinawa in a way that does not suppress but produces, even accentuates, internal differences.

• • •

In a manner that informs and is informed by the idea of radical appropriation, pro-base and anti-base residents of Henoko/Nago and beyond have indeed dramatically—and at least momentarily—united, owing to the latest development of the planned relocation of Futenma. I here want to specify the nature of this local protest against the background of the American post–cold war scheme of a "revolution in military affairs" (RMA), which, in the wake of the 9/11 "terrorist" attack on America, has taken on a specific global character.

Since the late 1990s it has become increasingly clear in the eyes of the U.S. strategic planners that the adversaries have changed from the large-scale, predictable, clearly defined enemy (e.g., the former Soviet Union) to the small-scale, unpredictable, amorphous "terrorists," "rebels," "dissenters" and so forth who would not attack the United States directly but challenge it asymmetrically by trying to exploit vulnerabilities such as its transportation systems, nuclear plants, and cyber spaces (Gongora and von Riekhoff 2000; Jablonsky 2001; Rumsfeld 2002; Umebayashi 2002: 199–228; Hardt and Negri 2004: 41–48). The events on September 11, 2001, became the clearest testimony to this change, in response to which the revolution in military affairs had to be articulated.

Thus, first, RMA involves the drastic makeover of military technology. It is no longer helpful to simply rely on weapons of mass destruction such as nuclear missiles and heavy armor developed during the cold war to fight the Soviet invasion. Instead, taking advantage of the innovation of information technology, the U.S. military must swiftly advance conventional capabilities on land, at sea, and in the air in order to achieve speed, precision, and effectiveness of the military activities inside and outside the U.S. territory. Second, RMA also means the revolution of operational concepts and doctrines. In the words of Secretary of Defense Donald Rumsfeld (2002: 27), "Our goal is not simply to fight and win wars; it is to prevent them." His words expressed the idea of preemptive war and were reflected in the 2002 Bush doctrine—formally known as "The National Security Strategy of the United States of America" (Bush et al., 2002)—which is "a marked departure from the policies of deterrence that generally characterized American foreign policy during the Cold War and brief period between the collapse of the Soviet Union and 9/11" (*Wikipedia*, s.v. "Bush Doctrine").

Third, RMA refers to the transformation of military organizational structure. Instead of reproducing a massive, hierarchical military structure characterized by a rigid chain of command, the U.S. military must transform itself into a constellation of flexible, rapidly deployable, fully integrated units. In short, the task of "harnessing new technologies, operational concepts and organizational structures to give U.S. forces greater mobility, flexibility and military capabilities so that they can dominate any future battlefield" (Department of Defense 1998a: 16) has become mandatory in the age of globalization.

In the Asia-Pacific region, RMA has been manifested since the middle-1990s as a project of integrating Japan tightly and thoroughly into the U.S. post–cold war security strategies, as exemplified by the revision of the bilateral defense guidelines in 1997, which gives the U.S. military access to airfields, ports, medical supports in Japan (see chapter 2) and, more recently, by the all-encompassing idea of using Japan as a "Power Projection Hub" (*Korea Times*, May 19, 2004; *Asahi.com*, September 22, 2004). In a manner that helped reinforce and accelerate the integration, the Japanese government sent the Self-Defense Forces to Cambodia, Zaire, the Golan Heights, and East Timor for peacekeeping operations (in the 1990s), and Afghanistan and Iraq to aid controversial U.S. military operations there (in the twenty-first century).[3] As the strategic integration of Japan into the U.S. continued, Richard Lee Armitage, influential Deputy Secretary of State under the Bush administration until 2004, argued in effect that the "peace constitution" of post–World War II Japan, which prohibits the nation from maintaining the military, was an obstacle to the fuller strategic collaborations between the United States and Japan (*Shinbun Akahata*, July 24, 2004). In other words, the peace constitution, originally created by the United States to suit, at least in part, its own convenience (demilitarization, democratization, and control of postwar Japan), is now to be abolished again to serve the post-9/11 U.S. strategic interests, according to this official. In the meantime, in December 2002, the U.S. government proposed that a discussion be initiated about the realignment of the U.S. military in Okinawa and Japan (Satō 2006), and a bilateral agreement was reached on this matter on October 29, 2005, in a manner that revealed the latest development of RMA in general and strategic integration of Japan in particular.

The agreement was presented as a "package deal." First, Futenma would be relocated not off the waters of Henoko (as in the case of the "airport" plan), but on the shore of Camp Schwab—i.e., along the barrack zone of Camp Schwab—by reclaiming part of waters of Henoko and its vicinity (*Okinawa Taimusu*, October 26, 2005). Here, the Japanese and U.S. governments allegedly accommodated the feelings of Okinawans, particularly anti-base Okinawans, because the new "coastal" plan, which does not require the extensive destruction of the coral reef, is more environment-friendly than the "airport" plan. Second, the modification of the planned relocation of Futenma came with the proposals to transfer eight thousand U.S. Marines to Guam; to return a number of major military facilities in central and southern Okinawa to Okinawa; and to transfer F-15 fighter airplanes from Kadena Air Force Base in central Okinawa to Self-Defense Forces bases in Kyushu of mainland Japan (*Okinawa Taimusu*, October 27, 2005). Third, the functions of Japan's Self-Defense Forces in Okinawa and mainland Japan would be more fully integrated into the U.S. military operations.[4] Finally, the Japanese government suggested an additional set of local economic development plans to persuade Okinawa to accept this bilateral agreement. President Bush comfortably stated that the package deal represents a "good faith effort" and a "positive development" (*Asahi. com*, November 10, 2005).

By accepting this package deal, Tokyo has chosen, essentially, to follow the footsteps of the U.S. global strategies, because, as Prime Minister Koizumi stated in the joint press conference with President Bush, who visited Japan and other Asian countries in November 2005, "The development of Japan lies in peace and security made possible by the U.S.-Japan security [system]" (*Asahi.com*, November 16, 2005). In other words, in a state bordering on blind faith in the doctrine of the "development of Japan," Tokyo has striven for the further fortification of the trans-Pacific intimate society, which is "dual, a society of me [the global, the U.S.] and you [the national, Japan, with Okinawa included but subordinated]. We are just among ourselves. Third parties are excluded" (Levinas 1998: 30). In order to accomplish this task, Tokyo has been considering, at least unofficially, a special law aiming at facilitating the Futenma relocation process, a law that would give "the central government power to approve matters usually left to local governments, such as environmental impact assessments and reclamation work on public waters" (*Daily Yomiuri Online*, October 29, 2005; English in original). By the same token, by taking advantage of the inexperience of the new mayor of Nago City, Shimabukuro Yoshikazu, who succeeded Kishimoto Tateo (who had been ill) in February 2006, Tokyo has contrived to revise the original coastal plan and to impose a new plan to construct a base of an even larger scale on the same shore of Camp Schwab. Immediately after the new mayor's acceptance of this revised coastal plan (May 1, 2006),[5] the entire package deal concerning the realignment of the U.S. military in Okinawa/Japan was sealed by Washington and Tokyo as the final agreement. From the perspective of strategic planners of the Japanese and U.S. governments, the mayor's acceptance might have been seen as the culmination of their prolonged political efforts to control and contain Okinawa's protest against the U.S. military presence there over the past eleven years after the 1995 rape incident.

From the perspective of the third person (local residents), however, the coastal plan meant the greater danger of noise, environmental destructions, and military accidents, because the new base would be built in a place (the shore of Camp Schwab) that would be far closer to the residential area of Henoko and its vicinity than the one proposed in the previous and already problematic "airport" plan. The agreement between Tokyo and Washington suggested the return of a number of bases in central and southern Okinawa, but this, when combined with the construction of a new base in Camp Schwab, also meant the further concentration of base functions in northern Okinawa which had already shouldered 70 percent of the U.S. bases in Okinawa. One should also be clear that the transference of eight thousand marines to Guam was proposed not for the sake of the well-being of Okinawans per se, but in order to enhance American military interests, thereby denying the very cause of the reorganization and reduction of the bases in Okinawa that was acknowledged after the 1995 rape incident. The ultimate sin that underlies these problems is that most Okinawans were not included in any of the discussions about the U.S. military realignment in Okinawa.

In short, the planned realignment of the U.S. military—the coastal plan particularly—has undermined the interests of Okinawans across the board, ironically and unexpectedly opening up opportunities for "radical appropriation," in which Okinawan citizens, both pro-base and anti-base, would reunite on the basis of the universal, but locally grounded, desire for democracy and a life without the military. Their voices, summarized below, have been radically appropriative, as they have exploded since the announcement of the coastal plan in October 2005, that is, *after* Okinawa received and used up "gifts" of development projects of various kinds provided by Tokyo after the 1995 rape incident.

Henoko's pro-base leaders expressed objections to and questions about the coastal plan in a manner that reconnected, at least implicitly, their voices to the traditional anti-base sentiment of Okinawa (e.g., *Okinawa Taimusu*, April 12, 2006). Former Nago City Mayer Kishimoto Tateo, before being succeeded by new Mayor Shimabukuro, explicitly rejected the coastal plan (*Okinawa Taimusu*, October 27, 2005). For the first time after being elected Nago City's mayor in 1998, pro-base Kishimoto even held hands of an old woman of the Society for the Protection of Life in Henoko (who visited the city hall for her protest against the coastal plan), and told her, "I am sorry that I have caused you so much trouble" (*Okinawa Times*, November 1, 2005).

Pro-Tokyo Governor Inamine Kei'ichi also rejected the coastal plan by saying, "unacceptable" (*Okinawa Taimusu*, October 27, 2005). Governor Inamine insisted that his own "airport" plan had been formulated as the best plan on the basis of strenuous conversations among Tokyo, Okinawa Prefecture, and Nago City/Henoko leaders; the Cabinet in Tokyo even officially endorsed this plan in December 1999. If this plan were to be abandoned, Inamine maintained, the only remaining solution would be to transfer Futenma to an area outside Okinawa. In addition, the Nago City Council and the Okinawa Prefectural Assembly, in both of which conservative pro-base assemblymen/women outnumbered reformist anti-base assemblymen/women, voted against the coastal plan (*Okinawa Taimusu*, November 21, 2005; December 16, 2005), and approximately 70 percent of Okinawans expressed objection to the coastal plan (*Okinawa Taimusu*, November 15, 2005; *Asahi.com*, May 16, 2006). Overall, Okinawa's anti-Tokyo, anti-base sentiment has become even more pervasive and deeper across the divide of pro-base and anti-base voices[6] because of the heartless attitude of Tokyo that has striven to realize global/national military-political interests at the expense of local life.

In the meantime, radical appropriation has ignited and has been ignited by broader, unexpected alliances between Okinawa and mainland Japan, because, as I have stated, the proposed realignment of the U.S. military in Okinawa is part of the package deal linked with the transference of some of the facilities/functions of the U.S. military and/or Japan's Self-Defense Forces to prefectures of mainland Japan—such as Kanagawa, Yamaguchi, Tokyo, and Kagoshima. Voices of opposition have multiplied in communities in these prefectures in a way that has created solidarity with Okinawa. For instance, Tokyo Governor Ishihara Shintarō, a right-wing nationalist who had seldom considered the interests of Okinawa, criticized the central government by saying that the realignment plan "is poorly done" (*Asahi.com*, October 28, 2005); Kanagawa Prefecture Governor Matsuzawa Narifumi led a symposium together with Okinawa Governor Inimine in order to oppose the basic scheme of the realignment (*Okinawa Taimusu*,

December 20, 2005); and Iwakuni City of Yamaguchi Prefecture held a referendum—a political weapon of the weak, once used in Nago City—wherein the overwhelming majority of the voters opposed the transference of a U.S. aircraft carrier unit to the already busy and noisy Iwakuni Marine Corps Air Station (*Asahi.com*, March 12, 2006).[7] Antipathy to the transnational form of power was shared by Okinawan and mainland Japanese taxpayers also when Tokyo agreed to spend their (taxpayers') money in the amount of 700 billion yen ($7 billion, or 59% of the total costs) to help the U.S. military transfer marines from Okinawa to Guam. Incidentally, this was only a segment of Tokyo's estimated overall payment of more than 2.6 trillion yen ($26 billion), requested by the U.S. to implement the entire realignment of its military in Okinawa/Japan (*Asahi.com*, April 24, 2006, *Okinawa Taimusu*, April 26, 2006).

In these and other ways, collaborations and interactions between the pro-base and anti-base movements and sentiments in Okinawa and between Okinawa and mainland Japan have helped us to catch a glimpse of the ideal of the oppositional public sphere. Indeed, in order to actualize this ideal, all interested parties should be invited to and included in the discussion of the U.S. military in Okinawa: working-class Okinawans (often adult men) who reluctantly support the new base and middle-class citizens (often adult men) who oppose it; women who view nature and peace as critical to the welfare of their children and senior citizens who have gone through the tragedy and atrocity of the battle of Okinawa; young residents in need of jobs and Japanese construction companies that would give them jobs; ecologists, activists, scholars, and students who protest the contemporary global order; and, indeed, U.S. Marines and the readers of this study. After all, what the U.S.-Japan alliance as a transnational regime of military-economic-political power is afraid of is not a contemporary multiplicity of opinions fragmented along the axes of class, gender, race, age, nationality, and so forth but the revolt of the public sphere—that is, the multiplicity of global citizenship that is grounded in and orchestrates a collectivity of cultural sensibilities and historical experiences within Okinawa, Japan, and beyond.

Needless to say, I am not suggesting that radical appropriation in Okinawa somehow automatically triggers the construction of an open, inclusive, and heterogeneous arena of discussion and action across local, national, and global levels. Certain qualifications must be made. The question of language is one obvious obstacle: how could Okinawa invent a common language through which citizens could express themselves on the matter of the U.S. military without simply reinforcing the power of global English? Put differently, while the circulation of Okinawan language of protest is currently confined to the local—and sometimes national—fields of public discourse, simply translating this language into English for American and international audience (which this project has done) may inadvertently reinforce the status of English as the norm of global communication. The question of place constitutes another problem. For, even though Okinawa Governor Inamine, together with the majority of Okinawans (*Okinawa Taimusu*, November 15, 2005), cites the relocation of Futenma to a place outside Okinawa as the solution to the current crisis, this proposal would actually result in only one of the following. The proposal would simply meet the objection from Washington and/or from Tokyo and as a result, Futenma, together with its problems—noise, accidents, crimes, and pollution—would be just sitting there for many years to come; or Futenma is transferred to another place in Japan or outside Japan, along with the problems (noise, pollution, crimes, and accidents) of this U.S. base. Either way, the global deployment and violence of the military would never cease; rather, it would be perpetuated across local, national, and global boundaries because the proposed solution lacks a larger, transnational scope.

Perhaps, the issues of language and place call for a political skill, or really an "art," with which to traverse, leap, and rework geocultural borders that often divide realms of local practices, national concerns, and global interests. It is in search of such an art that I address the question of positionality of the anthropologist at the final juncture of this study. Situating myself between the modern anthropological refusal to reveal the point of the view of the researcher, on the one hand, and the postmodern narcissism of talking about oneself, on the other, I want to carry out this exercise in order to sketch a number of specific possibilities and responsibilities of anthropology in the global public sphere.

Positionality

In 1996, placed within the critical tradition of cultural anthropology at Duke University (Allison 1994, 2000; Piot 1999; Starn 1999), which was radically problematizing nation-bound research paradigms that ignored transnational movements of people, goods, capital, and information, I chose the U.S. base problems in Okinawa as my dissertation research topic. Timing was crucial. The events that followed the 1995 rape incident, in highlighting precisely the complexities of the problems that are simultaneously local, national, and global, drew my attention. Now, after an extended period of fieldwork, writing, and theoretical inquiries, I am presenting this study with the recognition that the anthropological practices involve not only understanding the Other (the U.S. base problems in Okinawa) but also negotiating and re-crafting the anthropologist's own identity in the contexts of changing relations of power and history that produce this Other. Asad's old formulation (1973: 12)—"Anthropology does not merely apprehend the world in which it is located, but...the world also determines how anthropology will apprehend it"—is still apposite here if, and only if, we take both "anthropology" and "the world" as multidimensional processes that crisscross boundaries of the local, the national, and the global.

The ways in which (multidimensional) "anthropology" and "the (multidimensional) world" became crystallized and transformed in relation to one another can be perceived in the following counterpoint, which highlights interaction of two ethnographic—broadly defined—experiences of this writer, one in Okinawa and the other in the United States.

In the first, I was chatting with a group of older women under the eaves of an old Okinawan house in Henoko on a hot summer day in 1998. They talked about their deteriorating health, their children and grandchildren, and about me—urging me to find a wife in Henoko. Our conversation turned to Henoko's past, then eventually to the battle of Okinawa. We discussed the story related in chapter 5—of the woman who went mad as she ran away cradling her headless baby under the rain of U.S. bombs. Another woman talked about how Japanese soldiers had treated her family members as spies of the U.S. military. In the midst of this, one of the women turned to me and asked, "Do you know what kinds of things your fathers [the Japanese] did in and to Okinawa?"

The sense of intimacy the conversation had built disappeared at once, and was replaced by an unbridgeable distance between the women—Okinawans—and me—a Japanese. I even felt like I should apologize on behalf of the Japanese state. Yet at the same time, I resented this woman's construction of me simply as "the Japanese," the outsider. Indeed, through my politically committed research to Okinawa, I came to know certain—of course, not all—aspects of Okinawan social life perhaps better than any Okinawans ever could. While this Henoko woman "Japanized" me on the basis of her personal experience of the war, I found myself awkwardly fragmented into a Japanese self and something else, an Okinawan self, perhaps.

Across the Pacific, however, I now comprehend the Henoko woman's questioning—"Do you know what kinds of things your fathers did in and to Okinawa?"—against the background of identity fragmentation that I have experienced in the United States, owing to the persistent tendency in American society to thrust on the Other the responsibility of speaking for his or her own culture and identity (Gupta and Ferguson 1997: 17). In fact, my status as an academic from Japan has often overridden the fact that I was born in the United States and have American citizenship, and has forced me into the prison-house of self-Orientalization from which there is no exit. For instance, when I was a graduate student, I was once invited by a friendly and hospitable community college in the south to talk about "sumō" (Japanese style wrestling) about which I had no knowledge whatsoever. More recently, I was requested by a well-intentioned student of mine to perform, in front of a class, "origami" (Japanese style paper-folding) of which I knew nothing. I have often felt confined within the geopolitical and discursive space called "Japan" because of the very process by which I was physically removed, with my American passport, from Japan to the United States; I have simultaneously become Japanese and something else, American, perhaps.

When the Henoko woman's question, "Do you know what kinds of things your fathers did in and to Okinawa?" was added to and intersected with my experiences of identity disintegration in the United States, what became clear to me was that neither Okinawa, Japan, nor the United States could any longer or ever be called "my home, my inside" because all of them affected my intellectual practices and political agendas as "my field, my outside"; yet at the same time, neither Okinawa, Japan, nor the United States could be simply called "my field, my outside" because I reside—physically and metaphorically—in all of these places which have become at least partially "my home, my inside." In a way that displaces the conventional insider-outsider binary,[8] I have become arrested and suspended in a geopolitical and discursive space that is not quite Japanese, not quite Okinawan, and not quite American, precisely when the Henoko woman, on the one hand, and American society, on the other, have "Japanized" me in different ways.

One should be clear that I am discussing my experiences not in order to prescribe a solution to the pains of positionality. I do not mean to suggest, on the one hand, that the pains of positionality will somehow magically disappear if the third-world intellectuals like me—I see Japan as an intellectual, if not economic and cultural, third-world—make efforts to get rid of their distinctive local and national features and backgrounds to become more global/theoretical. Such a move may indeed perpetuate the binary between the observing/theorizing global and the observed/theorized national/local unless the radical separation between the global, the national, and the local itself is interrogated. Nor do I intend to suggest, on the other hand, that the pains of positionality will somehow disappear if the local intellectuals (like me) study one's own culture (e.g., Japan). That disappearance would not be possible, because one's own so-called culture can never be understood in itself; it is a construction within and against the language and hegemony of Western, white, middle-class men whose status is often unmarked, being assumed to be the global norm. The issue, perhaps, lies not in how to settle the problems and troubles of positionality once and for all. Indeed, I prefer to think about how these problems and troubles can be appropriated and utilized as a springboard for constructing a counter public sphere, that is, for "forging links between *different* knowledges that are possible from different locations and tracing lines of possible alliance and common purpose between them" (Gupta and Ferguson 1997: 39, emphasis in original). Formulated below are the two specific ways in which anthropology can (as its potentialities) and should (as its responsibilities) contribute to accomplishing this task. These pertain to fieldwork and writing, two arenas which, having been fundamental to the discipline of contemporary anthropology, correspond precisely to the problems of place and language I have mentioned above in my discussion of the public sphere in Okinawa.

First, I would like to discuss the problem of fieldwork (place) by inserting another field experience here. In Henoko I often crossed over the social fissures by talking with anti-base residents one day and pro-base residents the next. While I did so in an effort to reach a fuller understanding of Henoko, my behavior never escaped the eyes of watchful residents and came to be viewed, understandably, with suspicion. A Henoko woman against the offshore base once hesitantly asked me, "You are not a spy of the Japanese Ministry of Foreign Affairs or the CIA, right?" On another occasion, a young Henoko man who supported the new base told, or accused, me,

"Those who come from the outside like you agitate the anti-base movement whenever you like, but you will leave Okinawa when this turmoil ends. We have to live here though. Have you ever swum in our sea? No? Then, what qualifications do you have to say anything about Henoko and about Okinawa?!" Facing cross pressures between pro-base residents and anti-base advocates in Henoko, I was often caught in a double bind, which made conducting fieldwork almost physically impossible and mentally unbearable.

In retrospect, however, I feel fortunate that I continued to stay within this impossibility and unbearableness for some time, because, even though some residents accused me of flip-flopping, it is they who eventually kindly redefined my inconsistency as a sign of impartiality and openness to different opinions, and disclosed a great deal of personal information, feelings, and thoughts to me. In the process, I may have better understood the predicaments of Henoko by inadvertently sharing the same form of existential dilemma many residents (including those who explicitly stated their pro-base or anti-base positions) experienced: They found themselves agonizingly vacillating between accepting and rejecting the offshore base, just as I was uneasily situated between the anti-base camp and the pro-base camp. In doing so, I, like many anthropologists, learned that a field where one works is not simply a site of data collection, but rather a battlefield on which all the mutually struggling forces and identities (the pro-base vs. the anti-base, the local vs. the national vs. the global, the anthropologist vs. the informant) should meet, negotiate, and articulate one another. Put differently, "the field" is a public sphere in microcosm which the anthropologist is both privileged and obliged to intervene.

Second, the question of positionality enables (as a potentiality), even necessitates (as a responsibility), the anthropologist to confront the issues of writing, language, and power in the public sphere. Various institutional and methodological innovations helped constitute the authority of the modern professional Western anthropologist (see note 14 in chapter 1). One such innovation, according to Clifford (1988), concerned language. He highlighted anthropology's age-old problem of disregarding the importance of vernacular language, which, when combined with "an increased emphasis on the power of observation," on the one hand, and with "certain powerful theoretical abstractions" (Clifford 1988: 31), on the other, contributed to the model of fieldwork that was "centered in the *experience* of the participant-observing scholar" (p. 34). I concur with this analysis.

Then, Clifford proceeded to interweave the overshadowed experiences of the Other with the notion of ethnographic dialogue and polyphony. He suggests, "It becomes necessary to conceive ethnography not as the experience and interpretation of a circumscribed 'other' reality, but rather as a constructive negotiation involving at least two, and usually more, conscious, politically significant subjects. Paradigms of experience and interpretation are yielding to discursive paradigms of dialogue and polyphony" (Clifford 1988: 41). In discussing the notion of dialogue/polyphony, however, Clifford—and much of postmodern anthropology—passes unexamined the question of in *which* language the dialogue/polyphony is to take place. In other words, in talking of polyphony in general and "a utopia of plural authorship" (p. 51) in particular, Clifford appears to have in mind those voices that have already been translated into the discursive field of global English, however multiple and diverse its structure may be. For those whose first language is not English (myself included), however, this "utopia" can be a nightmare because it silences the questions of why, for instance, the debates among American, Japanese, and Okinawan intellectuals tend to be conducted in English (rather than "standard" Japanese or Okinawan "dialect").[9] Relatedly, by suppressing the question of language as power, Clifford's model of dialogue and polyphony may also perpetuate the ongoing problem of the inattention to regional (in this case, Okinawan and mainland Japanese) intellectual issues in the midst of the expansion of global metropolitan scholarship now (or, still) conducted predominantly in English. From this perspective, Clifford's "utopia" is exclusive and contradicts the very idea of the public sphere this conclusion has explored.

One way to start redressing this problem is for anthropologists to actively write and speak in the language of the Other. What I advocate here is not so much the mere translation of Euro-American works into non-Western languages, wherein translators/interpreters, often of third-world origins, are frequently used to mask and perpetuate the unequal power relations of language between the West (that speaks in its own language) and the rest (that is forced to speak two, often more, languages across the west-rest divide). I am instead advocating the possibility that anthropology will itself become multilingual, in order to traverse and connect different intellectual-political fields of actions and discourses, and to go beyond the terrain of a single academic community of which membership is often circumscribed by a single language. What language we use in dialogue, writing, and speech is already a political question that should be taken into consideration as a fundamental issue of the public sphere in this age of globalization.

Fieldwork/place and writing/language, the two foundational practices of contemporary anthropology, are thus also becoming the two (of many) points of entry into the public sphere, that lead into the acts of border-crossing. Frantz Fanon (1925–1961), among others, has already provided us with one of the best models of this border-crossing anthropology. As "the Martinique-born psychiatrist and activist for the Algerian National Liberation Front" (Williams and Chrisman 1994: 24), Fanon (1963, 1967) expressed his poignant desire for collective, as well as personal, emancipation from the voice of racism that the oppressed themselves had internalized; he expressed this desire by relentlessly traversing, leaping, and reworking colonial divides and contradictions.

Though situated in a different historical and geopolitical context, and exploring a different set of questions concerning identity, power, and history, I have also written this book from a structurally similar positionality of counter border-crossing. My own case—being not quite Japanese, not quite American, not quite Okinawan—is not an exception, but perhaps illustrates a larger global process of hybridization of the public sphere within and against power. That is to say, while various forces of globalization—of which the U.S. military is an integral part—have affected, penetrated, and, in varying degrees, controlled the lives of citizens in many parts of the world, these forces have also ironically connected the world in such a way as to open up new potentialities for a worldwide coalition of locally and nationally grounded but globally informed subjects—such as anthropologists—against the very global power that has constituted them. In a word, these subjects are unintended excesses, the third person, produced in the process of globalization. As one of those subjects, I have been and will continue to be situated in a position that is neither Okinawan, Japanese, nor American, and committed to communicating about Okinawa's predicaments within the global public sphere in which we are all, like it or not, already united.

NOTES

1. Introduction

1. The island of Okinawa, the main island of Okinawa Prefecture, is located approximately 1,500 kilometers (932 miles) away from Tokyo.

2. In 1994, the breakdown of 29,020 U.S. troops in Okinawa was as follows: Army—887 (3.1 percent), Navy—2,917 (10.0 percent), Air Force—7,483 (25.8 percent), and Marine Corps—17,733 (61.1 percent) (Okinawaken Sōmubu Chiji Kōshitsu Kichi Taisakushitsu 1998b: 20). It should be noted that the U.S. military in Okinawa has been slightly downsized since 1994, in part because of the partial implementation of the final report of the Special Action Committee on Okinawa (to be discussed shortly). In 1997, the total number of U.S. troops in Okinawa was 27,119 (Army—838 (3.1 percent), Navy—3,009 (11.1 percent), Air Force—6,881 (25.4 percent), Marine Corps—16,391 (60.4 percent)) (Okinawaken Sōmubu Chiji Kōshitsu Kichi Taisakushitsu 1998b: 10, 20). In 2000, the total number of U.S. troops in Okinawa was 24,858 (Army—832 (3.3 percent), Navy—1,854 (7.5 percent), Air Force—6,808 (27.4 percent), Marine Corps—15,364 (61.8 percent)) (Okinawaken Sōmubu Chiji Kōshitsu Kichi Taisakushitsu 2005: 20). In 2004, the total number of U.S. troops in Okinawa was 22,339 (Army—935 (4.2 percent), Navy—2,183 (9.8 percent), Air Force—6,163 (27.6 percent), Marine Corps—13,058 (58.5 percent)) (Okinawaken Sōmubu Chiji Kōshitsu Kichi Taisakushitsu 2005: 10, 21). The significance of downsizing in 2004, however, should not be overestimated

because U.S. troops (particularly Marines) in Okinawa were temporarily sent to Iraq and elsewhere.

3. The return of Futenma was announced in Tokyo by Prime Minister Hashimoto and Ambassador to Japan Mondale in April 1996 and then was made official in the final report of SACO issued in December 1996.

4. It should be added, however, that the number of crimes committed by U.S. military personnel in 2003—133, which is the highest after 1990 (*Okinawa Taimusu*, June 3, 2004)—is dramatically smaller than the number of crimes in years immediately after the reversion (e.g., 310 in 1973, 318 in 1974, 342 in 1977). This reflects changing relations of power between Okinawa and the U.S. military which I will touch upon in chapters 2 and 4.

5. My first visit to Okinawa was in the summer of 1996. I conducted fieldwork in Henoko and larger Nago City for fourteen months in 1997–98. For six years after this fieldwork, I continued to visit Okinawa, including Henoko and Nago City, virtually every summer and often in other seasons as well. My most recent visit to Okinawa was July 2004, and the correspondence with residents in Henoko has been kept up to date.

6. Some Henoko residents I interviewed insisted that they would "tolerate" (*ukeireru* or *yōninsuru*) the U.S. military for the sake of community development, while other residents held the belief that Henoko should "invite" (*yūchisuru*) the U.S. military for the same reason. Although the nuances of their beliefs were not necessarily the same, those "pro-base" residents tended to share worries about their financial futures as a fundamental reason for their endorsement of the U.S. military presence in Okinawa.

7. Scholars often entirely omit questions of the military from their discussions about globalization (see, for instance, Appadurai 1996, especially pp. 27–47; Featherstone, ed. 1990; Hannerz 1992).

8. In my view, the war on "terrorism"—recent abuse of the military forces by the Bush administration in Afghanistan and then Iraq—has not satisfied any of the above conditions.

9. To be more precise, rituals are performed at *kami ashage* ("the structure where god raises his foot and enters") right behind *kōminkan*.

10. As of 1998, Camp Schwab accommodated approximately 2,800 Marines and hosted the Headquarters of the 3rd Marine Division, which was in turn overseen by the 3rd Marine Expeditionary Forces (MEF). The 3rd MEF, with its Headquarters located in central Okinawa, operated a total of six camps (Camp Zukeran, Camp Kuwae, Camp McTureous, Camp Courtney, Camp Hansen, and Camp Schwab, from south to

north), along with the training fields adjacent to these camps, one service area (Makiminato Service Area), three airfields (Futenma Marine Corps Air Station, Ie Jima Auxiliary Airfield, Yomitan Auxiliary Airfield), and one ammunition depot (Henoko Ordinance Ammunition Depot). The 3rd MEF was the only one of its kind stationed overseas (i.e., the 1st MEF is based in California and the 2nd MEF in North Carolina), and was militarily responsible for the areas of the Far East, Indian Ocean, and Middle East (Umebayashi 1994, Camp Schwab 1998, Okinawaken Sōmubu Chiji Kōshitsu Kichi Taisakushitsu 1998a). Today, the above situation is basically unchanged.

11. Also, in 1982 a Marine from Camp Schwab murdered a woman in downtown Nago City.

12. The calculation is based on the $1 = 100 yen exchange rate (which more or less reflects the actual exchange rate in the 1990s). Whenever dealing with amounts of money after the 1972 reversion (i.e., after the U.S. dollar was replaced with the Japanese yen), I will convert yen to dollars accordingly. It should be added, however, that this conversion does not adjust to the fluctuations of the exchange rate between the yen and the dollar of the past thirty-plus years. In other words, the calculation is done solely for the purpose of conveying a general sense of how much increase or decrease Okinawans gained within the context of the yen.

13. I draw the meaning of appropriation from Clifford; it essentially means "'to make one's own,' from the Latin *proprius*, 'proper,' 'property'" (Clifford 1988: 221).

14. In light of the work of Malinowski ([1922] 1984) and Radcliffe-Brown ([1922] 1948], I take the 1920s as a rough starting point of modern anthropology. Because of what can be seen as an exhaustion of theoretical paradigms—including structural-functionalism (e.g., Fortes 1953, 1969), structuralism (e.g., Lévi-Strauss 1963, 1966, 1974), culture and personality (e.g., Mead 1935, Benedict 1934, 1946; Linton 1945, Whiting and Whiting 1975), cultural materialism (e.g., Harris 1979, 1987), practice theory (e.g., Bourdieu 1980), symbolic anthropology (e.g., Douglas 1966), interpretive anthropology (e.g., Geertz 1973, 1980, 1983), and Marxism (see note 15 below), I take the 1980s as an approximate ending point of modern anthropology. Ortner's well-known article titled "Theory in Anthropology since the Sixties" (1984) may have signaled this exhaustion of theoretical paradigms of modern anthropology. See Asad, ed. (1973), Fabian (1983), Marcus and Fischer (1986), Clifford and Marcus, eds. (1986), Clifford (1988), Gupta and Ferguson (1992, 1997), Rosald (1993), Dirks, Eley and Ortner (1994), and Coronil (1996), among others, for the critique of ethnographic writing and other innovations modern anthropology developed in order to talk about, deal with, and ultimately control and dominate the Others.

15. I have learned a great deal about long-standing Marxist, nationalist, and feminist critiques of power by reading, among others, (1) Tucker's (1978) edited volume of the writings of Marx and Engels, Marx ([1867] 1976), Lenin (1947), Thompson (1964), Gramsci (1971), Althusser (1971), Scott (1976), Wolf ([1982] 1997), and Laclau and Mouffe (1985) in the tradition of the Marxist revolutionary literature; (2) Fanon (1963, 1967), Senghor ([1970] 1994), Freire (1990), Guevara (1994), Nehru (1945), Gandhi ([1927] 1983)—also Nehrū and Gandhi as discussed by Chatterjee (1986)—Fukuzawa ([1875] 1997), Kita (1926), and Hashikawa ([1985] 2000) in the tradition of the nationalist/anticolonial/liberation literature; and (3) Etienne and Leacock, eds. (1980), Spivak ([1988] 1994), Enloe (1989), Shiva (1989), Ueno (1990), Mohanty, Russo and Torres, eds. (1991), Kandiyoti ([1991] 1994), and hooks (1992) in the tradition of the feminist (particularly the third-world feminist) literature.

16. My discussion here owes much to Derrida's (1978) reading of Levinas. It should be noted, however, Derrida ultimately rejects Levinas's movement and departure toward the third person, which I intend to explicitly rescue here.

17. Habermas (1989) locates the ideal type of public sphere—a critical sphere of discussion, communication, and deliberation against the state—in bourgeois societies of England, France, and Germany in the eighteenth and nineteenth centuries, while negatively viewing the expanded public sphere (i.e., the entrance of the masses into the public sphere) of the twentieth century as being a contaminated, deteriorated version of this ideal type. In other words, he sees the heterogeneity of the twentieth-century public sphere as a problem to be solved and overcome, and attempts to recover and recuperate a pristine public sphere on the basis of a Western, bourgeois model of rationality.

18. In Habermas's discussion of communicative action (1990), the actor is designated as a gender-and-race-unspecific "he," who, according to what I see as a European, bourgeois model of rationality, is to mediate his lifeworld—defined ahistorically as "background," as "a storehouse of unquestioned cultural givens" (p. 135)—and world—abstracted as a three-dimensional reference system of "interpersonally shared propositional knowledge" (corresponding to the domain of truth), "normative accord" (corresponding to the domain of justice), and "mutual trust" (corresponding to the domain of taste/art) (pp. 136-37), in order to reach a pristine agreement with other actors. See also Habermas (1985, 2000).

19. "The possibility of democracy on a global scale is emerging today for the very first time. This book is about that possibility, and what we call the project of the multitude. The project of the multitude not only expresses the desire for a world of equality and freedom, but also provides the means for achieving it" (Hardt and

Negri 2004: xi); "The multitude, although it remains multiple and internally different, is able to act in common and thus rule itself" (p. 100). The concept of the public sphere as used in this study shares with the project of the multitude its global democratic aspirations.

20. This study draws on and, simultaneously, radically redefines and thus departs from Habermas' ahistorical understanding of the "lifeworld" (1985, 1990: 135-141; 2000).

2. The Rape Incident and the Predicaments of Okinawan Identity

1. Linda Angst (2003) provides a vivid description about how the rape was committed. I owe the following narrative to her study, as well as other sources including Uehara M. (1995), *Ryukyu Shinpo* (November 7, November 8, December 27, 1995; March 8, 1996), *Ryukyu Shinpo Weekly News* (September 19 and November 14, 1995) and *Washington Post* (November 18, 1995). Needless to say, I assume full responsibility for the narrative I present here.

2. Privates Harp and Ledet were from two small towns in Georgia, and Navy Seaman Gill was from a town in Texas. The U.S. military provided them one of but a few social avenues for moving upward. *New York Times* (November 6, 1995) reported: "He always wanted to go into the Marine Corps," [Private Harp's] sister, Lillie Felton, 33, said today as she recalled that he had studied hard for a year before retaking the test. "That was his way out of this small town, his way to make something of himself. It was a great day for him and for me when he passed the test."

3. The Japanese Ministry of Foreign Affairs Chief, Kōno Yōhei, explicitly stated to Okinawa Governor Ota, who visited Tokyo to lodge a protest, that Tokyo was not considering the revision of SOFA (*Ryukyu Shinpo*, September 20, 1995).

4. During the same period, the U.S. military caused 121 aircraft accidents—including 36 crashes (Okinawa Prefectural Government 1995; cited in Ryukyu Shinpo 1995: 321).

5. On May 15, 1972, Governor Yara Chobyo stated in the reversion ceremony that "Now, the day of Okinawa's reversion has indeed arrived. Yet, when we look at the details of reversion in light of what we requested and what we experienced, it is also true that our earnest aspirations have not been necessarily met. We return to Japan along with various problems, including the problems concerning the situation of the U.S. bases. Accordingly, the severe situation may continue and we may face new hardships" (cited in Nanpō Dōhō Engokai 1972: 1000).

6. In 1972, immediately after the reversion of Okinawa, Tokyo enacted the Public Land Law to forcefully extend the contracts with Okinawa's anti-military landlords for five years. In 1977, Tokyo extended the Public Land Law for another five years. In 1982, Tokyo put into effect the Special Law concerning the Expropriation of Land for the U.S. Military (originally established in the 1950s to expropriate land in mainland Japan for the use of the U.S. military) to forcefully extend the contracts with anti-military landlords in Okinawa for another five years. In 1987, the Japanese government used the same law to forcefully extend the contracts with anti-military landlords in Okinawa for another ten years (Arasaki 1995).

7. As of March 1995, there were 2,919 anti-military landlords who refused to renew the land contracts (to be expired in May 1997) with the Japanese government (Defense Facilities Agency). After securing signatures from 279 landlords, in June 1995 the Defense Facilities Agency requested nine city/town/village mayors that they, in accordance with the law, sign and renew the land contracts as the proxy of the remaining 2,640 anti-military landlords. Six mayors agreed to the request, but the mayors of Naha City, Okinawa City, and Yomitan Village, who represented thirty-five anti-military landlords, refused. Then, in August 1995, in accordance with the law, the Defense Facilities Agency requested Governor Ota to sign and renew the contracts as their proxy.

8. The construction of a stone monument named *Heiwa no Ishiji* (Cornerstone for Peace) in Okinawa Prefectural Peace Memorial Park was a manifestation of Ota's anti-military stance. Unlike the Vietnam Veterans Memorial in Washington, DC, the monument is inscribed with and commemorates the names of all war dead in the battle of Okinawa regardless of nationality.

9. Murayama Tomi'ichi of the Social Democratic Party, who was succeeded by Hashimoto Ryūtarō of the Liberal Democratic Party in January 1996. By using the word "dumb" to describe the leadership of socialist Prime Minister Murayama, Hōshuyama appears to have been expressing his elitist distrust of socialists, workers, and the oppressed such as Okinawans. In 1994 Hōshuyama stated that "I would like Okinawa to coexist and cooperate with the bases" to stir Okinawans' indignation (Arasaki 1995: 221–24).

10. After the reversion of Okinawa, for instance, U.S. servicemen murdered a twenty-two-year-old prostitute in 1972, a thirty-seven-year-old hostess in 1972, a forty-three-year-old hostess in 1973, a fifty-two-year-old female bar owner in 1974, a thirty-three-year-old hostess in 1982 (Fukuchi 1995, Takazato and Kichi to Guntai wo Yurusanai Koudou suru Onnatachi no Kai 1996). As I stated earlier, U.S. military personnel committed 110 rapes over twenty-three years after the reversion.

11. *New York Times* (November 6, 1995) reported: "It's very disappointing and frustrating," said Kim Cannon, Private Ledet's sister, deputy sheriff in Felton County, GA. "It's political and it's racial. We're all black and we all come from small towns. I'm looking at three young black men who may face life in prison, and I just don't think this would be happening if they were white."

12. After the battle of Okinawa, B-52s took off from Okinawa to make air raids on major cities in mainland Japan until World War II ended (Nakano 1969: 1).

13. Part of Ordinance 109 read: "such owner or owners [of land who receive the Notice of Intent from USCAR] shall have thirty (30) days from the date of publication of the notice in which to accept or refuse the offer of the United States [i.e., compensation]. In the event of refusal, the owner(s) may within the said thirty (30) days appeal in writing to the Deputy Governor. Failing such appeal within said time the estate or interest shall be deemed transferred to the United States for the amount stated; in the event of appeal, only the issue of just compensation will be determined and such appeal shall not stay the right of the United States to file a Declaration of Taking" (USCAR 1953; cited in Gekkan Okinawasha 1983: 49).

14. These thirty-two families received little compensation. They were housed in a nearby school building for a while, and then, in their struggle to survive, eventually applied for an emigration program to Bolivia prepared by the Government of the Ryukyu Islands (GRI). (Kokuba 1973: 264, cited in Arasaki 1995: 65). For explanation of GRI, see p. 48.

15. The full text of the "Price Report" is stored in: http://www.niraikanai.wwma .net/pages/archive.html, prepared by John M. Purves (1995–2006).

16. The visa of Professor Nagazumi Yasuaki of Kobe University, who was invited to offer a course on Japanese literature at the University of the Ryukyus, was suspended in 1964 for this reason (Kano 1987: 200–262).

17. Data from 1955 show that an Okinawan man working as a laborer in a base construction site earned 9.50 B-yen to 20 B-yen an hour, a Japanese worker under similar working conditions 25 B-yen to 45 B-yen an hour, a Filipino worker/foreman 48 B-yen to 196.80 B-yen an hour, and an American worker/supervisor 125.20 B-yen to 752 B-yen an hour (Nakano 1969: 146). Cf. B-yen was used until 1958. The exchange rate was: $1 = 120 B-yen = 360 Japanese yen. In 1958 the dollar became the unit of currency in Okinawa (Makino 1987: 145–187).

18. In "Ryukyu Today," as Kano (1987: 161–99) has documented, Okinawan artists drew cover pictures, Okinawan professors wrote about the value of traditional arts, and Okinawan leaders in business and commerce discussed the prosperity of the U.S.-governed Ryukyu Islands. Kano also shows that *Shurei*, the Ryukyu Kingdom's

basic policy which literally meant "to observe courtesy," was appropriated by USCAR as part of the title of the magazine ("The Light of *Shurei*") to "teach" Okinawans about their own culture and personality. That is, they should "observe courtesy," i.e., not offend USCAR by conducting, for instance, protest activities. These magazines were ubiquitous. Combined, the monthly circulation of these two magazines reached 114,000 in 1968, on the islands of some 200,000 households (Kano 1987: 164).

19. The conservative ruling party, the Okinawa Liberal Democratic Party (OLDP)—established in 1959 and restructured as the Okinawa Democratic Party in 1964—operated outside *Fukkikyō*. OLDP's basic principle of actions is to represent and secure broader business interests of Okinawans; in accordance with this principle, it first advocated (somewhat vaguely) unification with Japan and then (more forcefully) reversion of Okinawa to Japan, while always seeking "concrete solutions through established official channels within the framework of cooperation with the U.S. and Japanese Governments" (Mi. Higa 1963: 56; see also Mi. Higa 1977).

20. See chapter 3 for the further discussion of the work of Pitts, Lebra, and Suttles (1955).

21. In actuality, boys below seventeen years of age and men over forty-five years of age were often included due to the shortage of soldiers.

22. Okinawan memories of the Japanese Imperial Army, which had not so much protected as shattered many lives of Okinawans, resurfaced in post-reversion Okinawa, when voices were pervasively raised against the appearance of Japan's Self-Defense Forces, the successor of the Imperial Army in postwar Japan (Takamine and Nagamoto 1995: 209–16).

23. The organized resistance of the Japanese Army ended in late June 1945, but sporadic fighting continued in July and August in some areas. The death toll among Okinawans would reach 150,000—about a quarter of the prefectural population—if those who died of malaria, illness, and starvation in the wake of the battle of Okinawa are included (Arashiro 1994: 253-54).

24. Post-reversion protests in the 1970s and 1980s have been made in terms of peace, the environment, the right to life and culture, freedom of thought, and other themes of "new" social movements. Examples include, but are not limited to, protests against the construction of tanks for crude oil stockpiling in Kin Bay and other areas, the U.S. military's target practice with live shells across Prefectural Route 104, the appearance of Japan's Self-Defense Forces (see note 22), forced extension of land contracts with anti-military landlords, noise pollution around Kadena Air Base, the construction of a commercial airport on Ishigaki Island, forced display of the Japanese flag in Okinawan schools, parachute-landing exercises at Yomitan Auxiliary

Airport, the Harrier Pad construction in Kunigami Village, the construction of a training facility for guerrilla warfare in Camp Hansen, the deployment of P-3C anti-submarine patrol aircrafts in Motobu Town (Arasaki 1992: 198–217). The term "silent revolution" is borrowed from the work of Inglehart (1977).

25. To anticipate my argument in chapter 8, the dispatch of SDF to Afghanistan and Iraq to aid controversial U.S. military operations there can be seen as another symptom of the dissolution and manipulation of the Japanese constitution by the global form of power.

26. This aid had been initiated in 1978 when the U.S. government called upon Tokyo for the financial assistance against the background of its budgetary difficulties and the weakening of the U.S. dollar.

27. Again, to anticipate my argument in chapter 8, the next and ultimate target is the peace constitution itself. Richard Lee Armitage, Deputy Secretary of State under the Bush administration till 2004, argued, for example, that this constitution is an obstacle to the fuller development of the U.S.–Japan Security alliance, that is, the complete integration of Okinawa and Japan's SFD into the U.S. military operations (*Shinbun Akahata*, July 24, 2004). In this way, the peace constitution, originally created to suit America's own convenience (demilitarization and democratization of postwar Japan), is about to be abolished again to accomplish the same.

28. The most obvious manifestation of the idea of "catching up with the mainland" is a series of *Okinawa Shinkō Kaihatsu Keikaku* (Okinawa Development Programs) sponsored by the Japanese government. Okinawa annually received from Tokyo an average of 169 billion yen ($1.69 billion) between 1972 and 1991 owing to the first (1972–1981) and second (1982–1991) Okinawa Development Programs (Arashiro 1994: 293). The third Okinawa Development Program began in 1992 and ended in 2001, and the fourth Okinawa Development Program (2002–2011) is under way.

29. Okinawan military landlords received annual rent in the amount of 3.1 billion yen ($31 million) from the U.S. in 1971. They received 17.7 billion yen ($177 million) in 1973, and 26.9 billion yen ($269 million) in 1975 from Tokyo. Two decades later, in 1996, the amount rose to 70.4 billion yen ($704 million).

3. Reduced to Culture without Politics and History

1. For example, see Miyata (1985), Ōtō (1990), and Yoshimoto (1995).

2. Murai Osamu (1992) relates the shift of Yanagita's focus to his earlier governmental career. Apparently, in the 1900s, Yanagita engaged in the drafting of

3. Reduced to Culture

colonial laws on agriculture and land in Korea as an elite bureaucrat of the Ministry of Agricultural Affairs. Far from being managed in the way Yanagita thought they would be, however, Koreans staged explosive resistance vis-à-vis Japan after Japan's "annexation" of Korea in 1910. Murai interprets Yanagita's silence about Asia from the 1920s on as a calculated attempt to mask and escape from his earlier, failed involvement in Korea. Murai's provocative thesis, however, remains to be substantiated on empirical grounds.

3. Yanagita was energetically traveling through various parts of Imperial Japan as an honorary editorial member of the *Asahi Shinbun* (News) Company when Tokyo assigned him a job in Geneva in 1921.

4. The rejection of Japan's proposal to include a provision of racial equality in the covenant of the League of Nations at the Paris Peace Conference in 1919 and the virtual prohibition of immigration from Japan to the U.S. in the mid-1920s are two of many other examples of the manifestation of discrimination against the "yellow race" in the early twentieth century (Dower 1986, especially chapters 7 and 8).

5. This is the basic trajectory of numerous Japanese *male* intellectuals since the days of Fukuzawa Yukichi ([1875]1997), Nitobe Inazō ([1905]1969), and Okakura Kakuzō ([1906]1956) in the Meiji period, of wartime nationalists like Kita Ikki (1926), of postwar cultural nationalists such as Doi Takeo (1971), Aida Yūji (1972), and Kawai Hayao (1982), and of contemporary critics such as Nisho Kanji, Fujioka Nobukatsu, and Kobayashi Yoshinori (Atarashii Rekishi Kyoukasho wo Tsukuru Kai, ed. 1997) who now promote the reactionary Liberal Historical View (*Jiyūshugi shikan*). These and other examples imply that we cannot adequately grasp the problem of Japanese cultural nationalism without taking the questions of masculinity, of racial and sexual identity of Japanese men, seriously. The task of the exploration of Japanese men's (including Yanagita's) sexual and racial identity in the global historical context, however, is beyond the scope of this study. I will undertake this task in a separate study.

6. As such, Yanagita's project was defined as the learning of one's own culture under the rubric of *aratanaru kokugaku* (new national learning) (Yanagita [1935]1968c: 314) or as *ikkoku minzokugaku* (one-nation folklore/ethnology) (Yanagita [1934]1968c: 339). "As far as the domain of what is called ethnology is concerned, I think it should be national" (Yanagita [1928]1968c: 244).

7. He wrote, "Japan is the foremost island country in the world" (Yanagita [1928]1968c: 136); "Japanese are themselves islanders" (p. 138). These are not so much innocent factual descriptions—it is difficult to "experience" that Japan is an

island nation unless one learns it as a piece of knowledge (Oguma 1995: 216–17)—as politically-loaded intellectual statements as I discuss below.

8. The term "Japanese" needs to be gender-specific, because in many cases only Japanese "men," not women, enjoyed the privileges. For the sake of avoiding cumbersomeness, I advisedly write "the Japanese."

9. The section titled "Military Employment" (pp. 204–16), from which this quote is taken, was written by Lebra.

10. Lebra's work in general, and this book in particular, exerts a strong influence upon Susan Sered's (1994, 1995, 1999) recent work (see chapter 5). In other words, the tradition of American anthropological studies on Okinawa in the 1950s and 1960s, so far from disappearing, has been reshaped in the present.

11. He also states that "the degree of their relationship [i.e., the Japanese and Okinawan languages] has been likened to that of French and Italian" (Lebra 1966: 8). The reference to Okinawans' physical features (e.g., hairiness), together with the comparison of the relationship between the Japanese and Okinawan languages to the relationship between European languages, was a noticeable trope of Okinawan studies in the United States that had appeared already in the *Handbook* (U.S. Navy Department 1944; for instance, see p. 43).

12. Maretzki was not the first one who lodged this challenge, however. *Post-War Okinawa* (Pitts, Lebra, and Suttles 1955) had already discussed Okinawa's pro-Japanese feeling (see pp. 215–216 and p. 222, for instance); this feeling, in my view, became a background against which Lebra attempted to discover Okinawan-ness away from Japan in his *Okinawan Religion* (1966).

13. Beillevaire (1999: 172) characterizes this dual process in the notion of "[Japanese] assimilation from within, [American] appropriation from without."

14. I here use the term "Ryukyuan/Okinawan" to designate the region Iha was referring to, the region that was once called the "Ryukyu" Kingdom and was transformed into "Okinawa" Prefecture by the Meiji government.

15. *Kojiki* is a history book compiled in the eighth century in mainland Japan; *Nihon Shoki* is another history book written in the eighth century in mainland Japan; and *Manyōshū* is a collection of poems compiled in the eighth century in mainland Japan.

16. The intimate interactions between Iha and Yanagita began when Yanagita visited Okinawa in 1921 (Kinjo and Takara 1984: 161–65); Yanagita genuinely encouraged Iha to study Okinawa's classical poems while he, in a way, used the results of Iha's research to advance Yanagita's own thesis of Okinawa as a foundational site of Japanese native ethnology.

3. Reduced to Culture

17. Here, I specifically draw on Fuss, who states "the radicality or conservatism of essentialism depends, to a significant degree, on *who* is utilizing it, *how* it is deployed, *where* its effects are concentrated" (1989: 20, emphasis in original).

4. *"We Are Okinawans of a Different Kind"*

1. For an analysis of how, in the United States, a local community interacted with the national twentieth-century history of war and peace, see Lutz' (2001) forceful and elegant ethnographic study of Fayetteville, NC.

2. Ages are taken as of January 1998. As I stated in "Note on Japanese Names and Translations" (p. xiii), local informants' names are mostly altered to protect their privacy except where specified (the real name is provided if his/her name has been publicly known). In this chapter, background information of certain local informants (e.g., family, work) is altered for the same reason.

3. In fact, Kushi village, since then, came to receive 70 percent of the total rent generated from Henoko's military land, while Henoko received 30 percent.

4. A portion of a family register compiled by the Henoko administration in 1969 shows that about half of the households were headed by men coming from outside Henoko.

5. As I stated in chapter 1, there were two other murders involving Henoko and Camp Schwab. In 1974 a U.S. Marine belonging to Camp Schwab murdered a female owner of a bar in Henoko, and in 1982 another Marine from Camp Schwab murdered a woman in downtown Nago City (Fukuchi 1995: 240–42; Okinawaken Sōmubu Chiji Kōshitsu Kichi Taisakushitsu 2003: 473).

6. According to aforementioned Yagaji Noriyuki, upon the construction of Camp Schwab most of the land owned by Henoko was evenly divided and distributed to the then existing households to help them launch into new commercial activities, which means that latecomers did not obtain plots of land.

7. It should be added, however, that the range of the rent was (and still is) huge among landlords, depending on how large their private land has been. Data show that in 1985, among holders of the military land in Camp Schwab—many of whom lived (and still live) mainly in Henoko, but some of whom lived (and still live) in nearby communities —196 landlords received less than 500,000 yen ($5,000), 80 received 500,000–1 million yen ($5,000–$10,000), 51 received 1–2 million yen ($10,000–$20,000), 8 received 2–3 million yen ($20,000–$30,000), 5 received 3–4 million yen ($30,000–$40,000), 1 received 4–5 million yen ($40,000–$50,000), 1

received 6–7 million yen ($60,000–$70,000), 2 received 7–8 million yen ($70,000–$80,000), 1 received 9–10 million yen ($90,000–$100,000), and 1 received 10–20 million yen ($100,000–$200,000), respectively (Okinawaken Gunyōchinado Jinushi Rengōkai 1988: 718).

8. The number of branch families can be one or many.

9. The aforementioned Yagaji Ippan was born into *Yagaji munchū*.

10. The average age of the HEC members in the late 1990s was approximately 54.

11. These five situations should not be taken as rigid markers, but rather as general guideposts to articulate multiplicity of women's experiences in Henoko.

12. This is his real name.

13. Non-Henoko residents like me cannot enter the base without a special permit.

14. Compare the positive view of the U.S. military among HYA members (who had no memory of the time before Camp Schwab had been created) with the more pungent feelings towards the U.S. military shared among the older pro-base residents who had experienced the war and/or the poverty of pre-Camp Schwab Henoko. For instance, Yagaji Noriyuki, one of the older leaders previously mentioned, told me, "I had a rather hostile feeling towards the servicemen because we were defeated in the war. But you had to put the past behind you. Otherwise the community would not prosper. I decided to make use of them—they needed us, and we needed them. But when crimes and accidents happened, I got angry. I feel the same, even now."

15. NHK has assumed the complex position of being a critical public TV station as well as a conservative state TV station. In this particular program, which was broadcast in the autumn of 1997 (after the plan to build an offshore base in Henoko was announced by the Japanese and U.S. governments), NHK revealed its state TV character by representing Henoko with a pro-base voice (Sueyoshi's), thereby implicitly supporting the governmental policy of building the new base there.

16. The HYA, which used to be a men-only organization, has recently allowed both men and women to join the group in order to increase the number of members.

17. They, for instance, set up and took down a non-permanent stage, and put podiums and chairs on it.

18. Family registers compiled by the Henoko administration, as well as my participation in and observation of the activities of young people in the community, suggest that at least two-thirds of the Henoko youth in their late-teens and twenties work and/or live outside of Henoko.

19. Since I was not allowed to attend this meeting, this description is on the basis of my observation of a similar social occasion which took place after the Dragon Boat festival in May, 1998, as well as the document prepared by the Henoko/Schwab Friendship Council (1998).

20. In the 1990s, more than half of Camp Schwab Marines rotated every three to six months, as they belonged to the Unit Deployment Program, in which numerous units were sent back and forth between Okinawa, Camp Lejeune in North Carolina, Camp Pendleton in California, and other locations (Umebayashi 1994).

21. This is a quote from an internal report based on interviews with 3,200 servicemen in seven bases in Japan (including Okinawa), Korea, and Alaska, which was submitted to U.S. Defense Secretary William Perry in September 1995 (after the rape incident in Okinawa).

22. I hasten to add that the boundaries of friendship were often crossed. For instance, a substantial number of Vietnam War veterans (five to ten in the late 1990s) had been residing in Henoko. They bridged the gap between the base and the community in many different ways—some married Henoko women; others taught English to residents; and still others actively participated in social functions in Henoko and beyond. However, typically, their command of the local language remained at a minimal conversational level, and thus they could not fully communicate with residents. An episode involving an old woman in Henoko and her thirty-nine-year-old daughter, whom I happened to meet in a Henoko bar, provided a graphic example of the communication gap. They rarely spoke to one another, sitting together in silence. It turned out this was the first time they had met in thirty-two years, and they could not converse because of their language difference. The mother had separated from her then American husband living in Henoko because she was fed up with his womanizing, had taken all of her six children to the United States when the daughter, whom she now saw in the Henoko bar, was seven years old, and then had returned to Okinawa alone. Since then, the mother and her children had not met at all. This episode shows that crossing the boundaries of friendship has often created even more insurmountable problems of race, culture, and language.

5. "We Are Okinawans"

1. The Japanese government filed a suit in the Naha District Court against Governor Ota in December 1995 on the grounds that he had refused to follow the governmental order to sign the land contracts. The judgment was given in March

1996 and went in favor of the Japanese government. Ota appealed to the Supreme Court immediately to reassert his position. In August 1996, the Supreme Court dismissed Ota's appeal.

2. The bill passed the Japanese Diet in April 1997, and then was revised in March 1999 to reinforce the power of the central government over Okinawa (*Okinawa Taimusu*, April 17, 1997, and March 26, 1999).

3. In fact, the return of Naha Military Port, as agreed upon between the U.S. and Japanese governments in 1974, has not yet been realized because of the impossibility of finding a relocation site within Okinawa.

4. In the case of Japan, I observe the mixture of internationalism and nationalism.

5. *Narrative of the Expedition of an American Squadron to the China Seas and Japan*, from which the above quote is taken, was compiled from the original notes and journals of Commodore Perry and his officers, at his request, and under his supervision, by Francis L. Hawks. Notably, Perry's squadron anchored at the Naha port of the Ryukyu Kingdom in May 1853 on his way to Edo (Perry 1857: 151–196, 215–227; Arashiro 1994: 160–163) in order to establish a coal station on the island of Okinawa. After this visit, Perry's squadron visited the Kingdom four more times. Incidentally, an Okinawan woman was raped by three American sailors during one of these visits (in 1854). One of the sailors was killed by angry Okinawans (Takara K. 1984: 91–98).

6. In *Multitude*, a sequel to *Empire* (2000), however, Hardt and Negri (2004) seem to slightly modify their position by more critically exploring the roles the United States and its military have played in the age of "armed globalization." See, particularly, pp. 41–62 and pp. 312–24 of *Multitude*.

7. This means, however, that less than 60 percent of the eligible voters came to the polls. Looking at the light turnout, some conservative critics called the referendum a failure. On SOFA, see chapter 1.

8. Some of the men from Haebaru *munchū* worked in Camp Schwab and elsewhere as laborers, and others started their own business in Henoko just like Haebaru Kenji who was himself a professional painter/plumber.

9. The term was popularized by Ahagon Shōkō, a legendary Okinawan antiwar landlord on Ie Island (off the coast of the Motobu peninsula of northwestern Okinawa), who played a central role in the development of the island-wide protest in the 1950s. This term helped Ahagon to epitomize his resistance to the pressures of USCAR (before the 1972 reversion) and the Japanese government (after the reversion) to sign the lease of his land for the use of the U.S. military, which, according to him, takes, not respects, life (Ahagon 1973, 1992).

10. She was also the wife of one of the most influential leaders in Henoko—Yagaji Ippan, who became something of a monarch of a communal dynasty (Henoko) in the 1960s; see chapter 4.

11. Micronesia was put under a German trusteeship before World War I and a Japanese trusteeship after World War I.

12. Knowing how important education was, he kept saying to me, evidently without clearly understanding the educational system in the United States, that "you've got to finish school and get your Ph.D., whatever that is."

13. Around the time of Okinawa's reversion in 1972, approximately ten *kaminchu* existed; as of 1997–98, there were only four actively performing religious functions—one of whom, however, died during my fieldwork.

14. A central problem in structural-functionalist theory has been to determine how a society, seen as a bounded, homogeneous, timeless unit, is kept together. But the argument is often circular. To the question "why is this society held together?" structural-functionalists typically answer, "Because they have rituals." But to the question "why do rituals exist?," structural-functionalist typically answer, "Because this society is held together." The argument is also indeterminate: It does not explain why one form of cohesion is chosen over another in a specific society (See Piot 1999: 10–11). Sered's analysis suffers these problems of structural-functionalist theory.

15. On this matter, see the concluding chapter of this book.

16. This is the translation of a Japanese saying, *kane no kireme wa en no kireme*, which was also used by a pro-base resident of Henoko (see chapter 4, the end of the section titled "Lonely Marines"), for whom it took on a slightly different meaning.

6. Nago City Referendum

1. To reiterate, the Japanese government wanted to hide the opposition of local inhabitants in order to reinforce the U.S.-Japan security alliance, and the mayor and conservative municipal assemblymen wanted to do the same because they needed money for the development of Nago City. See chapter 5.

2. During and after the war, the U.S. either converted the old bases of the former Japanese military into their own bases or constructed the new bases in Okinawa from scratch by confiscating its land. All existing U.S. bases in Okinawa are thus created regardless of Okinawans' opinions and wills; see chapter 2.

3. In the midst of the campaign for the referendum, Tokyo suddenly promoted Kakazu to the rank of Vice Director of the Okinawa Development Agency so as to have him work on the offshore base issues.

4. The rate of exchange is 100 yen to the dollar. See note 12 in chapter 1.

5. The economic benefit of the base construction for Okinawa at large was specifically foregrounded when, for instance, Prime Minister Hashimoto Ryūtarō came to Okinawa (November 1997) to announced the "Economic Development 21st Century Plan" which included the expansion of the free trade zone, the facilitation of tourism and international research programs, and the development of infrastructure.

6. Suzuki Muneo was also on stage, as a guest, at a concert by Matsuyama Chiharu, a Japanese folk singer, who was invited to Nago by the pro-base group to help foster, according to the words on an advertisement banner, "lofty ambitions and visions of the future" among the local youth.

7. For instance, he stated in an interview, "I don't think it's OK for local residents to suffer from…the violation of the right to life for the sake of the nation. The referendum is the first step to bring this issue up from the bottom…. In the past, Okinawa's military bases were created by bayonets and bulldozers [which were used to enclose and expropriate Okinawa's land]. Today, a new base is about to be created together with development projects. Bayonets and bulldozers have simply been replaced by money…. As Nago *shimin*, let us actively decide on the matter, and let us express our will in which sovereignty resides" (*Ryukyu Shinpo*, July 14, 1997).

8. Since the reversion of Okinawa to Japan, the traditional working class has thinned. In 1972 more than 35 percent of workers joined the unions, but today less than 14 percent join (*Okinawa Taimusu*, January 15, 2003). My observation also suggests that teachers, once a "key group in the moulding of public opinion" (Pitts, Lebra, and Suttles 1955: 219), have lost influences they once had.

9. The officials never used the words "military base." This may have been a verbal strategy to cover up the actual functions of the new "facility."

10. The women's group formally remained a unit within the Association of the Ten Districts Not Wanting the Offshore Base.

11. The development of the women's activities of *Jan'nu Kai* became linked with the broader women's network within Okinawa and beyond. Supporters from various fields and backgrounds, including housewives, photographers, reporters, civil servants, politicians, writers, and university instructors, came from all over Okinawa to help build up the women's movement. Groups such as *Yarukīzu* (Go-for-it),

Kodomo no Mirai wo Mamoru Matsuda Fubo no Kai (Society of Parents in Matsuda District in Ginoza Village [near Henoko] for Protecting the Future of Children), *Kamadūguwa no Tsudoi* (Meetings in a Small Okinawan Kitchen), etc., were created to support and extend the efforts of *Jan'nu Kai*. Ties between *Jan'nu Kai* and the older women of Henoko were also (if not tightly) established in the process. Ultimately, *Jan'nu Kai* became joined with Okinawa's women's movement at large, which had long been led by Naha City Assemblywoman Takazato Suzuyo and others. Takazato Suzuyo had been a popular, leading spokeswoman, who, before and after the 1995 rape incident, publicized the violence of the U.S. military presence in Okinawa from the perspective of women in Okinawa, mainland Japan, and beyond (see Takazato and Kichi to Guntai wo Yurusanai Koudou suru Onnatachi no Kai (1996) for example. See also Enloe (2000: 111–123) and Angst (2003) on Takazato and Okinawan feminism).

12. For instance, *Asahi Shinbun*, a major mainland Japanese newspaper (circulating 8 million copies daily), dispatched eighteen reporters and photographers to Nago City. Similarly, more than a hundred reporters and photographers were also dispatched by NHK (Japan Broadcasting Corporation) (*Okinawa Taimusu*, December 22, 1997).

7. The Nago City Mayoral Election and the Changing Tide of Okinawan Resistance

1. In addition, upon choosing Tamaki, the selection committee requested that he renounce his affiliation with the Okinawa Socialist Democratic Party, as a way to dissolve the historical conflict (dating back to the 1950s) between the revolutionary Communist Party and the non-Communist reformist parties supported by labor unions (Mi. Higa 1963).

2. It should be added, though, that Kyoda Kiyoka was sympathetic to the difficult position mayoral candidate Tamaki Yoshikazu had been put into. In my discussion with him following the mayoral election in which he was, ultimately, defeated (see below), the usually gentle Tamaki burst out angrily, saying, "I'm not a dress-up doll! One day a prefectural assemblyman, the next day a candidate for mayor, and then a candidate for prefectural assemblyman again?" In fact, after being defeated in the mayoral election, Tamaki was asked by the political parties and unions to run for by-election to fill a vacancy in the Okinawa Prefectural Assembly.

3. I worked as an interpreter in this forum.

4. The U.S. General Accounting Office issued a report in March 1998, cautioning against the construction of the new base in Henoko's sea from an ecological (and financial) point of view (U.S. General Accounting Office 1998).

8. Conclusion

1. As I have made clear in chapter 1, I do not reject the use of military force under all circumstances.

2. See, for example, editorials of May 14, 1997; December 22, 1997; February 7, 1998; April 30, 1999; and July 24, 2000.

3. The prospect of the SDF's active involvement in global military operations, even if subservient to the command of the U.S. military, has meant to give some confidence and national pride to ever wealthy but uncertain Japanese, whose lives are increasingly atomized and dictated by the logic of global-cum-American market capitalism.

4. For instance, it was proposed that U.S. Army's 1st Corps Headquarters in Washington State would be integrated with the Central Collective Headquarters of the Ground Self-Defense Forces of Japan (responsible for terrorist attacks in Japan) at U.S. Army Camp Zama in Kanagawa Prefecture; and that the Headquarters of the Air Self-Defense Forces would be integrated with the Headquarters of the 5th U.S. Air Force in Yokota Air Base in Tokyo (*Asahi.com*, October 27, 2005).

5. In March 2006, the new mayor declared that Nago City would not accept the coastal plan as long as aircrafts departing from and arriving to this newly constructed base would fly above residential areas of the thirteen districts of the city's east coast, because that would jeopardize the safety and well-being of the residents living there. In April 2006, the Japanese government cunningly responded to the mayor's adamant call by presenting a revised coastal plan that consisted of two—instead of one, as in the case of the original coastal plan—runways precisely in the name of "the safety and well-being of the residents," whereas one runway should be used for arriving aircrafts to avoid flying above three coastal districts south of Camp Schwab, and the other should be utilized for departing aircrafts to avoid flying above ten coastal districts north of Camp Schwab. Outwitted by the Japanese government, Nago City mayor was forced to accept this plan (together with the governmental promise to provide additional subsidies), and in doing so, assisted Tokyo in constructing a base of an even larger scale—with two, instead of one, runways—for the U.S. military. Mayors of other northern Okinawan cities and villages

followed suit. Governor Inamine reluctantly and somewhat ambiguously gave his partial approval to the revised coastal plan thereafter in May 2006. In the meantime, former Nago City Mayor Kishimoto, who, in spite of his pro-base position, had at least shown the spirit of Okinawan resistance by requesting the government to restrict the use of the bifunctional "airport" to fifteen years, passed away due to illness in March 2006.

6. The divide of pro-base and anti-base voices was also dramatically overcome in one of the grassroots meetings, titled *Gomen! Wajitte Ika?* (Sorry, but Can We be Angry?), which was held on a college campus in central Okinawa in the winter of 2005 and was attended by more than three hundred people. In this meeting, a former civil servant working *for* the Defense Facilities Agency in the 1997 Nago City Referendum and a Nago's anti-base intellectual working *against* the government in that referendum found themselves collaborating to show their opposition to the new agreement (*Okinawa Times*, December 19, 2005).

7. From a slightly different perspective, ongoing efforts to initiate ecologically-minded public works in Okinawa and elsewhere (e.g., Ui 1991, Makishi 1998) may be unexpectedly linked to the projects of the construction industry in Tokyo in a way that would benefit the former. The reason behind this potential collaboration is that the construction industry no longer necessarily shares the same interests with the Japanese government; the central government is now obsessed with downsizing itself (i.e., accepting the U.S. demand for privatization of public assets, market capitalism, deregulation, and neoliberal globalization) and cutting the budget for public construction works.

8. Until the 1980s (Simmel 1950, Flores-Meiser 1980, Fahim and Helmer 1980, Messerschmidt 1981, Fahim, ed. 1982), the relationship between the insider (i.e., an anthropologist who is native to the community being studied) and the outsider (i.e., an anthropologist who is not native to the community being studied) was generally characterized in such a way that the advantages of one were the disadvantages of the other and vice versa. Within this theoretical model, the advantages of being an insider (which an outsider was not assumed to possess) included the ease of establishing rapport with the informants, better understanding of the subtleties and nuances of cultural meanings, and a critical perspective of Western theoretical models of understanding the Other. Conversely, the advantages of being an outsider (which an insider does not possess, according to this theoretical model) included the ease of being able to keep a certain distance between him/her from the informants necessary to conduct good fieldwork, freedom from the cultural values and norms of the community that tend to cloud the objectivity of a study, the possibility of build-

ing a universal analytical framework, and leeway to play innocent. More recently, anthropologists have complicated, subverted, and deconstructed the either-insider-or-outsider model by showing interactions across the divide as well as internal differentiations and historical changes within the category of the inside and/or that of the outside (e.g., Kondo 1990, Jacobs-Huey 2002, Jackson 2004).

9. An informal conference that took place at the University of Ryukyus in May 1998 is an important exception. At this event, five American scholars including Steve Rabson, Michael Molaski, and Gregory Smits presented their papers in Japanese and carried out conversations with the Okinawan audience after their presentations.

CHRONOLOGY

Premodern Okinawa

14th-16th centuries:	The "golden age" of the Ryukyu Kingdom. Flourished by participating in a trans-Asian trade network structured by the Ming dynasty.
1609:	Invasion of the Ryukyu Kingdom by Satsuma, the southernmost feudal clan of the Tokugawa regime in mainland Japan.
17th–19th centuries:	For 270 years following this invasion, the kingdom, while keeping up its appearances as an independent state whose status was formally sanctioned by China, was in actuality politically and economically subordinated to Satsuma, and by implication, Tokugawa Japan.

Prewar Okinawa (1870s–1940s)

1872–1879:	The Ryukyu Measures were implemented by the Meiji government. The Ryukyu Kingdom

was abolished and turned into Okinawa
Prefecture.

Late 19th–Early 20th Centuries: Assimilation programs were implemented
in Okinawa by the Japanese government.

1920s: Economic crisis in Okinawa, accompanied
by the "cycad hell."

Late 1930s—early 1940s: The rise of militarism in Okinawa. The
Japanese government introduced various
policies to indoctrinate Okinawans as
imperial subjects.

Postwar Okinawa (1945–1980s)

March–June 1945:   The battle of Okinawa. The U.S.
occupation of Okinawa began.

1952:   The San Francisco Peace Treaty
came into effect. Japan's mainland
regained independence. Japan's
"residual sovereignty" over
Okinawa was acknowledged,
which gave the United States
power to administer Okinawa.

1956–1958:   The "island-wide protest" occurred
against USCAR's requisition of
Okinawan land.

1960s: The reversion movement unfolded.

1972:   The reversion of Okinawa from the
United States to Japan. Continued
presence of U.S. bases, mandated by the
U.S.-Japan security agreement.

1970s–1980s: Tokyo implemented the *hondonami*
(catching up with the mainland) project as
political compensation for the continued
presence of U.S. bases. Okinawa's living
standards improved dramatically.

1990s: Affluence of Okinawa

Chronology

Okinawa After the Rape Incident

September 1995:	The abduction and rape of a 12-year-old Okinawan school by three U.S. servicemen. Govenor Ota refused to sign and renew the contracts for the U.S. military as the proxy of anti-military landlords.
October 1995:	The Okinawan people's rally against the rape incident was held, in which 85,000 people participated.
November 1995:	The U.S. and Japanese governments established the Special Action Committee on Okinawa (SACO) to deal with the Okinawa base issues.
March 1996:	Naha District Court ordered Ota to sign and renew the land contracts as the proxy of anti-military landlords.
April 1996:	Prime Minister Hashimoto and Ambassador to Japan Mondale announced returning 500-hectare Futenma Marine Corps Air Station to Okinawa by the year 2003.
August 1996:	The Supreme Court dismissed the claim of Governor Ota, who had appealed against the Naha District Court's decision in March 1996.
September 1996:	A majority of Okinawans expressed their approval of the reorganization and reduction of U.S. bases in the prefectural referendum. Governor Ota gave his consent to renew the land contracts as the proxy of anti-military landlords.
December 1996.	SACO made the return of Futenma conditional on the construction of a new military facility off the east coast of the island of Okinawa.
Summer 1997:	Nago residents mobilized a movement to conduct a citywide referendum concerning the construction of the offshore base.

December 1997:	The anti-base group won in the Nago City referendum.
February 1998:	The pro-base candidate (Kishimoto Tateo) won in the Nago City mayoral election.
November 1998:	Governor Ota was defeated in the gubernatorial election by Inamine Kei'ichi.
November 1999:	Governor Inamine struck a deal with Tokyo to construct a military-commercial "airport" in Henoko, Nago City. Mayor Kishimoto Tateo followed suit in December 1999 and agreed to the construction. The Japanese government authorized the "airport" plan.
2000–2002:	Preparations for the construction of the new "airport" in Henoko were under way.
2003:	Seven years have passed since SACO issued the final report. The operations of Futenma remain intact.
2003- 2005:	Preparations for the construction of the new airport in Henoko have continued, while the actual construction has not begun owing in part to Okinawan citizens' resistance.
October 2005:	Tokyo and Washington reached an agreement concerning U.S. military realignment in Okinawa and mainland Japan. A new cycle of Okinawan resistance has begun.

REFERENCES

Books and Articles

Abelmann, Nancy. 1995. *Ethics of the Past, Epics of Dissent: A South Korean Social Movement.* Berkeley, CA: University of California Press.

——. 1997. "Reorganizing and Recapturing Dissent in 1990s South Korea: The Case of Farmers." In R. G. Fox and O. Starn, eds., *Between Resistance and Revolution: Cultural Politics and Social Protest,* pp. 251–278. New Brunswick, NJ: Rutgers University Press.

Abu-lughod, Lila. "The Romance of Resistance: Tracing Transformations of Power through Bedouin Women." *American Ethnologist* 17(1): 41–54.

Ahagon Shōkō. 1973. *Beigun to Nōmin* (The U.S. Military and the Peasantry). Tokyo: Iwanami Shoten.

——. 1992. *Inochi Koso Takara: Okinawa Hansen no Kokoro* (Life is Treasure: The Heart of Okinawan Anti-base Movement). Tokyo: Iwanami Shoten.

Aida Yūji. 1972. *Nihonjin no Ishikikozo* (The Structure of the Japanese Consciousness). Tokyo: Kōdansha.

Akamine Hidemitsu. 1983. s.v. "Saipan." In *Okinawa Daihyakka Jiten,* pp. 97–98. Okinawa: Okinawa Taimususha.

Aldous, Christopher. 2003. "'Mob rule' or popular activism? The Koza Riot of December 1970 and the Okinawan Search for Citizenship." In G. D. Hook and

R. Siddle, eds., *Japan and Okinawa: Structure and Subjectivity*, pp. 148–166. New York: Routledge.

Allen, Matthew. 2002. *Identity and Resistance in Okinawa*. Lanham, MD: Rowman and Littlefield.

Allison, Anne. 1994. *Nightwork: Sexuality, Pleasure, and Corporate Masculinity in a Tokyo Hostess Club*. Chicago, IL: University of Chicago Press.

———. 2000. *Permitted and Prohibited Desires : Mothers, Comics, and Censorship in Japan*. Berkeley, CA: University of California Press.

Althusser, Louis. 1971. "Ideology and Ideological State Apparatuses." In B. Brewster, trans., *Lenin and Philosophy, and Other Essays*, pp. 127–186. New York: Monthly Review.

Altinay, Ayse Gül. 2004. *The Myth of the Military-Nation: Militarism, Gender, and Education in Turkey*. New York: Palgrave Macmillan.

Alvarez, Sonia E. 1997. "Reweaving the Fabric of Collective Action: Social Movements and Challenges to 'Actually Existing Democracy' in Brazil." In R. G. Fox and O. Starn, eds., *Between Resistance and Revolution: Cultural Politics and Social Protest*, pp. 83–112. New Brunswick, NJ: Rutgers University Press.

Alvarez, Sonia E., Evelina Dagnino, and Arturo Escobar, eds. 1998. *Cultures of Politics, Politics of Cultures: Re-visioning Latin American Social Movements*. Boulder, CO: Westview Press.

Anderson, Benedict. [1983]1991. *Imagined Communities*. New York: Verso.

Angst, Linda Isako. 2003. "The Rape of a Schoolgirl." In L. Hein and M. Selden, eds., *Islands of Discontent: Okinawan Responses to Japanese and American Power*, pp.135–157. Lanham, MD: Rowman and Littlefield.

Appadurai, Arjun. 1996. *Modernity at Large: Cultural Dimensions of Globalization*. Minneapolis, MN: University of Minnesota Press.

Arakawa Akira. 1981a. *Ryukyu Shobun Igo Jyō* (After the Ryukyu Measures: Book 1). Tokyo: Asahi Shinbunsha.

———. 1981b. *Ryukyu Shobun Igo Ge* (After the Ryukyu Measures: Book 2). Tokyo: Asahi Shinbunsha.

———. 2000. *Okinawa, Tōgō to Hangyaku* (Okinawa, Integration and Resistance). Tokyo: Chikuma Shobō.

Arasaki Moriteru. 1969. *Dokyumento Okinawa Tōsō* (Documents on Okinawan Struggles). Tokyo: Aki Shobō.

———. 1982. *Ryukyuko no Shitenkara* (From the Perspective of the Ryukyu Archipelago). Tokyo: Gaifūsha.

——. 1992. *Okinawa Dōjidaishi dai 4 kan: 1988–1990—Yawarakai Shakai wo Motomete* (Contemporary Okinawan History Volume 4: 1988–1990— In search of an Inclusive Society). Tokyo: Gaifūsha.

——. 1995. *Okinawa Hansen Jinushi* (Okinawa's Anti-Military Landlords). Tokyo: Kōbunken.

——. 1998. "On One-tsubo Antiwar Landlords." *JPRI Critique* V(3): http://www.jpri.org/publications/critiques/critique_V_3.html#Arasaki

Arashiro Toshiaki. 1994. *Ryukyu-Okinawa Shi* (History of the Ryukyus and Okinawa). Okinawa: Okinawaken Rekishi Kyōiku Kenkyūkai.

Asad, Talal. 1973. Introduction to *Anthropology and the Colonial Encounter*, pp. 9–19. Atlantic Highlands, NJ: Humanities Press.

Asad, Talal, ed. 1973. *Anthropology and the Colonial Encounter*. Atlantic Highlands, NJ: Humanities Press.

Atarashii Rekishi Kyoukasho wo Tsukuru Kai, ed. 1997. *Atarashii Nihon no Rekishi ga Hajimaru: "Jigyakushikan" wo Koete* (A New Japanese History Begins: Beyond the "Self-Torturing" View of History). Tokyo: Gentōsha.

Beillevaire, Patrick. 1999. "Assimilation from Within, Appropriation from Without: The Folklore-Studies and Ethnology of Ryukyu/Okinawa." In J. van Bremen and A. Shimizu, eds., *Anthropology and Colonialism in Asia and Oceania*, pp. 172–196. Surrey, UK: Curzon Press.

Benedict, Ruth. 1934. *Patterns of Culture*. Boston MA: Houghton Mifflin.

——. 1946. *The Chrysanthemum and the Sword*. Boston, MA: Houghton Mifflin.

Bhabha, Homi K. 1994. *The Location of Culture*. New York: Routledge.

Bourdieu, Pierre. 1980. *The Logic of Practice* (R. Nice, trans.). Stanford, CA: Stanford University Press.

Burd, William W. 1952. *Scientific Investigations in the Ryūkyū Islands (SIRI): Karimata—A Village in the Southern Ryukyus*. Washington, DC: Pacific Science Board, National Research Council.

Bush, George W. et al. 2002. *The National Security Strategy of the United States of America*. Washington, DC: White House.

Calhoun, Craig. 1992. "Introduction. In C. Calhoun, ed., *Habermas and the Public Sphere*, pp. 1–48. Cambridge, MA: MIT Press.

Camp Schwab. 1998. Printed material provided to the author. Okinawa: Camp Schwab.

Camp Schwab Public Relations Officer. 1998. Personal communication.

References

Castells, Manuel. 1997. *The Information Age: Economy, Society and Culture, Volume 2, The Power of Identity*. Malden, MA: Blackwell.

———. 1998. *The Information Age: Economy, Society and Culture, Volume 3, End of Millennium*. Malden, MA: Blackwell.

Chatterjee, Partha. 1986. *Nationalist Thought and the Colonial World: A Derivative Discourse*. Minneapolis, MN: University of Minnesota Press.

Christy, Alan. 1993. "The Making of Imperial Subjects in Okinawa." *Positions* 1 (3): 607–639.

Clifford, James. 1988. *The Predicament of Culture: Twentieth-Century Ethnography, Literature, and Art*. Cambridge, MA: Harvard University Press.

———. 1994. Diasporas. *Cultural Anthropology* 9 (3): 302–338.

Clifford, James, and George E. Marcus, eds. 1986. *Writing Culture: The Poetics and Politics of Ethnography*. Berkeley, CA: University of California Press.

Cohen, Jean L. 1985. "Strategy or Identity: New Theoretical Paradigms and Contemporary Social Movements." *Social Research* 52 (4): 663–716.

Coronil, Fernando. 1996. "Beyond Occidentalism: Toward Nonimperial Geohistorical Categories." *Cultural Anthropology* 11 (1): 51–87.

Department of Defense. 1992. *A Strategic Framework for the Asian Pacific Rim: Report to Congress 1992*. Washington, DC: Department of Defense.

———. 1995. *United States Security Strategy for the East Asia-Pacific Region*. Washington, DC: Office of International Security Affairs.

———. 1998. *United States Security Strategy for the East Asia-Pacific Region*. Washington, DC: Office of International Security Affairs.

Derrida, Jacques. 1978. "Violence and Metaphysics: An Essay on the Thought of Emmanuel Levinas." In A. Bass, trans., *Writing and Difference*, pp. 79–153. Chicago, IL: University of Chicago Press.

Dirks, Nicholas, Geoff Eley, and Sherry Ortner. 1994. "Introduction." In N. Dirks, G. Eley, and S. Ortner, eds., *Culture/Power/History: A Reader in Contemporary Social Theory*, pp. 3–45. Princeton, NJ: Princeton University Press.

Dirlik, Arif. 1994a. *After the Revolution: Walking to Global Capitalism*. Hanover, NH: Wesleyan University Press.

———. 1994b. "The Postcolonial Aura: Third World Criticism in the Age of Global Capitalism." *Critical Inquiry* 20 (2): 328–356.

———. 1996. "Chinese History and the Question of Orientalism." *History and Theory* 35: 96–118.

———. 1999. "Place-Based Imagination: Globalism and the Politics of Place." *Review* 22(2): 151–187.

Doi Takeo. 1971. *Amae no Kōzō* (The Structure of Dependence). Tokyo: Kōbundō.

Douglas, Mary. 1966. *Purity and Danger: An Analysis of Concepts of Pollution and Taboo*. London: Routledge & K. Paul.

Dower, John W. 1986. *War without Mercy: Race and Power in the Pacific War*. New York, NY: Pantheon Books.

Eldridge, Robert D. 2001. *The Origins of the Bilateral Okinawa Problem: Okinawa in Postwar US-Japan Relations, 1945–1952*. New York: Garland.

Enloe, Cynthia. 1989. *Bananas, Beaches and Bases: Making Feminist Sense of International Politics*. Berkeley, CA: University of California Press.

———. 2000. *Maneuvers: The International Politics of Militarizing Women's Lives*. Berkeley, CA: University of California Press.

Epstein, Barbara. 1990. "Rethinking Social Movement Theory." *Socialist Review* 20(1): 35–65.

Escobar, Arturo, and Sonia E. Alvarez, eds. 1992. *The Making of Social Movements in Latin America: Identity, Strategy, and Democracy*. Boulder, CO: Westview Press.

Etienne, Mona, and Eleanor Leacock, eds. 1980. *Women and Colonization: Anthropological Perspectives*. New York: Praeger.

Fabian, Johannes. 1983. *Time and the Other: How Anthropology Makes its Object*. New York: Columbia University Press.

Fahim, Hussein, ed. 1982. *Indigenous Anthropology in Non-Western Countries*. Forest Hills Station, NC: Carolina Academic Press.

Fahim, Hussein and Katherine Helmer. 1980. "Indigenous Anthropology in non-Western Countries: A Further Elaboration." *Current Anthropology* 21(5): 644–663.

Fanon, Franz. 1963. *The Wretched of the Earth* (C. Farrington, trans.). New York: Grove Press.

———. 1967. *Black Skin, White Masks* (C. L. Markmann, trans.). New York: Grove Press.

Featherstone, Mike, ed. 1990. *Global Culture: Nationalism, Globalization and Modernity*. Newbury Park, CA: SAGE Publications.

Field, Norma. 1991. *In the Realm of a Dying Emperor*. New York: Pantheon Books.

Figal, Gerald A. 2000. *Civilization and Monsters: Spirits of Modernity in Meiji Japan*. Durham, NC: Duke University Press.

References

Flores-Meiser, Enya P. 1980. "Doing Fieldwork in One's Own Community." *Association of Third World Anthropologists (ATWA) Research Bulletin* 2: 24–28.

Fortes, Meyer. 1953. "The Structure of Unilineal Descent Groups." *American Anthropologist* 55: 17–41.

———. 1969. *Kinship and the Social Order*. Chicago, IL: Aldine Publishing.

Foucault, Michel. [1978]1990. *The History of Sexuality, Volume 1: An Introduction* (R. Hurley, trans.). New York: Vintage Books.

Foweraker, Joe. 1995. *Theorizing Social Movements*. Boulder, CO: Pluto Press.

Fox, Richard G., and Orin Starn, eds. 1997. *Between Resistance and Revolution: Cultural Politics and Social Protest*. New Brunswick, NJ: Rutgers University Press.

Fraser, Nancy. 1992. "Rethinking the Public Sphere: A Contribution to the Critique of Actually Existing Democracy." In C. Calhoun, ed., *Habermas and the Public Sphere*, pp. 109–142. Cambridge, MA: MIT Press.

———. 2004. "Culture and the Public Sphere." *Anthropology News* (March 2003): 6–7.

Freire, Paulo. 1990. *Pedagogy of the Oppressed* (M. B. Ramos, trans.). New York: Continuum.

Fukuchi Hiroaki. 1995. *Okinawa ni Okeru Beigun no Hanzai* (Crimes Committed by the U.S. Military in Okinawa). Tokyo: Dōjidaisha.

Fukuzawa Yukichi. [1875]1997. *Bunmeiron no Gairyaku* (An Outline of the Civilization Theory). Tokyo: Iwanami Shoten.

Furuie Shinpei. 1994. *Hi to Mizu no Minzokubunkashi* (A Historical Ethnography of Fire and Water). Tokyo: Yoshikawa Kōbunkan.

Fuss, Diana. 1989. *Essentially Speaking: Feminism, Nature and Difference*. New York: Routledge.

Futenma Hikōjō Isetsu Taisaku Honbu. 1997. *Kaijyōheripōto: Kurashi to Shizen wo Kangaete* (Offshore Heliport: Thinking Human Life and the Environment). Okinawa: Futenma Hikōjō Isetsu Taisaku Honbu.

Gabe Masa'aki. 1975. "60nendai Fukki Undō no Tenkai" (The Development of the Reversion Movement in the 60s). In S. Miyazao, ed., *Sengo Okinawa no Seiji to Hō: 1945–72nen* (Politics and Law in Postwar Okinawa: 1945–1972), pp. 153–211. Tokyo: Tokyo Daigaku Shuppankai.

Gandhi, Mahatma [1927]1983. *An Autobiography: The Story of my Experiments with Truth* (M. Desai, trans.). New York: Dover.

Geertz, Clifford. 1973. *The Interpretation of Cultures; Selected Essays*. New York, NY: Basic Books.

———. 1980. *Negara: The Theatre State in Nineteenth-Century Bali*. Princeton, NJ: Princeton University Press.

———. 1983. *Local Knowledge: Further Essays in Interpretive Anthropology*. New York, NY: Basic Books.

Gekkan Okinawasha. 1983. *America no Okinawa Touchikankeihōki Sōran* (Laws and Regulations during the U.S. Administration of Okinawa). Okinawa: Gekkan Okinawasha.

Giddens, Anthony. 1991. *Modernity and Self-identity: Self and Society in the Later Modern Age*. Stanford, CA: Stanford University Press.

Gilroy, Paul. 1987. *'There Ain't No Black in the Union Jack': The Cultural Politics of Race and Nation*. Chicago, IL: The University of Chicago Press.

———. 1993. *The Black Atlantic: Modernity and Double Consciousness*. Cambridge, MA: Harvard University Press.

Glacken, Clarence J. 1955. *The Great Loochoo: A Study of Okinawan Village Life*. Berkeley, CA: University of California Press.

Gongora, Thierry, and von Rickhoff, Harald. 2000. "Introduction: Sizing up the Revolution in Military Affairs." In T. Gongora and H. von Riekhoff, eds., *Toward a Revolution in Military Affairs?*, pp. 1–20. Westport, CT: Greenwood.

Gramsci, Antonio. 1971. *Selections from the Prison Notebooks of Antonio Gramsci* (Q. Hoare and G. N. Smith, eds. and trans.). New York: International Publishers.

Guevara, Ernesto. 1994. *The Bolivian Diary of Ernesto Che Guevara* (Mary-Alice Waters, ed. and trans.). New York: Pathfinder.

Gupta, Akhil, and James Ferguson. 1992. "Beyond 'Culture': Space, Identity, and the Politics of Difference." *Cultural Anthropology* 7(1): 6–23.

———. 1997. "Discipline and Practice: 'The Field' as Site, Method, and Location in Anthropology." In A. Gupta and J. Ferguson, eds., *Anthropological Locations: Boundaries and Grounds of a Field Science*, pp. 1–46. Berkeley, CA: University of California Press.

Habermas, Jürgen. 1985. *The Theory of Communicative Action, Volume 2: Lifeworld and System, A Critique of Functionalist Reason* (T. McCarthy, trans.). Boston, MA: Beacon Press.

———. 1989. *The Structural Transformation of the Public Sphere: An Inquiry into a Category of Bourgeois Society* (T. Burger, trans., with assistance of F. Lawrence). Cambridge, MA: MIT Press.

———. 1990. *Moral Consciousness and Communicative Action* (C. Lenhardt and S. W. Nicholsen, trans.). Cambridge, MA: MIT Press.

———. 2000. "Kindai—Mikan no Purojekuto" (Modernity—an Unfinished Project). In *Kindai—Mikan no Purojekuto* (Modernity—an Unfinished Project) (Mishima K., ed. and trans), 3–45. Tokyo: Iwanami Shoten.

Hall, Start. [1990]1994. "Cultural Identity and Diaspora." In P. Williams and L. Chrisman, eds., *Colonial Discourse and Post-Colonial Theory: A Reader*, pp. 392–403. New York: Columbia University Press.

Hannertz, Ulf. 1992. *Cultural Complexity: Studies in the Social Organization of Meaning*. New York: Columbia University Press.

Hardt, Michael, and Antonio Negri. 2000. *Empire*. Cambridge, MA: Harvard University Press.

———. 2004. *Multitude: War and Democracy in the Age of Empire*. New York: Penguin Press.

Haring, Douglas G. 1952. *Scientific Investigations in the Ryukyu Islands (SIRI): The Island of Amami Ōshima in the Northern Ryūkyūs*. Washington, DC: Pacific Science Board, National Research Council.

Harootunian, Harry D. 2000. *Overcome by Modernity: History, Culture, and Community in Interwar Japan*. Princeton, NJ: Princeton University Press.

Harris, Marvin. 1979. *Cultural Materialism: The Struggle for a Science of Culture*. New York: Random House.

———. 1987. *Cultural Anthropology (2nd ed.)*. New York: Harper and Row.

Harvey, David. 1990. *The Condition of Postmodernity: An Enquiry into the Origins of Cultural Change*. Cambridge, MA: Blackwell.

Hashikawa Bunzō. [1985]2000. "Nihon Nashonarizumu no Genryū" (The Origin of Japanese Nationalism). In *Hashikawa Bunzō Chosakushū Dai 2kan* (The Complete Works of Hashikawa Bunzō Volume 2), pp. 1–225. Tokyo: Chikuma Shobō.

Hein, Laura, and Mark Selden, eds. 2003. *Islands of Discontent: Okinawan Responses to Japanese and American Power*. Lanham, MD: Rowman and Littlefield.

Henoko District. 1997. Personal Communication (with Henoko District Mayer).

———. 1998. *Henokoshi* (History and Culture of Henoko) (Shimabukuro K., ed.). Okinawa: Henoko District.

———. Not Dated. Documents found in the Henoko Administration Office in Spring 1998.

Henoko/Schwab Friendship Council. 1998. Printed material provided to the author. Okinawa: Henoko/Schwab Friendship Council.

Higa Masao. 1987. *Jyosei Yūi to Dankei Genri: Okinawa no Minzoku Shakai Kōzō* (Spiritual Superiority of Women and Patrilineality: The Structure of Okinawan Folkloristic Society). Tokyo: Gaifūsha.

Higa, Mikio. 1963. *Politics and Parties in Postwar Okinawa*. Vancouver, Canada: University of British Columbia.

———. 1977. "The Okinawa Reversion." In C. Hosoya, ed., *Okinawa Reversion: Occasional Paper # 12*, pp. 1–24. Pittsburgh, PA: International Studies Association.

Hirai Gen. 1998. "*Koza no Nagai Kage: Uta no Senjyō wo Reikisuru*" (A Long Shadow of Koza: Imagining the Battlefield of Music). In DeMusik Inter, ed., *Otono Chikara: Koza Futtōhen* (The Power of Music: On Koza That Boiled), pp. 21–56. Tokyo: Impact Shuppankai.

Hirschkind, Charles. 2001. "Civic Virtue and Religious Reason: An Islamic Counterpublic." *Cultural Anthropology* 16(1): 3–34.

Hiyane Teruo. 1981. *Kindai Nihon to Iha Fuyū* (Modern Japan and Iha Fuyū). Tokyo: San'ichi Shobō.

———. 1996. *Kindai Okinawa no Seishinshi* (A History of Thoughts in Modern Okinawa). Tokyo: Shakai Hyōronsha.

Hook, Glenn D. and Richard Siddle, eds. 2003. *Japan and Okinawa: Structure and Subjectivity*. New York: Routledge.

hooks, bell. 1992. *Black Looks: Race and Representation*. Boston, MA: South End Press.

Iha Fuyū. [1906]1974a. "Ryūkyūjin no Sosen ni Tsuite" (On the Ancestry of the Ryukyuans). In Hattori S., Nakama S., and Hokama S., eds., *Iha Fuyu Zenshū Dai 1kan* (The Complete Works of Iha Fuyū Volume 1), pp. 17–48. Tokyo: Heibonsha.

———. [1907]1974a. "Ryūkyūshi no Sūsei" (The Trend in Ryukyuan History). In Hattori S., Nakama S., and Hokama S., eds., *Iha Fuyu Zenshū Dai 1kan* (The Complete Works of Iha Fuyū Volume 1), pp. 49–63. Tokyo: Heibonsha.

———. [1914]1974a. "Ryūkyū Shobun ha Isshu no Doreikaihō nari" (The Ryukyu Measures are a kind of Emancipation of Slaves). In Hattori S., Nakama S., and Hokama S., eds., *Ihu Fuyu Zenshū Dai 1kan* (The Complete Works of Iha Fuyū Volume 1), pp. 491–495. Tokyo: Heibonsha.

———. [1921]1974a. "Koryukyū no Seiji" (The Politics of the Ancient Ryukyus). In Hattori S., Nakama S., and Hokama S., eds., *Iha Fuyu Zenshū Dai 1kan* (The Complete Works of Iha Fuyū Volume 1), pp. 419–490. Tokyo: Heibonsha

———. [1938]1973a. *Onarishin no Shima 1* (The Island of Goddesses Book 1). Tokyo: Heibonsha.

———. [1939]1973b. *Onarishin no Shima 2* (The Island of Goddesses Book 2). Tokyo: Heibonsha.

———. [1947]1974b. "Okinawa Rekishi Monogatari: Nippon no Shukuzu" (Okinawa Historical Story: A Miniature of Japan). In Hattori S., Nakama S., and Hokama S., eds., *Iha Fuyu Zenshū Dai 2kan* (The Complete Works of Iha Fuyū Volume 2), pp. 329–457. Tokyo: Heibonsha.

Imai Hajime. 1997. *Jyūmin Tōhyō* (Referendum). Osaka: Nikkei Osaka PR Kikaku Shppanbu.

Inglehart, Ronald. 1977. *The Silent Revolution: Changing Values and Political Styles among Western Publics*. Princeton, NJ: Princeton University Press.

Inoue, Masamichi. 1998. "Kaijyō Herikichi Mondai to Nihon Jinruigaku: Okinawaken Nagoshi Henoko deno Fīrudowāku no Oboegaki" (Offshore Base Issues and Japan Anthropology: Notes from the Field in Henoko, Nago City, Okinawa). *Gendai Shisō* 26 (7): 228–244.

———. 1999. "U.S. Military Bases in Okinawa: Problems of Local-National-Global Articulation." *The Ryukyuanist: A Newsletter on Ryukyuan/Okinawan Studies* 44: 2–5.

———. 2002a. "Gurōbaruka no nakano Okinawa Inishiachibu Ronsō: Kioku, Aidentiti, Kichimondai" (The Debate over the 'Okinawa Initiative' in the Age of Globalization: Collective Memory, Identity, and the Base Problems). *Shisō* 933: 246–267.

———. 2002b. "Mainichi ga Fīrudowāku: Yanbaru to Watashi" (Fieldwork as an Everyday Act: Yanbaru and I). *Kēshikaji* 36: 38–39.

———. 2004a. "'We are Okinawans but of a different kind': New/Old Social Movements and the U.S. military in Okinawa." *Current Anthropology* 45(1): 85–104.

———. 2004b. "Tōjisha no Kyōdōtai, Kenryoku, Shmin no Kōkyōkūkan: Ryūyōron no Atarashī Kaitei to Kichimondai" (The Community of Subjects, Power, and the Public Sphere of Citizens: A New Stage of the Theory of Appropriation and the U.S. Base Problems in Okinawa). *Minzokugaku Kenkyū* 68(4): 534–554.

Inoue, Masamichi, Sebastian, John Purves, and Mark Selden. 1997. "Okinawa Citizens, U.S. Bases, and the Dugong." *Bulletin of Concerned Asian Scholars* 29 (4): 82–86.

Isa Chihiro. 1996. *Okinawa no Ikari: Koza Jiken, Shōjo Bōkō Jiken* (The Anger of Okinawa: The Koza Riot and the Rape Incident). Tokyo: Bungei Shunjyūsha.

Ishikawa Iwao. 1995. "*Kakanai noga Jinkenhōdō ka*" (Not to Write is to Protect Human Rights?). *Ryukyu Shinpo*, October 24, 1995.

References

Ishikawa Mao. 1998. *Okinawa Kaijyō Herikichi: Kyohi to Yūchi ni Yureru Machi* (The Offshore Base in Okinawa: A Town Torn between Rejection and Acceptance). Tokyo: Kōbunken.

Ishikawa Mao, Kuniyoshi Kazuo, and Nagatomo Tomohiro. 1996. *Korega Okinawa no Beigunda: Kichi no Shima ni Ikiru Hitobito* (This is the U.S. Military in Okinawa: People Living in the Island of Bases). Tokyo: Kōbunken.

Ito Mikiharu, and Kamishima Jiro. 1974. "Yanagita Kunio no Gakumon" (Scholarship of Yanagita Kunio). In Ito M. and Kamishima J., eds., *Nihon no Meicho 50: Yanagita Kunio* (50 Great Books of Japan: Yanagita Kunio), pp. 5–38. Tokyo: Chūō Kōronsha.

Ivy, Marilyn. 1995. *Discourses of the Vanishing: Modernity, Phantasm, Japan*. Chicago, IL: University of Chicago Press.

Iwamoto Yoshiteru. 1983. *Zoku Yanagita Kunio: Minzokugaku no Shūhen* (Sequel to the Study of Yanagita Kunio: In the Fringes of Folklore Studies). Tokyo: Kashiwa Shobō

Jablonsky, David. 2001. "Army Transformation: A Tale of Two Doctrines." In C. C. Crane, ed., *Transforming Defense*, pp. 45–88. Carlisle, PA: Strategic Studies Institute.

Jackson, John L. Jr. 2004. "An Ethnographic *Film*flam: Giving Gifts, Doing Research, and Videotaping the Native Subject/Object." *American Anthropologist* 106(1): 32–42.

Jacobs-Huey, Lanita. 2002. "The Natives are Gazing and Talking Back: Reviewing the Problematics of Positionality, Voice, and Accountability among 'Native' Anthropologists." *American Anthropologist* 104(3): 791–804.

Jameson, Fredric. 1992. *Postmodernism, Or, the Cultural Logic of Late Capitalism*. Durham, NC: Duke University Press.

Johnson, Chalmers. 1999. "The 1995 Rape Incident and the Rekindling of Okinawan Protest against the American Bases." In C. Johnson, ed., *Okinawa: Cold War Island*, pp. 109–132. Cardiff, CA: Japan Policy Research Institute.

Johnson, Chalmers, ed. 1999. *Okinawa: Cold War Island*. Cardiff, CA: Japan Policy Research Institute.

Kandiyoti, Deniz. [1991]1994. "Identity and its Discontents: Women and the Nation." In P. Williams and L. Chrisman, eds., *Colonial Discourse and Post-Colonial theory: A Reader*, pp. 376–391. New York: Columbia University Press.

Kano Masanao. 1987. *Sengo Okinawa no Shisōzō* (Thoughts in Postwar Okinawa). Tokyo: Asahi Shinbunsha.

———. 1993. *Okinawa no Fuchi* (Borders of Okinawa). Tokyo: Iwanami Shoten.

Kato Sango. [1916]1971. *Ryūkyū no Kenkyū* (A Study of the Ryukyu Islands). Okinawa: Okinawa Kyōdobunka Kenkyūkai.

Kawai Hayao. 1982. *Mukashibanashi to Nihonjin no Kokoro* (Old Tales and the Japanese Mind). Tokyo: Iwanami Shoten.

Kawase Mitsuyoshi. 1998. "Okinawa Fukki Seisaku to Jichitai Zaisei" (Okinawa Reversion Policies and the Finance of the Local Self-Governing Bodies). *Toshi Mondai* 89(5): 87–113.

Kerr, George H. 1958. *Okinawa: The History of an Island People*. Rutland, VT: Charles E. Tuttle.

Kinchō to Kichi Henshū Īnkai. 1991. *Kinchō to Kichi* (Kin Town and the Base). Okinawa: Kinchō to Kichi Henshū Īnkai.

Kinjo Seitoku, and Takara Kurayoshi. 1984. *'Okinawagaku' no Chichi Iha Fuyū* (Iha Fuyū, the Founding Father of 'Okinawan Studies'). Tokyo: Shimizushoin.

Kita Ikki. 1926. *Nihon Kaizō Hōan Taikō* (The Basic Plan for the Reorganization of Japan). Tokyo: Nishida Zei.

Kokuba Kōtarō. 1973. *Okinawa no Ayumi* (The History of Okinawa). Tokyo: Maki Shoten.

Kondo, Dorinne K. 1990. *Crafting Selves: Power, Gender, and Discourses of Identity in a Japanese Workplace*. Chicago, IL: University of Chicago Press.

Kurima Yasuo. 1998. *Okinawa Keizai no Gensō to Genjitu* (Myths and Realities of the Okinawan Economy). Tokyo: Nihon Keizaihyōronsha.

Kyoda Kiyoka. 1998. "Korekaraha Tanpopo no Yōni" (From Now On, Like a Dandelion). *Sekai* 649: 313–316.

Kyūgakkai Rengō Okinawa Chōsa Īnkai. 1976. *Okinawa: Shizen, Bunka, Shakai* (Okinawa: Nature, Culture, Society). Tokyo: Kyūgakkai Rengō Okinawa Chōsa Īnkai.

Laclau, Ernesto, and Chantal Mouffe. 1985. *Hegemony and Socialist Strategy: Toward a Radical Democratic Politics*. London: Verso.

Lanman, Ingelise L. 1998. "Okinawa's unique community centers: *Aza*-Kōminkan." *Ryukyuanist: A Newsletter on Ryukyuan/Okinawan Studies* 40: 5–6.

Lebra, William P. 1966. *Okinawan Religion: Belief, Ritual and Social Structure*. Honolulu, HI: University of Hawaii Press.

Lenin, Vladimir I. 1947. *Imperialism, the Highest Stage of Capitalism (A Popular Outline)*. Moscow: Foreign Languages Publishing House.

Levinas, Emmanuel. 1998. *Collected Philosophical Papers* (A. Lingis, ed. and trans). Pittsburgh, PA: Duquesne University Press.

Lévi-Strauss, Claude. 1963. *Structural Anthropology* (C. Jacobson and B. G. Schoepf, trans.). New York: Basic Books.

———. 1966. *The Savage Mind*. Chicago, IL: University of Chicago Press.

———. 1974. *Tristes Tropiques: An Anthropological Study of Primitive Societies in Brazil* (J. Russell, trans.). New York: Atheneum.

Linton, Ralph. 1945. *The Cultural Background of Personality*. New York, London: D. Appleton-Century.

Lovell, Nadia. 1998. "Introduction." In N. Lovell ed., *Locality and Belonging*, pp. 1–24. New York: Routledge.

Lutz, Catherine. 2001. *Homefront: A Military City and the American Twentieth Century*. Boston, MA: Beacon Press.

Mabuchi, Tōichi. 1964. "Spiritual Predominance of the Sister." In A.H. Smith, ed., *Ryukyuan Culture and Society: A Survey*, pp. 79–91. Honolulu, HI: University of Hawaii Press.

Makino Hirotaka. 1987. *Sengo Okinawa no Tsūka, Jyō* (The Currencies of Postwar Okinawa, Volume 1). Okinawa: Hirugisha.

———. 1996. *Saikō: Okinawa Kēzai (Rethinking the Okinawan Economy)*. Okinawa: Okinawa Taimususha.

Makishi Kōichi. 1998. "Jyūmin Undō wa Ima" (The Present of Residents' Movements). In Ikehara S. and Kato Y., eds., *Okinawa no Shizen wo Shiru* (Understanding Okinawa's Nature), pp. 214–232. Tokyo: Tsukiji Shokan.

Malinowski, Bronislaw [1922]1984. *Argonauts of the Western Pacific: An Account of Native Enterprise and Adventure in the Archipelagoes of Melanesian New Guinea.* Prospect Heights, IL: Waveland Press.

Marcus, George E. and Michael M. J. Fischer. 1986. *Anthropology as Cultural Critique: An Experimental Moment in the Human Sciences*. Chicago, IL: University of Chicago Press.

Maretzki, Thomas W. 1962. "Dai 2ji Sekai Taisengo no Beikokujinruigakusha ni yoru Ryūkyū Kenkyū" (Okinawan Studies by American Anthropologists after W.W. II). (Minzokugaku Kenkyū, trans.) *Minzokugaku Kenkyū* 27(1): 431–436.

———. 1964. "Personality in Rural Okinawa." In A.H. Smith, ed., *Ryukyuan Culture and Society: A Survey*, pp. 99–111. Honolulu, HI: University of Hawaii Press.

Maretzki, Thomas W. and Hatsumi Maretzki. 1966. *Taira: An Okinawan Village.* New York: John Wiley and Sons.

Márquez, García G. [1970]1998. *One Hundred Years of Solitude* (G. Rabassa, trans.). New York: Harper and Row.

Marx, Karl. [1867]1976. *Capital, Volume 1* (B. Fowkes, trans.). New York: Vintage Books.

McCormack, Gavan. 1999. "Okinawan Dilemmas: Coral Islands—Concrete Islands." In C. Johnson, ed., *Okinawa: Cold War Island*, pp. 261–282. Cardiff, CA: Japan Policy Research Institute.

Mead, Margaret. 1935. *Sex and Temperament in Three Primitive Societies*. New York: Morrow Quill Paperbacks.

Medoruma Shun. 1996. "Okinawa no Bunkajyōkyō no Genzai ni Tsuite" (On Cultural Conditions of Present-Day Okinawa). *Kēshikazji* 13: 28–29.

———. 2000. *Suiteki* (Water Drops). Tokyo: Bungei Shunjyūsha.

Melucci, Alberto. 1985. "The Symbolic Challenge of Contemporary Movements." *Social Research* 52 (4): 789–816.

———. 1996a. *Challenging Codes: Collective Action in the Information Age*. Cambridge, UK: Cambridge University Press.

———. 1996b. *The Playing Self: Person and Meaning in the Planetary Society*. Cambridge, UK: Cambridge University Press.

Mertes, Tom. 2003. "Grass-Roots Globalism." In G.Balakrishnan, ed., *Debating Empire*, pp. 144–154. London: Verso.

Messerschmidt, Donald A. 1981. "On Anthropology 'at Home.'" In D. A. Messerschmidt, ed., *Anthropologists at Home in North America: Methods and Issues in the Study of One's Own Society*, pp. 3–14. Cambridge (United Kingdom): Cambridge University Press.

Military Government Headquarters. Not Dated. *Leaflet X-4*. Okinawa: Military Government Headquarters.

Miyagi Etsujirō. 1982. *Senryōsha no Me: Amerikajin ha Okinawa wo dō Mitaka* (The Gaze of the Ruler: How did Americans see Okinawans?). Okinawa: Naha Shuppansha.

Miyagi Shinji. [1938]1987. *Yanbaru, Sono Mura to Ie to Hito to* (Northern Okinawa, its Villages, Homes, and People). Okinawa: Nago City.

Miyamoto Ken'ichi. 2006. Notes from Sustainable Okinawa 111, posted on January 26, 2006, in the mailing list <Sustainable_OKINAWA@yahoogroups.jp>

Miyamoto Ken'ichi, and Sasaki Masayuki, eds. 2000. *Okinawa, 21seiki eno Chōsen* (Okinawa: Challenges to the Twenty-first Century). Tokyo: Iwanami Shoten.

Miyata Noboru. 1985. *Nihon no Minzokugaku* (Japanese Folklore). Tokyo: Kōdansha.

Miyazato Seigen. 1975. "Amerika no tai Okinawa Seisaku no Keisei to Tenkai" (The Formation and Development of the U.S. Policies over Okinawa). In Miyazao S., ed., *Sengo Okinawa no Seiji to Hō: 1945–72nen* (Politics and Law in Postwar Okinawa: 1945–1972), pp. 3–116. Tokyo: Tokyo Daigaku Shuppankai.

Mohanty, Chandra Talpade, Ann Russo, and Lourdes Torres, eds. 1991. *Third World Women and the Politics of Feminism.* Bloomington, IN: Indiana University Press.

Molasky, Michael S. 1999. *The American Occupation of Japan and Okinawa: Literature and Memory.* New York: Routledge.

———. 2003. "Modoruma Shun: The Writer as Public Intellectual in Okinawa Today." In L. Hein and M. Selden, eds., *Islands of Discontent: Okinawan Responses to Japanese and American power*, pp. 161–191. Lanham, MD: Rowman and Littlefield.

Morris-Suzuki, Tessa. 1998. *Re-Inventing Japan: Time, Space, Nation.* Armonk, New York: M. E. Sharpe.

———. 2000. For and Against NGOs: The Politics of the Lived World. *New Left Review* 2 (March/April): 63–84.

Moskos, Charles C., and Frank R. Wood, eds. 1988. *The Military: More than just a Job?* Washington, DC: Pergamon-Brassey's International Defense Publishers.

Murai Osamu. 1992. *Nantō Ideologī no Hassei: Yanagita Kunio to Shokuminchi Shugi* (The Birth of the Southern Islands Ideology: Yanagita Kunio and Colonialism). Tokyo: Ota Shuppan.

Nago Shimin Tōhyō Hōkokushū Kankō Inkai. 1999. *Nagoshimin Moyu: Aratana Kichi ha Iranai* (Nago Citizens Burning with Anger: No More Bases in Okinawa). Okinawa: Kaijō Herikichi Hantai, Heiwa to Nago Shisei Minshuka wo Motomeru Kyōgikai.

Nagoshishi Hensan Inkai. 1988. *Nagoshishi Honpen 11: Waga Machi, Waga Mura* (The History of Nago City Volume 11: Our Town, Our Village). Okinawa: Nago City.

———. 2001a. *Nagoshishi Honpen 9: Minzoku 1* (The History of Nago City Volume 9: Folklore 1). Okinawa: Nago City.

———. 2001b. *Nagoshishi Honpen 9: Minzoku 2* (The History of Nago City Volume 9: Folklore 2). Okinawa: Nago City.

Nago Shiyakusho. 1996. *Nagoshi Gunyōchi Ichiranhyō* (Rent of Military Land in Nago City: A List). Okinawa: Nago City.

Nakamatsu Yashū. [1968]1990. *Kami to Mura* (God and Village). Tokyo: Fukurōsha.

———. 1979. *Kosō no Mura: Okinawa Minzoku Bunkaron* (Village in a Deep Layer: On Okinawa's Folkloristic Culture). Okinawa: Okinawa Taimususha.

Nakano Yoshio. 1969. *Sengo Shiryō Okinawa* (Historical Records of Postwar Okinawa). Tokyo: Nihon Hyōronsha.

Nakasone Seizen. [1982]1995. *Himeyuri no Tō wo meguru Hitobito no Shuki* (Memoranda of the Students in reference to the Tower for the Lily Corps). Tokyo: Kadokawa Bunko.

Nanpō Dōhō Engokai. 1972. "Okinawafukki Shikiten deno Yara Okinawakenchiji Aisatsu" (Okinawa Governor Yara's Statement at the Okinawa Reversion Ceremony). In Nanpō Dōhō Engokai, ed., *Okinawa Fukki no Kiroku* (The Records of Okinawa Reversion), pp. 1000–1001. Tokyo: Nanpō Dōhō Engokai.

Nehru, Jawaharlal. 1945. *An Autobiography.* London: J. Lane.

Nelson, Christopher. 2003. "*Nuchi nu Sūji*: Comedy and Everyday Life in Postwar Okinawa." In G. D. Hook and R. Siddle, eds., *Japan and Okinawa: Structure and Subjectivity*, pp. 208–224. New York: Routledge.

Nitobe, Inazō. [1905]1969. *Bushido, the Soul of Japan.* Rutland, VT: Tuttle Publishing.

Nye, Joseph S. Jr. 1995. "East Asian Security: The Case for Deep Engagement." *Foreign Affairs* 74 (4): 90–102.

Offe, Claus. 1985. "New Social Movements: Challenging the Boundaries of Institutional Politics." *Social Research* 52 (4): 817–868.

Ogata Nobuo. 1997. "Kakushin Hyōron (Commentary coming to the Core of the Issue)." In *Okinawa Times*, December 26, 1997, p. 3.

Ogden, David A.D. "Keystone of the Pacific." 1954. *Army Information Digest* 9(1): 42–48.

Ōgo Kin'ichi. 1962. "Hokubu Okinawa no Shakai Soshiki (Social Organization in Northen Okinawa)." *Minzokugaku Kenkyū* 27(1): 371–381.

Oguma Eiji. 1995. *Tan'itsu Minzoku Shinwa no Kigen* (The Origin of the Myth of Homogeneous Japan). Tokyo: Shinyōsha.

———. 1998. *Nihonjin no Kyōkai: Okinawa, Ainu, Taiwan, Chōsen— Shokuminchi Shihai kara Fukki Undō made* (The Boundaries of the Japanese: Okinawa, Ainu, Taiwan, Korea—From Colonial Control to the Reversion Movement). Tokyo: Shinyōsha.

———. 2002. *Minshu to Aikoku: Sengo Nihon no Nashonarizumu to Kōkyōsei* (Democracy and Patriotism: Nationalism and Publicness in Postwar Japan). Tokyo: Shinyōsha.

Okakura, Kakuzō. [1906]1956. *The Book of Tea.* Rutland, VT: C.E. Tuttle.

Okaya Kōji. 1991. *Yanagita Kunio no Seishun* (Yanagita Kunio's Youth). Tokyo: Chikuma Shobō.

Okinawaken Chijikōshitsu Kōhōka. 1996. *Okinawa karano Messēji* (A Message from Okinawa). Okinawa: Okinawaken Chijikōshitsu Kōhōka.

Okinawaken Gunyōchinado Jinushi Rengōkai. 1988. *Tochiren 30nen no Ayumi* (The Progress of the Military Landlords' Association over 30 Years). Okinawa: Okinawaken Gunyōchinado Jinushi Rengōkai.

Okinawaken Kyōiku Īinkai. 1974a. *Okinawa Kenshi 9* (History of Okinawa Prefecture Volume 9). Okinawa: Okinawaken Kyōiku Īinkai.

———. 1974b. *Okinawa Kenshi 10* (History of Okinawa Prefecture Volume 10). Okinawa: Okinawaken Kyōiku Īinkai.

Okinawakenritsu Toshokan Shiryō Henshūshitu. 1996. "Documents concerning Psychological Warfare in the Battle of Okinawa." In *Okinawa Kenshi Shiryouhen Dai 2kan* (Materials on the History of Okinawa Prefecture Volume 2), 149–323. Okinawa: Okinawaken Kyōiku Īinkai.

Okinawaken Sokoku Fukki Kyōgikai. 1960. "Okinawaken Sokoku Fukki Kyōgikai Katsudō Hōshin" (Activity Principles of the Council for the Reversion of Okinawa Prefecture to the Homeland). Okinawa: Okinawaken Sokoku Fukki Kyōgikai.

Okinawaken Sōmubi Chiji Kōshitu Kichi Taisakushitu. 1998a. *Okinawa no Beigunkichi Heisei 10nen 3gatsu* (The U.S. Bases in Okinawa, March 1998). Okinawa: Okinawaken Sōmubi Chiji Kōshitu Kichi Taisakushitu.

———. 1998b. *Okinawa no Beigun oyobi Jieitaikichi (Tōkeishiryōshū): Heisei 10nen 3gatsu* (Bases of the U.S. Military and Japan's Self-Defense Forces in Okinawa, Statistical Materials, March 1998). Okinawa: Okinawaken Sōmubi Chiji Kōshitu Kichi Taisakushitu.

———. 2003. *Okinawa no Beigunkichi Heisei 15nen 3gatsu* (The U.S. Bases in Okinawa, March 2003). Okinawa: Okinawaken Sōmubi Chiji Kōshitu Kichi Taisakushitu.

———. 2005. *Okinawa no Beigun oyobi Jieitaikichi (Tōkeishiryōshū): Heisei 17nen 3gatsu* (Bases of the U.S. Military and Japan's Self-Defense Forces in Okinawa, Statistical Materials, March 2005). Okinawa: Okinawaken Sōmubi Chiji Kōshitu Kichi Taisakushitu.

Okinawa Prefectural Government. 1995. *Protest Advertising* (published on October 29 on major Japanese news papers). Okinawa: Okinawa Prefectural Government.

———. 1997. *U.S. Military Bases in Okinawa: A Message from the Land of Courtesy.* Okinawa: Military Base Affairs Office, Okinawa Prefectural Government.

Okinawa Prefectural Peace Memorial Museum [OPPMM]. 2001. *Okinawaken Heiwakinen Shiryōkan Sōgōan'nai* (Okinawa Prefectural Peace Memorial Museum Comprehensive Guide). Okinawa: Okinawan Prefectural Peace Memorial Museum.

References

Okinawa Shichōson 30 Nenshi Henshū Īnkai.1982. *Okinawa Shichōson 30 Nenshi* (30 Years of History of Okinawan Cities, Towns, and Villages). Okinawa: Okinawa Shichōson 30 Nenshi Henshū Īnkai.

Okinawa Shiyakusho. 1994. *Okinawashishi Shiryōshū 4: Rokku to Koza* (Okinawa City Historical Materials 4: Rock and Koza City). Okinawa: Okinawa Shiyakusho.

Okinawa Taimusu. [1950]1980. *Okinawa Senki: Tetsu no Bōfū* (Recording the Battle of Okinawa: The Typhoon of Steel). Okinawa: Okinawa Taimususha.

———. 1970. *Okinawa to 70nendai* (Okinawa and the 1970s). Okinawa: Okinawa Taimususha.

———. 1997a. *127 Man'nin no Jikken* (An Experiment of 1.27 Million People). Okinawa: Okinawa Taimususha.

———. 1997b. *Okinawa kara: Beigun Kichi Mondai no Shinsou* (From Okinawa: A Deep Structure of the U.S. Base Problems). Okinawa: Okinawa Taimususha.

Onga Takashi. 1998. "Koza no Jidai wo Kangaeru: Kichi ni yotte Tsukurareta Machi" (Thinking about the Era of Koza: The Town created by the U.S. base). *Koza Bunka Box* 1: 25–30.

Ōnishi Masayuki. 2001. "Jugon no Genzai" (The Present of the Dugong). *Okinawa Taimusu*, June 15 and 16, 2001. Okinawa: Okinawa Taimususha.

Ortner, Sherry. 1984. "Theory in Anthropology since the Sixties." *Comparative Studies in Society and History* 26(1): 126–166.

———. 1995. "Resistance and the Problem of Ethnographic Refusal." *Comparative Studies in Society and History* 37(1): 173–193.

Ōshiro Shōho. 1995. "Okinawasen no ato wo Tadoru" (Visiting the Ruins of the Battle of Okinawa). In Arasaki M. et al. eds., *Shinpan: Kankō Kōsudenai Okinawa (Okinawa beyond Commercial Tourism)*, pp. 159–216. Tokyo: Kōbunken.

Ota Chōfu. 1995. *Ota Chōfu Senshū, Chūkan* (Selected Works of Ota Chōfu, Volume 2) (Hiyane T. and Isa S., eds.). Tokyo: Dai'ichi Shobō.

Ota Masahide. 1972. *Okinawa no Kokoro* (Okinawa's Heart). Tokyo: Iwanami Shoten.

———. 1976. *Okinawa no Minshū Ishiki* (Okinawa's Popular Consciousness). Tokyo: Shinsensha.

———. 1996a. "Okinawa ga Kataru 1: Ota Masahide." *Weekly Asahi Graph* 3855 (March 29): 10–13.

———. 1996b. *Okinawa no Teiō: Kōtōbenmukan* (The King of Okinawa, High Commissioner). Tokyo: Asahi Shinbunsha.

———. 1999. "Governor Ota at the Supreme Court of Japan." In C. Johnson, ed., *Okinawa: Cold War Island*, pp. 205–214. Cardiff, CA: Japan Policy Research Institute.

Ota, Yoshinobu. 1997. "Appropriating Media, Resisting Power: Representations of Hybrid Identities in Okinawan Popular Culture." In R. G. Fox and O. Starn, eds., *Between Resistance and Revolution: Cultural Politics and Social Protest*, pp. 145–170. New Brunswick, NJ: Rutgers University Press.

———. 1998. *Toransupojishon no Shisō* (Thoughts on Trans-Position). Tokyo: Sekaishisousha.

Ōtō Tokihiko. 1990. *Nihonminzokugaku Shiwa* (Historical Stories of Japanese Folklore). Tokyo: San'ichi Shobō.

Perry, Matthew Calbraith. 1857. *Narrative of the Expedition of an American Squadron to the China Seas and Japan*. New York: D. Appleton.

Piot, Charles. 1999. *Remotely Global: Village Modernity in West Africa*. Chicago: University of Chicago Press.

Pitts, Forest R., William. P. Lebra, and Wayne P. Suttles. 1955. *Post-War Okinawa*. Washington, DC: Pacific Science Board, National Research Council.

Piven, Frances Fox, and Richard A. Cloward. 1977. *Poor People's Movements: Why They Succeed, How They Fail*. New York: Vintage.

Pratt, Mary L. 1992. *Imperial Eyes: Travel Writing and Transculturation*. New York: Routledge.

Purves, John M. 1995–2006. *The Contemporary Okinawa Website: Archive*. http://www.niraikanai.wwma.net/pages/archive.html

Rabson, Steve. 1989. *Okinawa: Two Postwar Novellas*. Berkeley, CA: Institute of East Asian Studies, University of California.

Radcliffe-Brown, A. R. [1922]1948. *The Andaman Islanders*. Glencoe, IL: Free Press.

Roberson, James E. 2001. "Uchinaa pop: Place and Identity in Contemporary Okinawan Popular Music." *Critical Asian Studies* 33(2): 211–242.

Rosald, Renato. 1993. *Culture and Truth: The Remaking of Social Analysis*. Boston, MA: Beacon Press.

Rumsfeld, Donald. 2002. "Transforming the Military." *Foreign Affairs* 81(3): 20–32.

Ryukyu Shinpo. 1995. *Igi Mōshitate: Kichi Okinawa* (Okinawa's Protests against the U.S. Military). Okinawa: Ryukyu Shinposha.

Said, Edward W. 1978. *Orientalism*. New York: Vintage Books.

Saito Jun'ichi. 2000. *Kōkyōsei* (Publicness). Tokyo: Iwanami Shoten.

Sakai, Naoki. 1996a. "Multi-ethnic nation and Japanese Culturalism: on Cultural Studies and Internationalism." Paper presented at International Symposium "Dialogue with Cultural Studies" at the University of Tokyo, Tokyo, on March 17, 1996.

———. 1996b. *Shizan Sareru Nihongo, Nihonjin: "Nihon" no Rekishi–Chiseiteki Hai-chi* (The Aborted Japanese Language and People: A History of "Japan" and its Configuration). Tokyo: Shinyōsha.

Sanjek, Roger. 1991. "The Ethnographic Present." *Man* 26(4): 609–628.

Sarup, Madan. 1996. *Identity, Culture and the Postmodern World*. Edinburgh, UK: Edinburgh University Press.

Satō Taketsugu. 2006. "Taibeikyōgi—Nihonseifu no Meisō" (Negotiations with the U.S.—Confusions of the Japanese Government). *Sekai* 751: 135–143.

Scarry, Elaine. 1985. *The Body in Pain: The Making and Unmaking of the World*. Oxford, UK: Oxford University Press.

Scott, James C. 1976. *The Moral Economy of the Peasant: Subsistence and Rebellion in Southeast Asia*. New Haven: Yale University Press.

———. 1985. *Weapons of the Weak: Everyday Forms of Peasant Resistance*. New Haven, CT: Yale University Press.

Selden, Mark. 1974. "Okinawa and American Security Imperialism." In M. Selden, ed., *Remaking Asia: Essays on the American Uses of Power*, pp. 279–302. New York: Pantheon Books.

Senghor, Léopold S. [1970]1994. "Negritude: A Humanism of the Twentieth Century." In P. Williams and L. Chrisman, eds., *Colonial Discourse and Post-Colonial Theory: A Reader*, pp. 27–35. New York: Columbia University Press.

Sered, Susan S. 1994. *Priestess, Mother, Sacred Sister: Religions Dominated by Women*. Oxford, UK: Oxford University Press.

———. 1995. "Jyūzokusha ga Rīdosuru Toki: Okinawa to Isuraeru ni Okeru Jyosei no Shyūkyouteki Rīdāshhipu no Paradokkusu" (When the Subjugated Leads: A Paradox of Women's Religious Leadership in Okinawa and Israel) (M. Akamine, trans.). *Okinawa Minzoku Kenkyū* 15: 1–10.

———. 1999. *Women of the Sacred Groves: Divine Priestesses of Okinawa*. Oxford, UK: Oxford University Press.

Shiels, Frederic L. 1980. *America, Okinawa, and Japan: Case Studies for Foreign Policy Theory*. Washington, D.C.: University Press of America.

Shimabukuro Genshichi. [1927]1977. *Yanbaru no Dozoku* (Old Customs of Northern Okinawa). Tokyo: Meicho Shuppan.

Shimao Toshio. 1992. *Shinpen: Ryūkyūko no Shitenkara* (From the Perspective of the Ryukyu Archipelago: New Edition). Tokyo: Asahi Shinbunsha.

Shindo Ei'ichi. 1979. "Bunkatsu sareta Ryōdo—Okinawa, Chishima, soshite Anpo" (The Divided Territory—Okinawa, the Kuriles, and the U.S.-Japan Security Treaty). *Sekai* 401: 36–75.

Shiva, Vandana. 1989. *Staying Alive: Women, Ecology and Development*. Atlantic Highlands, NJ: Zed Books.

Simmel, Georg. 1950. *The Sociology of Georg Simmel* (K.H. Wolff, trans. and ed.). New York: Free Press.

Smith, Allan. 1952. *Scientific Investigations in the Ryukyu Islands (SIRI): Anthropological investigations in Yaeyama*. Washington, DC: Pacific Science Board, National Research Council.

Smith, Allan H. ed. 1964. *Ryukyuan Culture and Society: A Survey*. Honolulu, HI: University of Hawaii Press.

Sōrifu. 1995. *Kokusei Chōsa* (National Census). Tokyo: Sōrifu.

Special Action Committee on Okinawa [SACO]. [1996]1997. "Final Report." *Interjurist* 115: 28–37.

Special Subcommittee of the Armed Services Committee. 1956. *Report of a Special Subcommittee of the Armed Services Committee, House of Representatives, Following an Inspection Tour October 14 to November 23, 1955*. Washington, DC: Special Subcommittee of the Armed Services Committee.

Spencer, Caroline. 2002. "Townsville International Women's Conference." *Kēshikaji* 36: 64–65.

Spivak, Gayatri Chakravorty. [1988]1994. "Can the Subaltern Speak?" In P. Williams and L. Chrisman, eds., *Colonial Discourse and Post-Colonial Theory: A Reader*, pp. 66–111. New York: Columbia University Press.

Starn, Orin. 1999. *Nightwatch: The Politics of Protest in the Andes*. Durham, NC: Duke University Press.

Taira Takeshi. 1997. Personal communication. December 1997.

Takamine Chōichi and Nagamoto Tomohiro. 1995. "Gunjikichi wo Aruku" (Walking the Military Bases). In Arasaki M. et al. eds., *Shinpan: Kankō Kōsudenai Okinawa (Okinawa beyond Commercial Tourism)*, pp. 159–216. Tokyo: Kōbunken.

Takara Ben. 1996. *Uruma no Hasshin: Kunizakai no Shimajima kara* (Messages from the Ryukyu archipelago). Tokyo: Ochanomizu Shobō.

Takara Kurayoshi. 1975. "Rekishigaku" (Historiography). In *Okinawa Kenshi Dai 5kan* (History of Okinawa Prefecture Volume 5), pp. 833–880. Okinawa: Okinawaken Kyōiku Īinkai.

———. 1984. *Okinawa Rekishi Monogatari* (Okinawa Historical Story). Okinawa: Hirugisha.

———. 1993. *Ryūkyū Ōkoku* (The Ryukyu Kingdom). Tokyo: Iwanami Shoten.

References

Takara Kurayoshi, Ōshiro Tsuneyoshi, and Maeshiro Marisada. 2000. "Okinawa Inishiatibu: Ajia/Taiheiyou de Hatasu Yakuwari" (Okinawa Initiative: The Role Okinawa Plays in the Asia-Pacific Region). In *Okinawa Taimusu*, May 3, 4, 5, 7, 8, 10, and 11, 2000. Okinawa: Okinawa Taimususha.

Takazato Suzuyo, and Kichi to Guntai wo Yurusanai Koudou suru Onnatachi no Kai. 1996. *Buki ni Yoranai Kokusai Kankei* (International Relations not Depending on the Military). Okinawa: Okinawa Kichi to Guntai wo Yurusanai Koudou suru Onnatachi no Kai.

Takemura Takuji. 1965. "Kunigamison Uka wo Chūshin to suru Shinzokutaikei to Saishisoshiki" (The Kinship System and Ceremonial Organization in and around Uka of Kunigami Village). In Tokyo Toritudaigaku Nanseishotō Kenkyū Īinkai, ed., *Okinawa no Shakai to Shūkyō* (Society and Religion of Okinawa), pp. 59–89. Tokyo: Heibonsha.

Tanaka, Stefan. 1993. *Japan's Orient: Rendering Pasts into History*. Berkeley, CA: University of California Press.

Tanigawa Ken'ichi. 1972. "Okinawagaku no Tenkai no Tameni" (For the Development of Okinawan Studies). In Tanigawa K., ed., *Okinawagaku no Kadai* (Tasks in Okinawan Studies), pp. 1–10. Tokyo: Mokujisha.

———. 1975. "Sanchijin to Heichijin: Aru Zasetsu to Tenkō" (People in the Flatland and People in the Mountain: A Breakdown and Conversion). *Gendai Shisō* 3(4): 118–123.

———. 1996. *Okinawa*. Tokyo: Iwanami Shoten.

Tashiro Antei. [1894]1977. "Yaeyamaguntō Jyūmin no Gengo oyobi Shūkyō" (Language and Religion of the Islands of Yaeyama). In Hasebe K., ed., *Okinawa Yuinawakō* (A Study of Okinawan Straw Rope Making), pp. 4–7. Tokyo: Perikansha.

Tengan Morio. 1999. *Okinawa Senryō Beigun Hanzai Jikenbo* (Crimes Committed by the U.S. Military Occupying Okinawa). Okinawa: Gushikawa Bungu Ten.

Thompson, E. P. 1964. *The Making of the English Working Class*. New York: Pantheon Books.

Tilly, Charles. 1985. "Models and Realities of Popular Collective Action." *Social Research* 52(4): 717–748.

Tomiyama Ichiro. 1990. *Kindai Nihonshakai to 'Okinawajin'* (Modern Japanese Society and 'Okinawans'). Tokyo: Nippon Keizai Hyouronsha.

———. 1995. *Senjyō no Kioku* (Memories of the Battlefield). Tokyo: Nippon Keizai Hyouronsha.

———. 1996. "Reipu to Reishizumu" (Rape and Racism). *Impaction* 95: 50–58.

———. 1997. "Ryukyūjin toiu Shutai: Iha Fuyū niokeru Bōryoku no Yokan" (The Subject named the Ryukyuans: Anticipation of Violence in Iha Fuyu). *Shisō* 878: 5–33.

———. 2002. *Bōryoku no Yokan* (Anticipation of Violence). Tokyo: Iwanami Shoten.

Torii Ryūzō. [1894a]1976. "Nihonkodai no Misu to Miyakojima no Misu" (A Myth of Ancient Japan and a Myth of Miyako Island). In *Torii Ryūzō Zenshū 4* (The Complete Works of Torii Ryūzō Volume 4), pp. 609–610. Tokyo: Asahi Shinbunsha.

———. [1894b]1976. "Ryūkyūshotō Joshi Genyō no Hakedama oyobi Dōchihō Kushhutsu no Magatama" (Jewelry used by Females in the Islands of Okinawa). In *Torii Ryūzō Zenshū 4* (The Complete Works of Torii Ryūzō Volume 4), pp. 612–614. Tokyo: Asahi Shinbunsha.

Total War Research Institute. 1942. *Draft of Basic Plan for Establishment of Greater East Asia Co-Prosperity Sphere.* Tokyo: Total War Institute.

Touraine, Alain. 1985. "An Introduction to the Study of Social Movements." *Social Research* 52(4): 749–788.

———. 1988. *Return of the Actor: Social Theory in Postindustrial Society* (M. Godzich, trans.). Minneapolis, MN: University of Minnesota Press.

Tsing, Anna Lowenhaupt. 2005. *Friction: An Ethnography of Global Connection.* Princeton, NJ: Princeton University Press.

Tsuha Takashi. 1978. "Utakisaishi no Shudōsha: Okinawa no Kamiyakusoshiki ni kansuru Ichimondaiten" (Leaders of Religious Festivals: A Problem Concerning the Priestess Organization in Okinawa). *Minzokugaku Kenkyū* 43(3): 279–293.

———. 2001. "Haneji Chūbu: Nenchūsaishi no Minzokushi" (Central Haneji: A Folkloristic Study of Annual Functions). In Nagoshishi Hensan Iinkai, ed. *Nagoshishi Honpen 9: Minzoku 1* (The History of Nago City Volume 9: Folklore 1), pp. 431–506.

Tsunemi Jun'ichi. 1965. "Kunigamison Aha ni okeru Monchūseido no Hensen" (The Formation and Development of the *Munchū* System in Kunigami Village, Northern Okinawa). In Tokyo Toritudaigaku Nanseishotō Kenkyū Īnkai, ed. *Okinawa no Shakai to Shūkyō* (Society and Religion of Okinawa), pp. 25–58. Tokyo: Heibonsha.

Tsunoda, Ryusaku, Wm. Theodore de Bary, and Donald Keene, eds. 1958. *Sources of Japanese Tradition, Volume 2.* New York: Columbia University Press.

Tsurumi Kazuko. 1975. "Kaisetsu" (Commentary). In Tsurumi K., ed., *Kindai Nihon Shisō Taikei 14 Yanagita Kunio Shū* (An Outline of Modern Japanese Thought

References

Book 14, Selected Works of Yanagita Kunio), pp. 430–458. Tokyo: Chikuma Shobō.

Tucker, Robert C., ed. 1978. *The Marx-Engels Reader (2nd ed.)*. New York: W. W. Norton.

Turner, Terence S. 1991. "Representing, Resisting, Rethinking: Historical Transformations of Kayapo Culture and Anthropological Consciousness." In G. W. Stocking Jr., ed., *Colonial Situations: History of Anthropology, Volume 7*, pp. 285–313. Madison, WI: University of Wisconsin Press.

Uehara Kōsuke. 1982. *Kichi Okinawa no Kutō: Zengunrō Tōsōshi* (Okinawa against the U.S. Bases: Struggles of the All Okinawa Base Workers' Union). Tokyo: Sōkō.

Uehara Masatoshi. 1995. "Ryūkyū to Okinawa no Jiken to Gaikō" (Incidents and Diplomacy in the Ryukyu Kingdom and Okinawa). *Ryukyu Shinpo*, October 31 and November 1, 1995.

Ueno Chizuko. 1990. *Kafuchōsei to Shihonsei: Marukusushugi Feminizumu no Chihei* (Patriarchy and Capitalism: The Horizon of Marxist-Feminism). Tokyo: Iwanami Shoten.

Ui Jyun. 1991. *Kōgaijishukōza 15nen* (15 Years of the Self-Organized Seminar on Environmental Destruction). Tokyo: Aki Shobō.

———. 1998. "Omoiyari Yosan Iken Soshō ni Sanka shite" (Participating in a Litigation over the Unconstitutionality of the *Omoiyari* Budget). *Impaction* 108: 61–67.

Umebayashi Hiromichi. 1994. *Jyōhō Kōkaihō de Toraeta Okinawa no Beigun* (The U.S. military in Okinawa revealed by the Furnishing of Information Act). Tokyo: Kōbunken.

———. 2002. *Zainichi Beigun* (The U.S. Military in Japan). Tokyo: Iwanami Shoten.

USCAR (United States Civil Administration of the Ryukyu Islands). Not Dated. Documents found in the Henoko Administration Office in the spring of 1998. Okinawa: USCAR.

———. 1953. *Ordinance 109*. Okinawa: USCAR.

U.S. General Accounting Office. 1998. *Overseas Presence: Issues Involved in Reducing the Impact of the U.S. Military Presence on Okinawa*. Washington, DC: U.S. General Accounting Office.

U.S.-Japan Security Consultative Committee [1996]1997. "Joint Announcement." *Interjurist* 115: 26–28.

U.S. Navy Department. 1944. *Civil Affairs Handbook: Ryukyu (Loochoo) Islands*. Washington, DC: Office of the Chief of Naval Operations.

Vogel, Ezra. 1999. "Case for U.S. Troops in Okinawa." *Asian Studies Newsletter* 44(1): 11.

Watanabe Yoshio. 1971. "Okinawa Hokubu Nouson no Monchū Soshiki" (A *Munchū* Organization of a Northern Okinawan Village). *Nihon Minzokugaku* 74: 16–20.

———. 1990. *Minzokuchishikiron no Kadai: Okinawa no Chishiki Jinruigaku* (Tasks in the Studies of Folkloristic Knowledge: Anthropology of Knowledge in Okinawa). Tokyo: Gaifūsha.

Whiting, Beatrice B., and John W.M. Whiting. 1975. *Children of Six Cultures: A Psycho-Cultural Analysis.* Cambridge, MA: Harvard University Press.

Williams, Patrick and Laura Chrisman. 1994. "Introduction." In P. Williams and L. Chrisman, eds., *Colonial Discourse and Post-Colonial Theory: A Reader*, pp. 23–26. New York: Columbia University Press.

Williams, Raymond. 1983. *Keywords: A Vocabulary of Culture and Society, Revised Edition.* New York: Oxford University Press.

Wolf, Eric, R. [1982]1997. *Europe and the People without History (with a New Preface).* Berkeley, CA: University of California Press.

Yakabi Osamu. 2000. "Gama ga Souki suru Okinawasen no Kioku" (The Memory of the Battle of Okinawa Invoked by the Cave). *Gendai Shiso* 28 (7): 114–125.

Yanagita Kunio. [1910]1968a. "Tōno Monogatari" (Tales of Tōno). In *Yanagita Kunio Zenshū Dai 4kan* (The Complete Works of Yanagita Kunio Volume 4), pp. 1–58. Tokyo: Chikuma Shobō.

———. [1913]1968a. "Yamabito Gaiden Shiryō" (Supplementary Materials on the Mountain People). In *Yanagita Kunio Zenshū Dai 4kan* (The Complete Works of Yanagita Kunio Volume 4), pp. 449–472. Tokyo: Chikuma Shobō.

———. [1917]1968a. "Yamabitokō" (A Discourse on the Mountain People). In *Yanagita Kunio Zenshū Dai 4kan* (The Complete Works of Yanagita Kunio Volume 4), pp. 172–188. Tokyo: Chikuma Shobō.

———. [1925]1968d. "Kainan Shōki" (Minor Travel Accounts of the Southern Sea). In *Yanagita Kunio Zenshū Dai 1kan* (The Complete Works of Yanagita Kunio Volume 1), pp. 217–380. Tokyo: Chikuma Shobō.

———. [1928]1968c. "Seinen to Gakumon" (Youth and Learning). In *Yanagita Kunio Zenshū Dai 25kan* (The Complete Works of Yanagita Kunio Volume 25), pp. 83–260. Tokyo: Chikuma Shobō.

———. [1934]1968c. "Minkan Denshōron" (A Discourse on Popular Traditions). In *Yanagita Kunio Zenshū Dai 25kan* (The Complete Works of Yanagita Kunio Volume 25), pp. 329–357. Tokyo: Chikuma Shobō.

———. [1935]1968c. "Kyōdo Seikatsu no Kenkyūhō" (Methods for Studying Village Life). In *Yanagita Kunio Zenshū Dai 25kan* (The Complete Works of Yanagita Kunio Volume 25), pp. 261–328. Tokyo: Chikuma Shobō.

———. [1936]1974. "Meiji Taisho Shi Sesōhen" (Social and Cultural Conditions of the Meiji and Taisho periods). In Ito M. and Kamishima J., eds., *Nihon no Meicho 50: Yanagita Kunio* (50 Great Books of Japan: Yanagita Kunio), pp. 71–344. Tokyo: Chūō Kōronsha.

———. [1947]1968b. "Junēbu no Omoide" (Memories of Geneva). In *Yanagita Kunio Zenshū Dai 3kan* (The Complete Works of Yanagita Kunio Volume 3), pp. 307–314. Tokyo: Chikuma Shobō.

———. [1951]1968d. "Shima no Jinsei" (Life on the Island). In *Yanagita Kunio Zenshū Dai 1kan* (The Complete Works of Yanagita Kunio Volume 1), pp. 381–498. Tokyo: Chikuma Shobō.

———. [1961]1968d. "Kaijō no Michi" (The Passage on the Sea). In *Yanagita Kunio Zenshū Dai 1kan* (The Complete Works of Yanagita Kunio), pp. 1–216. Chikuma Shobō.

Yomitansonshi Henshūshitsu. 2002. "Shūdanjiketsu" (Compulsory Collective Suicide). In *Yomitansonshi Dai 5kan Shiryōhen 4, Senjikiroku Jyōkan* (History of Yomitan Village 5, Historical Materials 4, Records of the Battle of Okinawa 1), http://www.yomitan.jp/sonsi/vol05a/chap02/sec03/. Okinawa: Yomitanson.

Yoshimi Yoshiaki. 1995. *Jyūgun Ianfu* (Comfort Women). Tokyo: Iwanami Shoten.

Yoshimoto Taka'aki. 1995. *Teihon Yanagita Kunio Ron* (Standard Discourses on Yanagita Kunio). Tokyo: Yōsensha.

Newspapers and Popular Magazines

Asahi Shinbun: December 23, 1970.

Korea Times: May 19, 2004.

Mainichi Shinbun: December 11, 1997.

New York Times: 1995—November 6, November 18.

Okinawa Shinminpo: July 15, 1947.

Okinawa Taimusu:

1956—December 21.

1957— January 5.

1958— April 9.

References

1961— July 4.

1992— September 18.

1997— April 5, April 6, April 17, August 22, September 2, September 23, October 4, November 25, December 9, December 14, December 17, December 19, December 21, December 22, December 23, December 25, December 31.

1999— March 26.

2002— July 29.

2003— January 15.

2004— June 3.

2005— October 26, October 27, November 1, November 15, November 21, December 16, December 19, December 20.

2006— April 12, April 26.

Ryukyu Shinpo: 1956— June 26.

1995— September 12, September 20, September 25, September 29, October 3, October 7, October 19, October 22, October 31, November 7, November 8, December 12, December 27.

1996— March 8, March 25, July 11, November 26, December 3, December 8.

1997—January 16, January 22, April 11, April 19, July 14, November 30.

1998—February 5.

Ryukyu Shinpo Weekly News: 1995— September 19, October 17, November 14.

Shinbun Akahata: July 24, 2004.

Time: "Forgotten Island." The November 28, 1949 issue: 24–27.

Washington Post : November 18, 1995.

Yomiuri Shinbun : 1997— May 14, December 22.

1998— February 7.

1999— April 30.

2000— July 24.

Internet News Sites

Asahi.com http://www.asahi.com/

2004— April 28, September 22.

2005— October 27, October 28, November 10, November 16.

2006— March 12, April 24, May 16.

Asahi.com maitaun Okinawa http://www.asahi.com/okinawa

2006— January 12

Daily Yomiuri Online http://www.yomiuri.co.jp/dy/

2005— October 29

TV Programs

NHK (Nihon Hōsō Kyōkai) 1997. *Oi mo Wakaki mo Americahei mo: Okinawa, Kichi no Machi no Natsumatsuri* (Yong people, old people, and American servicemen: Everybody Participates in a Summer Festival in a Base Town in Okinawa). Aired on August 17, 1997. Tokyo: NHK.

INDEX

Page numbers in italics refer to pages with illustrations.

working-class, pro-base ideology ("we are Okinawans but of a different kind"), 18, 98–125, 126, 155, 161–64, 230*n*6; appropriation of power, 25–26; job concerns, 10, 30, 114–15, 188, 196, 209, 220; Nago City mayoral election and, 195–97; Nago City referendum and, 159–67; pyramidal mobilization structure, 166–67. *See also* Henoko Council for Facilitating Economic Activities; Invigoration Society

World War II: appropriation of "backward" Okinawan concept, 58–59; attempt to erase memories, 204–5; Okinawa as "rear area," 52; typhoon of steel (1945), 4; U.S. acquisitions, 59. *See also* battle of Okinawa

Wretched of the Earth, The (Fanon), 227

Yagaji Ippan, 108
Yagaji Kiyoko, 148, 190

Yagaji Masatoshi, 192
Yagaji Noriyuki, 99, 108, 115, 241*n*14
Yamabito Gaiden Shiryō (Yanagita), 71–72
Yamashiro Ei, 146–47
Yamashiro Fumi, 147–48
yamato (Japanese) race, 90
Yanagita Kunio, 70–79, 90, 237–38*n*2, 238–39*n*7, 238*nn*3, 4, 5, 239*n*16; categorization of ethnic materials, 73–76; cultural trauma, 72–73; inattention to China, 76–77; intellectual career, 71–72; *Kaijō no Michi*, 76; *Kainan Shōki*, 76; *Meiji Taishō Shi, Sesōhen*, 73; *Tōno Monogatari*, 71–72; *Yamabito Gaiden Shiryō*, 71–72
yellow peril discourses of, 72
Yomiuri Shinbun (newspaper), 211–12
Yoshinobu Ota, 95
youth, 48; mixed-blood children, 115–16
yume (dream) discourse, 162–64

CPSIA information can be obtained
at www.ICGtesting.com
Printed in the USA
LVOW13s0900061216

516023LV00012B/40/P